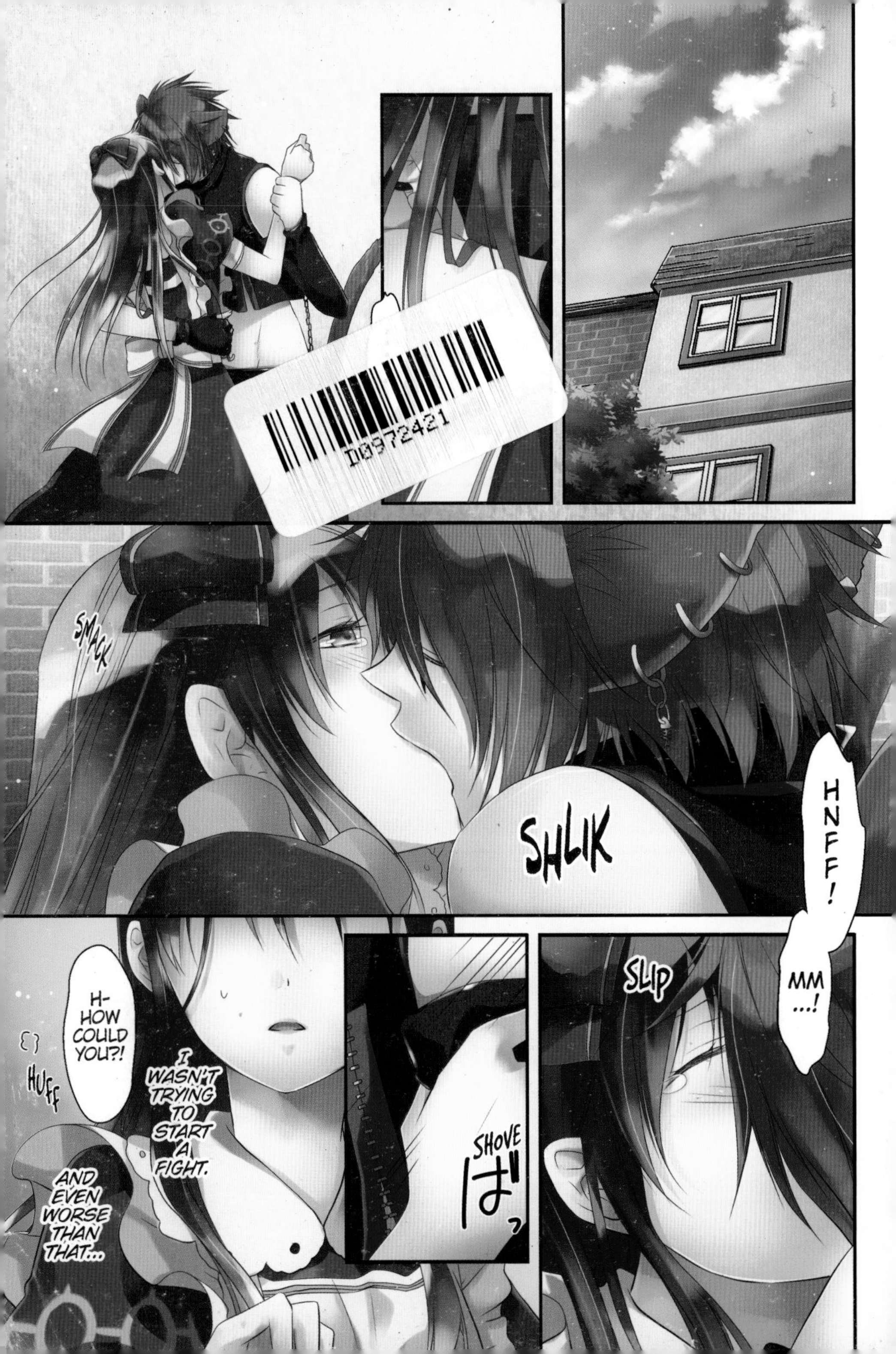
HNFF!
SMACK
SHLIK
MM...!
SLIP
SHOVE
ばっ
H-HOW COULD YOU?!
I WASN'T TRYING TO START A FIGHT.
HUFF
AND EVEN WORSE THAN THAT...

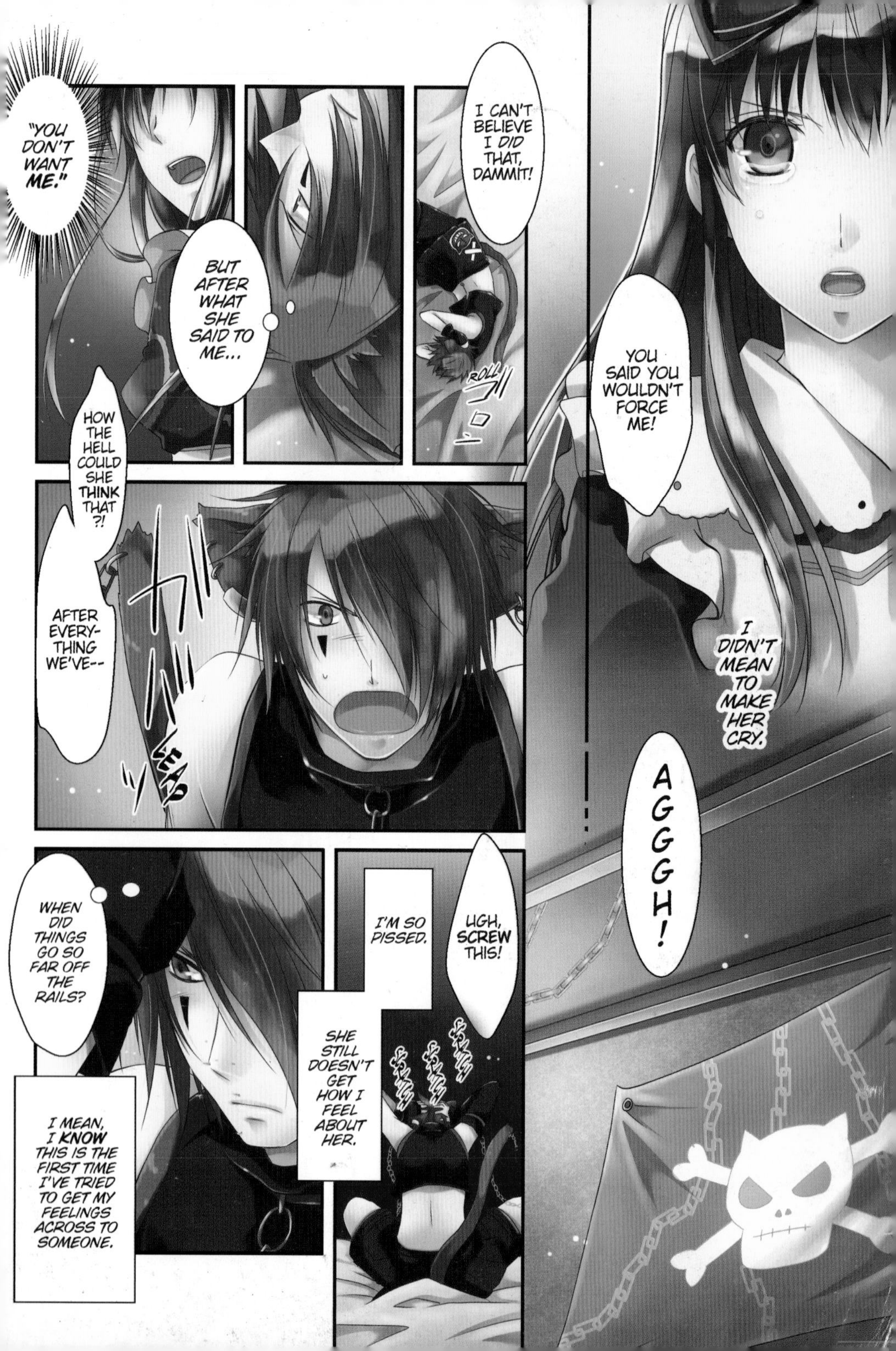
YOU SAID YOU WOULDN'T FORCE ME!
I DIDN'T MEAN TO MAKE HER CRY.
AGGGH!
I CAN'T BELIEVE I *DID* THAT, DAMMIT!
ROLL
BUT AFTER WHAT SHE SAID TO ME...
"YOU DON'T WANT **ME**."
HOW THE HELL COULD SHE **THINK** THAT?!
AFTER EVERY-THING WE'VE--
LEAP
UGH, **SCREW** THIS!
I'M SO PISSED.
SHE STILL DOESN'T GET HOW I FEEL ABOUT HER.
WHEN DID THINGS GO SO FAR OFF THE RAILS?
I MEAN, I **KNOW** THIS IS THE FIRST TIME I'VE TRIED TO GET MY FEELINGS ACROSS TO SOMEONE.

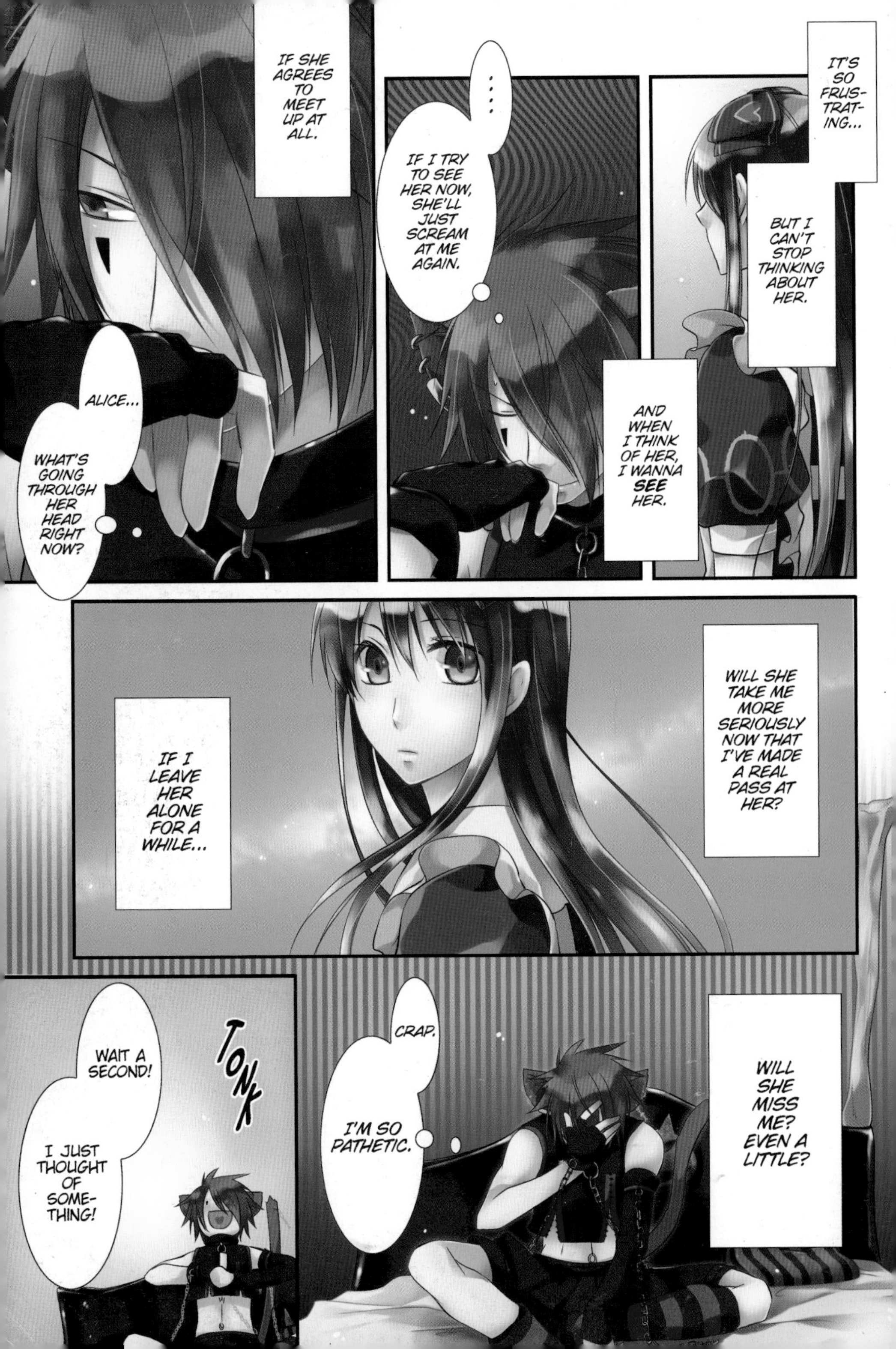
IT'S SO FRUS-TRAT-ING...
BUT I CAN'T STOP THINKING ABOUT HER.
AND WHEN I THINK OF HER, I WANNA **SEE** HER.
....
IF I TRY TO SEE HER NOW, SHE'LL JUST SCREAM AT ME AGAIN.
IF SHE AGREES TO MEET UP AT ALL.
ALICE...
WHAT'S GOING THROUGH HER HEAD RIGHT NOW?
WILL SHE TAKE ME MORE SERIOUSLY NOW THAT I'VE MADE A REAL PASS AT HER?
IF I LEAVE HER ALONE FOR A WHILE...
WILL SHE MISS ME? EVEN A LITTLE?
CRAP.
I'M SO PATHETIC.
TONK
WAIT A SECOND!
I JUST THOUGHT OF SOME-THING!

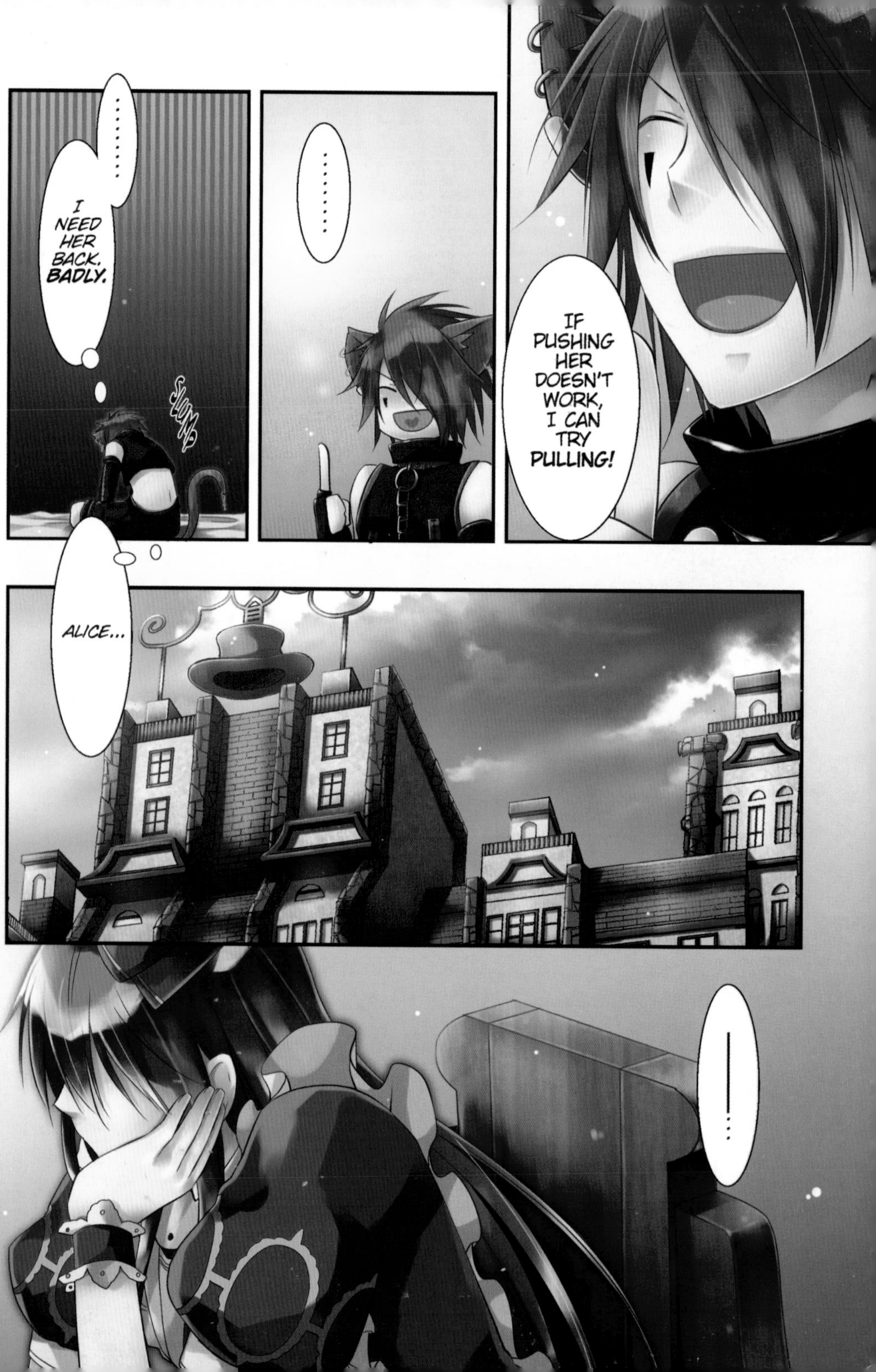

IF PUSHING HER DOESN'T WORK, I CAN TRY PULLING!
......
......
I NEED HER BACK. BADLY.
SLUMP
ALICE...
!......

Alice in the Country of Clover
~Cheshire Cat Waltz~ 2

Mamenosuke Fujimaru

藤丸 豆ノ介

Alice IN THE COUNTRY OF Clover
CHESHIRE CAT WALTZ
VOLUME 2

story by **QuinRose**
art by **Mamenosuke Fujimaru**

STAFF CREDITS

translation	**Angela Liu**
adaptation	**Lianne Sentar**
lettering	**Roland Amago**
layout	**Bambi Eloriaga-Amago**
cover design	**Nicky Lim**
copy editor	**Shanti Whitesides**
editor	**Adam Arnold**
publisher	**Jason DeAngelis**
	Seven Seas Entertainment

ALICE IN THE COUNTRY OF CLOVER: CHESHIRE CAT WALTZ VOL. 2
Copyright © Mamenosuke Fujimaru / QuinRose 2010
First published in Japan in 2010 by ICHIJINSHA Inc., Tokyo.
English translation rights arranged with ICHIJINSHA Inc., Tokyo, Japan.

ISBN: 978-1-935934-92-9

Printed in Canada

First Printing: September 2012

10 9 8 7 6 5 4 3

FOLLOW US ONLINE: www.gomanga.com

READING DIRECTIONS

This book reads from *right to left*, Japanese style.
If this is your first time reading manga, you start
reading from the top right panel on each page and
take it from there. If you get lost, just follow the
numbered diagram here. It may seem backwards
at first, but you'll get the hang of it! Have fun!!

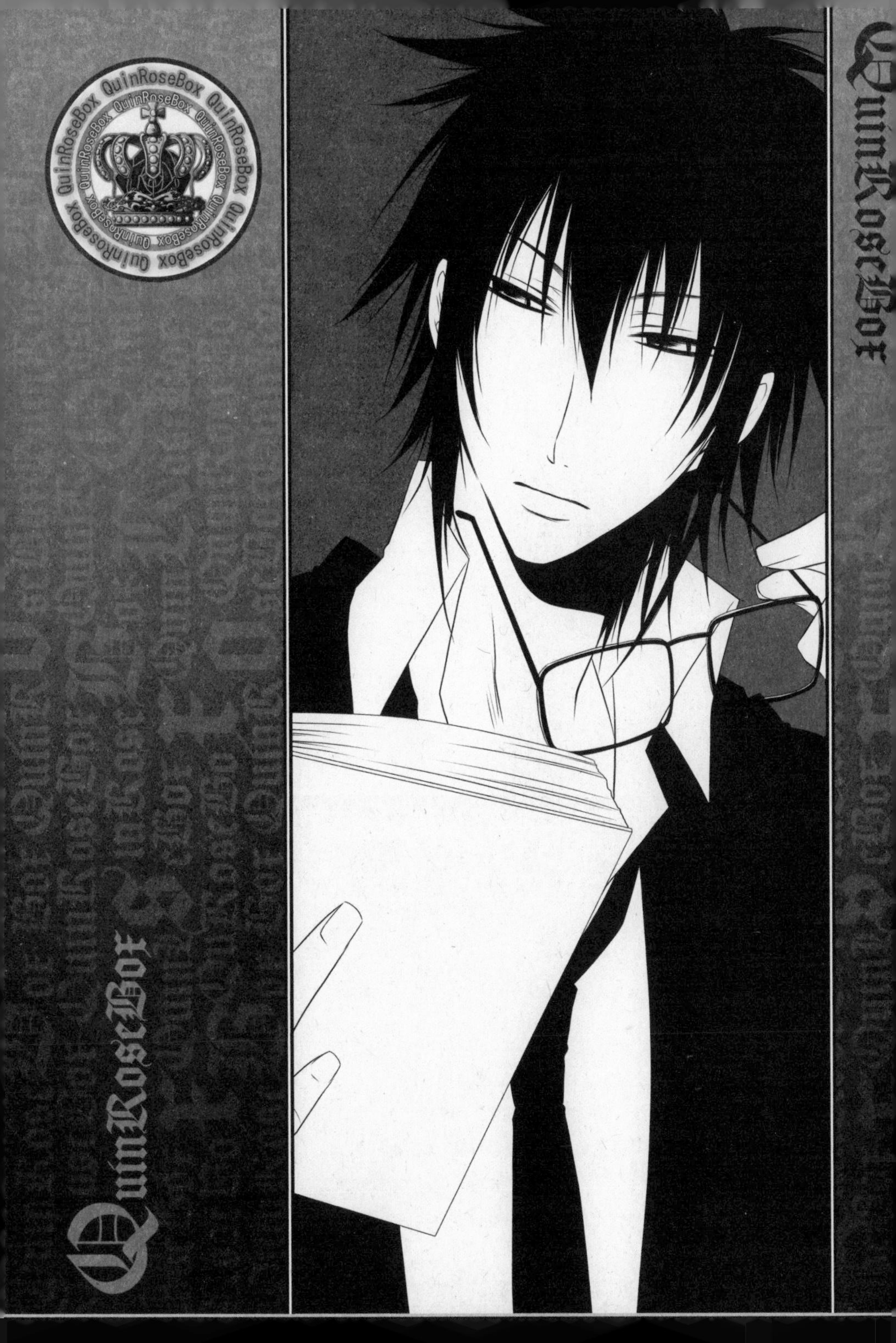
QuinRoseBox

Alice in the Country of Clover

クローバーの国の

アリス

~Wonderful Wonder World~

- STORY -

In *Alice in the Country of Clover*, the game starts with Alice having not fallen in love, but still deciding to stay in Wonderland.

She's acquainted with all the characters from the previous game, *Alice in the Country of Hearts*.

Since love would now start from a place of friendship rather than passion with a new stranger, she can experience a different type of romance from that in the previous game. Her dynamic with the characters is different through this friendship—characters can't always be forceful with her, and in many ways it's more comfortable to grow intimate. The relationships *between* the Ones With Duties have also become more of a factor.

In this game, the story focuses on the mafia. Alice attends the suited meetings (forcefully) and gets involved in various gunfights (forcefully), among other things.

Land fluctuations, sea creatures in the forest, and whispering doors—it's a game more fantastic and more eerie than the first.

Will our everywoman Alice be able to have a romantic relationship in a world devoid of common sense?

Alice in the Country of Clover
Character Information

Elliot March
VA: Tsuguo Mogami

Blood's right-hand man has a criminal past... and a temperamental present. But he's not as bad as he used to be, so that's something. Joining Blood has been good(?) for him.

Blood Dupre
VA: Katsuyuki Konishi

The head of the mafia Hatter Family, Blood is a cunning yet moody puppet-master. Alice now has the pleasure of having him for a landlord.

Alice Liddell
VA: Rie Kugimiya

A normal girl with a bit of a chip on her shoulder. Deciding to stay in the Wonderland she was carried to, she's adapted to her strange new lifestyle.

Vivaldi
VA: Yuuko Kaida

The beautiful Queen of Hearts has an unrivaled temper—which is really saying something in Wonderland. Although a picture-perfect Mad Queen, she cares for Alice as if Alice were her little sister...or a very interesting plaything.

Tweedle Dum
VA: Jun Fukuyama

The second "Bloody Twin" is equally cute and equally scary. In *Clover*, Dum can also turn into an adult.

Tweedle Dee
VA: Jun Fukuyama

One of the "Bloody Twin" gatekeepers of the Hatter territory, Dee can be cute when he's not being terrifying. In *Clover*, he sometimes turns into an adult.

Boris Airay
VA: Noriaki Sugiyama

This riddle-loving cat has a signature smirk—and in *Clover*, a new toy. One of his favorite pastimes is giving the Sleepy Mouse a hard time.

Ace
VA: Daisuke Hirakawa

The unlucky knight of Hearts was a former subordinate of Vivaldi and is perpetually lost. Even though he's depressed to be separated from his friend and boss Julius, he stays positive and tries to overcome it with a smile. He seems like a classic nice guy... or is he?

Peter White
VA: Kouki Miyata

The Prime Minister of Heart Castle—who has rabbit ears growing out of his head—invited (kidnapped) Alice to Wonderland. He loves Alice and hates everything else. His cruel, irrational actions are disturbing, but he acts like a completely different person (rabbit?) when in the throes of his love for Alice.

Gray Ringmarc
VA: Kazuya Nakai

Nightmare's subordinate in *Clover*. He used to have strong social ambition and considered assassinating Nightmare... but since Nightmare was such a useless boss, Gray couldn't help but feel sorry for him and ended up a dedicated assistant. He's a sound thinker with a strong work ethic. He's also highly skilled with his blades, rivaling even Ace.

Nightmare Gottschalk
VA: Tomokazu Sugita

A sickly nightmare who hates the hospital and needles. He has the power to read people's thoughts and enter dreams. Even though he likes to shut himself away in dreams, Gray drags him out to sulk from time to time. He technically holds a high position and has many subordinates, but since he can't even take care of his own health, he leaves most things to Gray.

Pierce Villiers
VA: Souichirou Hoshi

New to *Clover*, Pierce is an insomniac mouse who drinks too much coffee. He loves Nightmare (who can help him sleep) and hates Boris (who terrifies him). He dislikes Blood and Vivaldi for discarding coffee in favor of tea. He likes Elliot and Peter well enough, since rabbits aren't natural predators of mice.

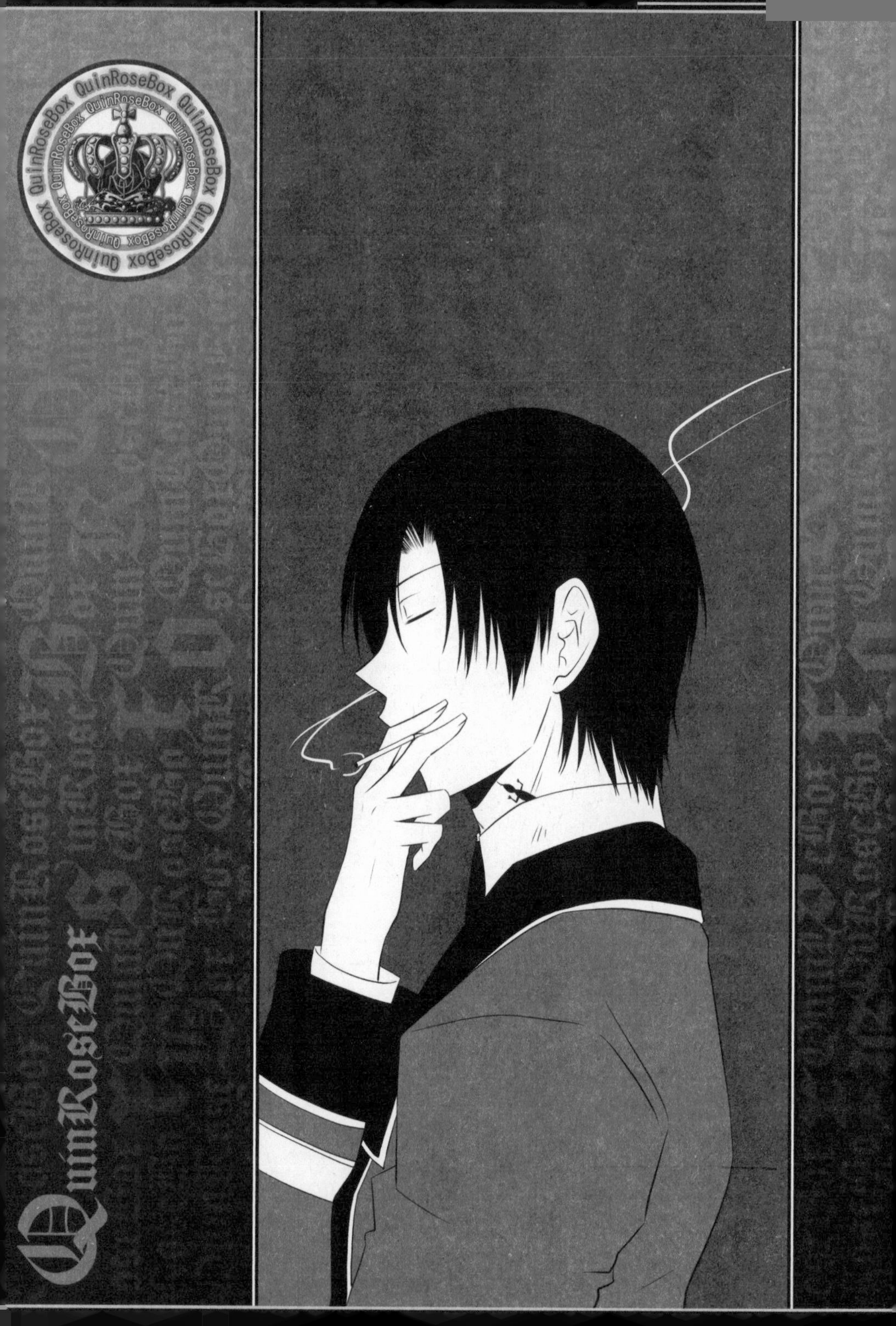
QuinRoseBox

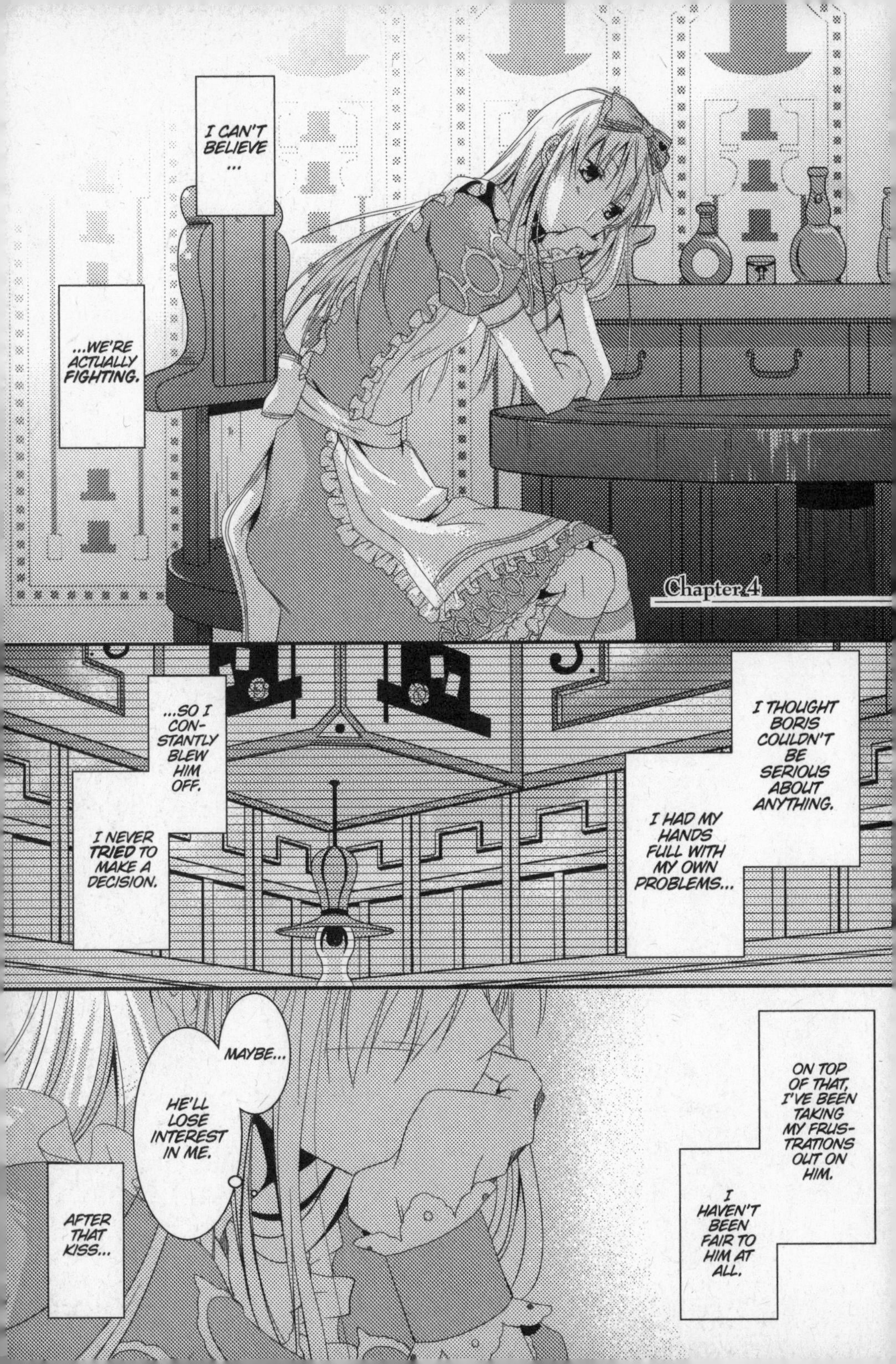

I CAN'T BELIEVE ...
...WE'RE ACTUALLY FIGHTING.
Chapter 4
I THOUGHT BORIS COULDN'T BE SERIOUS ABOUT ANYTHING.
I HAD MY HANDS FULL WITH MY OWN PROBLEMS...
...SO I CON-STANTLY BLEW HIM OFF.
I NEVER TRIED TO MAKE A DECISION.
ON TOP OF THAT, I'VE BEEN TAKING MY FRUS-TRATIONS OUT ON HIM.
I HAVEN'T BEEN FAIR TO HIM AT ALL.
MAYBE... HE'LL LOSE INTEREST IN ME.
AFTER THAT KISS...

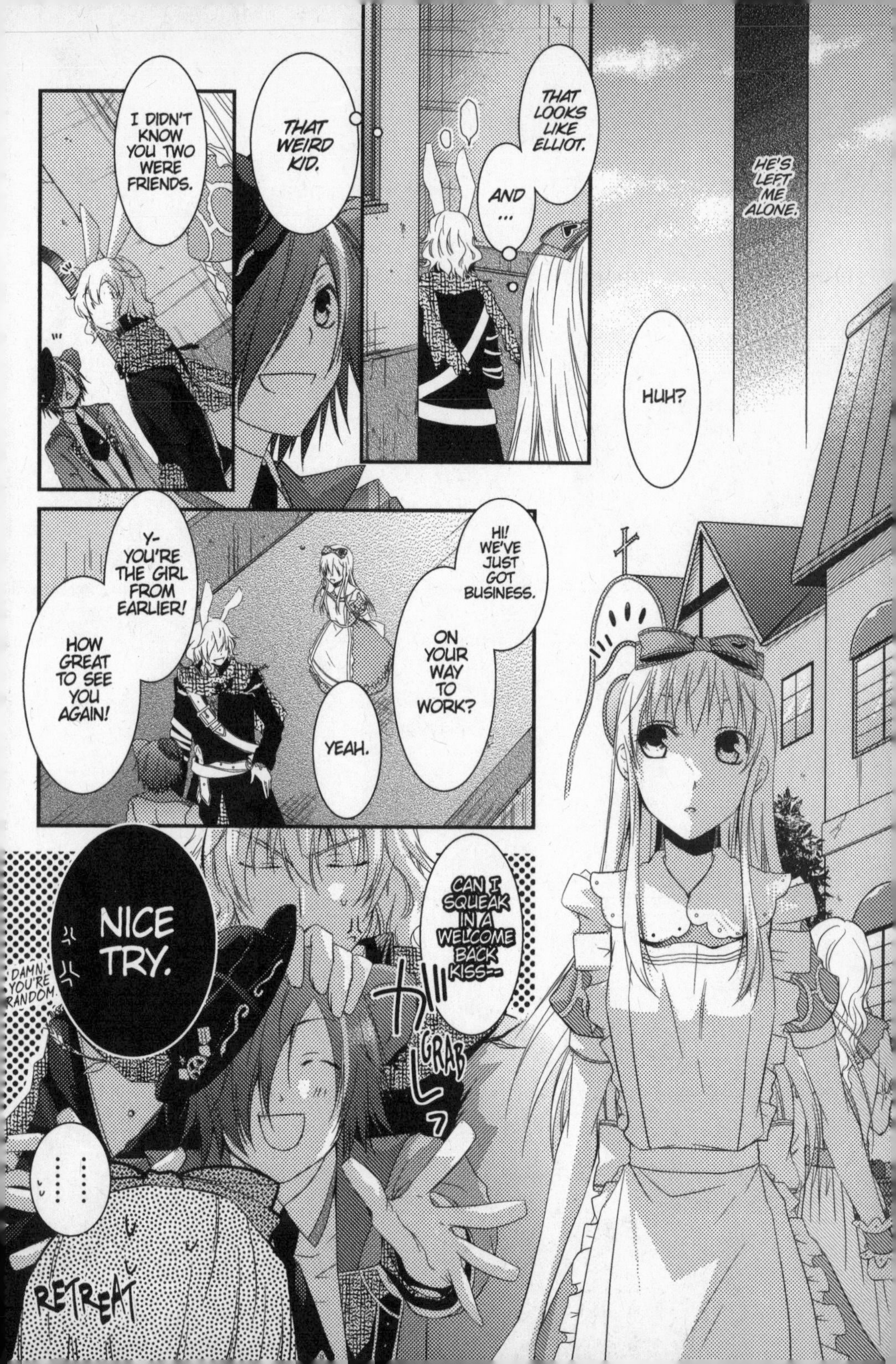
HE'S LEFT ME ALONE.
HUH?
THAT LOOKS LIKE ELLIOT.
AND ...
THAT WEIRD KID.
I DIDN'T KNOW YOU TWO WERE FRIENDS.
HI! WE'VE JUST GOT BUSINESS.
ON YOUR WAY TO WORK?
YEAH.
Y-YOU'RE THE GIRL FROM EARLIER!
HOW GREAT TO SEE YOU AGAIN!
CAN I SQUEAK IN A WELCOME BACK KISS--
GRAB
NICE TRY.
DAMN, YOU'RE RANDOM.
......
RETREAT

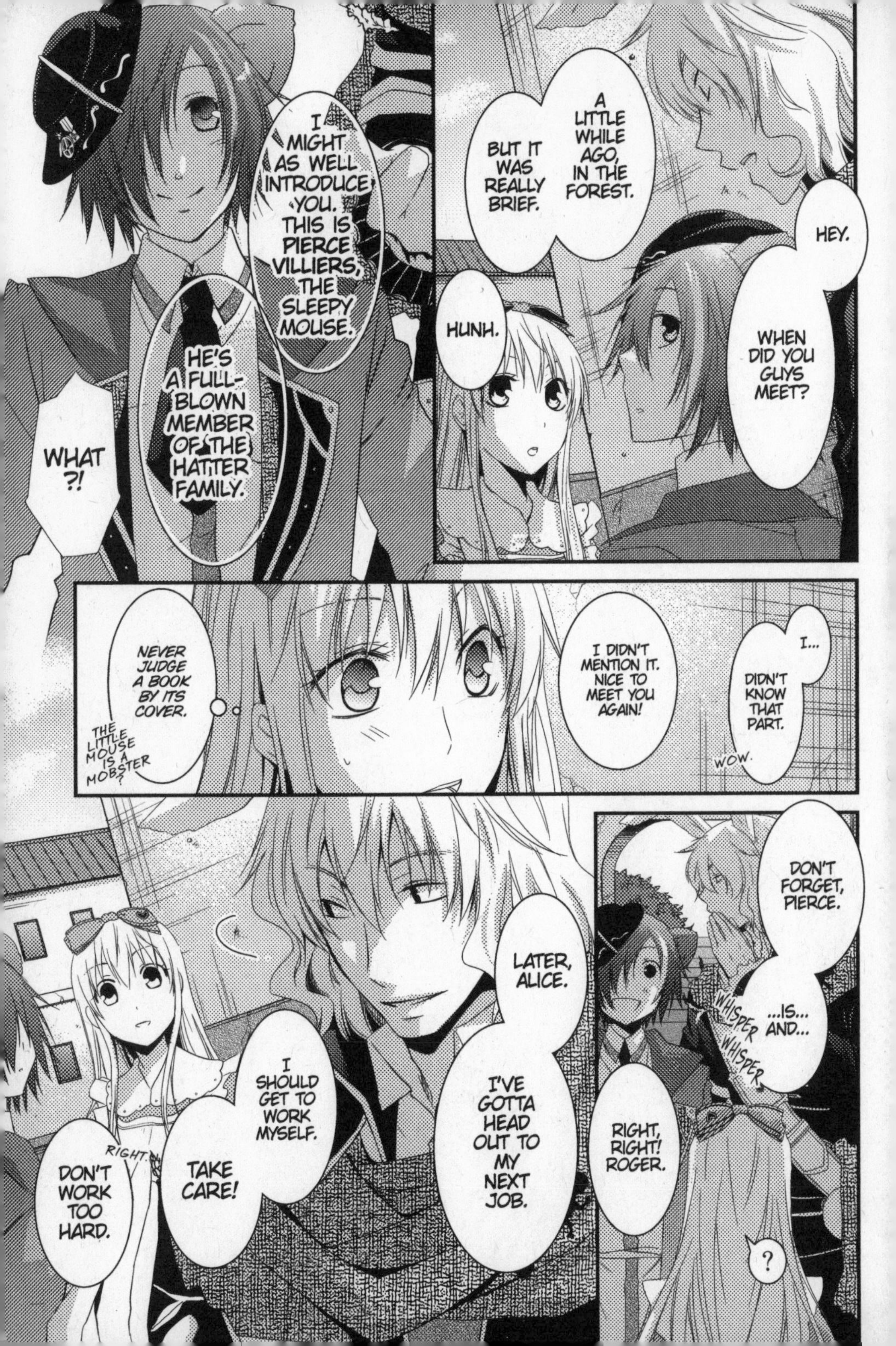
HEY.
WHEN DID YOU GUYS MEET?
A LITTLE WHILE AGO, IN THE FOREST.
BUT IT WAS REALLY BRIEF.
HUNH.
I MIGHT AS WELL INTRODUCE YOU. THIS IS PIERCE VILLIERS, THE SLEEPY MOUSE.
HE'S A FULL-BLOWN MEMBER OF THE HATTER FAMILY.
WHAT ?!
I... DIDN'T KNOW THAT PART.
WOW.
I DIDN'T MENTION IT. NICE TO MEET YOU AGAIN!
NEVER JUDGE A BOOK BY ITS COVER.
THE LITTLE MOUSE IS A MOBSTER?
DON'T FORGET, PIERCE.
...IS... AND...
WHISPER WHISPER
RIGHT, RIGHT! ROGER.
?
LATER, ALICE.
I'VE GOTTA HEAD OUT TO MY NEXT JOB.
I SHOULD GET TO WORK MYSELF.
TAKE CARE!
RIGHT.
DON'T WORK TOO HARD.

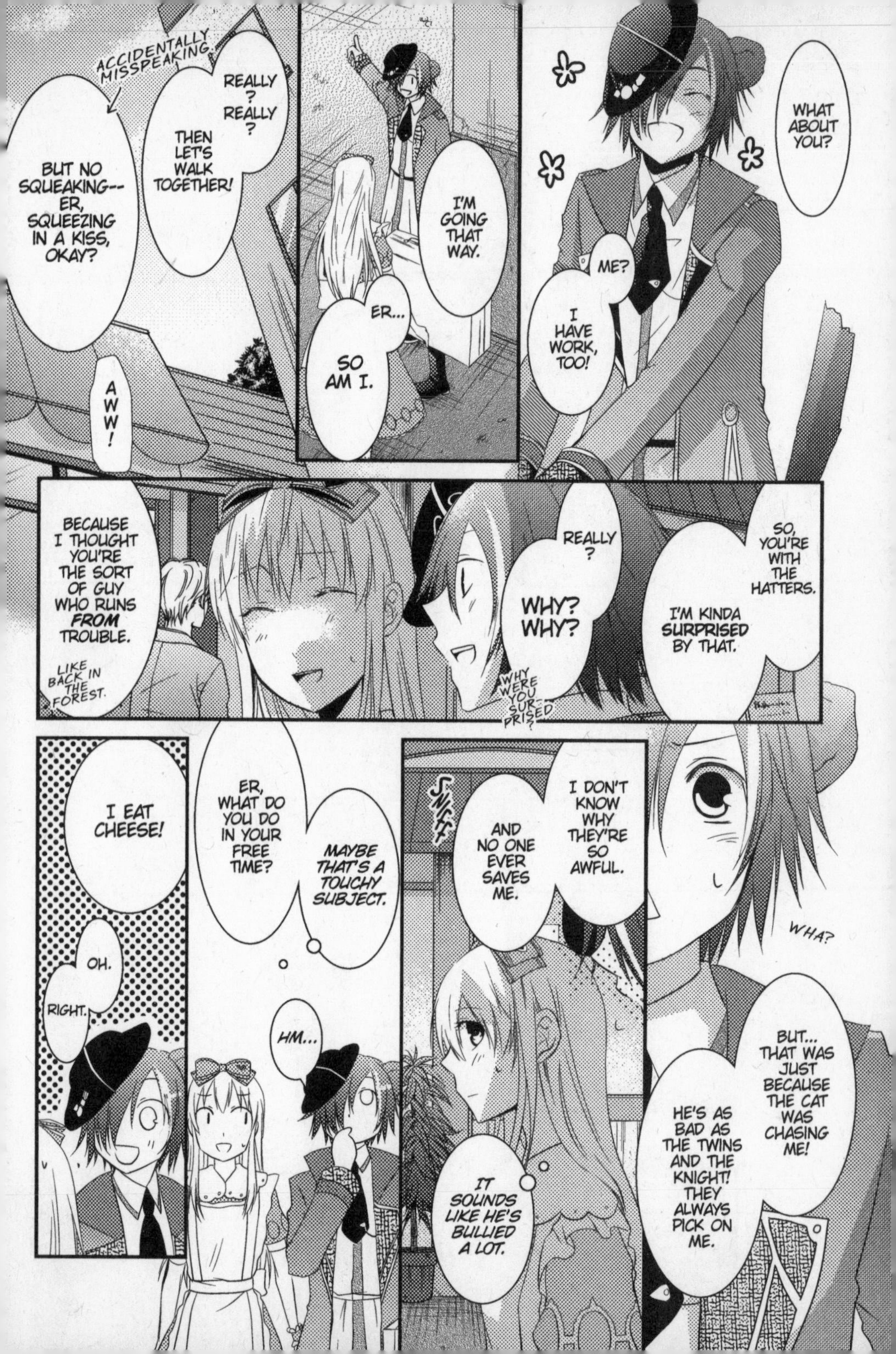
WHAT ABOUT YOU?
ME?
I HAVE WORK, TOO!
I'M GOING THAT WAY.
ER...
SO AM I.
REALLY? REALLY?
THEN LET'S WALK TOGETHER!
ACCIDENTALLY MISSPEAKING
BUT NO SQUEAKING-- ER, SQUEEZING IN A KISS, OKAY?
AWW!
SO, YOU'RE WITH THE HATTERS.
I'M KINDA SURPRISED BY THAT.
REALLY?
WHY? WHY?
WHY WERE YOU SURPRISED?
BECAUSE I THOUGHT YOU'RE THE SORT OF GUY WHO RUNS FROM TROUBLE.
LIKE BACK IN THE FOREST.
WHA?
BUT... THAT WAS JUST BECAUSE THE CAT WAS CHASING ME!
HE'S AS BAD AS THE TWINS AND THE KNIGHT! THEY ALWAYS PICK ON ME.
I DON'T KNOW WHY THEY'RE SO AWFUL.
AND NO ONE EVER SAVES ME.
SNIFF
IT SOUNDS LIKE HE'S BULLIED A LOT.
ER, WHAT DO YOU DO IN YOUR FREE TIME?
MAYBE THAT'S A TOUCHY SUBJECT.
HM...
I EAT CHEESE!
OH.
RIGHT.

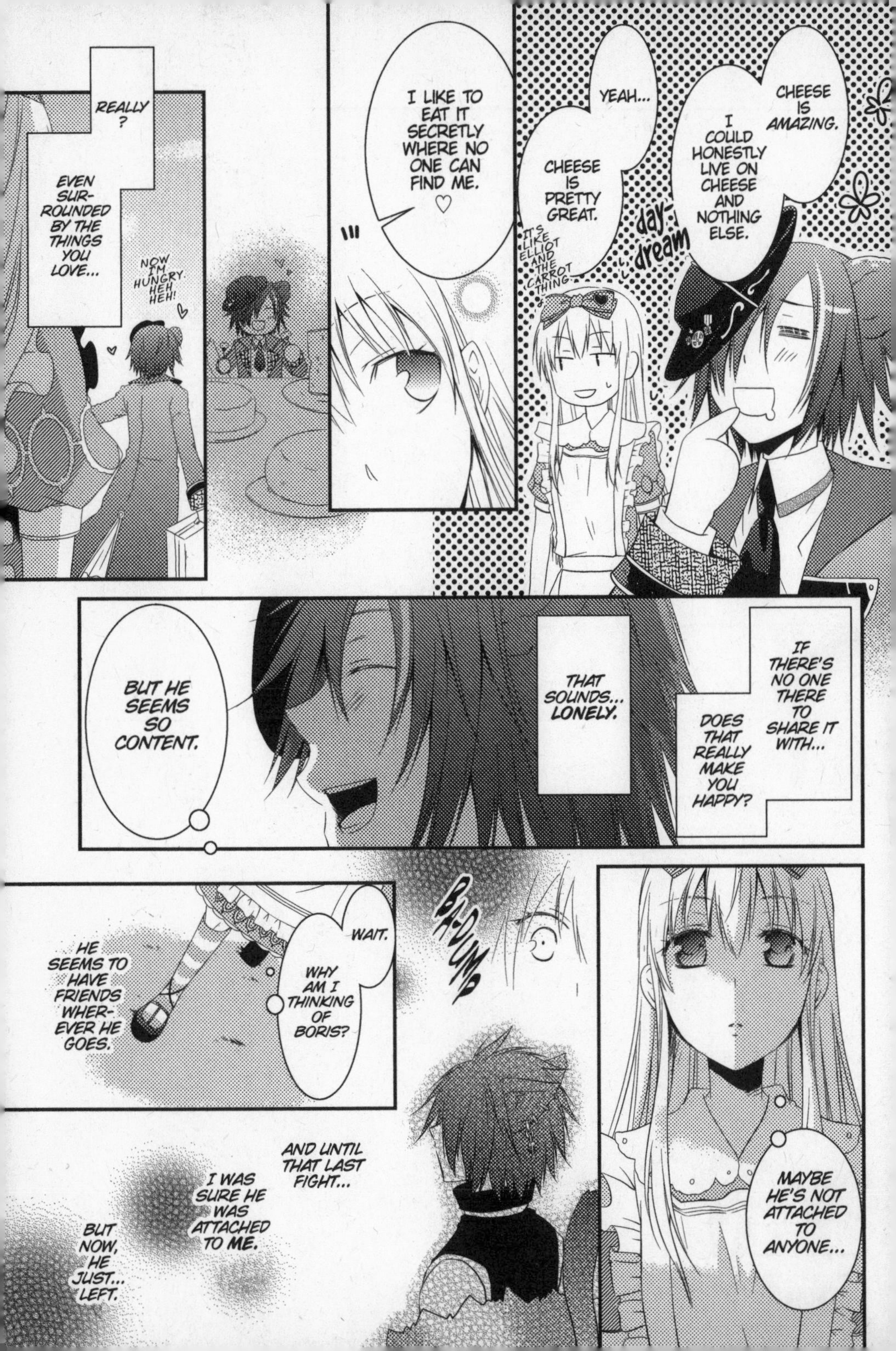
CHEESE IS AMAZING.
I COULD HONESTLY LIVE ON CHEESE AND NOTHING ELSE.
day-dream
YEAH...
CHEESE IS PRETTY GREAT.
IT'S LIKE ELLIOT AND THE CARROT THING.
I LIKE TO EAT IT SECRETLY WHERE NO ONE CAN FIND ME. ♡
REALLY?
EVEN SUR-ROUNDED BY THE THINGS YOU LOVE...
NOW I'M HUNGRY. HEH HEH!
IF THERE'S NO ONE THERE TO SHARE IT WITH...
DOES THAT REALLY MAKE YOU HAPPY?
THAT SOUNDS... LONELY.
BUT HE SEEMS SO CONTENT.
MAYBE HE'S NOT ATTACHED TO ANYONE...
BA-DUMP
WAIT.
WHY AM I THINKING OF BORIS?
HE SEEMS TO HAVE FRIENDS WHER-EVER HE GOES.
AND UNTIL THAT LAST FIGHT...
I WAS SURE HE WAS ATTACHED TO ME.
BUT NOW, HE JUST... LEFT.

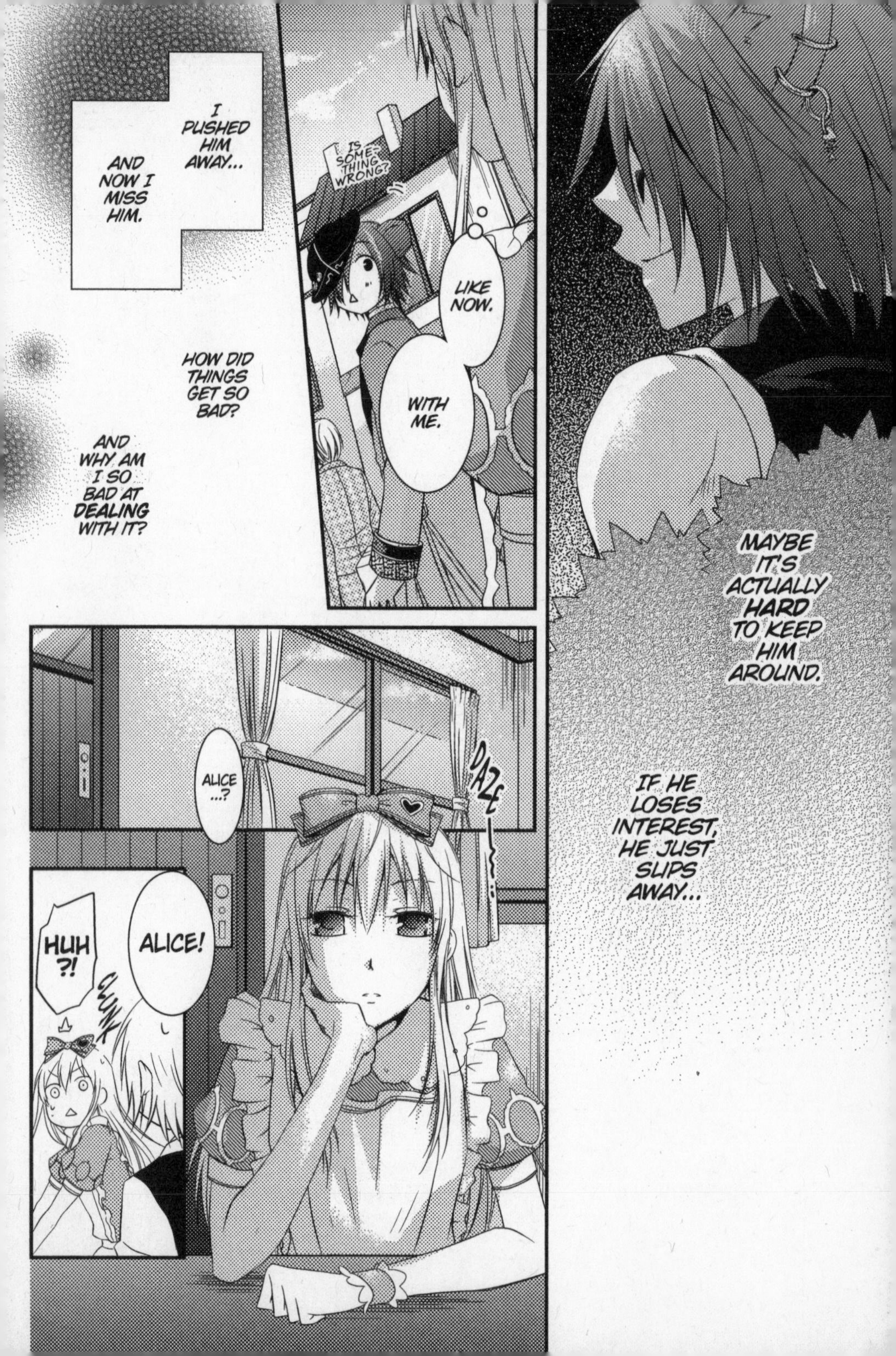
MAYBE IT'S ACTUALLY HARD TO KEEP HIM AROUND.
IF HE LOSES INTEREST, HE JUST SLIPS AWAY...
IS SOME-THING WRONG?
LIKE NOW.
WITH ME.
I PUSHED HIM AWAY...
AND NOW I MISS HIM.
HOW DID THINGS GET SO BAD?
AND WHY AM I SO BAD AT DEALING WITH IT?
ALICE ...?
DAZE~
ALICE!
HUH ?!
CLUNK

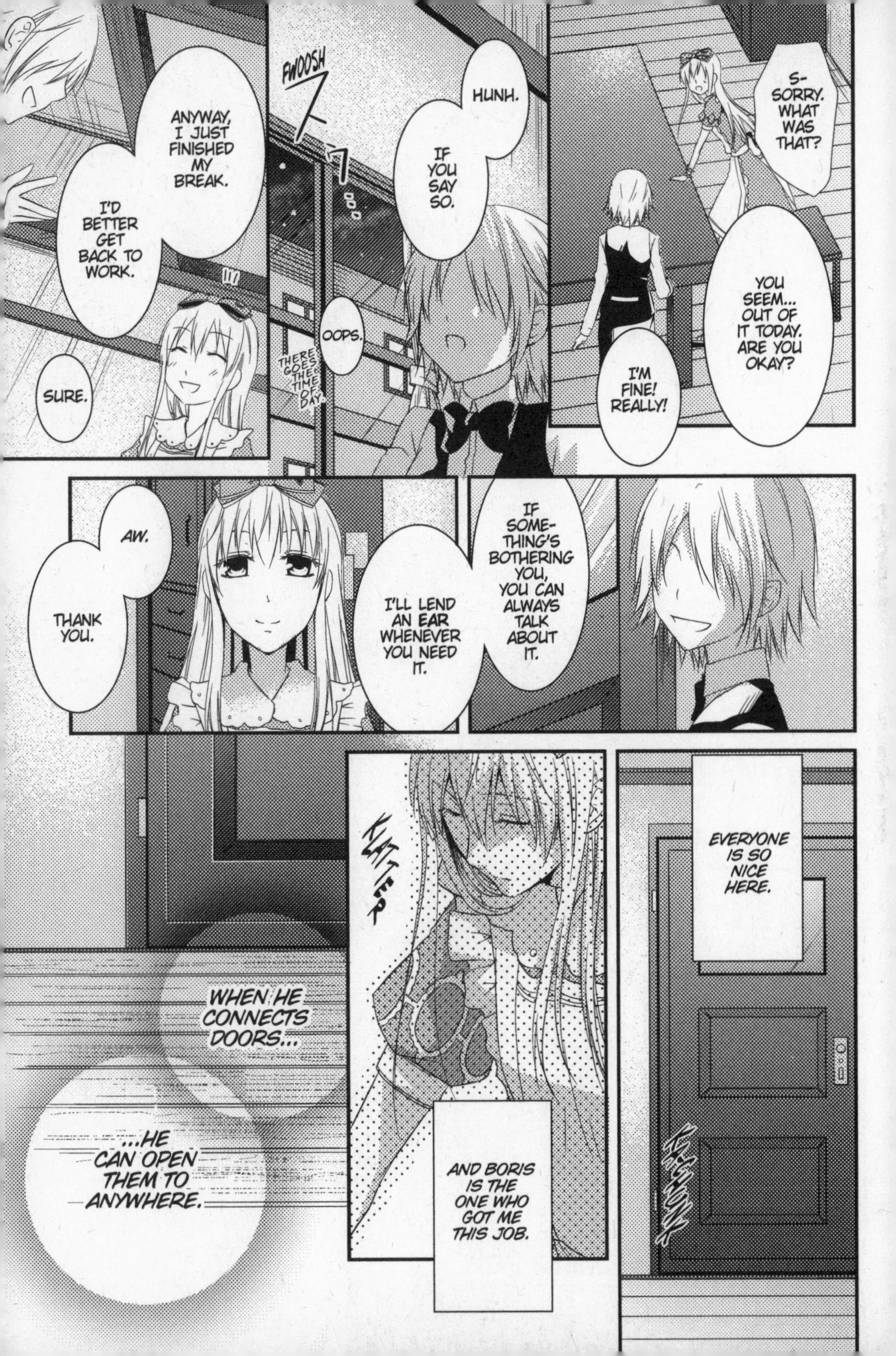
S-SORRY. WHAT WAS THAT?
YOU SEEM... OUT OF IT TODAY. ARE YOU OKAY?
I'M FINE! REALLY!
HUNH.
IF YOU SAY SO.
FWOOSH
OOPS.
THERE GOES THE TIME OF DAY.
ANYWAY, I JUST FINISHED MY BREAK.
I'D BETTER GET BACK TO WORK.
SURE.
IF SOMETHING'S BOTHERING YOU, YOU CAN ALWAYS TALK ABOUT IT.
I'LL LEND AN EAR WHENEVER YOU NEED IT.
AW.
THANK YOU.
EVERYONE IS SO NICE HERE.
KACHUNK
KLATTER
AND BORIS IS THE ONE WHO GOT ME THIS JOB.
WHEN HE CONNECTS DOORS...
...HE CAN OPEN THEM TO ANYWHERE.

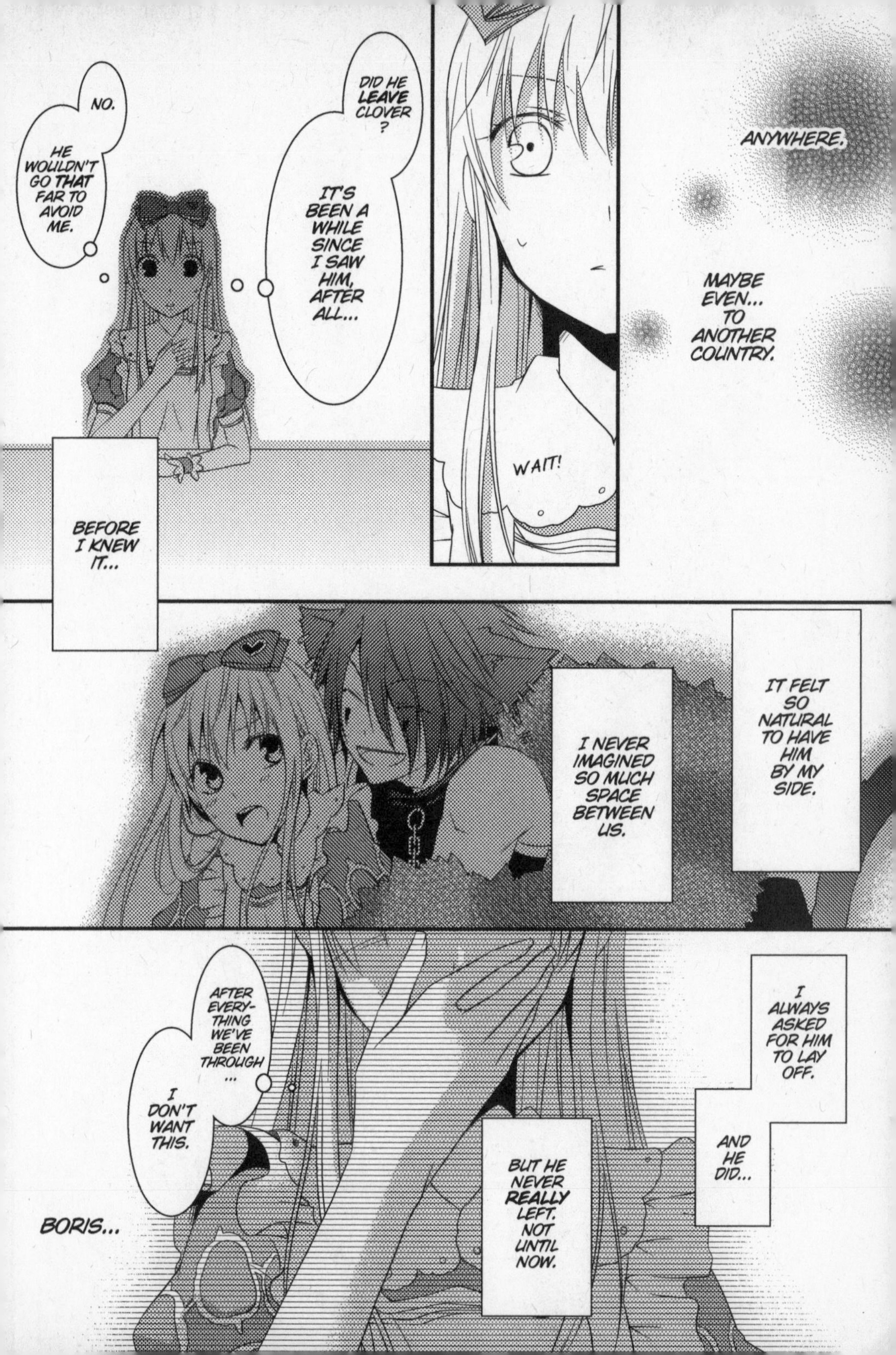
ANYWHERE.
MAYBE EVEN... TO ANOTHER COUNTRY.
WAIT!
DID HE LEAVE CLOVER?
IT'S BEEN A WHILE SINCE I SAW HIM, AFTER ALL...
NO.
HE WOULDN'T GO THAT FAR TO AVOID ME.
BEFORE I KNEW IT...
IT FELT SO NATURAL TO HAVE HIM BY MY SIDE.
I NEVER IMAGINED SO MUCH SPACE BETWEEN US.
I ALWAYS ASKED FOR HIM TO LAY OFF.
AND HE DID...
BUT HE NEVER REALLY LEFT. NOT UNTIL NOW.
AFTER EVERYTHING WE'VE BEEN THROUGH...
I DON'T WANT THIS.
BORIS...

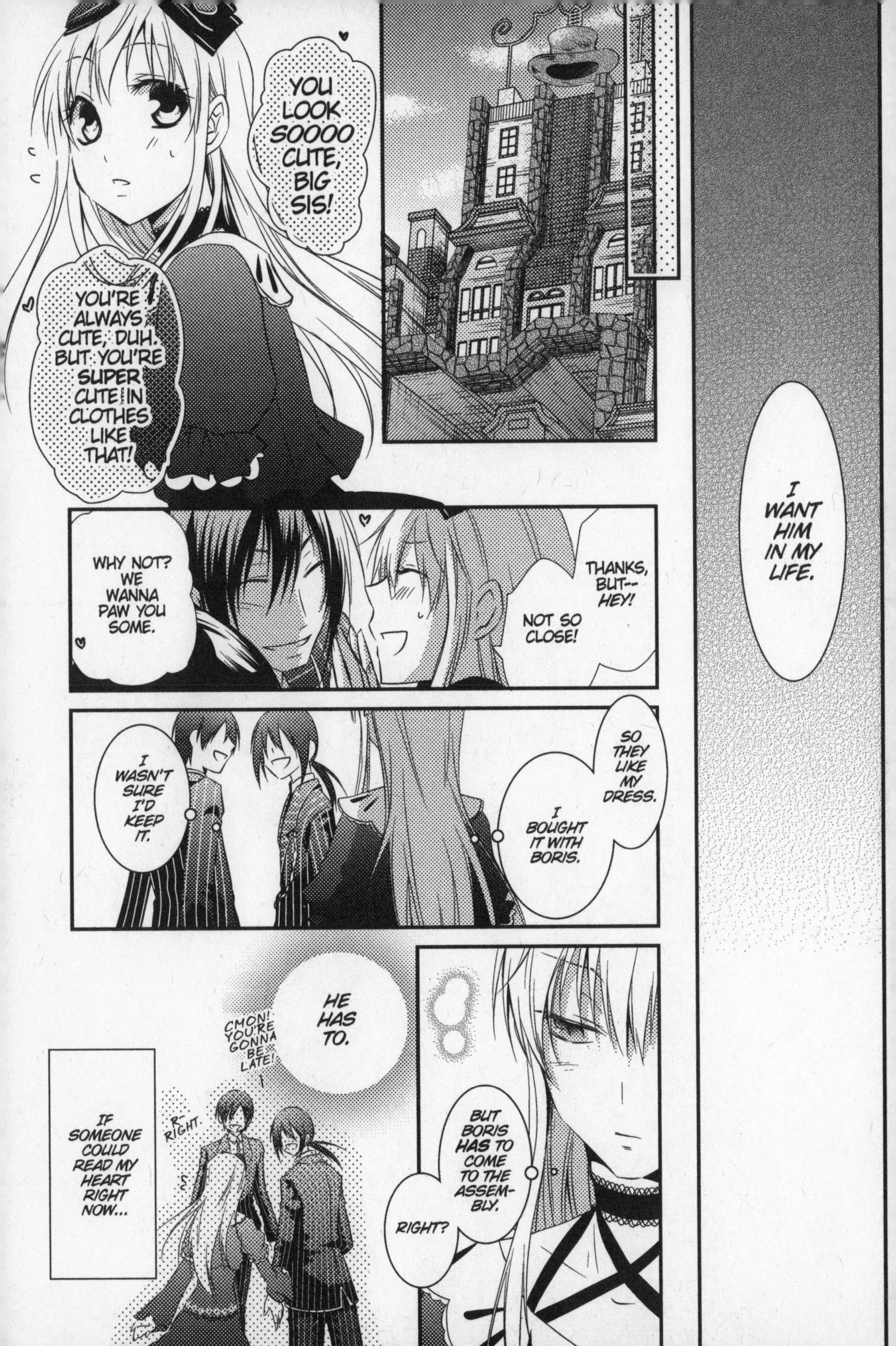
I WANT HIM IN MY LIFE.
YOU LOOK SOOOO CUTE, BIG SIS!
YOU'RE ALWAYS CUTE, DUH. BUT YOU'RE SUPER CUTE IN CLOTHES LIKE THAT!
THANKS, BUT-- HEY!
NOT SO CLOSE!
WHY NOT? WE WANNA PAW YOU SOME.
SO THEY LIKE MY DRESS.
I BOUGHT IT WITH BORIS.
I WASN'T SURE I'D KEEP IT.
BUT BORIS HAS TO COME TO THE ASSEMBLY.
RIGHT?
HE HAS TO.
CMON! YOU'RE GONNA BE LATE!
R-RIGHT.
IF SOMEONE COULD READ MY HEART RIGHT NOW...

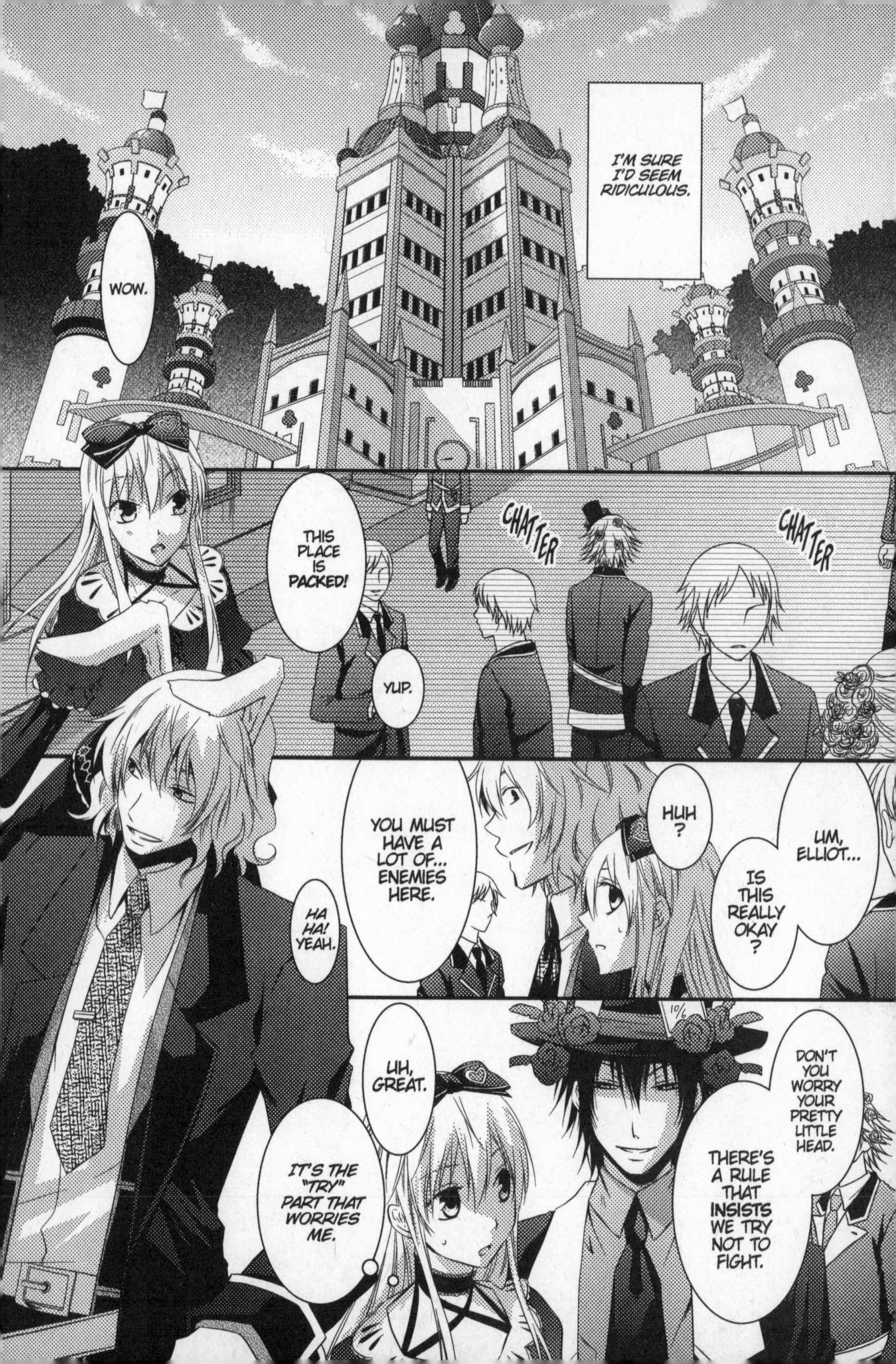

I'M SURE I'D SEEM RIDICULOUS.
WOW.
CHATTER
CHATTER
THIS PLACE IS PACKED!
YUP.
UM, ELLIOT...
IS THIS REALLY OKAY?
HUH?
YOU MUST HAVE A LOT OF... ENEMIES HERE.
HA HA! YEAH.
DON'T YOU WORRY YOUR PRETTY LITTLE HEAD.
THERE'S A RULE THAT INSISTS WE TRY NOT TO FIGHT.
UH, GREAT.
IT'S THE "TRY" PART THAT WORRIES ME.

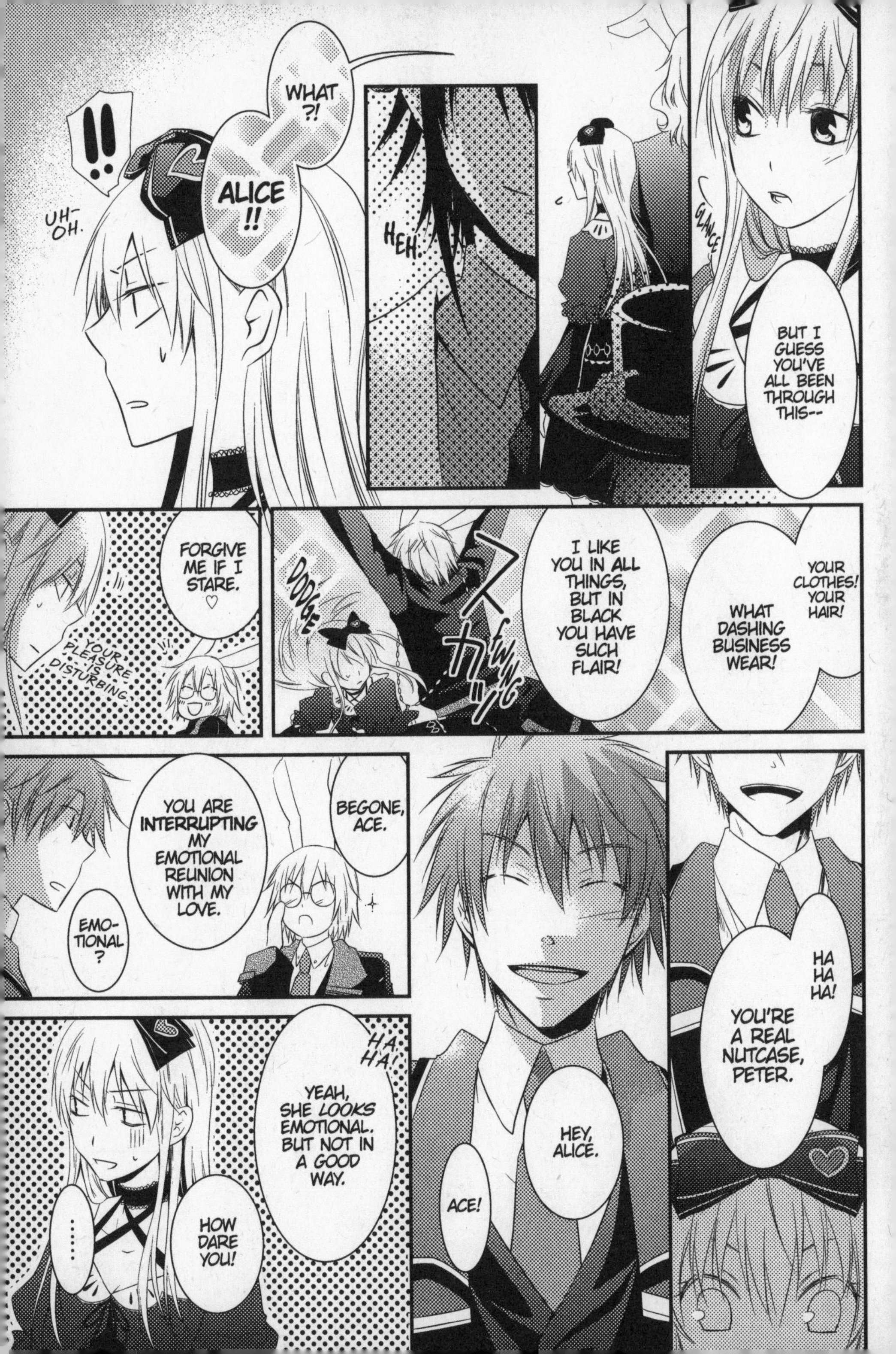
GLANCE
BUT I GUESS YOU'VE ALL BEEN THROUGH THIS--
HEH.
WHAT ?!
ALICE !!
!!
UH-OH.
YOUR CLOTHES! YOUR HAIR!
WHAT DASHING BUSINESS WEAR!
I LIKE YOU IN ALL THINGS, BUT IN BLACK YOU HAVE SUCH FLAIR!
DODGE
FWING
FORGIVE ME IF I STARE. ♡
YOUR PLEASURE IS DISTURBING.
HA HA HA!
YOU'RE A REAL NUTCASE, PETER.
HEY, ALICE.
ACE!
BEGONE, ACE.
YOU ARE INTERRUPTING MY EMOTIONAL REUNION WITH MY LOVE.
EMO-TIONAL ?
HA HA!
YEAH, SHE LOOKS EMOTIONAL. BUT NOT IN A GOOD WAY.
HOW DARE YOU!
......

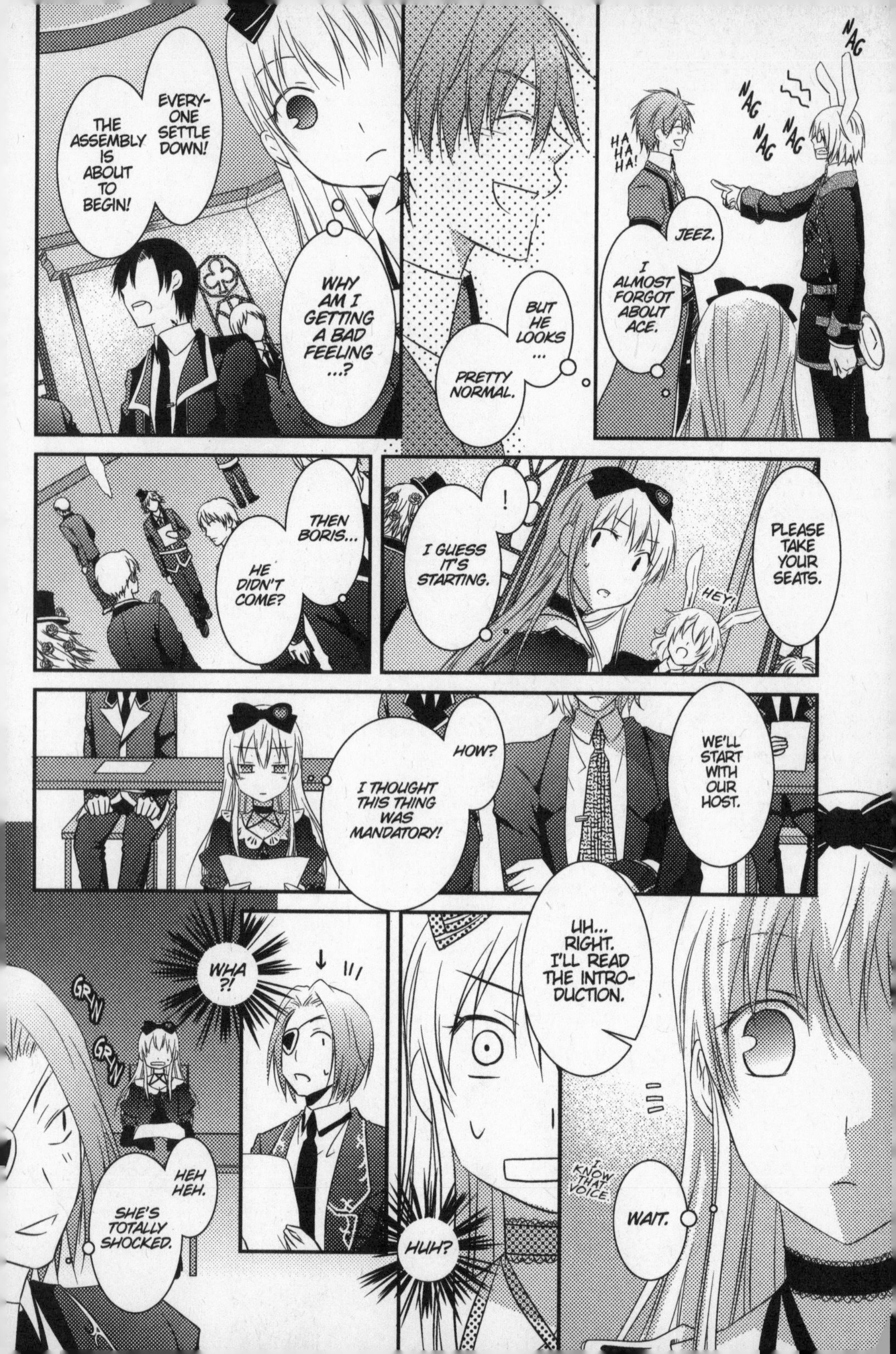
NAG NAG NAG NAG
HA HA HA!
JEEZ.
I ALMOST FORGOT ABOUT ACE.
BUT HE LOOKS...
PRETTY NORMAL.
EVERY-ONE SETTLE DOWN!
THE ASSEMBLY IS ABOUT TO BEGIN!
WHY AM I GETTING A BAD FEELING...?
PLEASE TAKE YOUR SEATS.
HEY!
!
I GUESS IT'S STARTING.
THEN BORIS...
HE DIDN'T COME?
WE'LL START WITH OUR HOST.
HOW?
I THOUGHT THIS THING WAS MANDATORY!
UH... RIGHT. I'LL READ THE INTRO-DUCTION.
I KNOW THAT VOICE.
WAIT.
WHA?!
HUH?
GRIN GRIN
HEH HEH.
SHE'S TOTALLY SHOCKED.

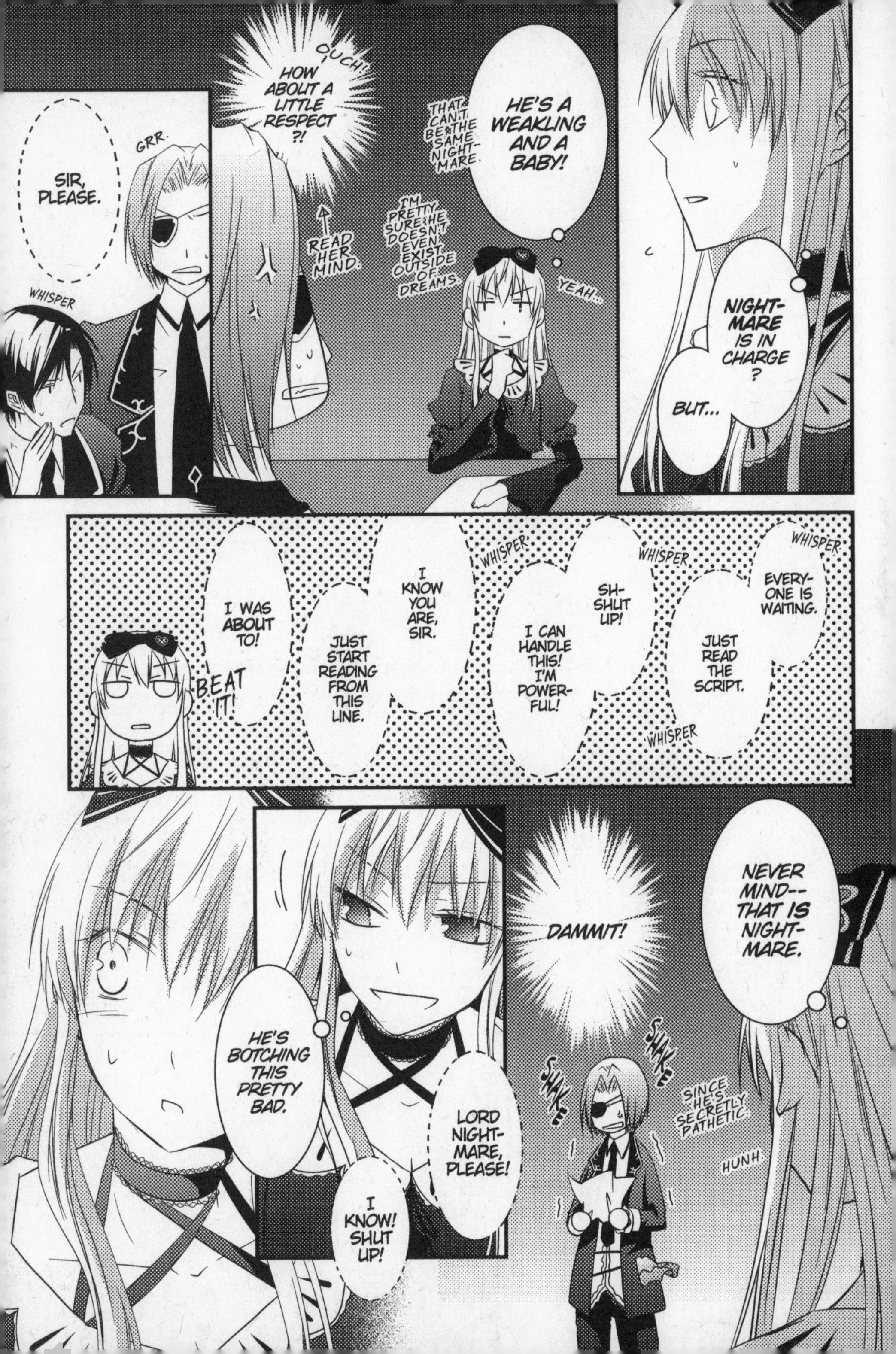
NIGHT-MARE IS IN CHARGE?
BUT...
HE'S A WEAKLING AND A BABY!
THAT CAN'T BE THE SAME NIGHT-MARE.
I'M PRETTY SURE HE DOESN'T EVEN EXIST OUTSIDE OF DREAMS.
YEAH...
READ HER MIND.
OUCH!
HOW ABOUT A LITTLE RESPECT?!
GRR.
SIR, PLEASE.
WHISPER
WHISPER
EVERY-ONE IS WAITING.
JUST READ THE SCRIPT.
WHISPER
WHISPER
SH-SHUT UP!
I CAN HANDLE THIS! I'M POWER-FUL!
WHISPER
I KNOW YOU ARE, SIR.
JUST START READING FROM THIS LINE.
I WAS ABOUT TO!
BEAT IT!
NEVER MIND--THAT IS NIGHT-MARE.
SINCE HE'S SECRETLY PATHETIC.
HUNH.
DAMMIT!
SHAKE
SHAKE
LORD NIGHT-MARE, PLEASE!
I KNOW! SHUT UP!
HE'S BOTCHING THIS PRETTY BAD.

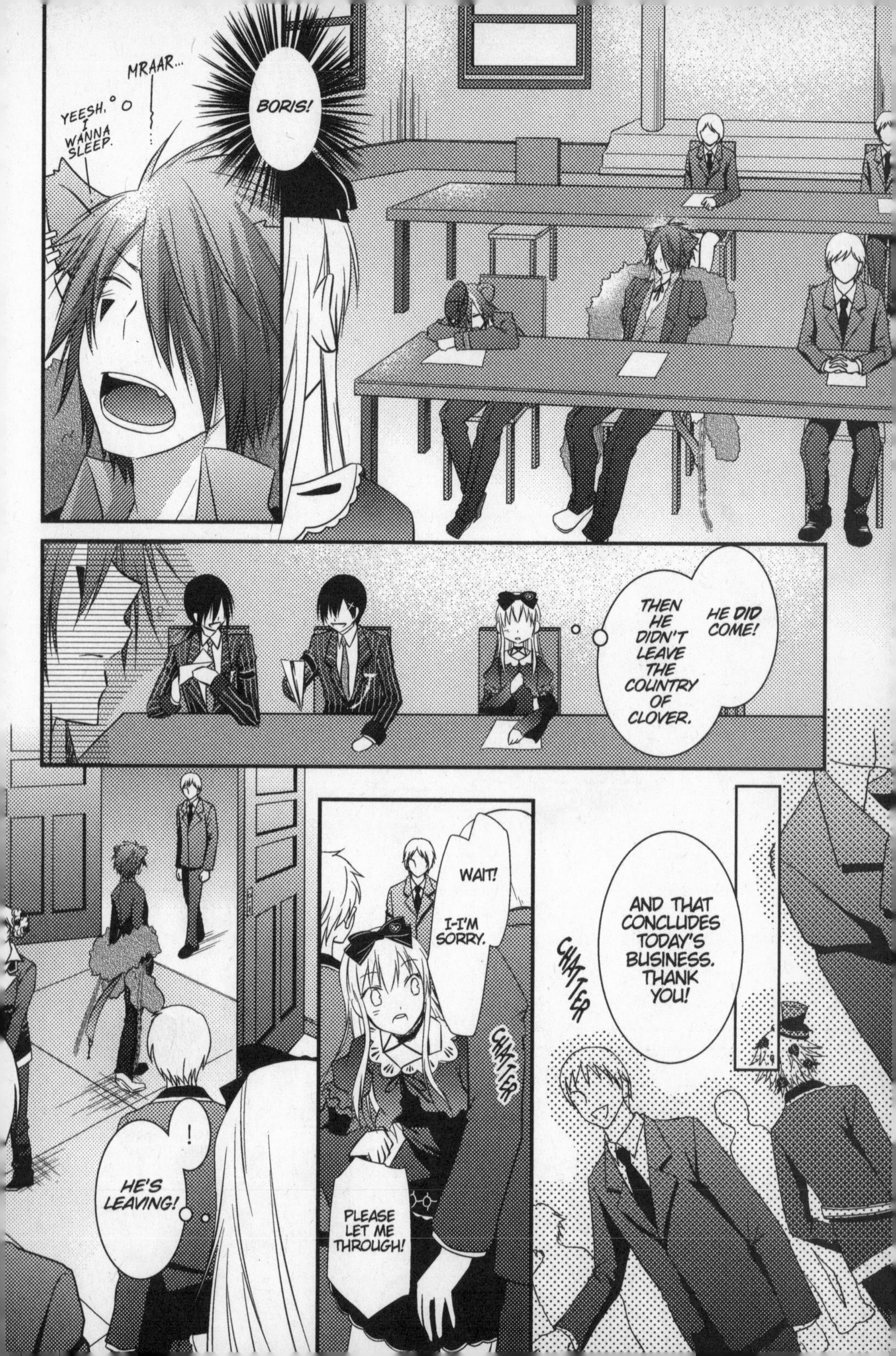
BORIS!
MRAAR...
YEESH, I WANNA SLEEP.
HE DID COME!
THEN HE DIDN'T LEAVE THE COUNTRY OF CLOVER.
AND THAT CONCLUDES TODAY'S BUSINESS. THANK YOU!
CHATTER
WAIT!
I-I'M SORRY.
CHATTER
PLEASE LET ME THROUGH!
!
HE'S LEAVING!

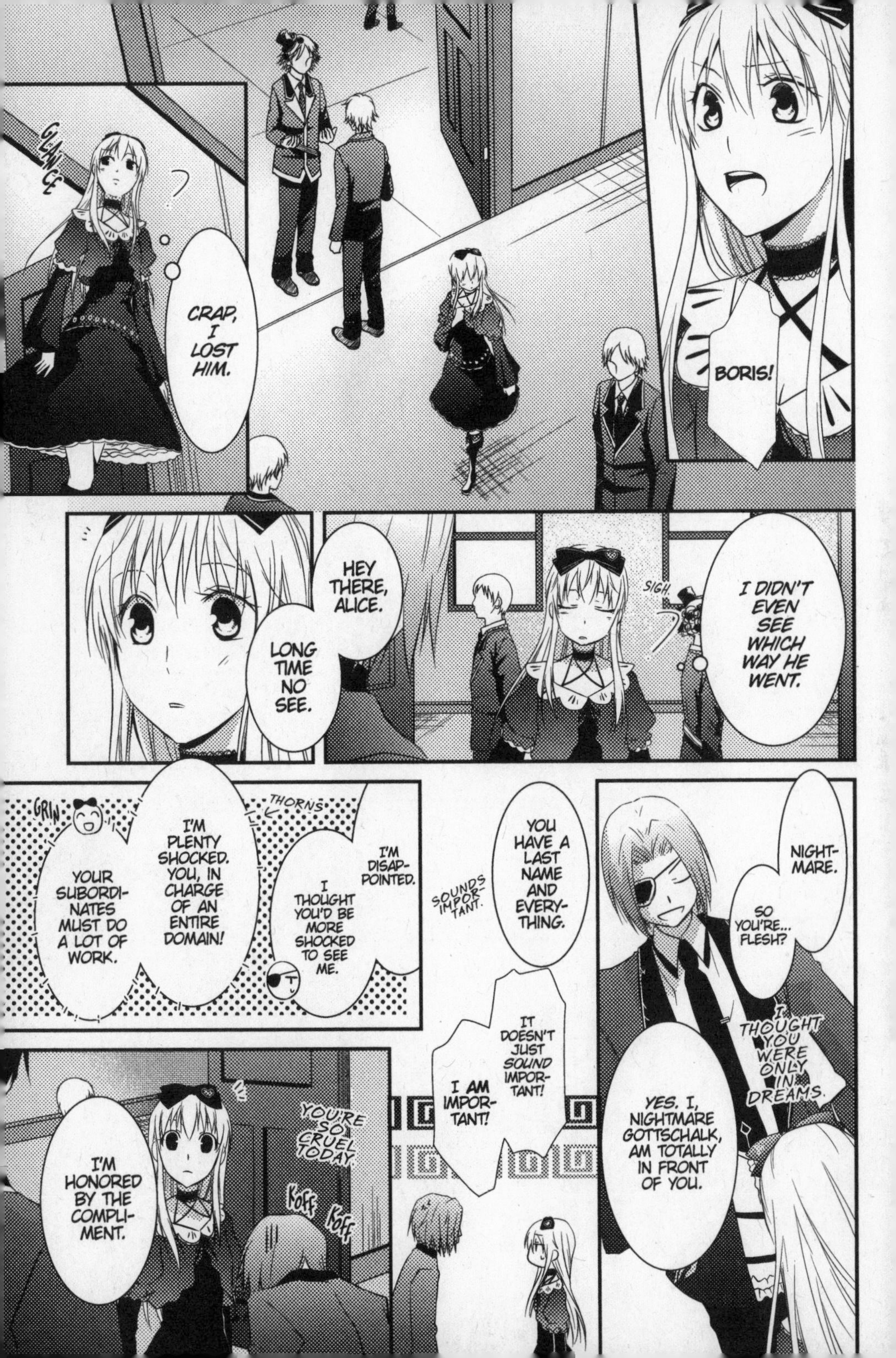
BORIS!
GLANCE
CRAP, I LOST HIM.
SIGH.
I DIDN'T EVEN SEE WHICH WAY HE WENT.
HEY THERE, ALICE.
LONG TIME NO SEE.
NIGHTMARE.
SO YOU'RE... FLESH?
I THOUGHT YOU WERE ONLY IN DREAMS.
YES. I, NIGHTMARE GOTTSCHALK, AM TOTALLY IN FRONT OF YOU.
YOU HAVE A LAST NAME AND EVERYTHING.
SOUNDS IMPORTANT.
I'M DISAPPOINTED.
I THOUGHT YOU'D BE MORE SHOCKED TO SEE ME.
THORNS
I'M PLENTY SHOCKED. YOU, IN CHARGE OF AN ENTIRE DOMAIN!
GRIN
YOUR SUBORDINATES MUST DO A LOT OF WORK.
IT DOESN'T JUST SOUND IMPORTANT!
I AM IMPORTANT!
YOU'RE SO CRUEL TODAY.
KOFF KOFF
I'M HONORED BY THE COMPLIMENT.

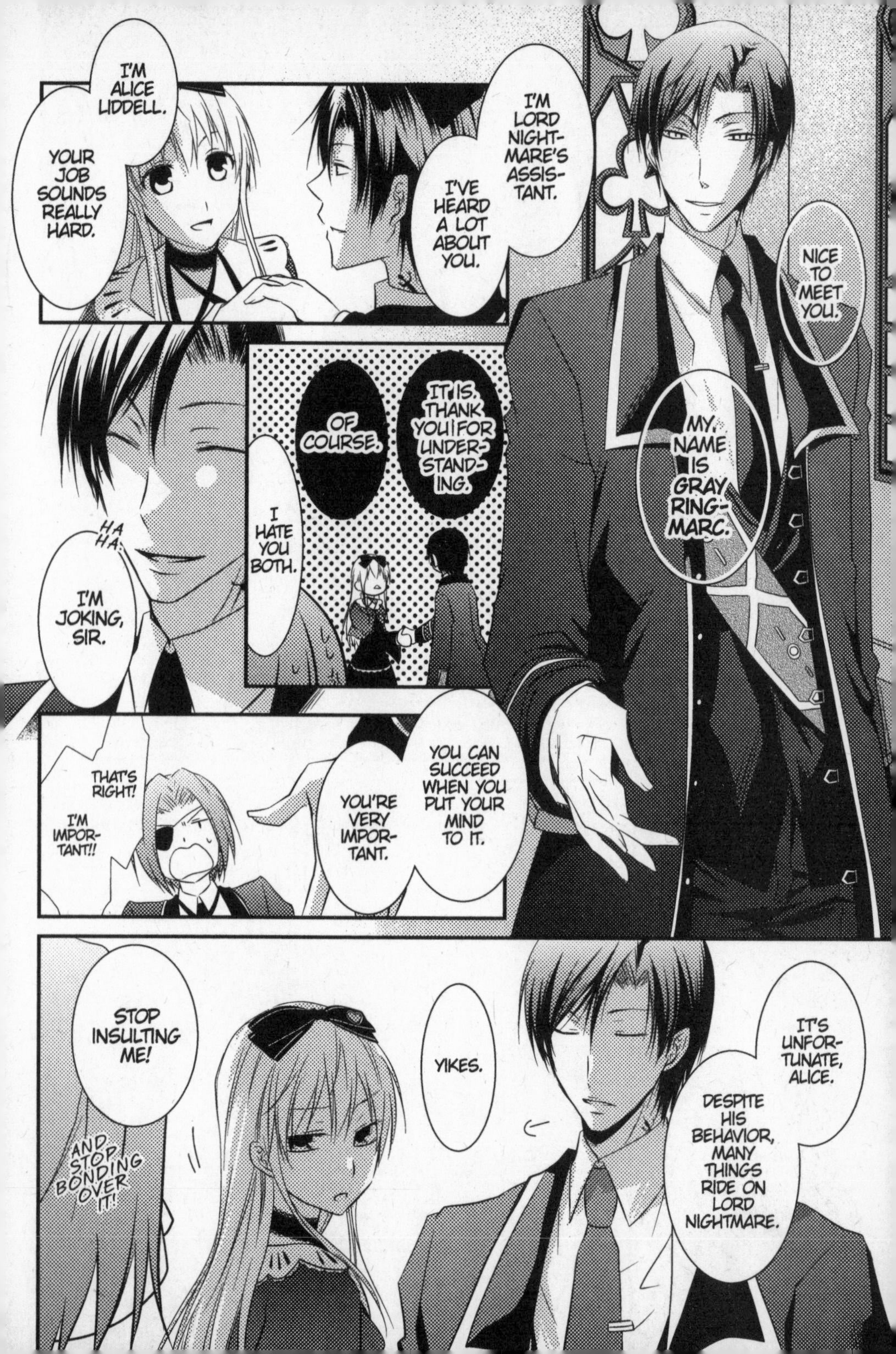
NICE TO MEET YOU.
MY NAME IS GRAY RING-MARC.
I'M LORD NIGHT-MARE'S ASSIS-TANT.
I'VE HEARD A LOT ABOUT YOU.
I'M ALICE LIDDELL.
YOUR JOB SOUNDS REALLY HARD.
IT IS. THANK YOU FOR UNDER-STAND-ING.
OF COURSE.
I HATE YOU BOTH.
HA HA.
I'M JOKING, SIR.
YOU CAN SUCCEED WHEN YOU PUT YOUR MIND TO IT.
YOU'RE VERY IMPOR-TANT.
THAT'S RIGHT!
I'M IMPOR-TANT!!
IT'S UNFOR-TUNATE, ALICE.
DESPITE HIS BEHAVIOR, MANY THINGS RIDE ON LORD NIGHTMARE.
YIKES.
STOP INSULTING ME!
AND STOP BONDING OVER IT!

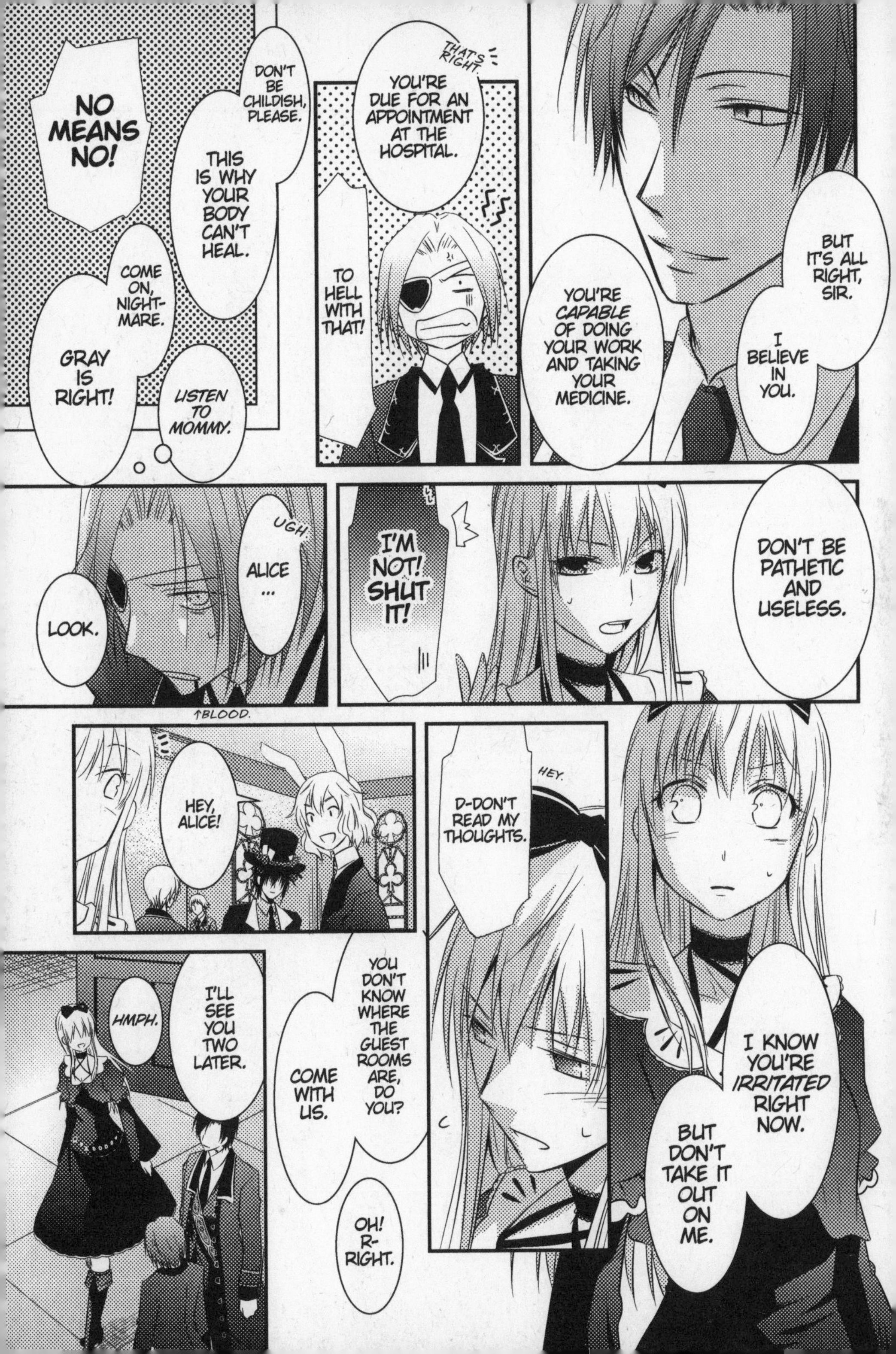
BUT IT'S ALL RIGHT, SIR.
I BELIEVE IN YOU.
YOU'RE CAPABLE OF DOING YOUR WORK AND TAKING YOUR MEDICINE.
THAT'S RIGHT.
YOU'RE DUE FOR AN APPOINTMENT AT THE HOSPITAL.
TO HELL WITH THAT!
DON'T BE CHILDISH, PLEASE.
THIS IS WHY YOUR BODY CAN'T HEAL.
NO MEANS NO!
COME ON, NIGHT-MARE.
LISTEN TO MOMMY.
GRAY IS RIGHT!
DON'T BE PATHETIC AND USELESS.
I'M NOT! SHUT IT!
UGH.
ALICE ...
LOOK.
↑BLOOD.
HEY.
D-DON'T READ MY THOUGHTS.
HEY, ALICE!
I KNOW YOU'RE IRRITATED RIGHT NOW.
BUT DON'T TAKE IT OUT ON ME.
YOU DON'T KNOW WHERE THE GUEST ROOMS ARE, DO YOU?
COME WITH US.
OH! R-RIGHT.
I'LL SEE YOU TWO LATER.
HMPH.

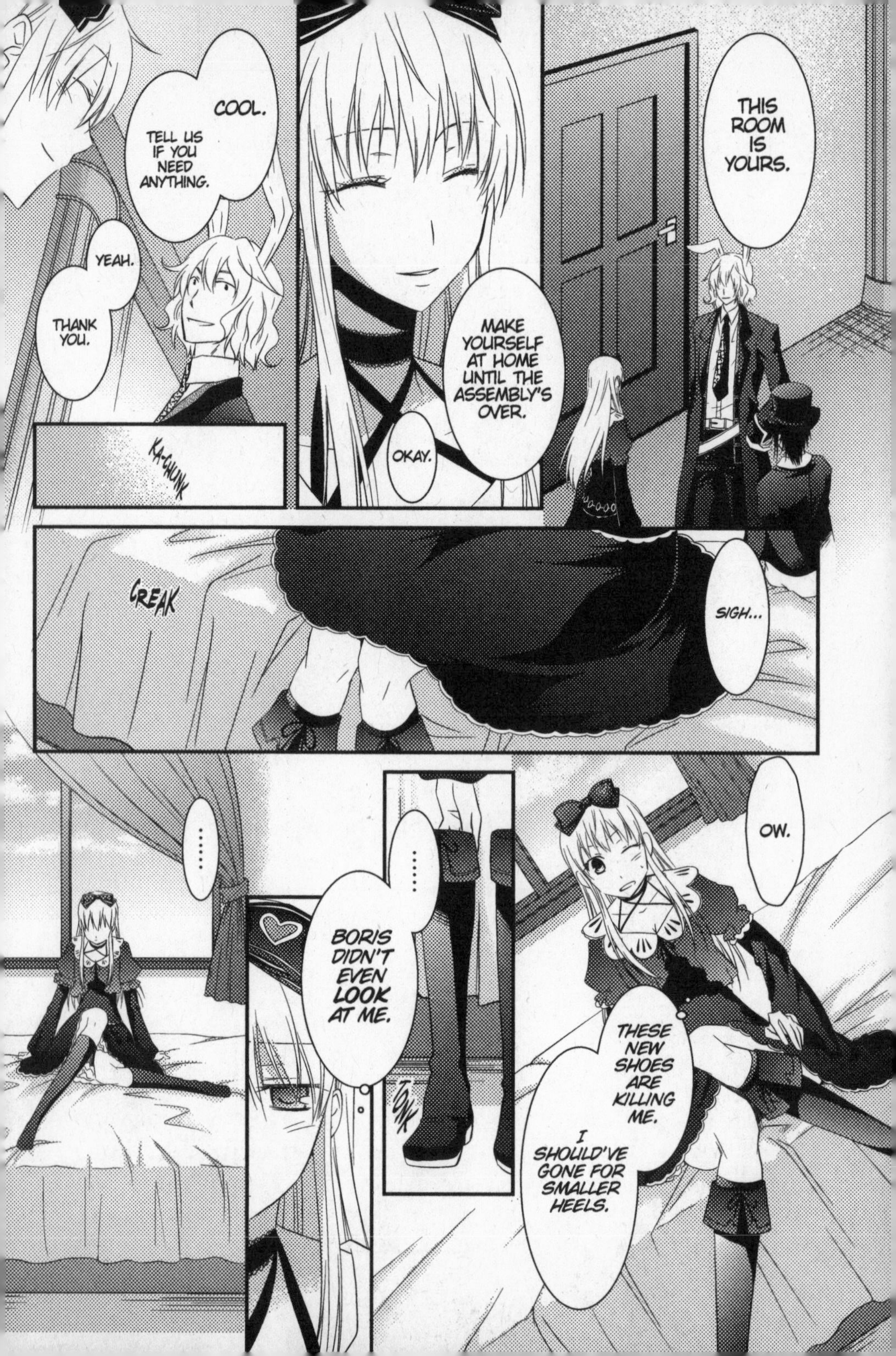
THIS ROOM IS YOURS.
MAKE YOURSELF AT HOME UNTIL THE ASSEMBLY'S OVER.
OKAY.
COOL.
TELL US IF YOU NEED ANYTHING.
YEAH.
THANK YOU.
KA-CHUNK
SIGH...
CREAK
OW.
THESE NEW SHOES ARE KILLING ME.
I SHOULD'VE GONE FOR SMALLER HEELS.
......
BORIS DIDN'T EVEN LOOK AT ME.
TONK
......

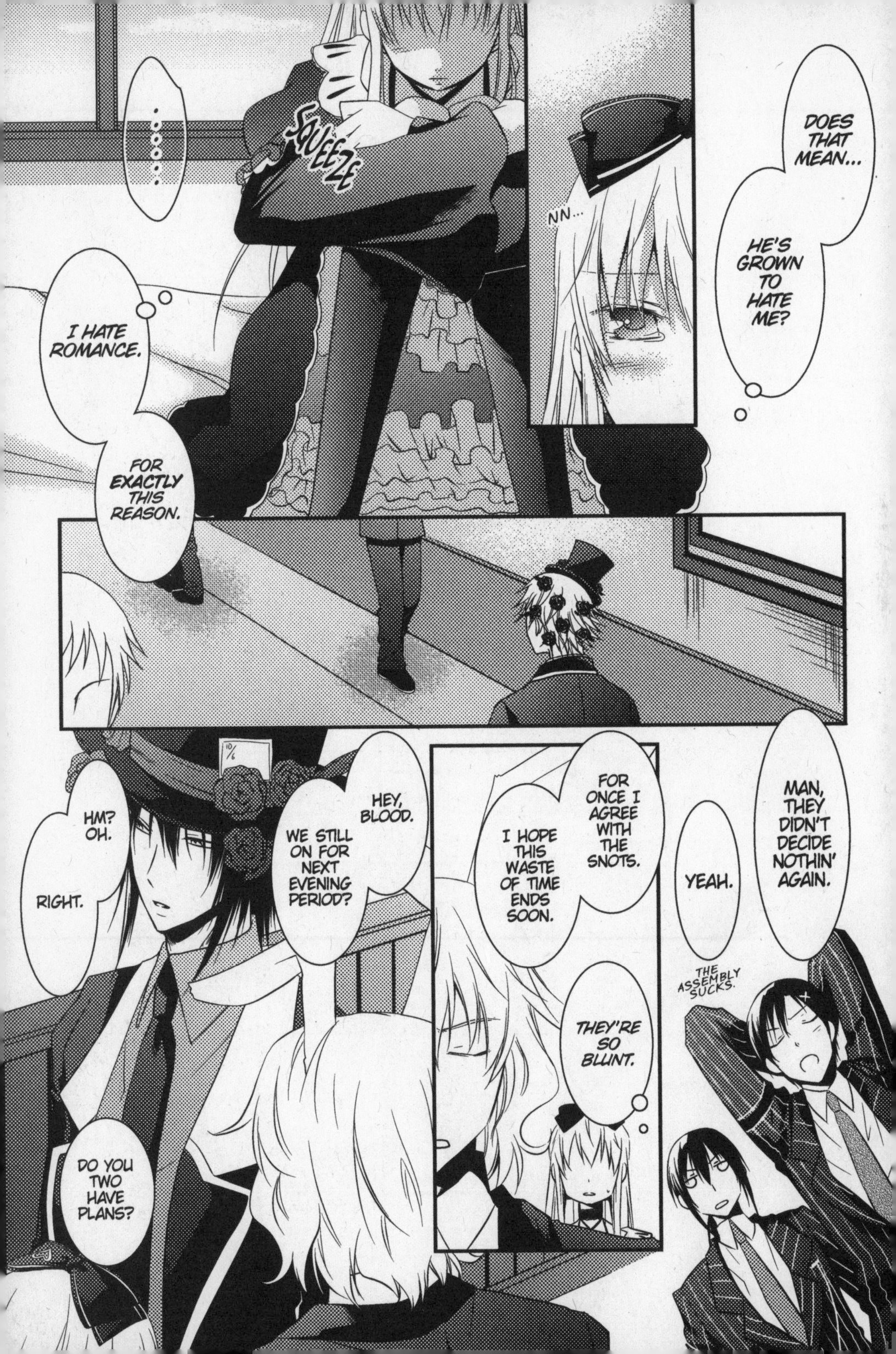
DOES THAT MEAN...
NN...
HE'S GROWN TO HATE ME?
......
SQUEEZE
I HATE ROMANCE.
FOR EXACTLY THIS REASON.
MAN, THEY DIDN'T DECIDE NOTHIN' AGAIN.
YEAH.
THE ASSEMBLY SUCKS.
FOR ONCE I AGREE WITH THE SNOTS.
I HOPE THIS WASTE OF TIME ENDS SOON.
THEY'RE SO BLUNT.
HEY, BLOOD.
WE STILL ON FOR NEXT EVENING PERIOD?
10/6
HM? OH.
RIGHT.
DO YOU TWO HAVE PLANS?

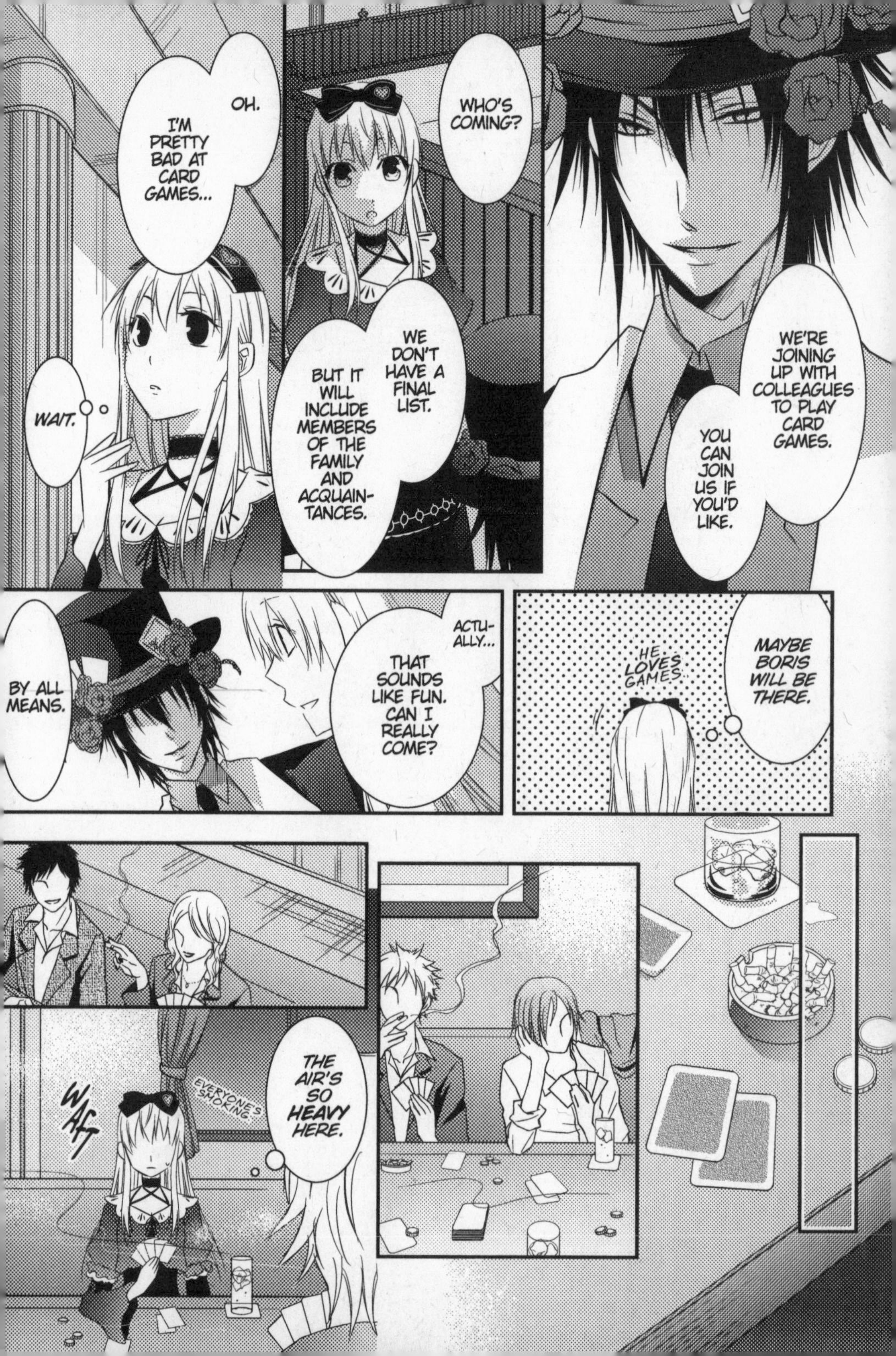
WE'RE JOINING UP WITH COLLEAGUES TO PLAY CARD GAMES.
YOU CAN JOIN US IF YOU'D LIKE.
WHO'S COMING?
WE DON'T HAVE A FINAL LIST.
BUT IT WILL INCLUDE MEMBERS OF THE FAMILY AND ACQUAIN-TANCES.
OH.
I'M PRETTY BAD AT CARD GAMES...
WAIT.
MAYBE BORIS WILL BE THERE.
HE LOVES GAMES...
ACTU-ALLY...
THAT SOUNDS LIKE FUN. CAN I REALLY COME?
BY ALL MEANS.
THE AIR'S SO HEAVY HERE.
EVERYONE'S SMOKING.
WAFT

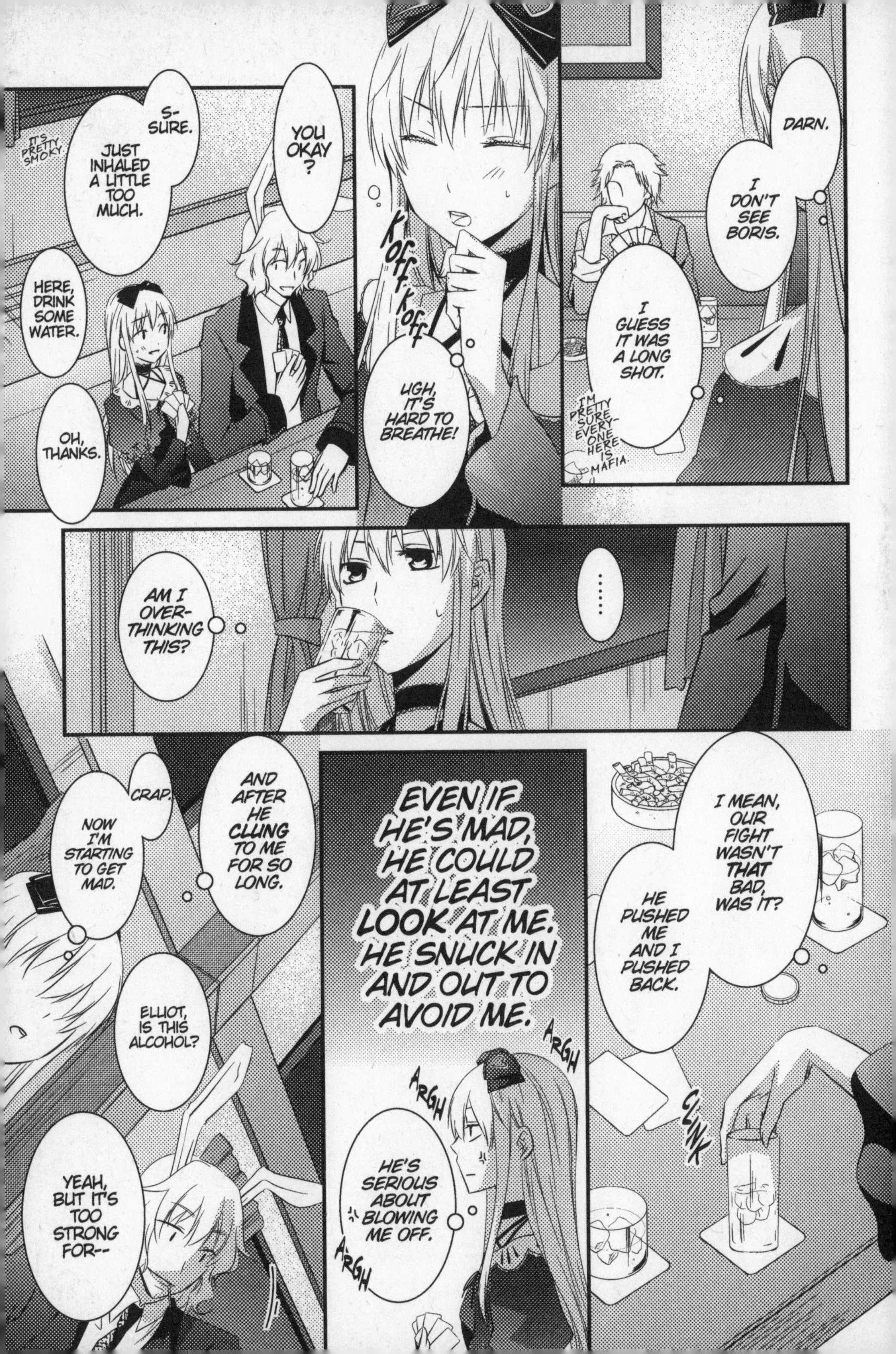
DARN.
I DON'T SEE BORIS.
I GUESS IT WAS A LONG SHOT.
I'M PRETTY SURE EVERYONE HERE IS MAFIA.
KOFF KOFF
UGH, IT'S HARD TO BREATHE!
YOU OKAY?
S-SURE.
JUST INHALED A LITTLE TOO MUCH.
IT'S PRETTY SMOKY.
HERE, DRINK SOME WATER.
OH, THANKS.
......
AM I OVERTHINKING THIS?
I MEAN, OUR FIGHT WASN'T THAT BAD, WAS IT?
HE PUSHED ME AND I PUSHED BACK.
CLINK
EVEN IF HE'S MAD, HE COULD AT LEAST LOOK AT ME. HE SNUCK IN AND OUT TO AVOID ME.
ARGH
ARGH
HE'S SERIOUS ABOUT BLOWING ME OFF.
ARGH
AND AFTER HE CLUNG TO ME FOR SO LONG.
CRAP.
NOW I'M STARTING TO GET MAD.
ELLIOT, IS THIS ALCOHOL?
YEAH, BUT IT'S TOO STRONG FOR--

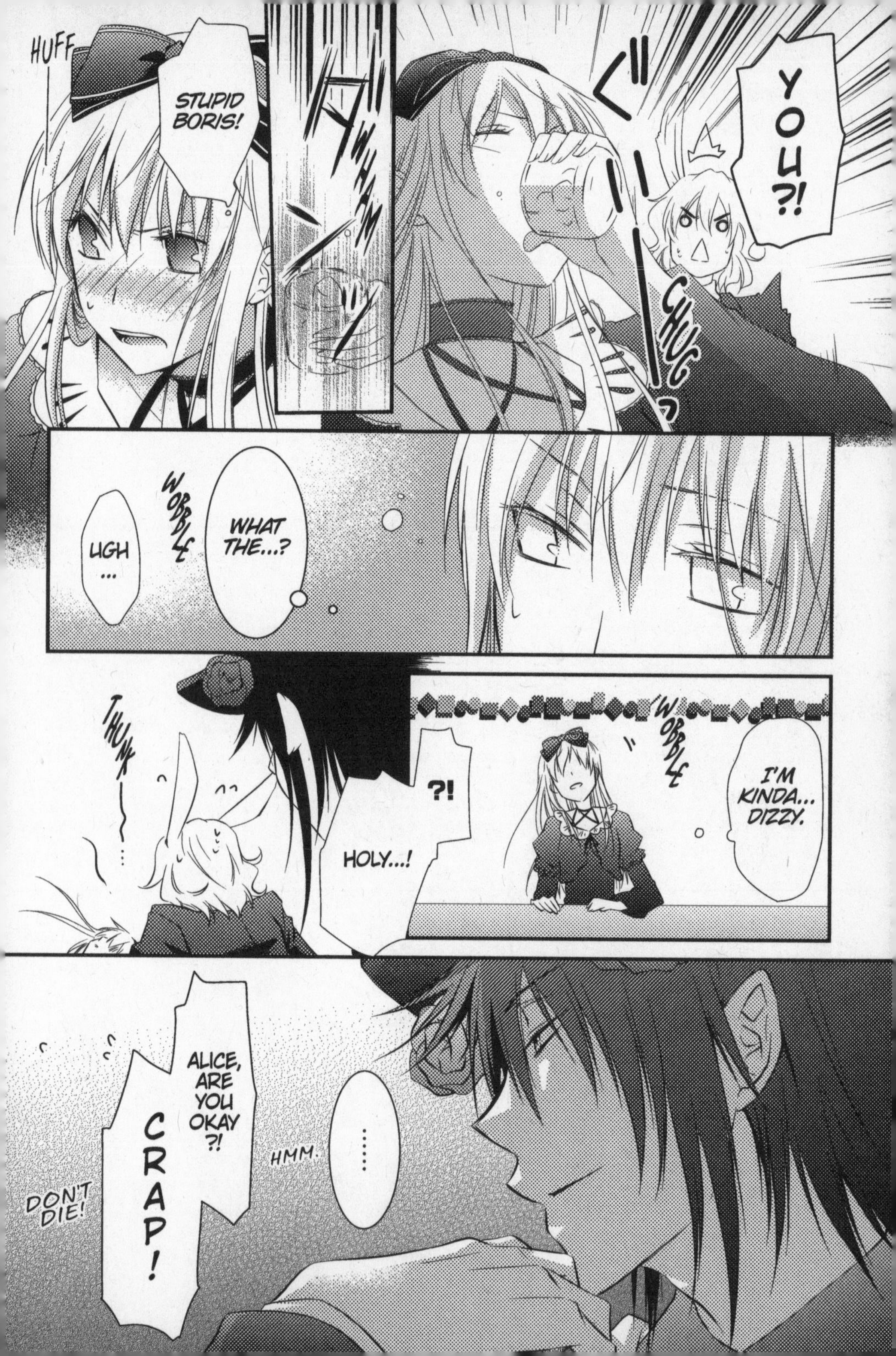
YOU?!
CHUG
HUFF
STUPID BORIS!
WHAT THE...?
WOBBLE
UGH ...
I'M KINDA... DIZZY.
WOBBLE
?!
HOLY...!
THUNK
......
HMM.
ALICE, ARE YOU OKAY?!
CRAP!
DON'T DIE!

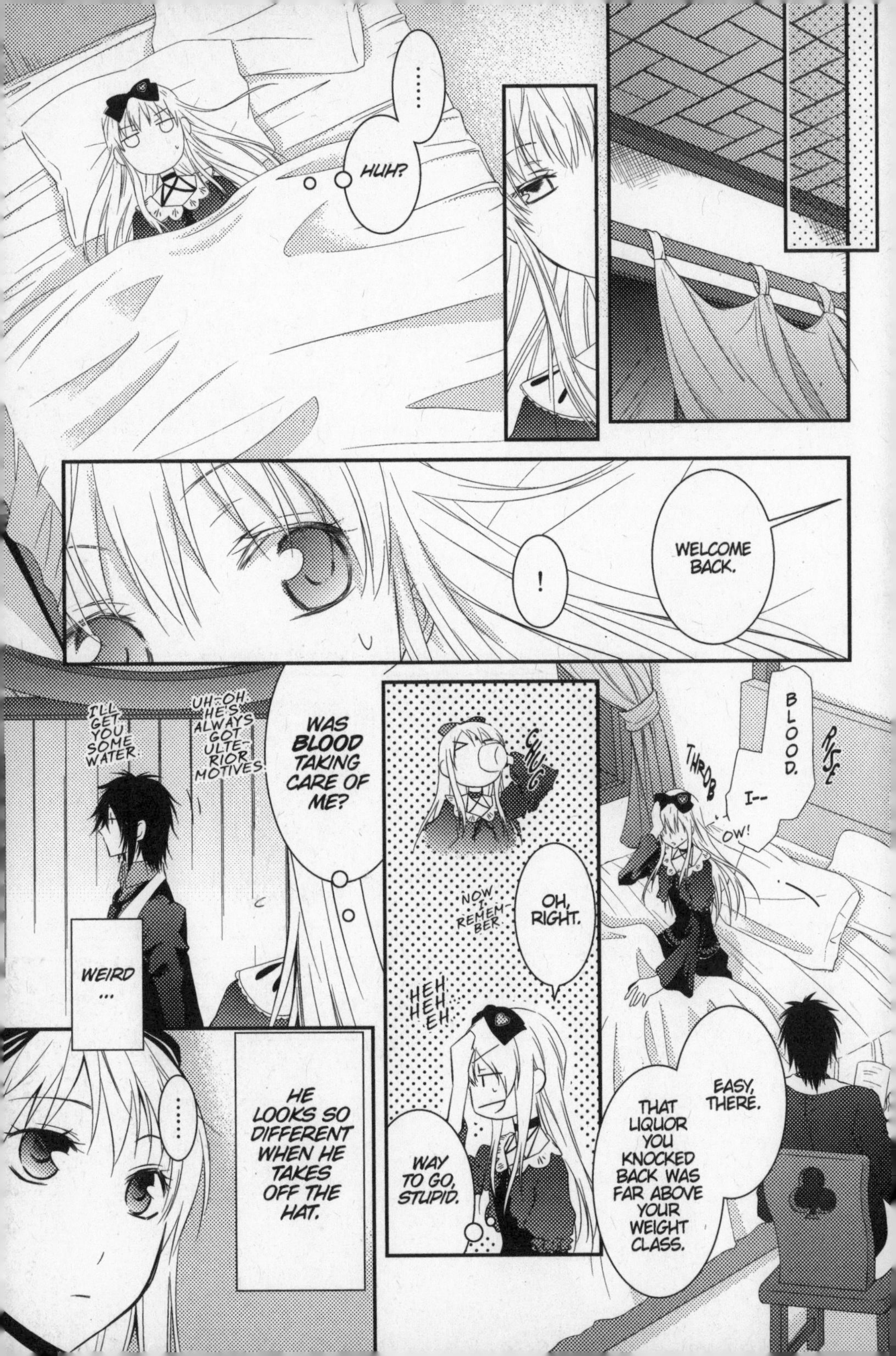
......
HUH?
WELCOME BACK.
!
BLOOD.
RISE
THROB
I--
OW!
EASY, THERE.
THAT LIQUOR YOU KNOCKED BACK WAS FAR ABOVE YOUR WEIGHT CLASS.
CHUG
OH, RIGHT.
NOW I REMEMBER
HEH HEH EH...
WAY TO GO, STUPID.
WAS BLOOD TAKING CARE OF ME?
UH-OH. HE'S ALWAYS GOT ULTERIOR MOTIVES!
I'LL GET YOU SOME WATER.
WEIRD...
......
HE LOOKS SO DIFFERENT WHEN HE TAKES OFF THE HAT.

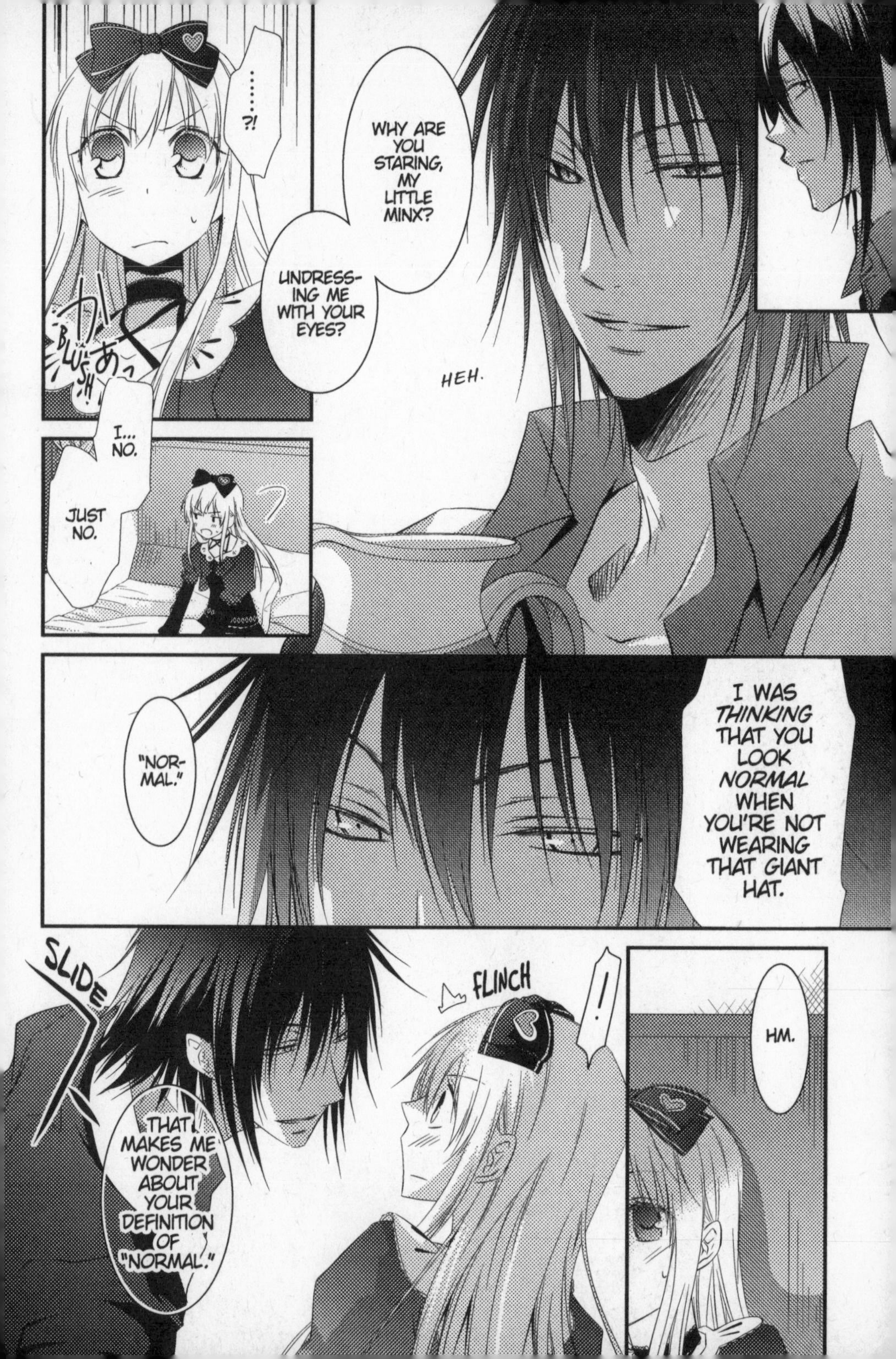
WHY ARE YOU STARING, MY LITTLE MINX?
UNDRESSING ME WITH YOUR EYES?
HEH.
......?!
BLUSH
I... NO.
JUST NO.
I WAS *THINKING* THAT YOU LOOK *NORMAL* WHEN YOU'RE NOT WEARING THAT GIANT HAT.
"NORMAL."
HM.
FLINCH
!
SLIDE
THAT MAKES ME WONDER ABOUT YOUR DEFINITION OF "NORMAL."

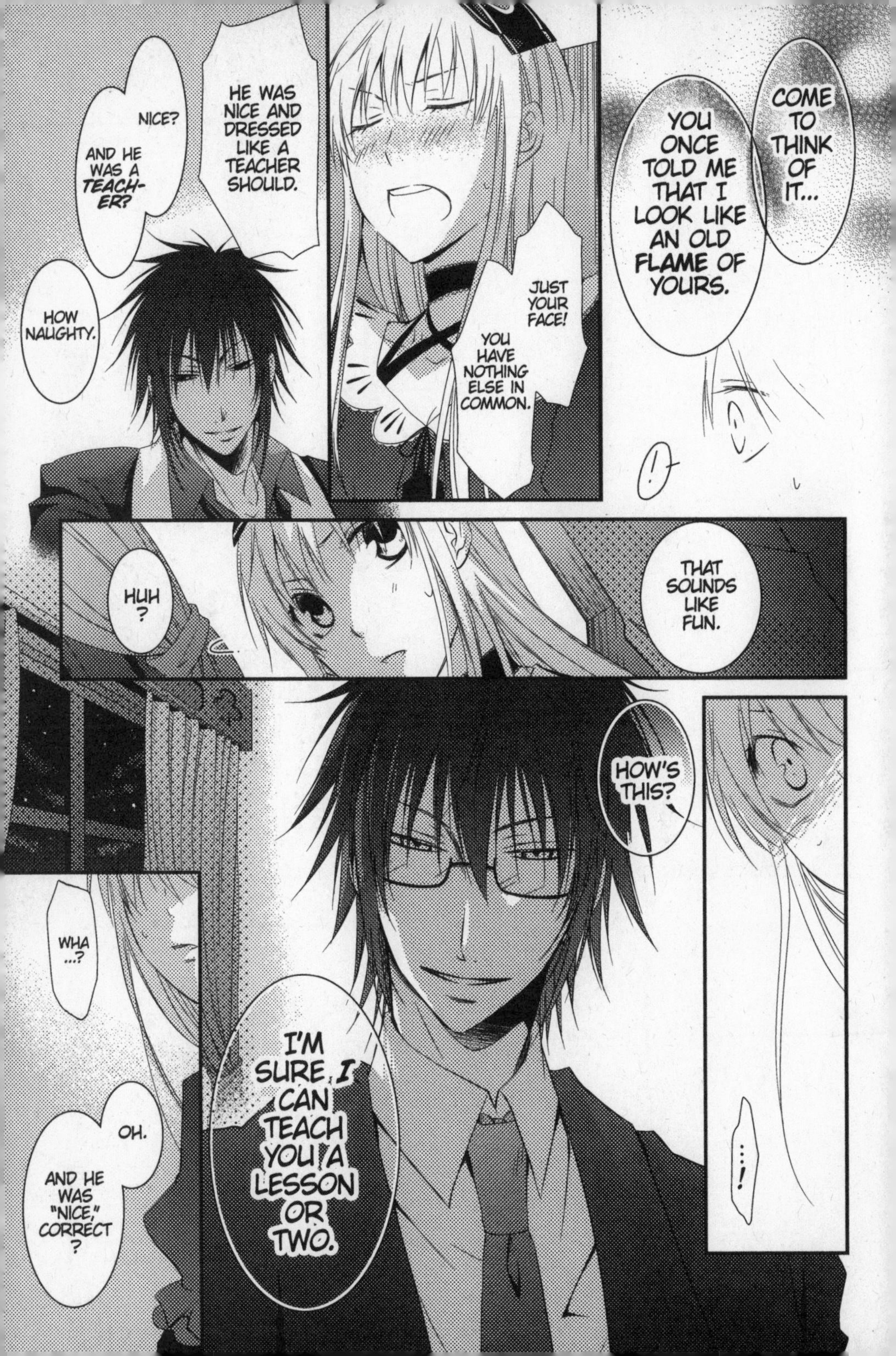
COME TO THINK OF IT...
YOU ONCE TOLD ME THAT I LOOK LIKE AN OLD FLAME OF YOURS.
!
JUST YOUR FACE!
YOU HAVE NOTHING ELSE IN COMMON.
HE WAS NICE AND DRESSED LIKE A TEACHER SHOULD.
NICE?
AND HE WAS A *TEACHER?*
HOW NAUGHTY.
THAT SOUNDS LIKE FUN.
HUH?
HOW'S THIS?
WHA...?
OH.
AND HE WAS "NICE," CORRECT?
I'M SURE *I* CAN TEACH YOU A LESSON OR TWO.
...!

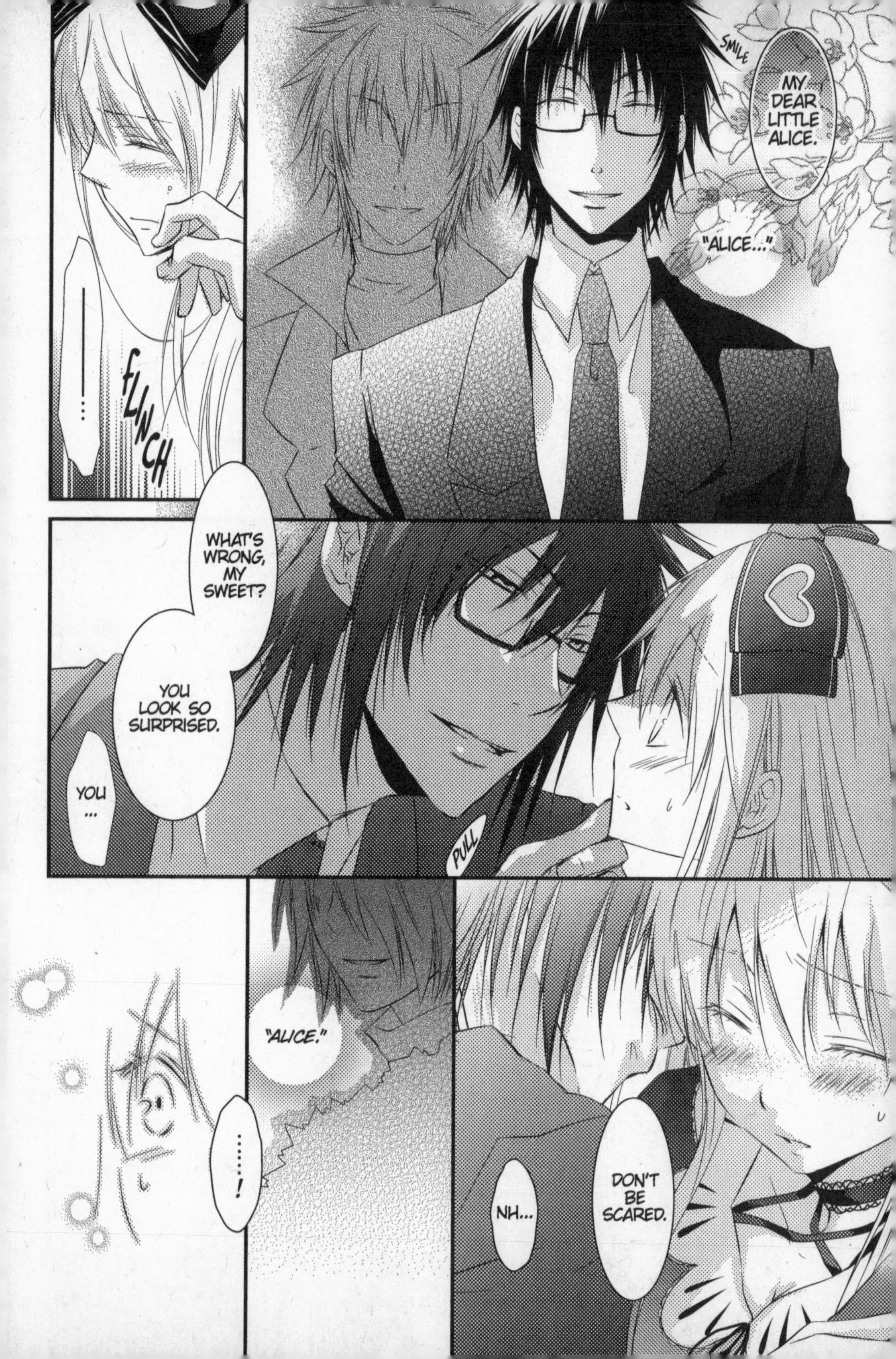
SMILE
MY DEAR LITTLE ALICE.
"ALICE..."
......
FLINCH
WHAT'S WRONG, MY SWEET?
YOU LOOK SO SURPRISED.
PULL
YOU ...
DON'T BE SCARED.
NH...
"ALICE."
......!

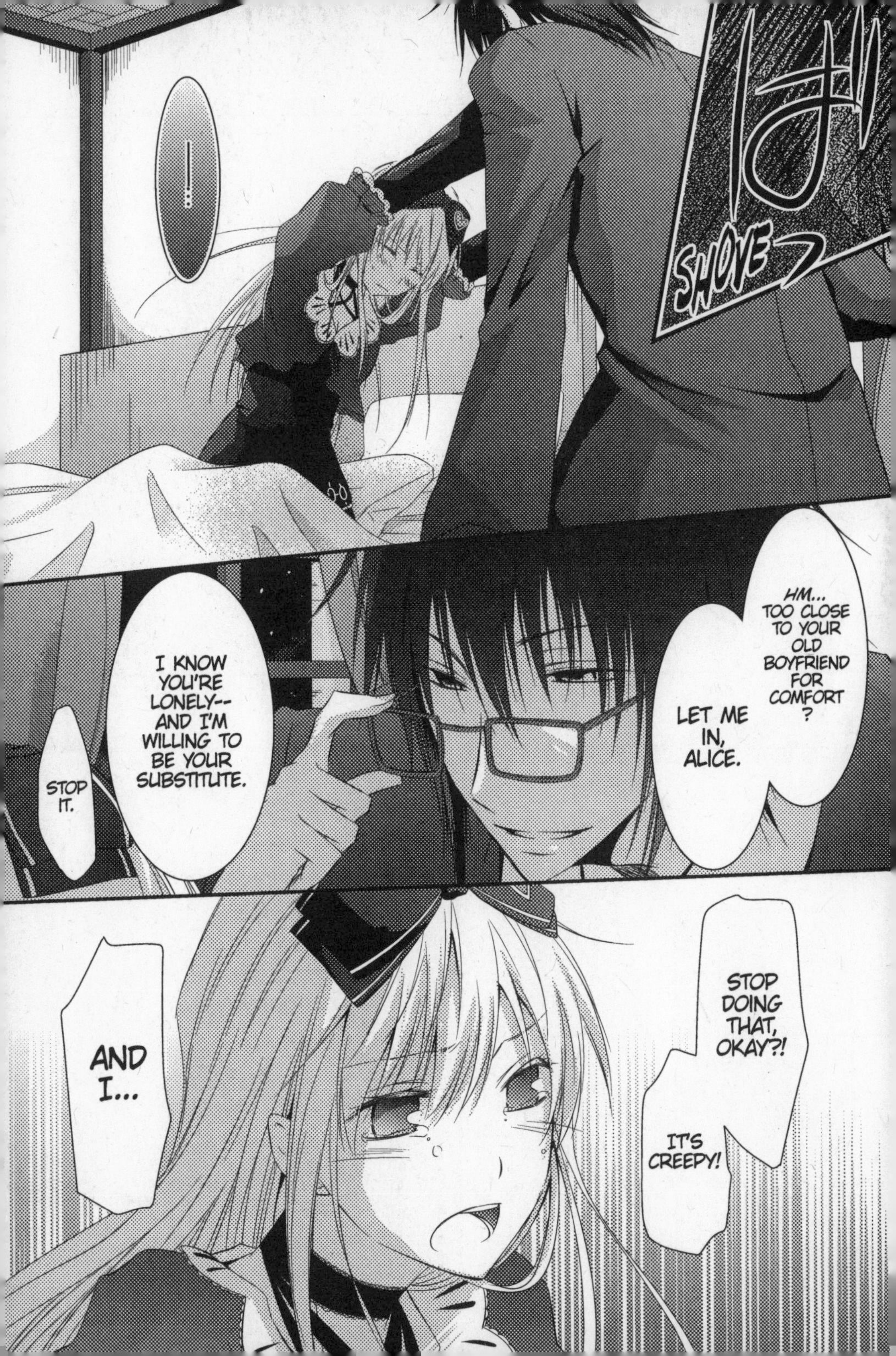
ばっ
SHOVE
...!
HM... TOO CLOSE TO YOUR OLD BOYFRIEND FOR COMFORT?
LET ME IN, ALICE.
I KNOW YOU'RE LONELY-- AND I'M WILLING TO BE YOUR SUBSTITUTE.
STOP IT.
STOP DOING THAT, OKAY?!
IT'S CREEPY!
AND I...

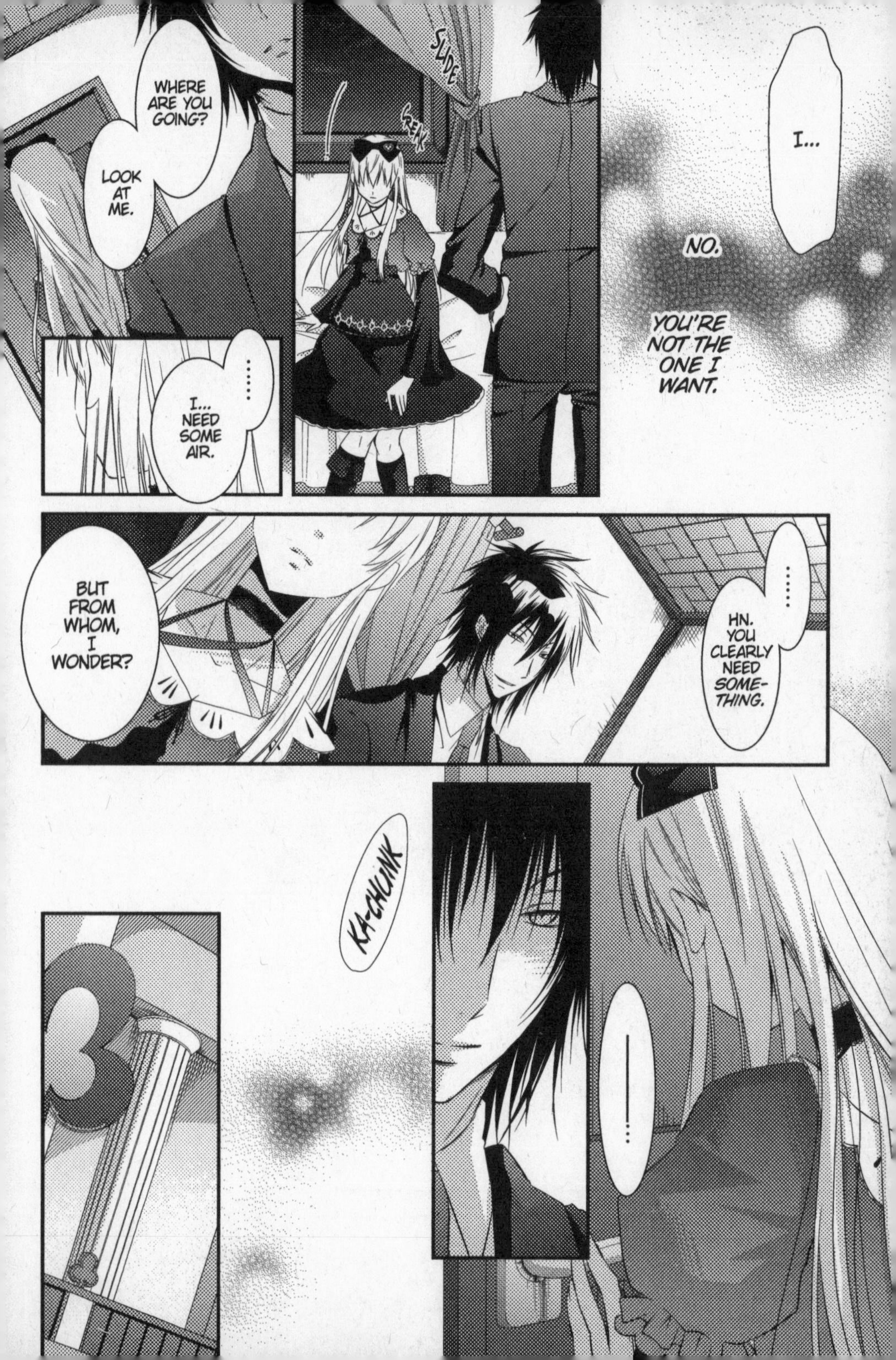
I...
NO.
YOU'RE NOT THE ONE I WANT.
SLIDE
CREAK
WHERE ARE YOU GOING?
LOOK AT ME.
......
I... NEED SOME AIR.
......
HN. YOU CLEARLY NEED SOME-THING.
BUT FROM WHOM, I WONDER?
KA-CHUNK

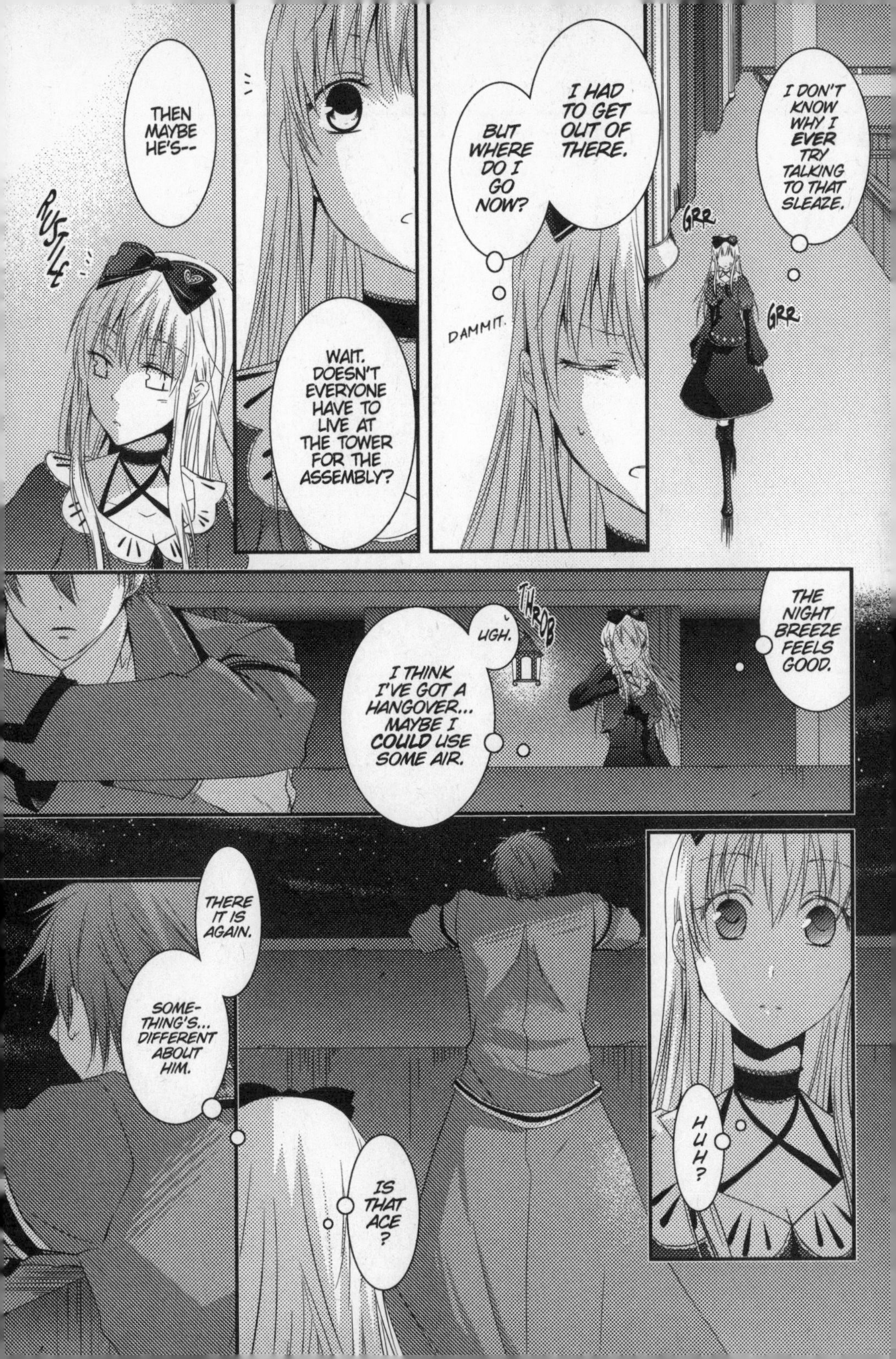

I DON'T KNOW WHY I EVER TRY TALKING TO THAT SLEAZE.
GRR
GRR
I HAD TO GET OUT OF THERE.
BUT WHERE DO I GO NOW?
DAMMIT.
WAIT. DOESN'T EVERYONE HAVE TO LIVE AT THE TOWER FOR THE ASSEMBLY?
THEN MAYBE HE'S--
RUSTLE
THE NIGHT BREEZE FEELS GOOD.
THROB
UGH.
I THINK I'VE GOT A HANGOVER... MAYBE I COULD USE SOME AIR.
HUH?
IS THAT ACE?
THERE IT IS AGAIN.
SOME-THING'S... DIFFERENT ABOUT HIM.

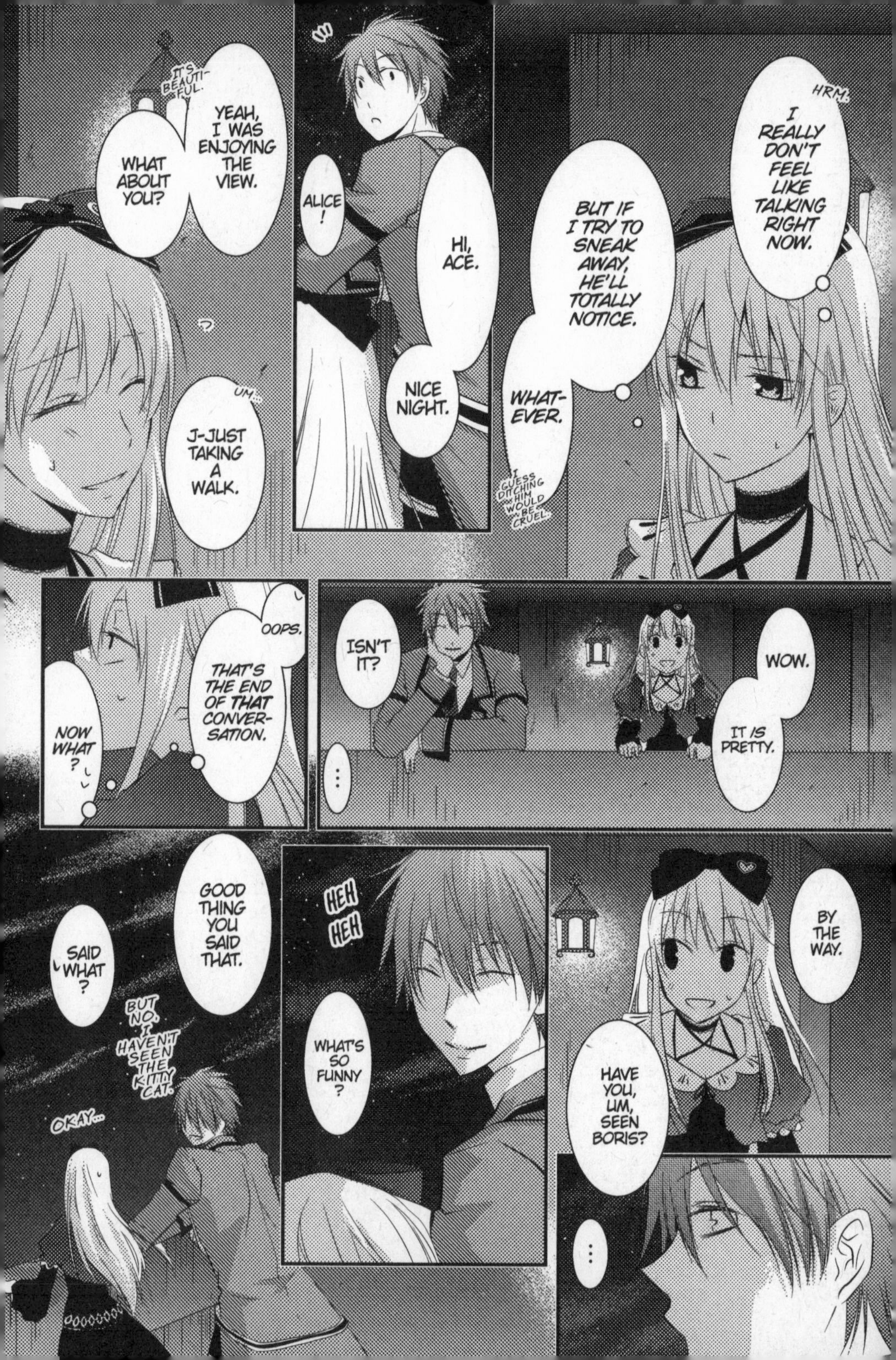
HRM.
I REALLY DON'T FEEL LIKE TALKING RIGHT NOW.
BUT IF I TRY TO SNEAK AWAY, HE'LL TOTALLY NOTICE.
WHAT-EVER.
I GUESS DITCHING HIM WOULD BE CRUEL.
ALICE!
HI, ACE.
NICE NIGHT.
YEAH, I WAS ENJOYING THE VIEW.
IT'S BEAUTI-FUL.
WHAT ABOUT YOU?
UM...
J-JUST TAKING A WALK.
WOW.
IT IS PRETTY.
ISN'T IT?
...
OOPS.
THAT'S THE END OF THAT CONVER-SATION.
NOW WHAT?
BY THE WAY.
HAVE YOU, UM, SEEN BORIS?
...
HEH HEH
WHAT'S SO FUNNY?
GOOD THING YOU SAID THAT.
SAID WHAT?
BUT NO, I HAVEN'T SEEN THE KITTY CAT.
OKAY...

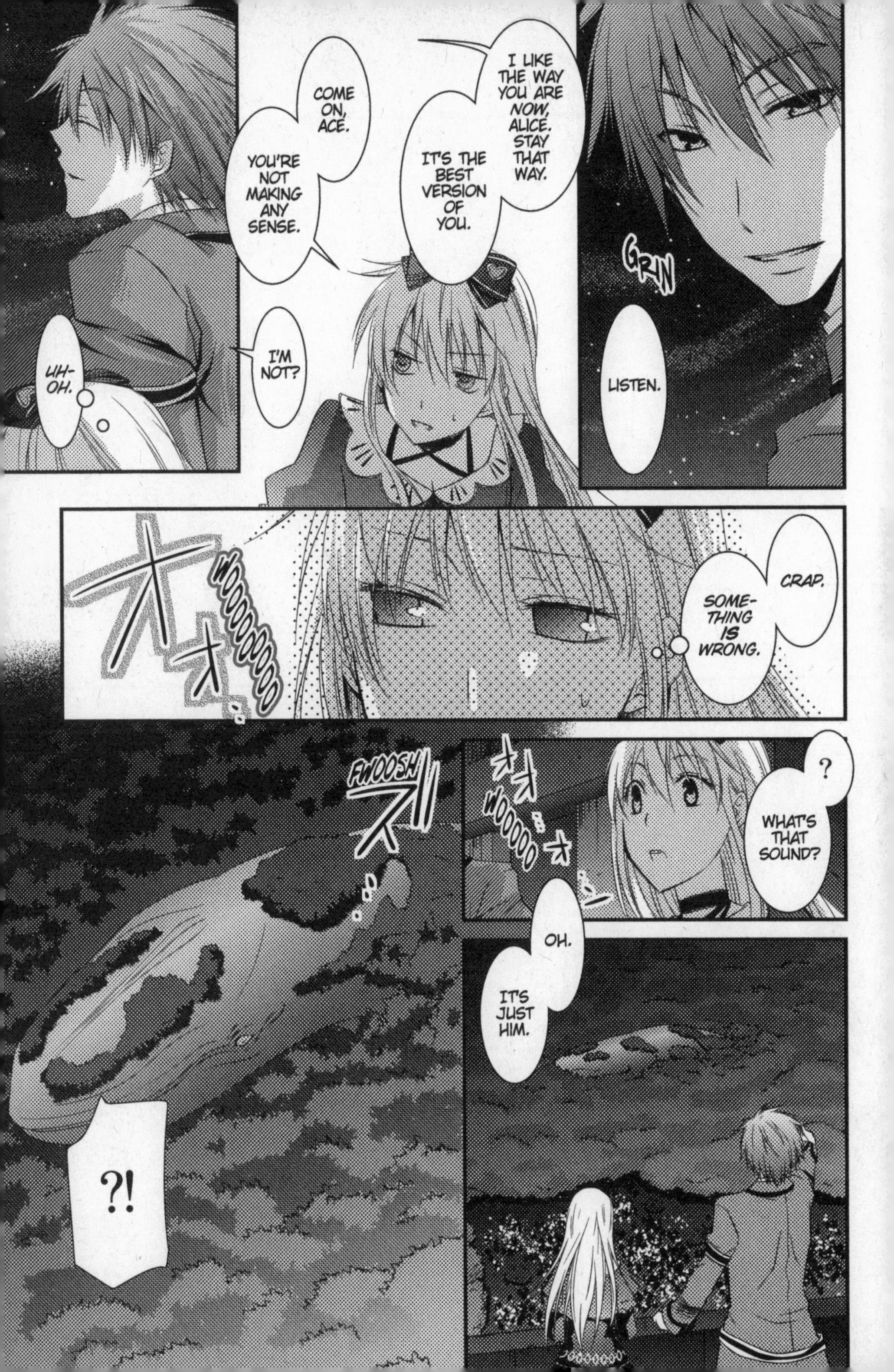

GRIN
LISTEN.
I LIKE THE WAY YOU ARE NOW, ALICE. STAY THAT WAY.
IT'S THE BEST VERSION OF YOU.
COME ON, ACE.
YOU'RE NOT MAKING ANY SENSE.
I'M NOT?
UH-OH.
CRAP.
SOMETHING IS WRONG.
WOOOOOOOOO
?
WHAT'S THAT SOUND?
WOOOOO
OH.
IT'S JUST HIM.
FWOOSH
?!

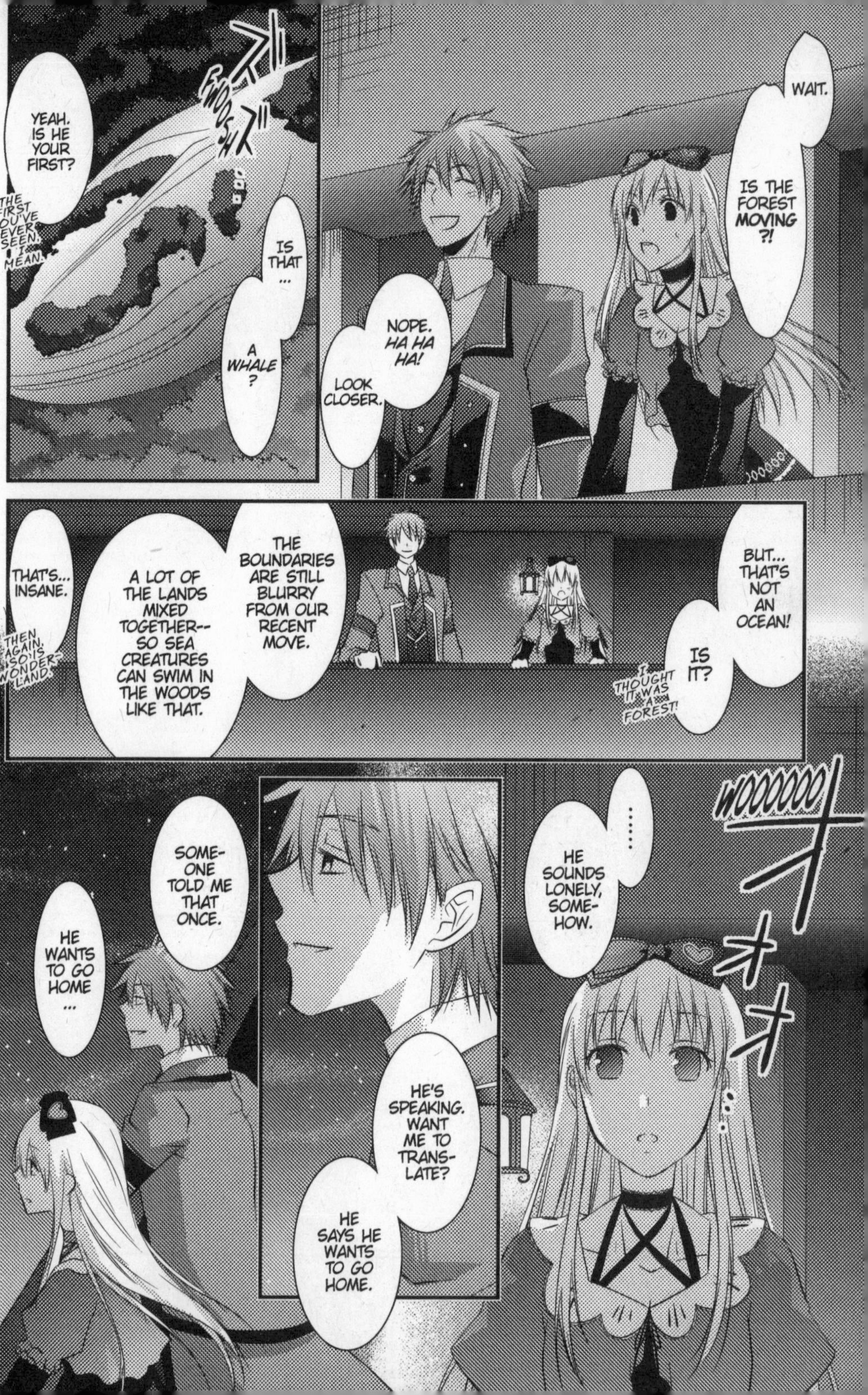
WAIT.
IS THE FOREST MOVING?!
NOPE. HA HA HA!
LOOK CLOSER.
WOOSH
IS THAT... A WHALE?
YEAH. IS HE YOUR FIRST?
THE FIRST YOU'VE EVER SEEN, I MEAN.
BUT... THAT'S NOT AN OCEAN!
IS IT?
I THOUGHT IT WAS A FOREST!
THE BOUNDARIES ARE STILL BLURRY FROM OUR RECENT MOVE.
A LOT OF THE LANDS MIXED TOGETHER-- SO SEA CREATURES CAN SWIM IN THE WOODS LIKE THAT.
THAT'S... INSANE.
THEN AGAIN, SO IS WONDERLAND.
WOOOOOO
......
HE SOUNDS LONELY, SOME-HOW.
HE'S SPEAKING. WANT ME TO TRANS-LATE?
HE SAYS HE WANTS TO GO HOME.
SOME-ONE TOLD ME THAT ONCE.
HE WANTS TO GO HOME...

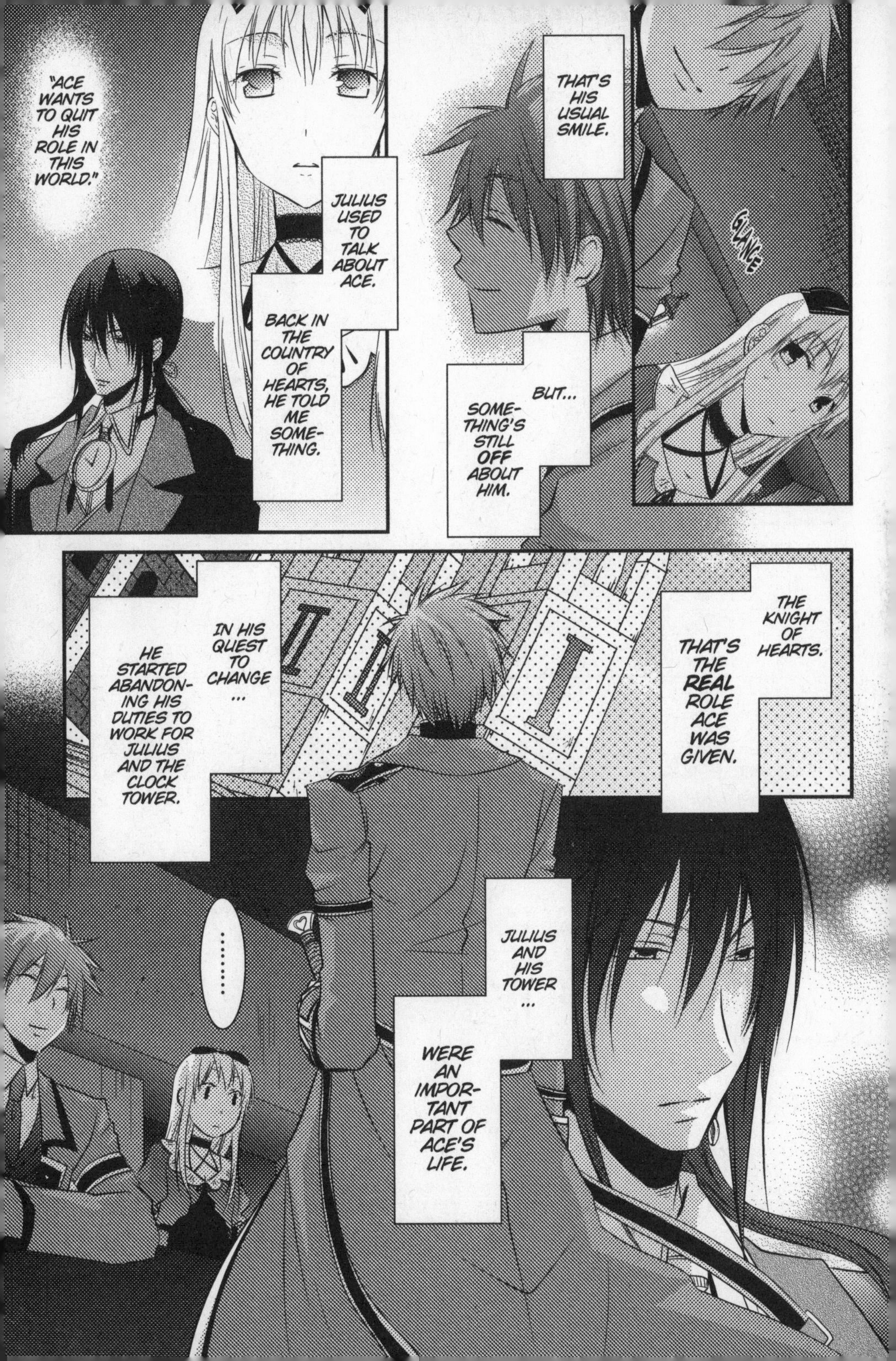
GLANCE
THAT'S HIS USUAL SMILE.
BUT...
SOMETHING'S STILL OFF ABOUT HIM.
JULIUS USED TO TALK ABOUT ACE.
BACK IN THE COUNTRY OF HEARTS, HE TOLD ME SOMETHING.
"ACE WANTS TO QUIT HIS ROLE IN THIS WORLD."
THE KNIGHT OF HEARTS.
THAT'S THE REAL ROLE ACE WAS GIVEN.
IN HIS QUEST TO CHANGE...
HE STARTED ABANDONING HIS DUTIES TO WORK FOR JULIUS AND THE CLOCK TOWER.
JULIUS AND HIS TOWER...
WERE AN IMPORTANT PART OF ACE'S LIFE.
......

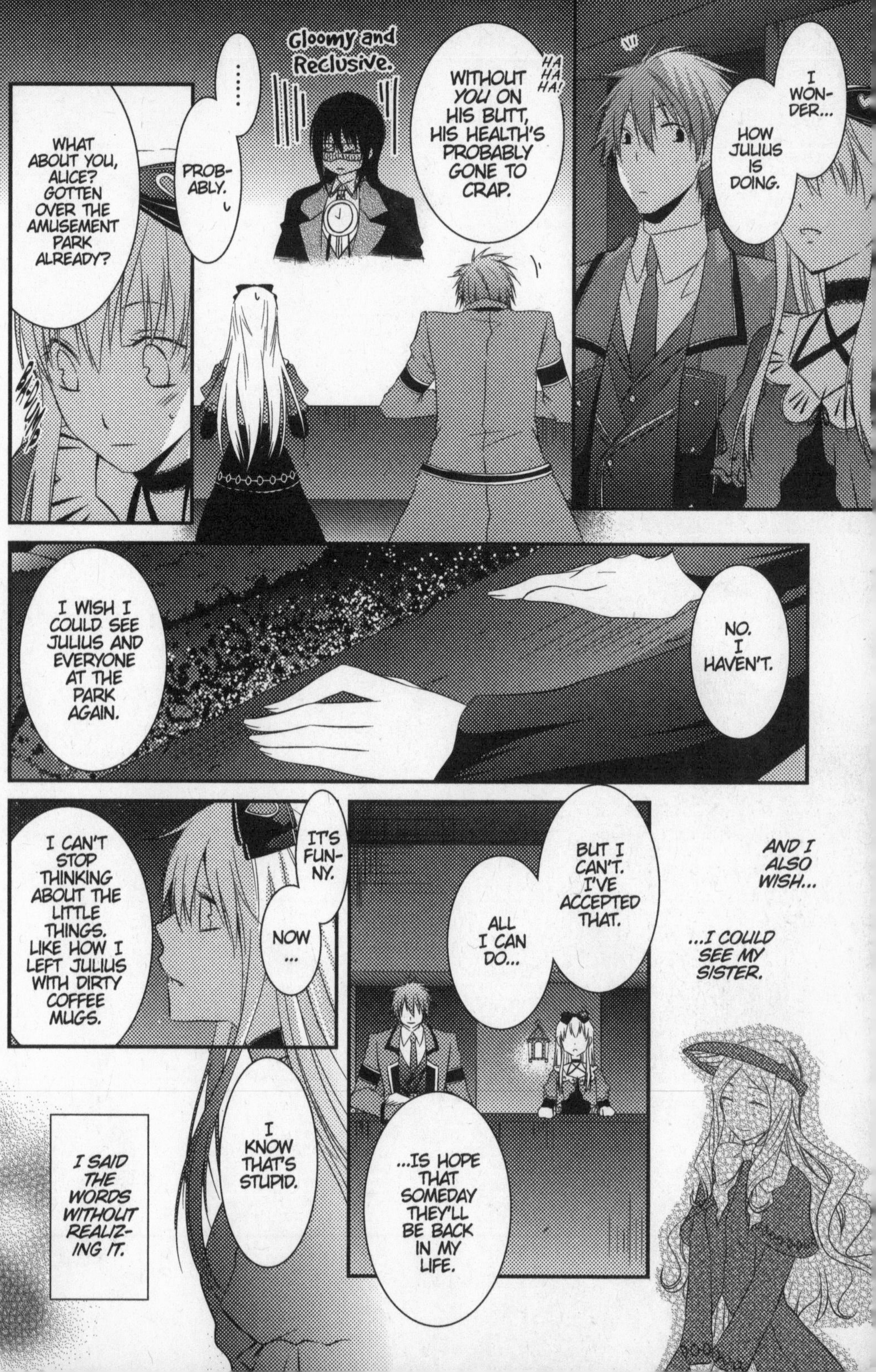
I WONDER...
HOW JULIUS IS DOING.
WITHOUT YOU ON HIS BUTT, HIS HEALTH'S PROBABLY GONE TO CRAP.
HA HA HA!
Gloomy and Reclusive.
......
PROBABLY.
WHAT ABOUT YOU, ALICE? GOTTEN OVER THE AMUSEMENT PARK ALREADY?
BA-DUMP
NO. I HAVEN'T.
I WISH I COULD SEE JULIUS AND EVERYONE AT THE PARK AGAIN.
AND I ALSO WISH...
...I COULD SEE MY SISTER.
BUT I CAN'T. I'VE ACCEPTED THAT.
ALL I CAN DO...
...IS HOPE THAT SOMEDAY THEY'LL BE BACK IN MY LIFE.
IT'S FUNNY.
NOW...
I CAN'T STOP THINKING ABOUT THE LITTLE THINGS. LIKE HOW I LEFT JULIUS WITH DIRTY COFFEE MUGS.
I KNOW THAT'S STUPID.
I SAID THE WORDS WITHOUT REALIZING IT.

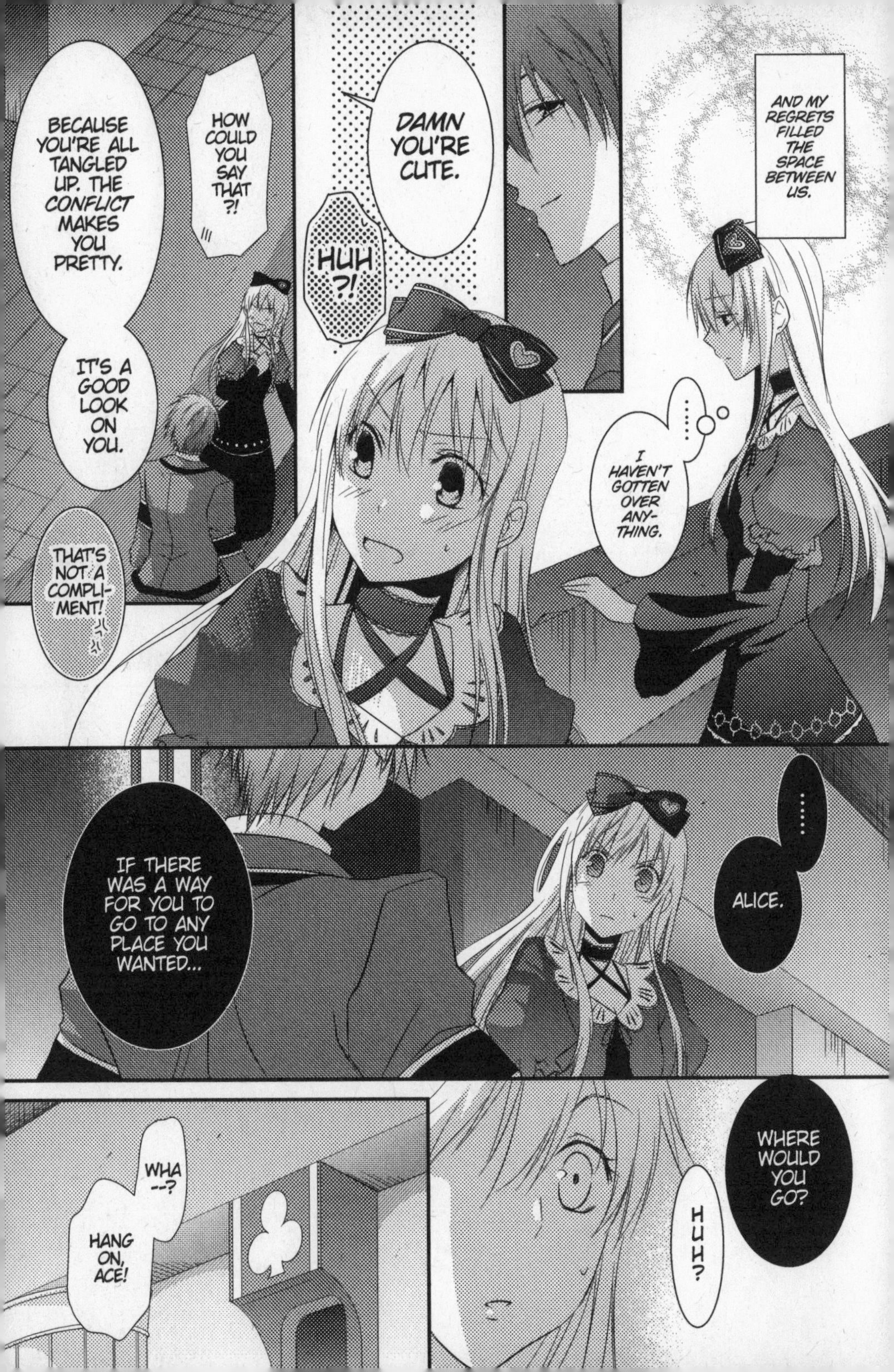

AND MY REGRETS FILLED THE SPACE BETWEEN US.
......
I HAVEN'T GOTTEN OVER ANYTHING.
DAMN YOU'RE CUTE.
HUH ?!
HOW COULD YOU SAY THAT ?!
BECAUSE YOU'RE ALL TANGLED UP. THE CONFLICT MAKES YOU PRETTY.
IT'S A GOOD LOOK ON YOU.
THAT'S NOT A COMPLI-MENT!
......
ALICE.
IF THERE WAS A WAY FOR YOU TO GO TO ANY PLACE YOU WANTED...
WHERE WOULD YOU GO?
HUH?
WHA --?
HANG ON, ACE!

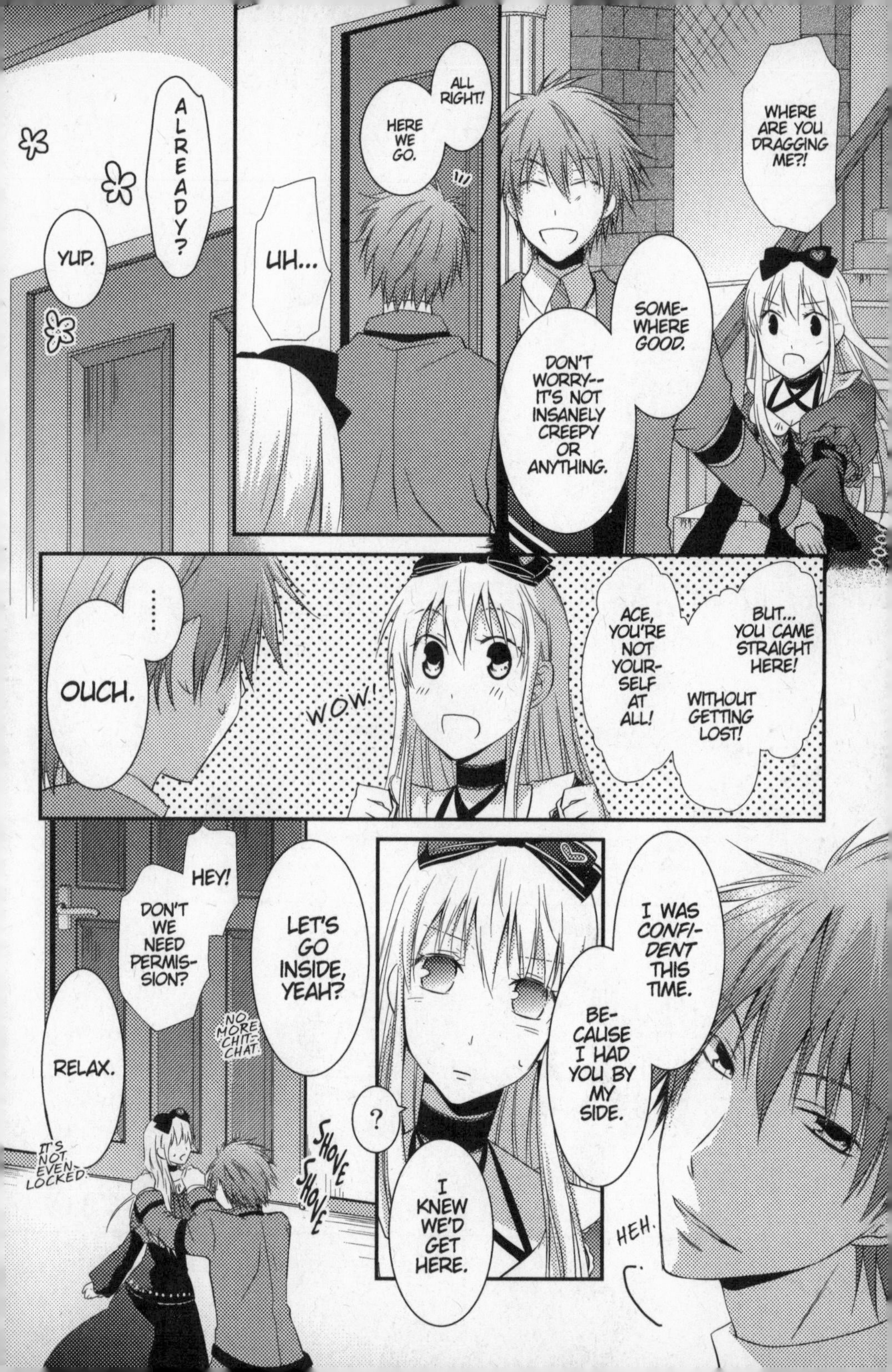
WHERE ARE YOU DRAGGING ME?!
SOME-WHERE GOOD.
DON'T WORRY-- IT'S NOT INSANELY CREEPY OR ANYTHING.
ALL RIGHT!
HERE WE GO.
!!
UH...
ALREADY?
YUP.
BUT... YOU CAME STRAIGHT HERE!
WITHOUT GETTING LOST!
ACE, YOU'RE NOT YOURSELF AT ALL!
WOW!
......
OUCH.
I WAS CONFI-DENT THIS TIME.
BE-CAUSE I HAD YOU BY MY SIDE.
HEH.
LET'S GO INSIDE, YEAH?
?
I KNEW WE'D GET HERE.
HEY!
DON'T WE NEED PERMIS-SION?
NO MORE CHIT-CHAT.
SHOVE SHOVE
RELAX.
IT'S NOT EVEN LOCKED.

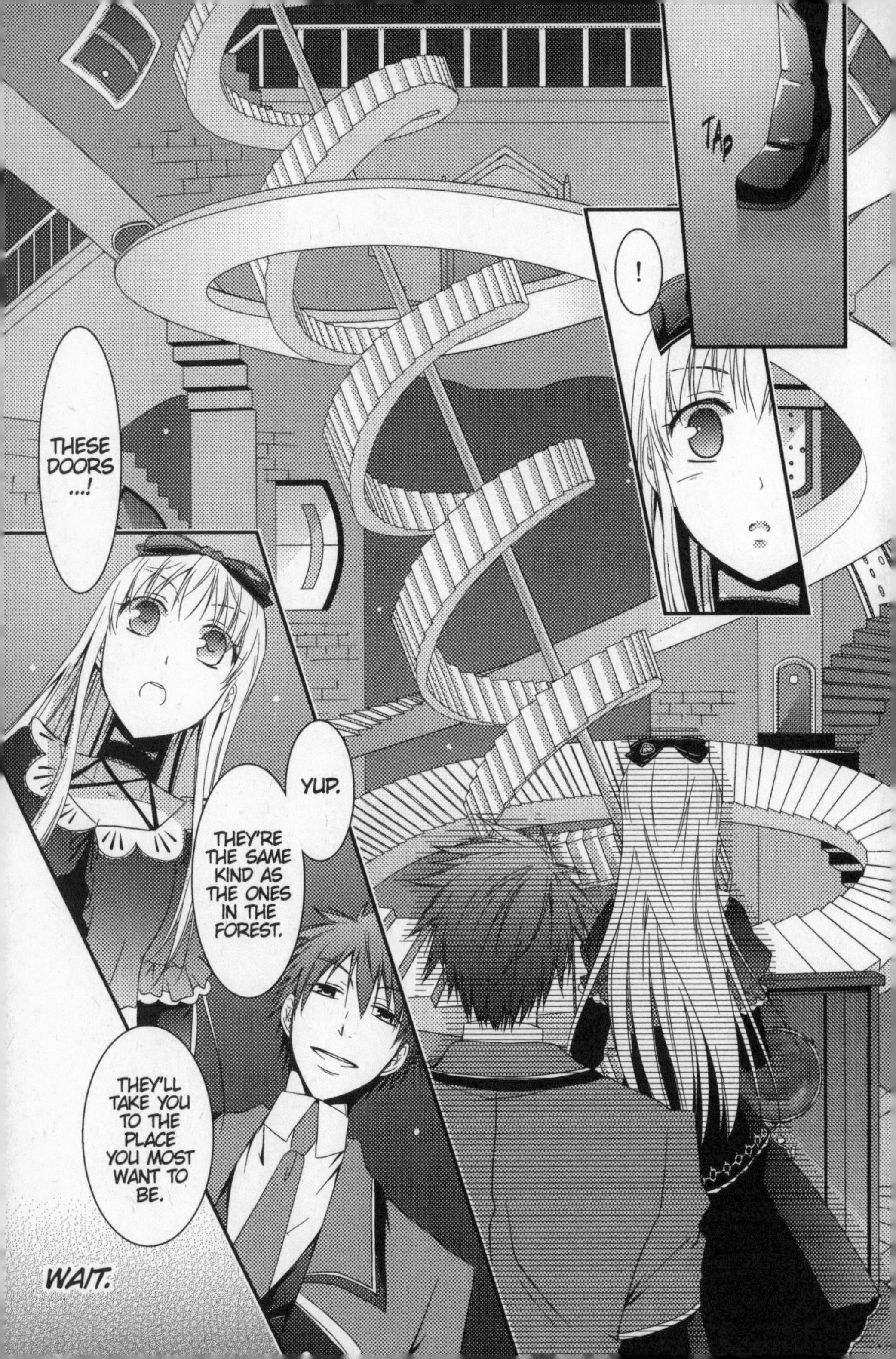
TAP
!
THESE DOORS ...!
YUP.
THEY'RE THE SAME KIND AS THE ONES IN THE FOREST.
THEY'LL TAKE YOU TO THE PLACE YOU MOST WANT TO BE.
WAIT.

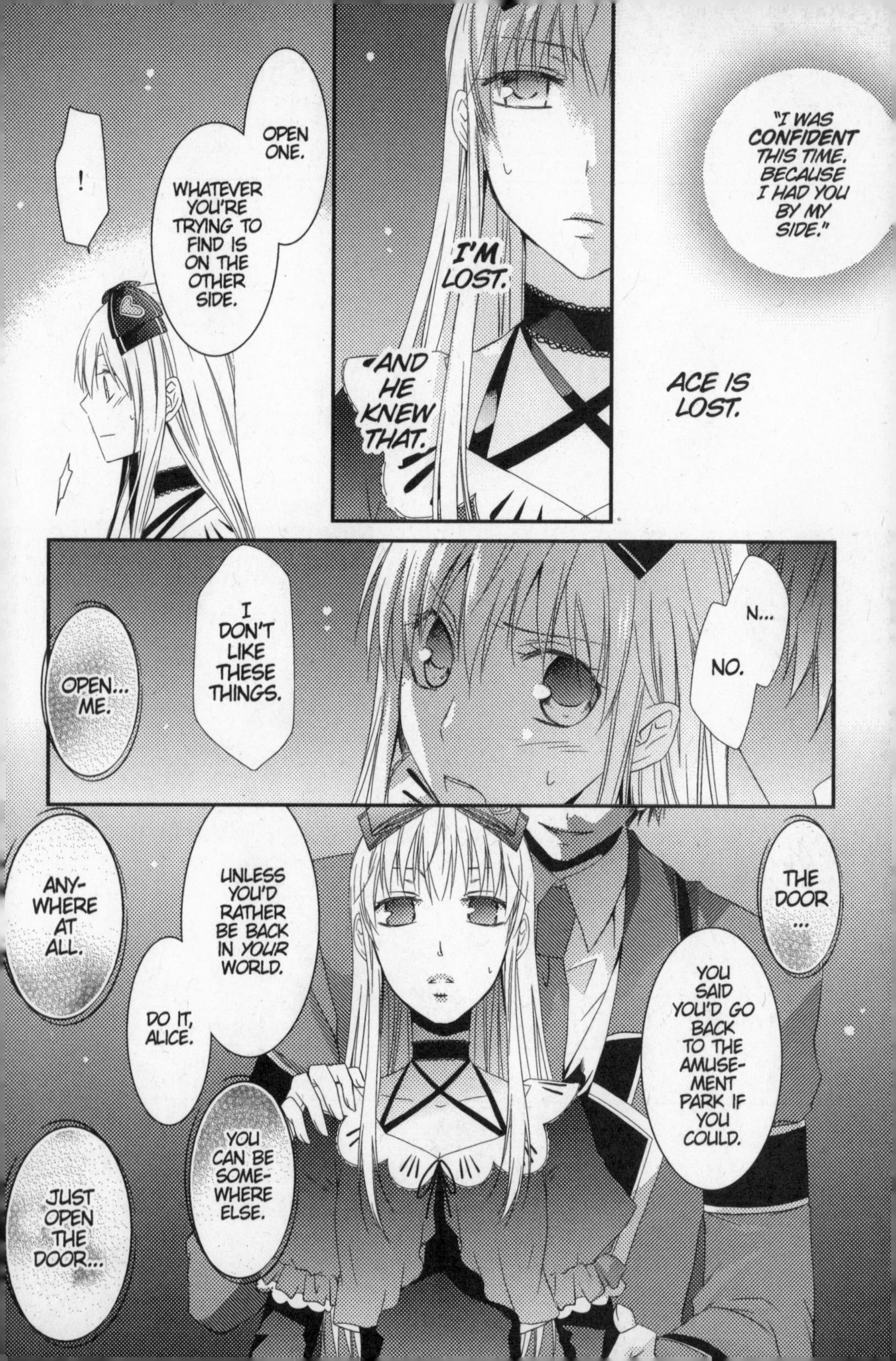
"I WAS CONFIDENT THIS TIME. BECAUSE I HAD YOU BY MY SIDE."
ACE IS LOST.
I'M LOST.
AND HE KNEW THAT.
OPEN ONE.
WHATEVER YOU'RE TRYING TO FIND IS ON THE OTHER SIDE.
!
N... NO.
I DON'T LIKE THESE THINGS.
OPEN... ME.
THE DOOR...
YOU SAID YOU'D GO BACK TO THE AMUSEMENT PARK IF YOU COULD.
UNLESS YOU'D RATHER BE BACK IN *YOUR* WORLD.
DO IT, ALICE.
ANYWHERE AT ALL.
YOU CAN BE SOMEWHERE ELSE.
JUST OPEN THE DOOR...

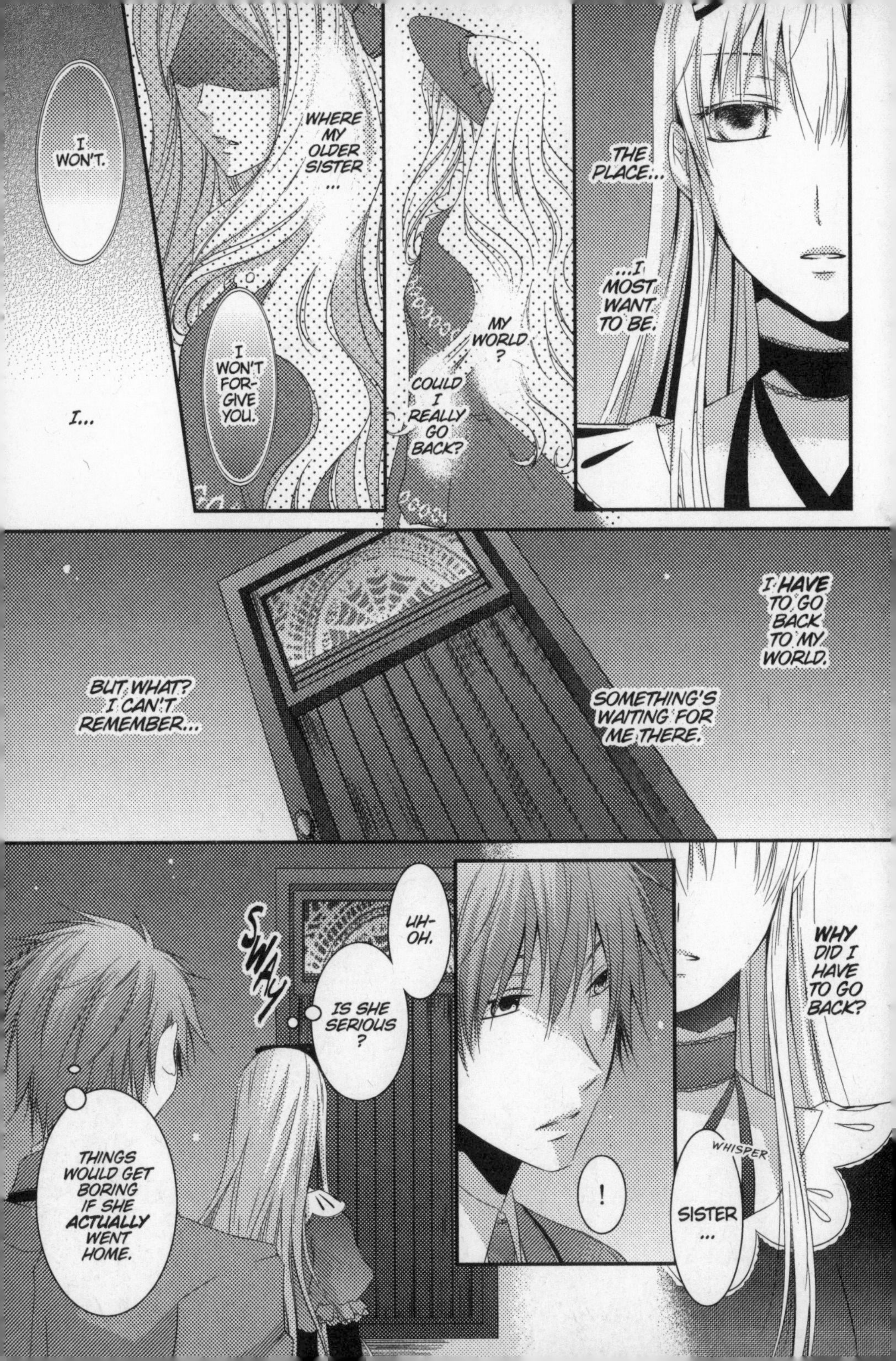
THE PLACE...
...I MOST WANT TO BE.
MY WORLD?
COULD I REALLY GO BACK?
WHERE MY OLDER SISTER...
I WON'T FORGIVE YOU.
I WON'T.
I...
I HAVE TO GO BACK TO MY WORLD.
SOMETHING'S WAITING FOR ME THERE.
BUT WHAT? I CAN'T REMEMBER...
WHY DID I HAVE TO GO BACK?
WHISPER
SISTER...
!
UH-OH.
IS SHE SERIOUS?
SWAY
THINGS WOULD GET BORING IF SHE ACTUALLY WENT HOME.

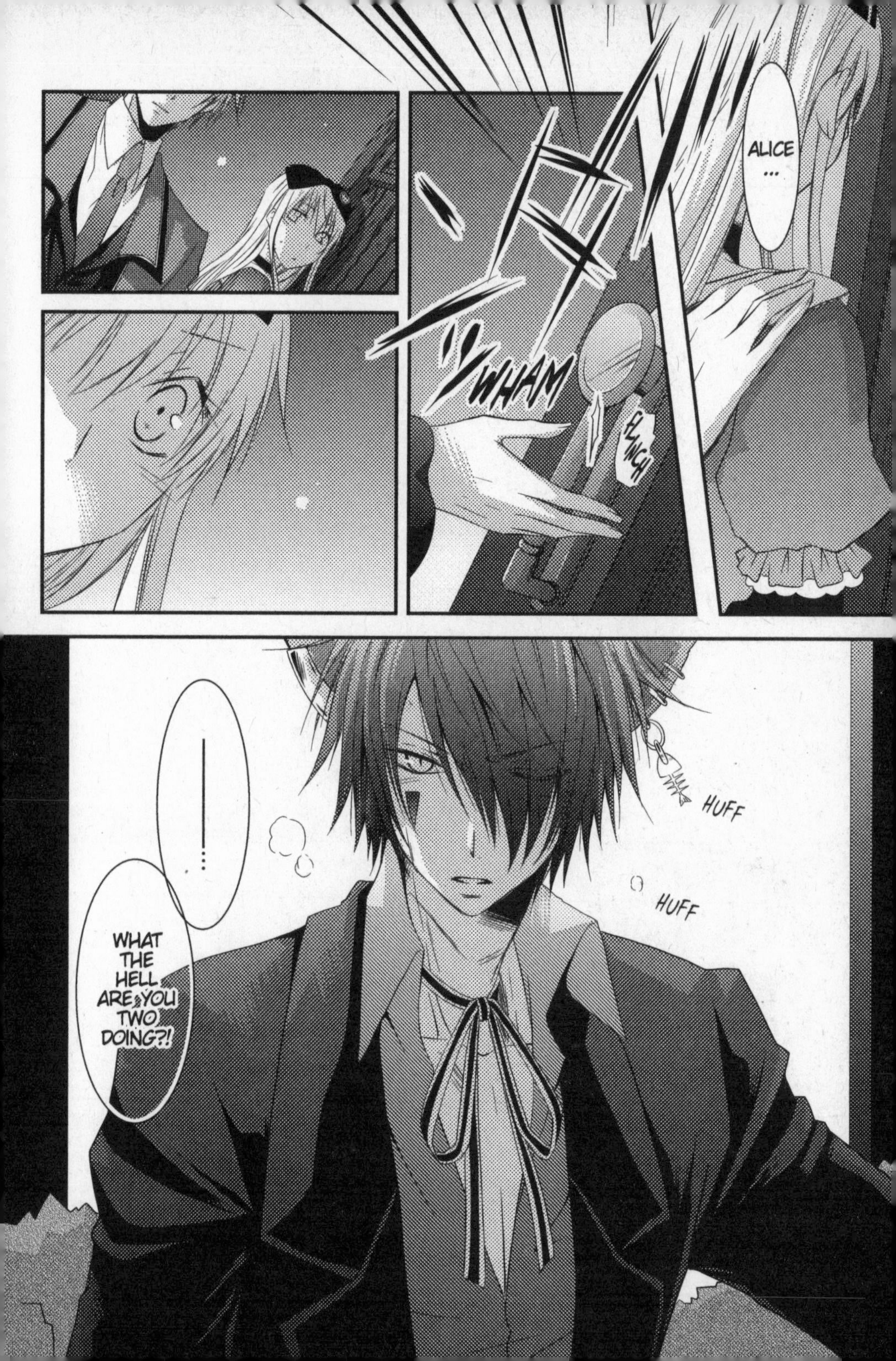
ALICE ...
WHAM
FLINCH
......!
WHAT THE HELL ARE YOU TWO DOING?!
HUFF
HUFF

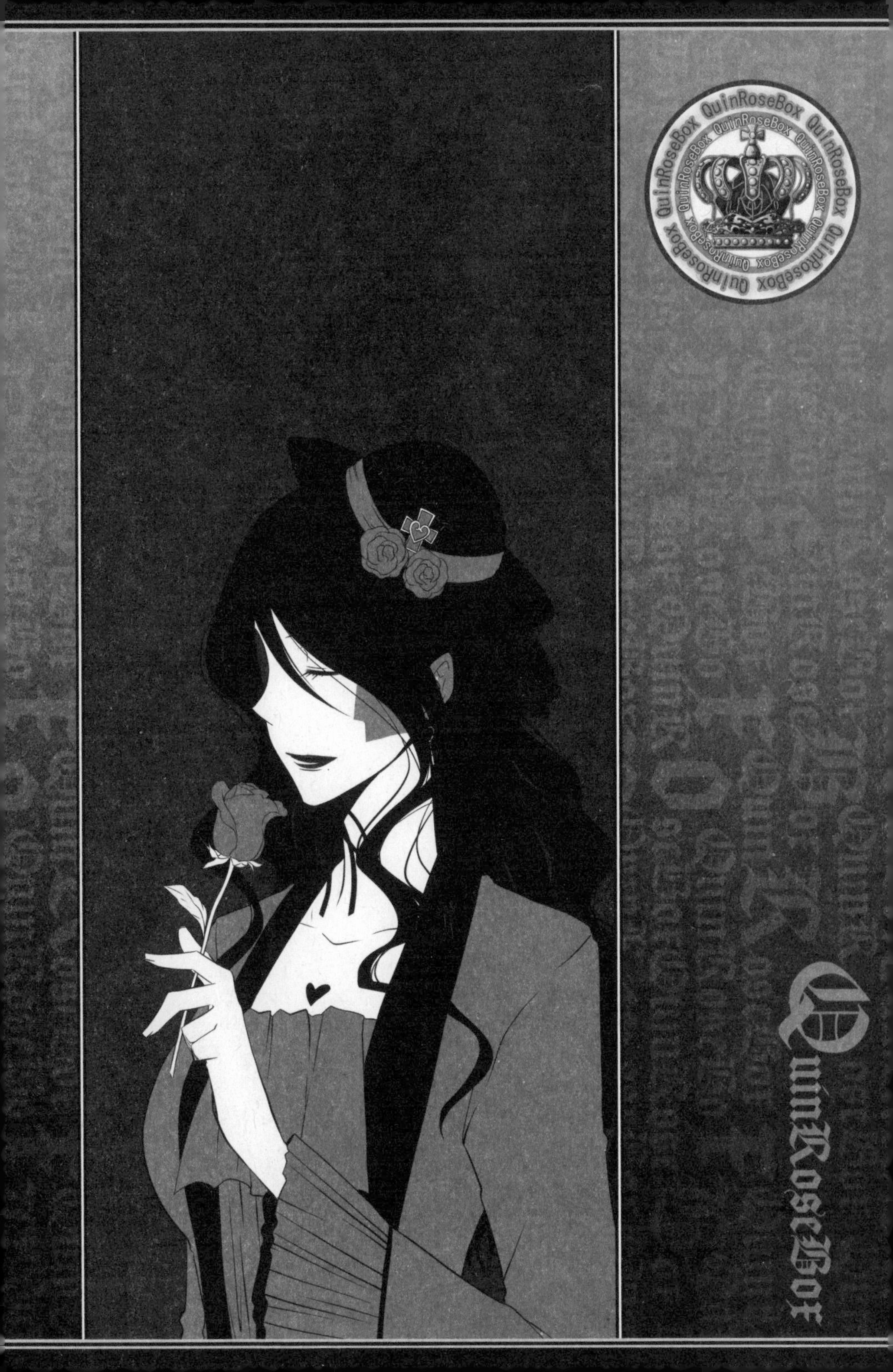
QuinRoseBox

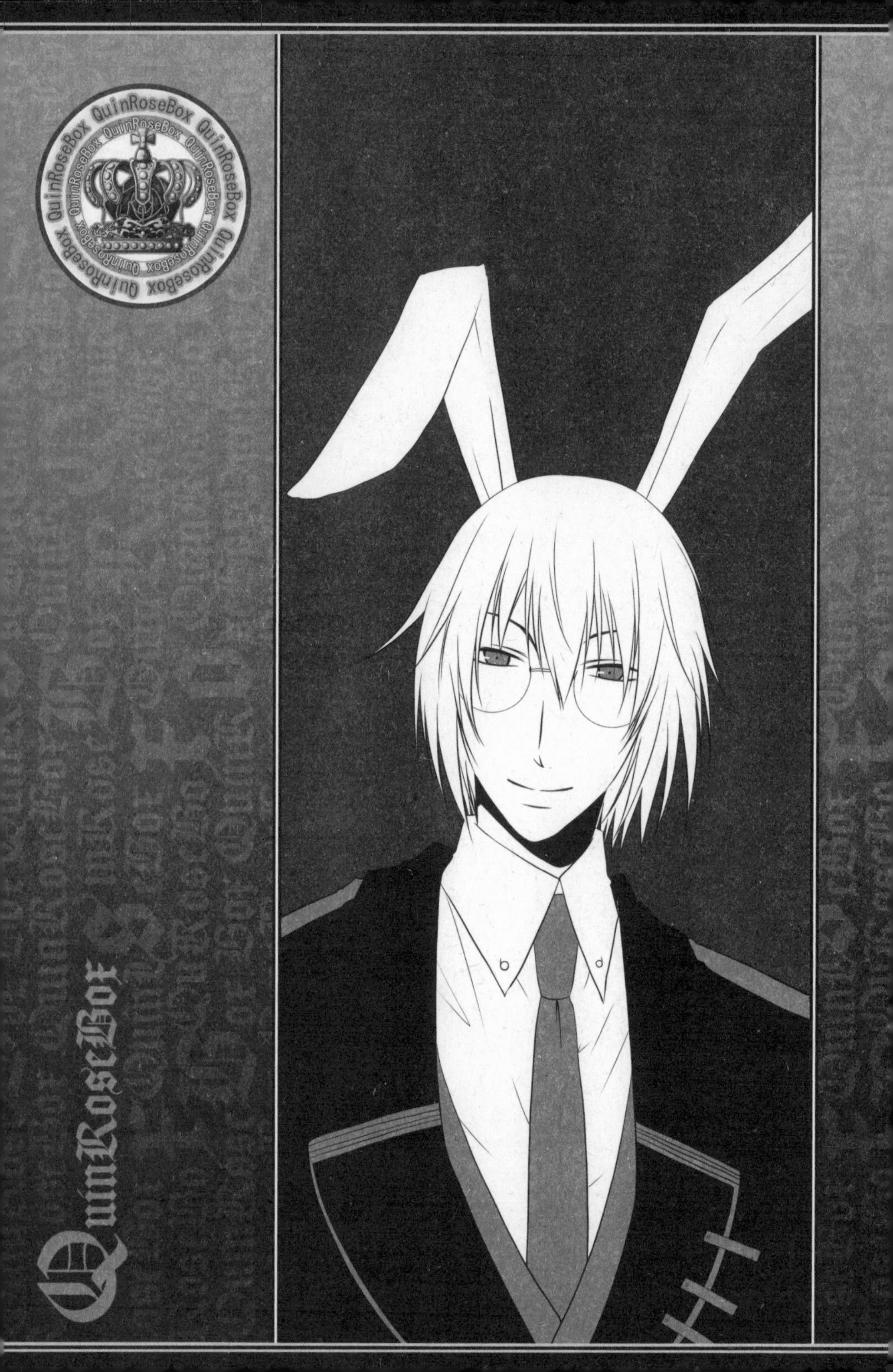
QuinRoseBox

Chapter 5

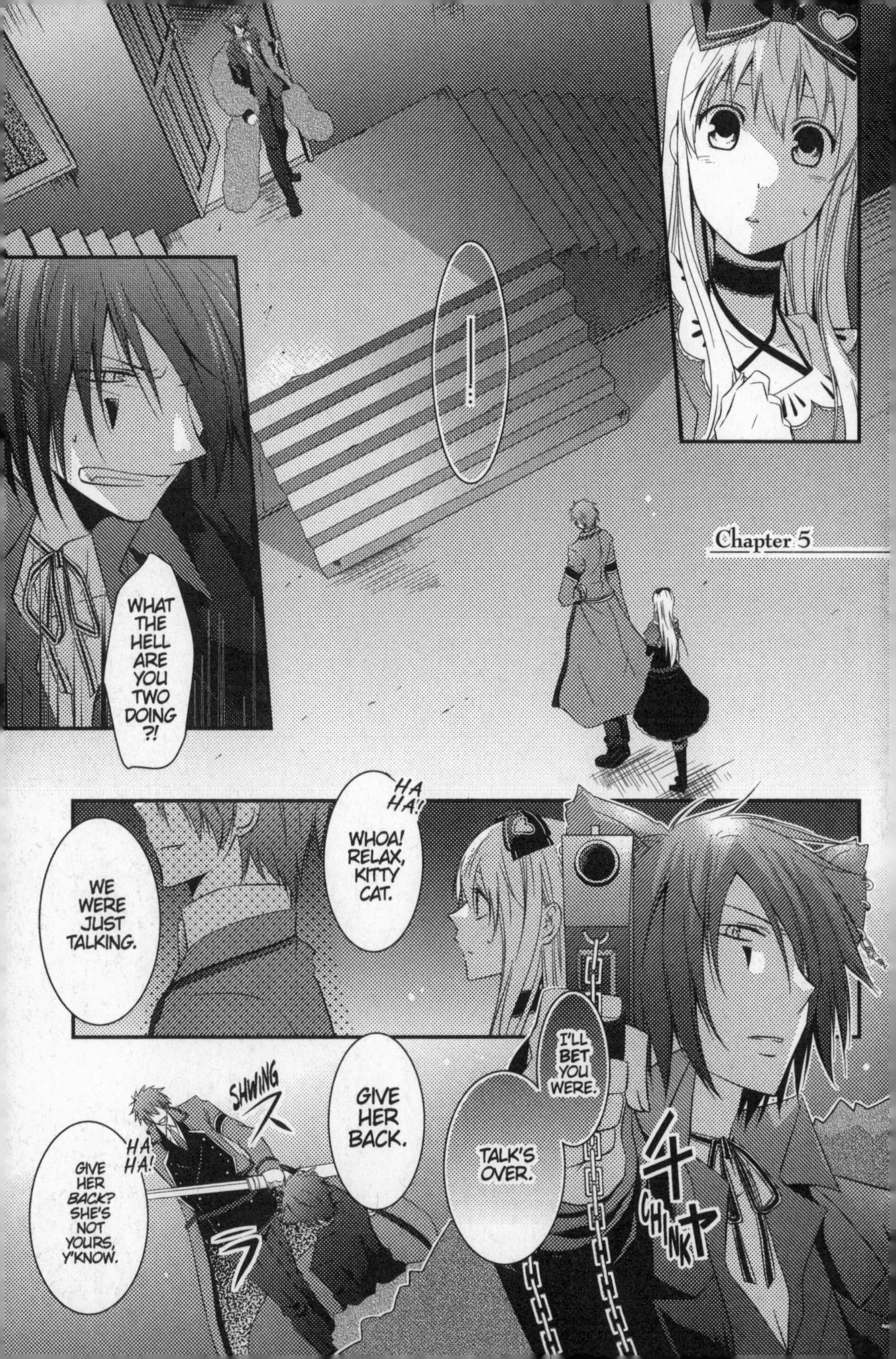
...!
WHAT THE HELL ARE YOU TWO DOING?!
HA HA!
WHOA! RELAX, KITTY CAT.
WE WERE JUST TALKING.
I'LL BET YOU WERE.
TALK'S OVER.
CHINK
GIVE HER BACK.
SHWING
HA HA!
GIVE HER BACK? SHE'S NOT YOURS, Y'KNOW.

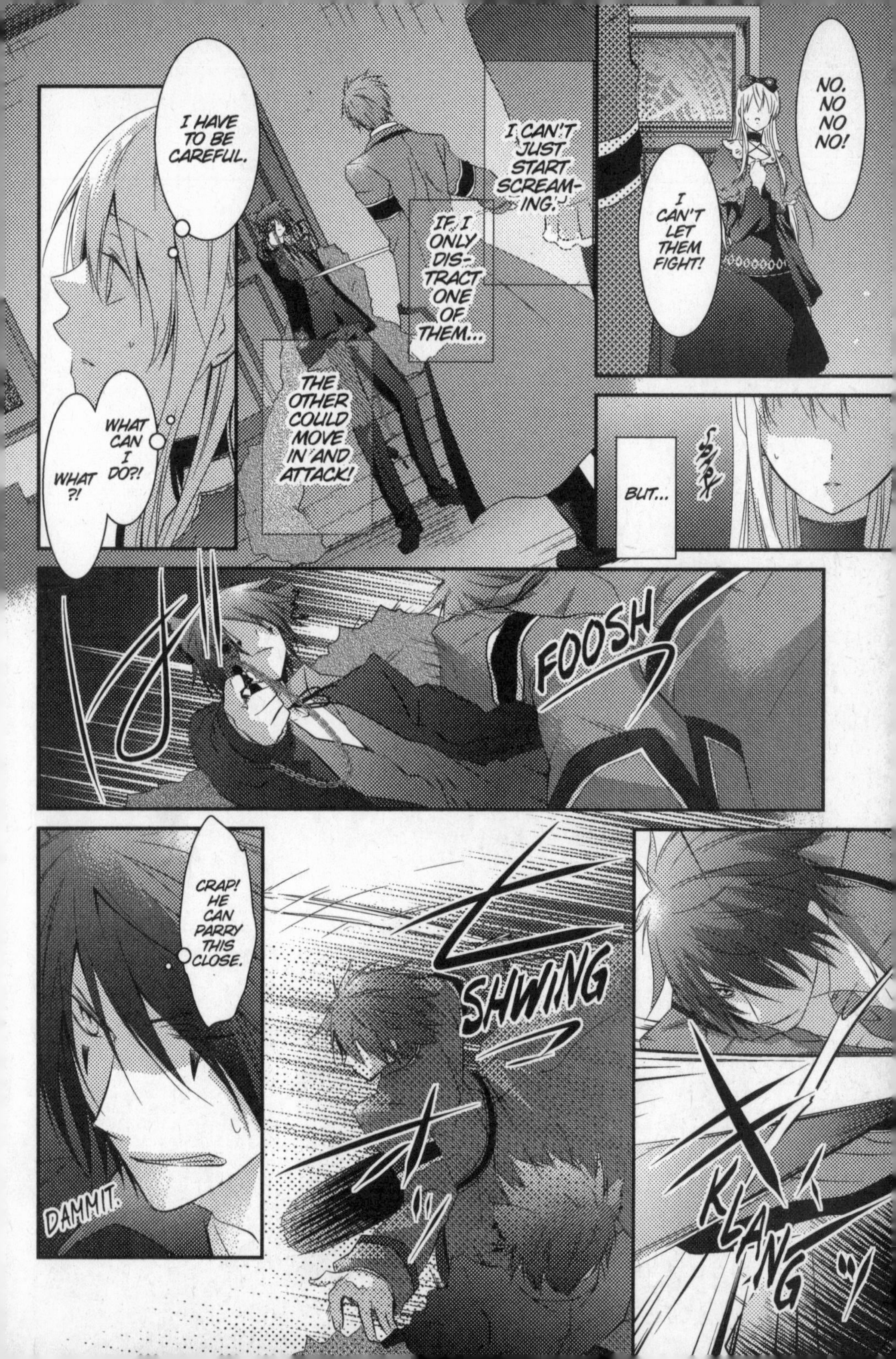
NO. NO NO NO!
I CAN'T LET THEM FIGHT!
BUT...
I CAN'T JUST START SCREAMING.
IF I ONLY DISTRACT ONE OF THEM...
THE OTHER COULD MOVE IN AND ATTACK!
I HAVE TO BE CAREFUL.
WHAT CAN I DO?!
WHAT?!
FOOSH
KLANG
SHWING
CRAP! HE CAN PARRY THIS CLOSE.
DAMMIT.

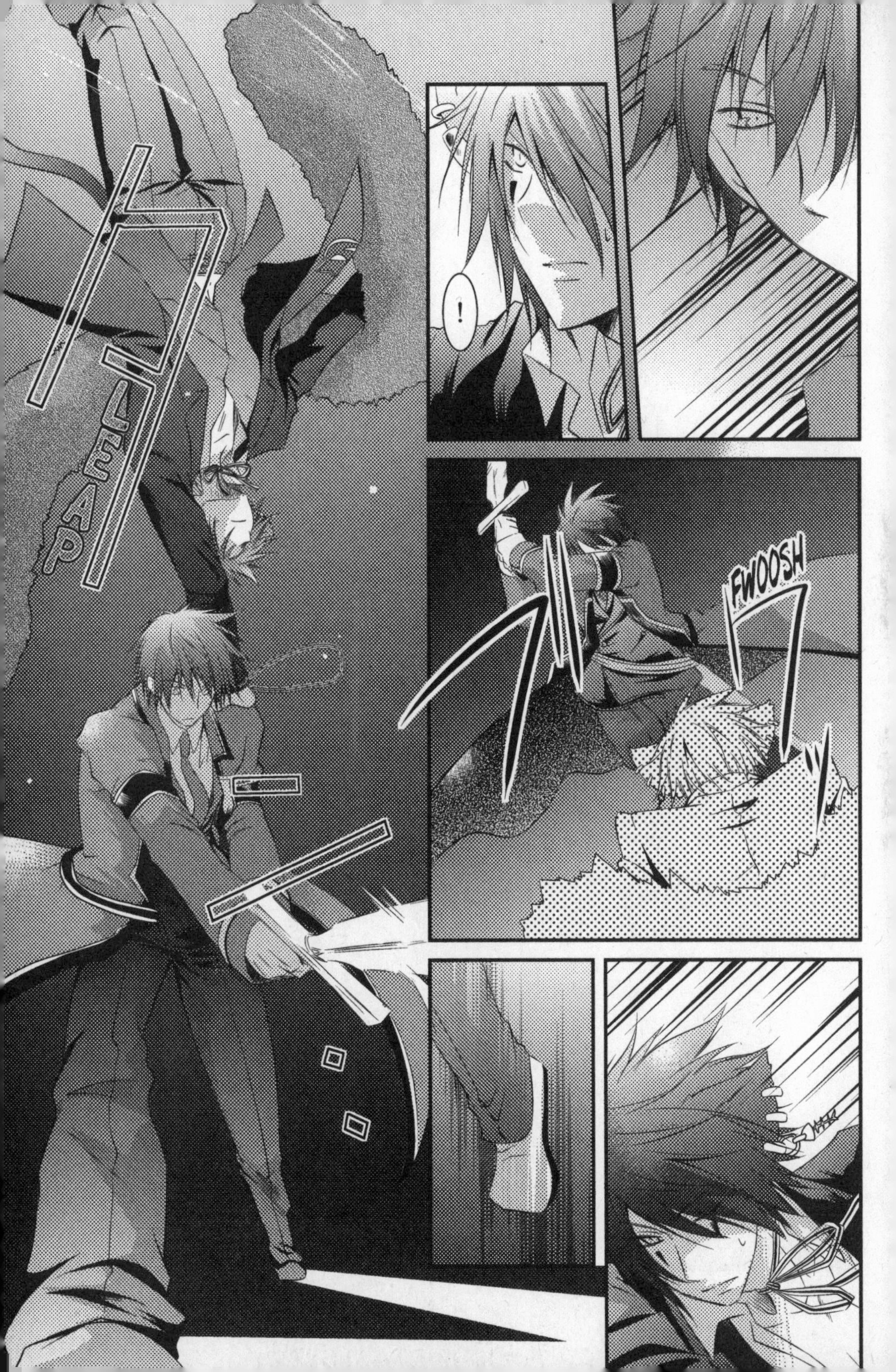
!
LEAP
FWOOSH

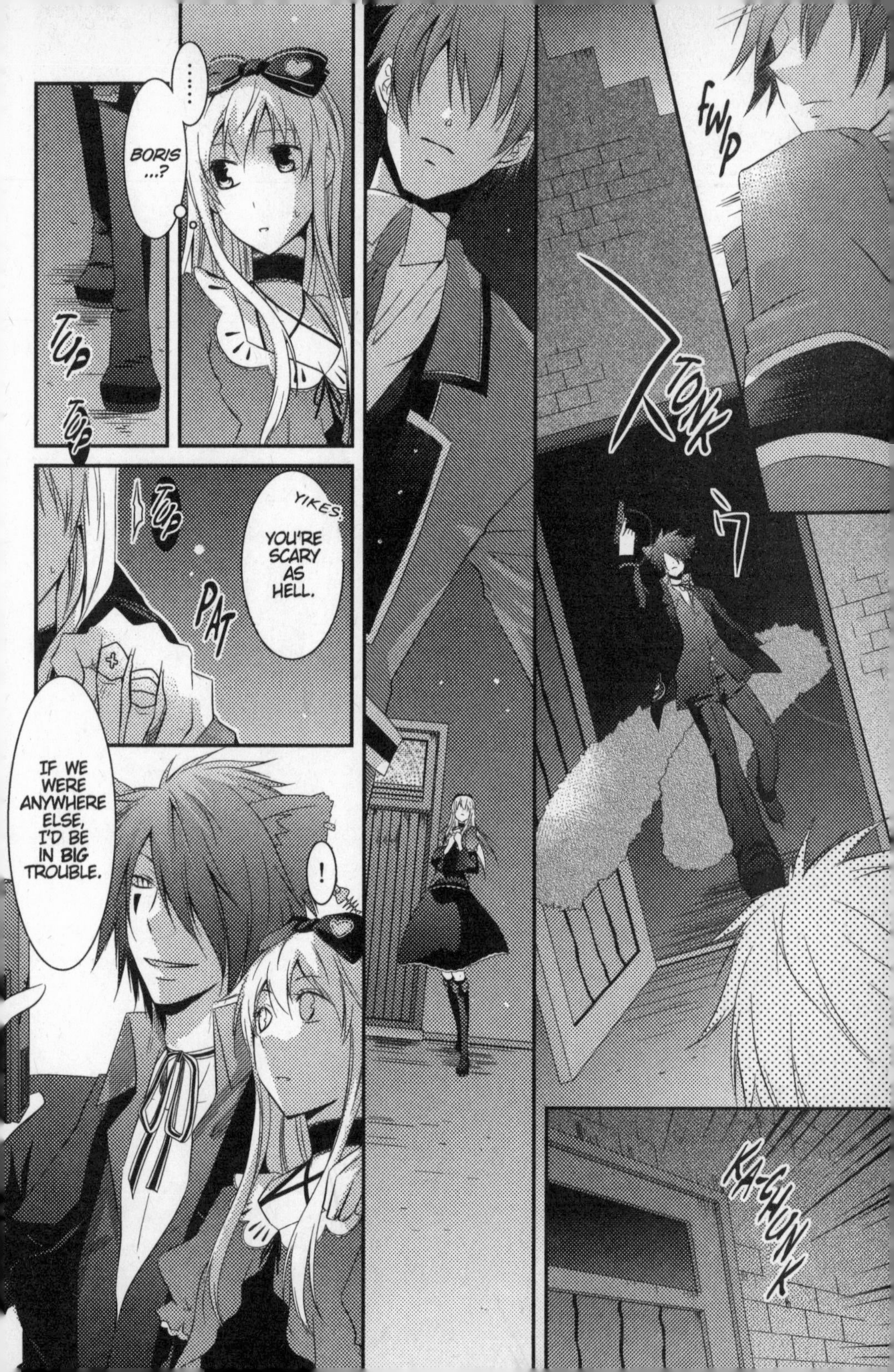
FWIP
TONK
KA-CHUNK
......
BORIS ...?
TUP
TUP
TUP
PAT
YIKES.
YOU'RE SCARY AS HELL.
IF WE WERE ANYWHERE ELSE, I'D BE IN BIG TROUBLE.
!

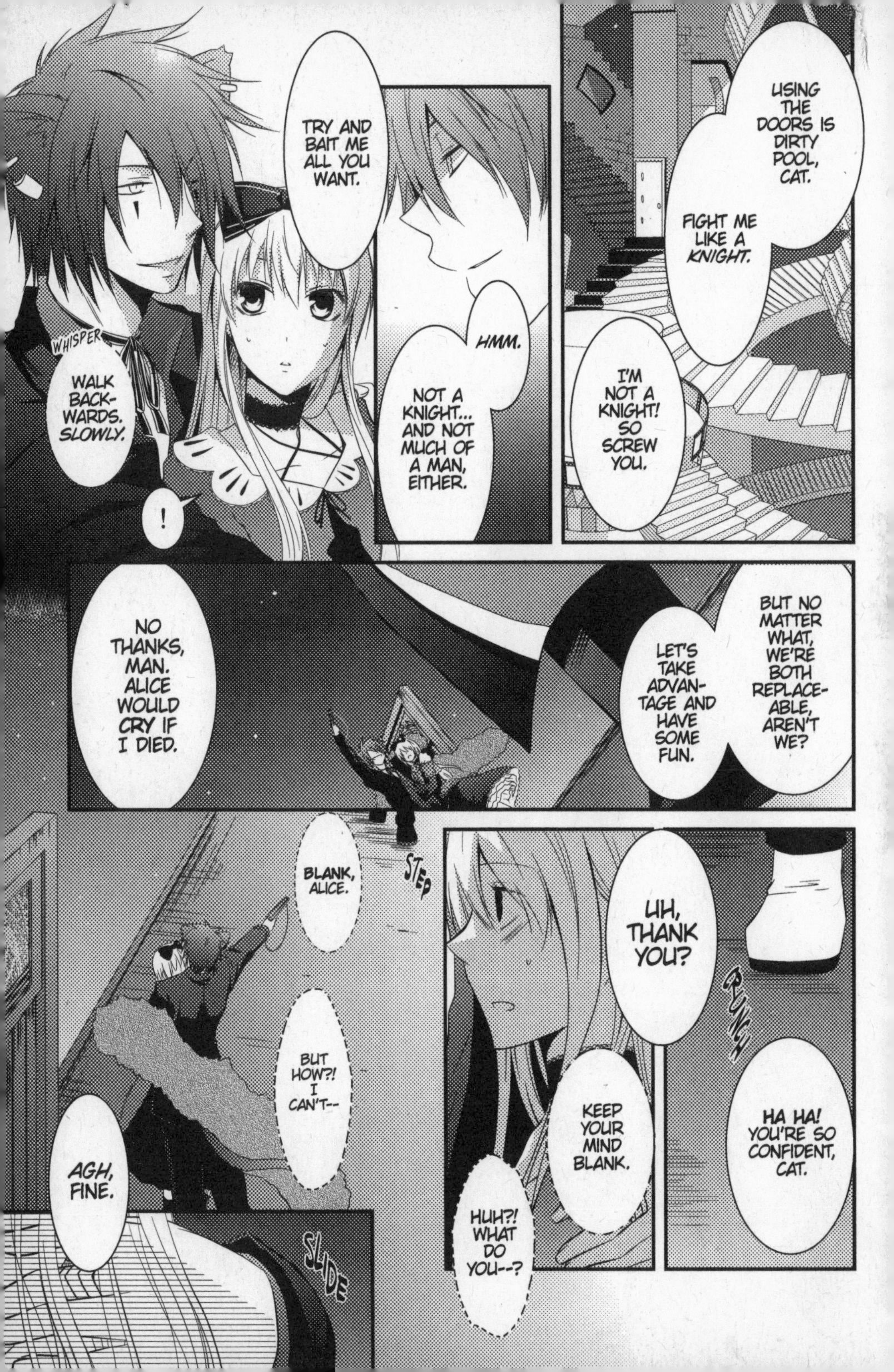
USING THE DOORS IS DIRTY POOL, CAT.
FIGHT ME LIKE A KNIGHT.
I'M NOT A KNIGHT! SO SCREW YOU.
TRY AND BAIT ME ALL YOU WANT.
HMM.
NOT A KNIGHT... AND NOT MUCH OF A MAN, EITHER.
WHISPER
WALK BACK-WARDS. SLOWLY.
!
BUT NO MATTER WHAT, WE'RE BOTH REPLACE-ABLE, AREN'T WE?
LET'S TAKE ADVAN-TAGE AND HAVE SOME FUN.
NO THANKS, MAN. ALICE WOULD CRY IF I DIED.
HA HA! YOU'RE SO CONFIDENT, CAT.
CRUNCH
UH, THANK YOU?
KEEP YOUR MIND BLANK.
HUH?! WHAT DO YOU--?
STEP
BLANK, ALICE.
BUT HOW?! I CAN'T--
AGH, FINE.
SLIDE

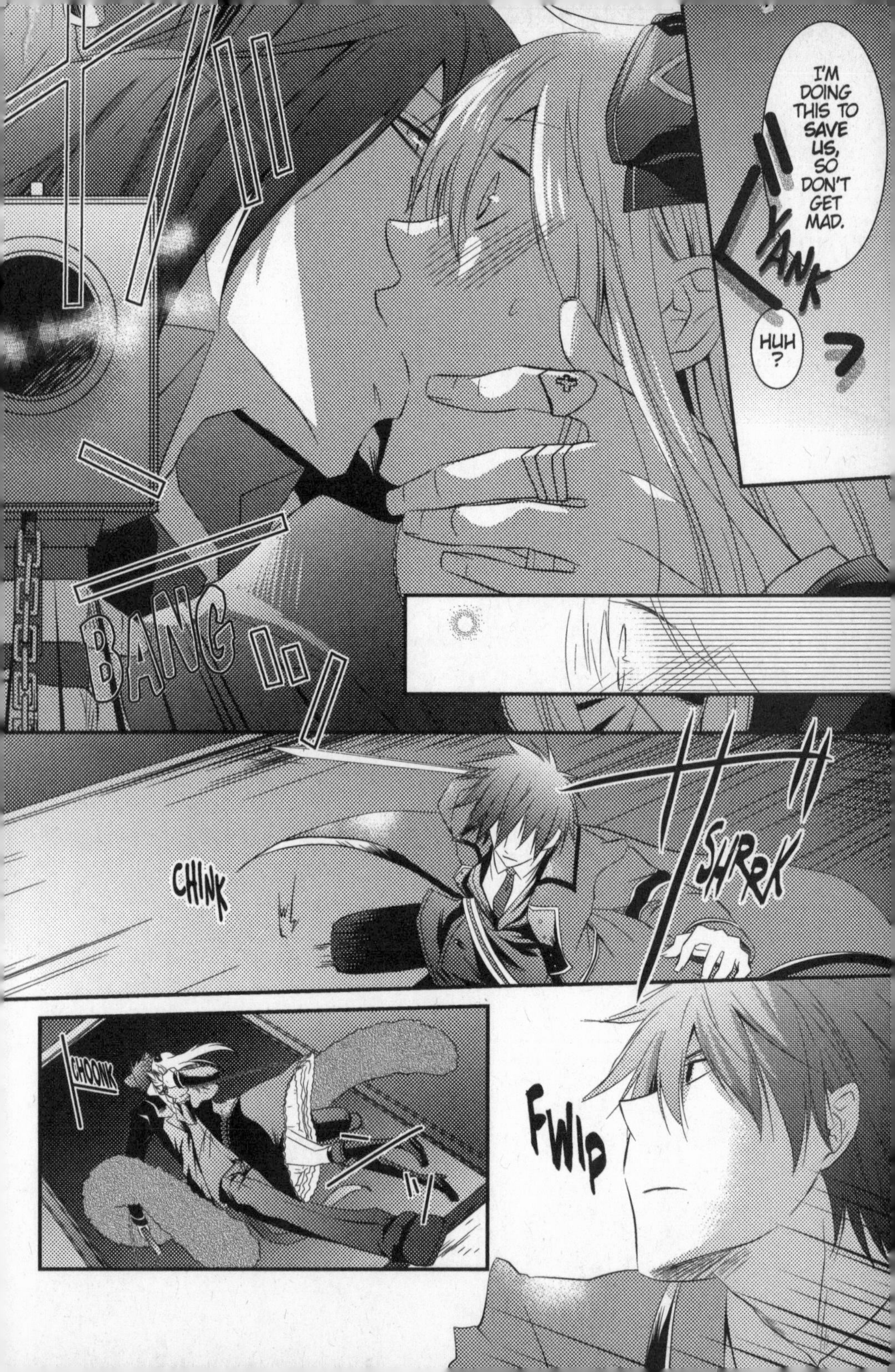
I'M DOING THIS TO SAVE US, SO DON'T GET MAD.
YANK
HUH?
BANG
SHRRK
CHINK
FWIP
CHOONK

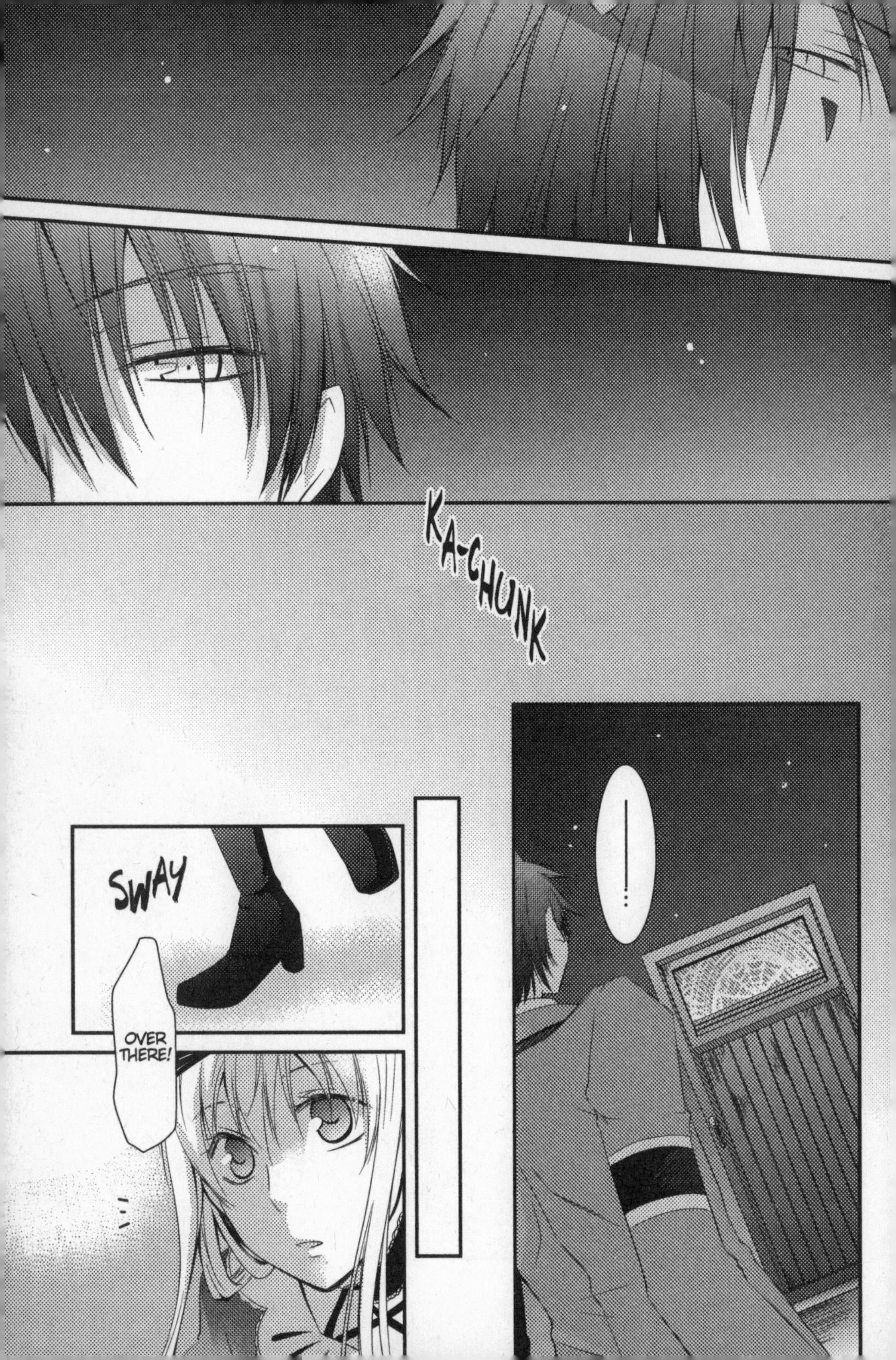
KA-CHUNK
SWAY
OVER THERE!

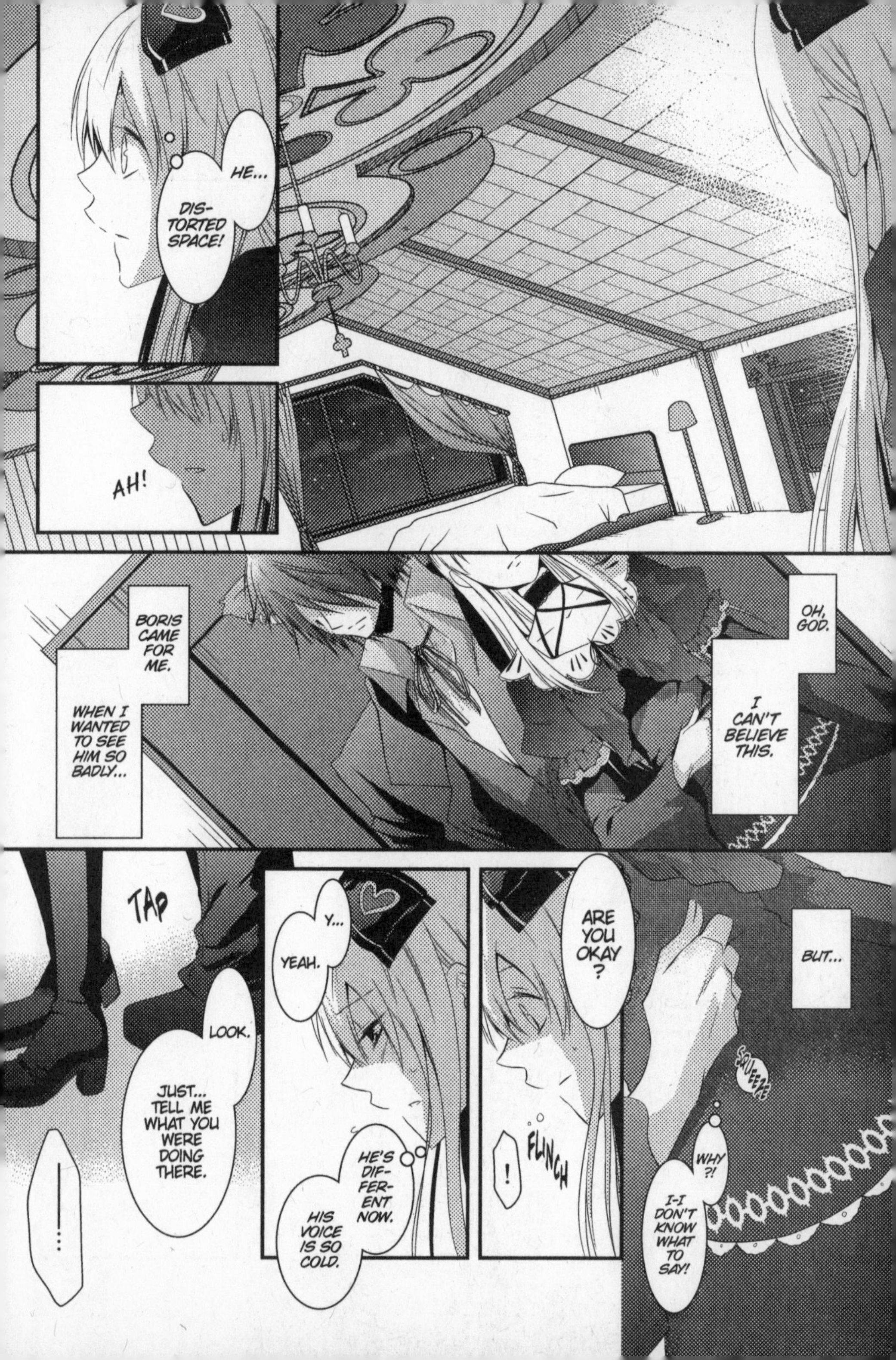
HE... DISTORTED SPACE!
AH!
OH, GOD.
I CAN'T BELIEVE THIS.
BORIS CAME FOR ME.
WHEN I WANTED TO SEE HIM SO BADLY...
BUT...
SQUEEZE
WHY?!
I-I DON'T KNOW WHAT TO SAY!
ARE YOU OKAY?
!
FLINCH
Y...
YEAH.
HE'S DIFFERENT NOW.
HIS VOICE IS SO COLD.
TAP
LOOK.
JUST... TELL ME WHAT YOU WERE DOING THERE.
......

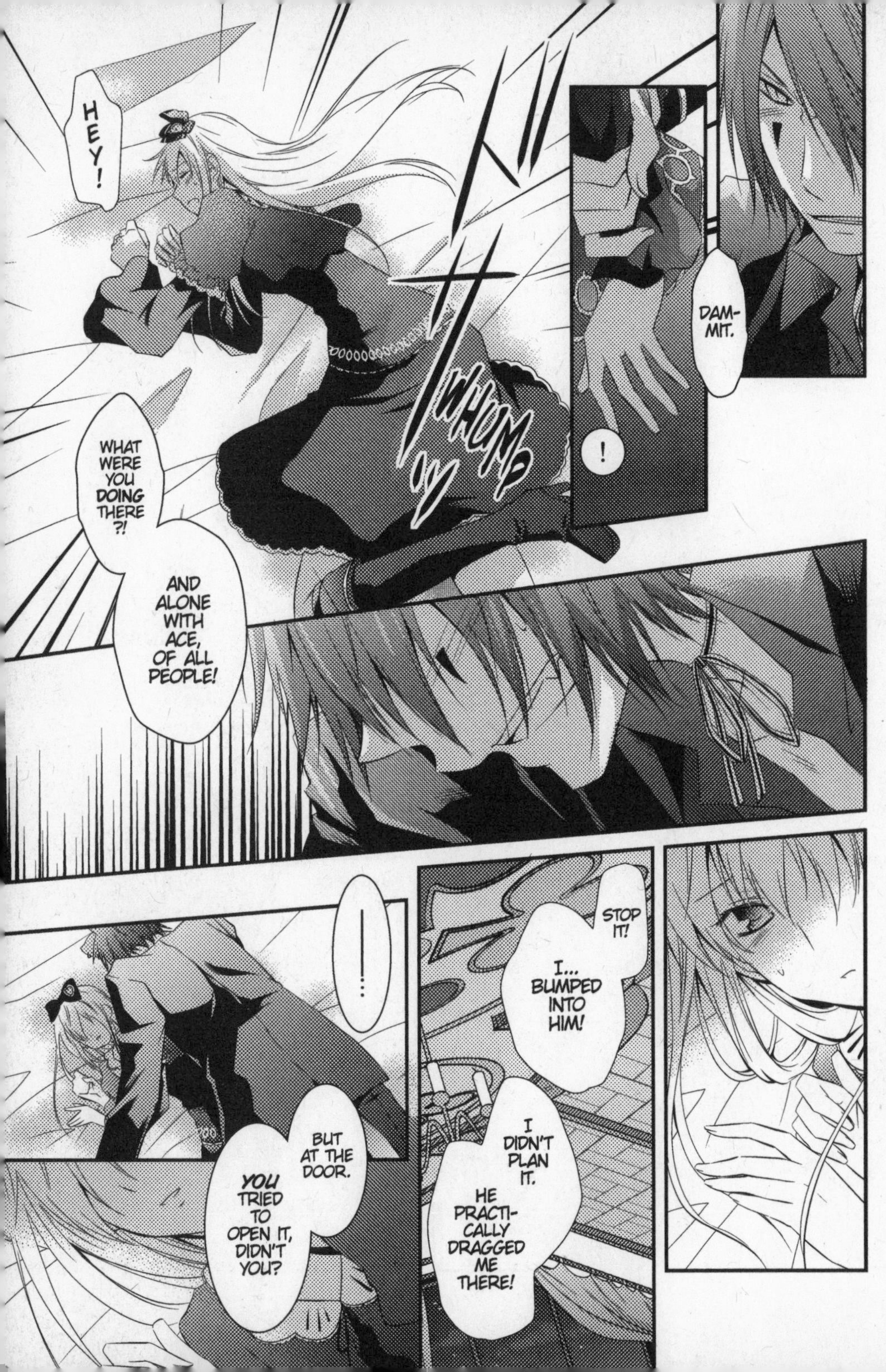
DAM-MIT.
!
HEY!
WHAT WERE YOU DOING THERE?!
AND ALONE WITH ACE, OF ALL PEOPLE!
STOP IT!
I... BUMPED INTO HIM!
I DIDN'T PLAN IT.
HE PRACTICALLY DRAGGED ME THERE!
!...
BUT AT THE DOOR.
YOU TRIED TO OPEN IT, DIDN'T YOU?

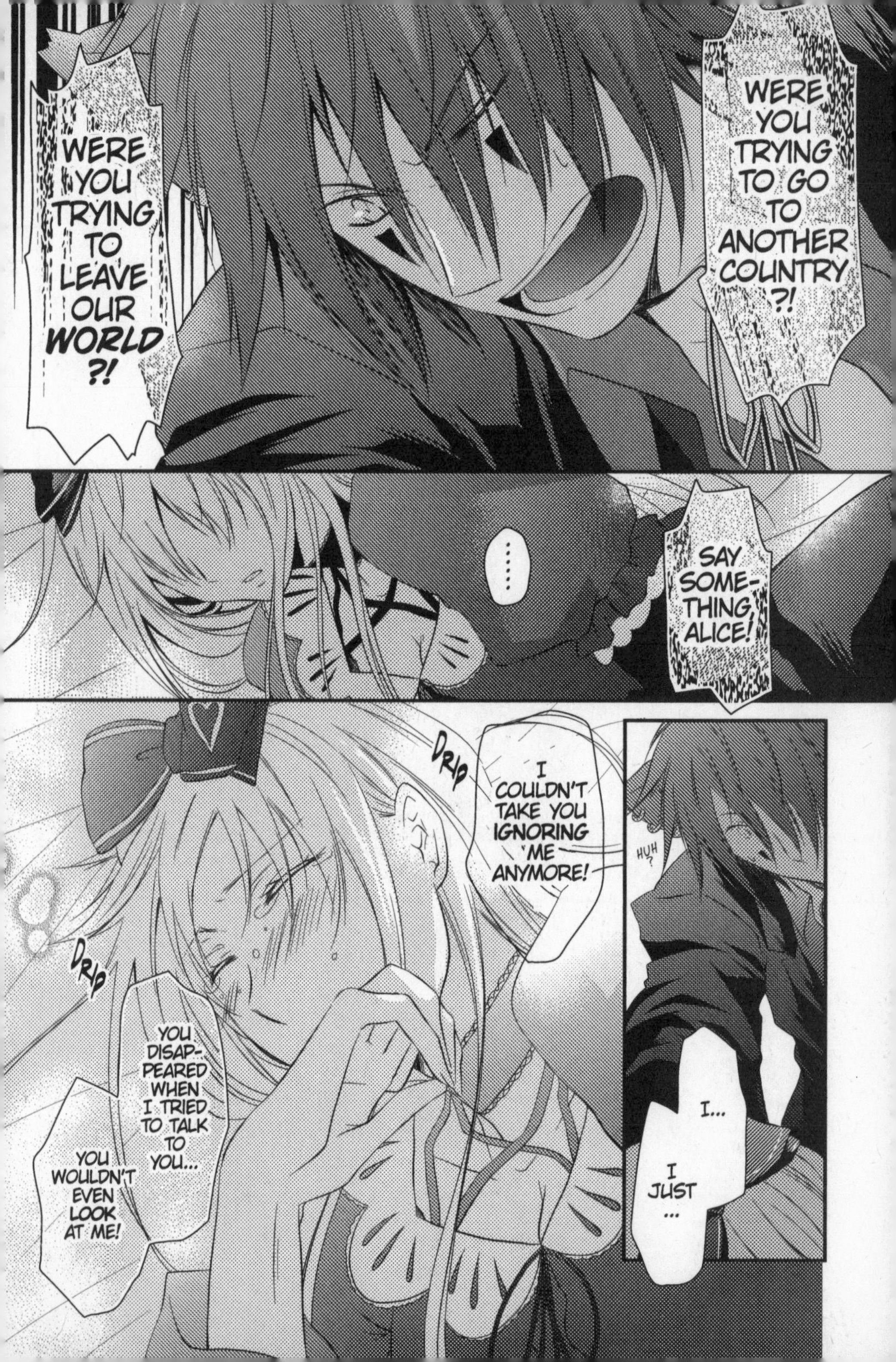
WERE YOU TRYING TO GO TO ANOTHER COUNTRY?!
WERE YOU TRYING TO LEAVE OUR WORLD?!
SAY SOME-THING, ALICE!
......
HUH?
I...
I JUST ...
DRIP
I COULDN'T TAKE YOU IGNORING ME ANYMORE!
DRIP
YOU DISAP-PEARED WHEN I TRIED TO TALK TO YOU...
YOU WOULDN'T EVEN LOOK AT ME!

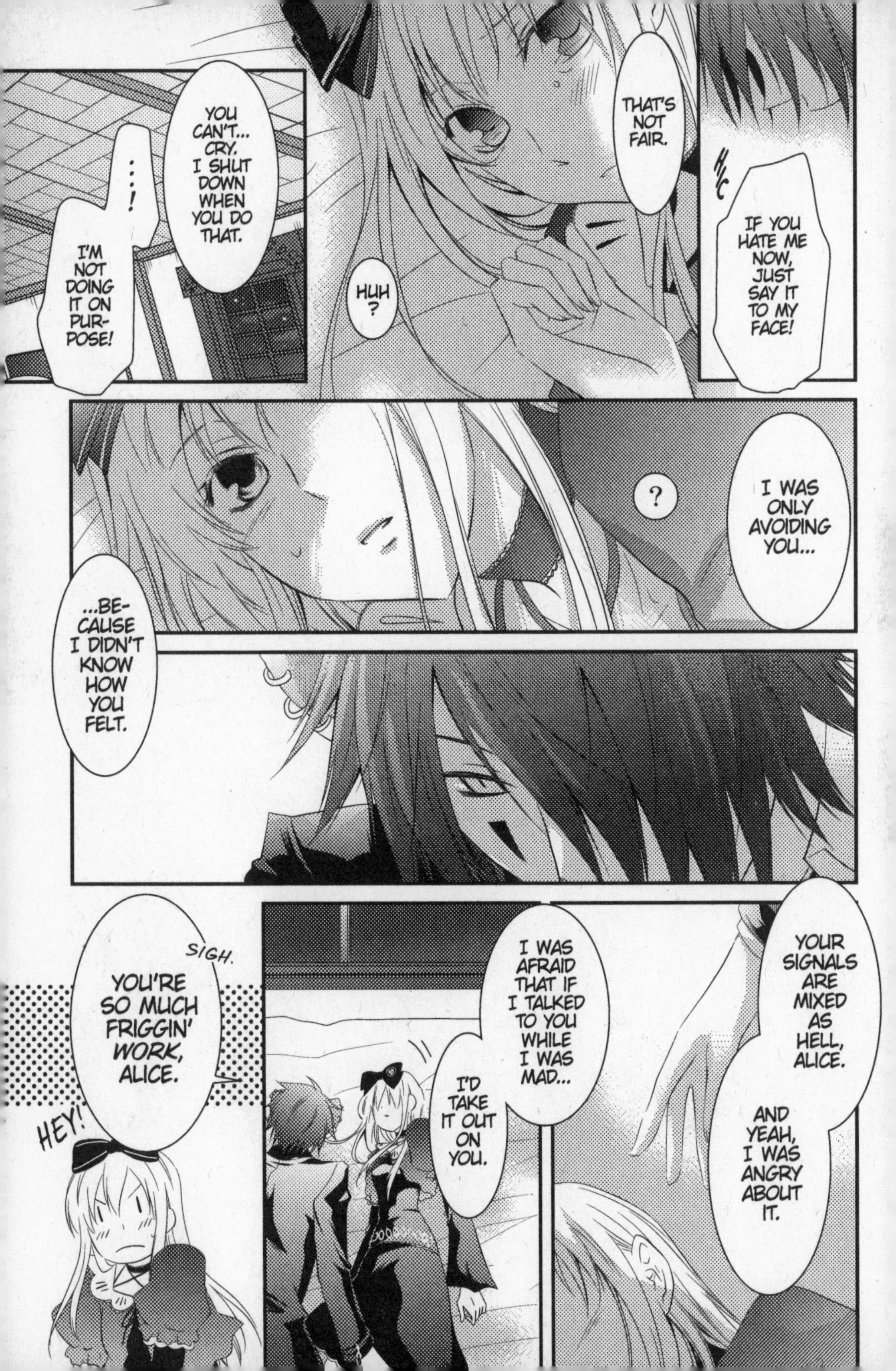
HIC
IF YOU HATE ME NOW, JUST SAY IT TO MY FACE!
THAT'S NOT FAIR.
HUH?
YOU CAN'T... CRY. I SHUT DOWN WHEN YOU DO THAT.
...!
I'M NOT DOING IT ON PUR-POSE!
?
I WAS ONLY AVOIDING YOU...
...BE-CAUSE I DIDN'T KNOW HOW YOU FELT.
YOUR SIGNALS ARE MIXED AS HELL, ALICE.
AND YEAH, I WAS ANGRY ABOUT IT.
I WAS AFRAID THAT IF I TALKED TO YOU WHILE I WAS MAD...
I'D TAKE IT OUT ON YOU.
SIGH.
YOU'RE SO MUCH FRIGGIN' WORK, ALICE.
HEY!

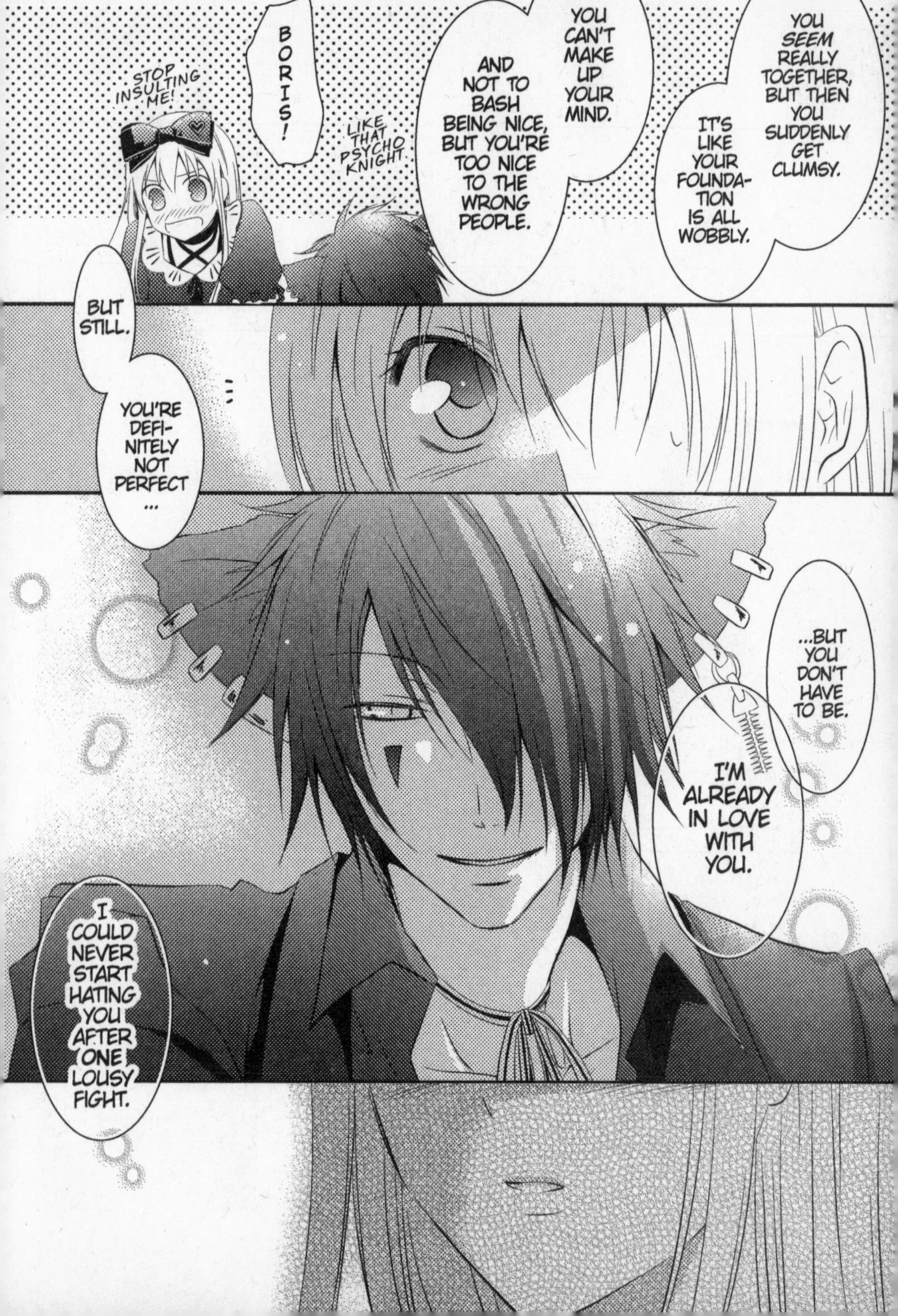
YOU SEEM REALLY TOGETHER, BUT THEN YOU SUDDENLY GET CLUMSY.
IT'S LIKE YOUR FOUNDATION IS ALL WOBBLY.
YOU CAN'T MAKE UP YOUR MIND.
AND NOT TO BASH BEING NICE, BUT YOU'RE TOO NICE TO THE WRONG PEOPLE.
LIKE THAT PSYCHO KNIGHT.
BORIS!
STOP INSULTING ME!
BUT STILL.
YOU'RE DEFINITELY NOT PERFECT...
...BUT YOU DON'T HAVE TO BE.
I'M ALREADY IN LOVE WITH YOU.
I COULD NEVER START HATING YOU AFTER ONE LOUSY FIGHT.

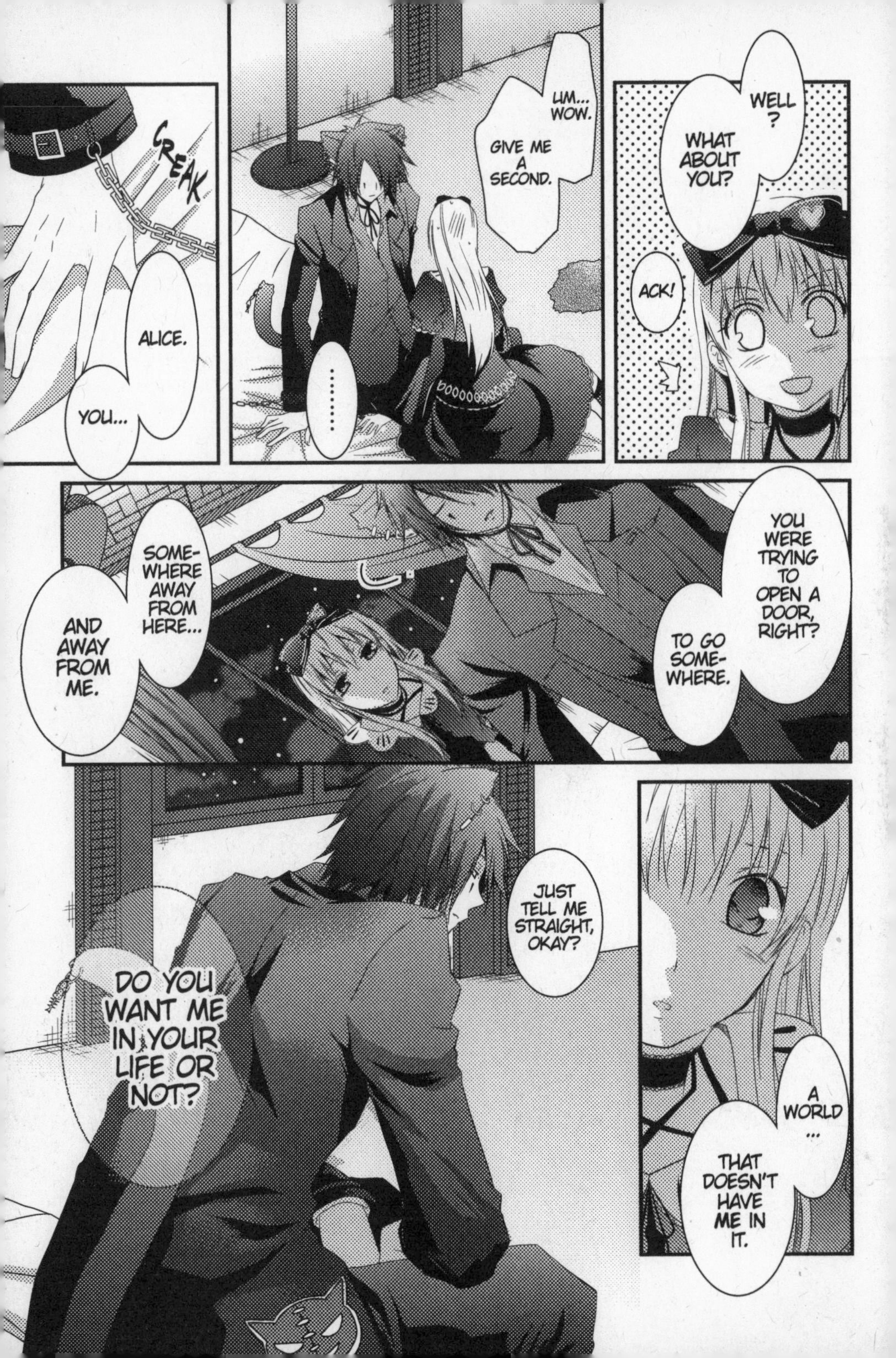
WELL?
WHAT ABOUT YOU?
ACK!
UM... WOW.
GIVE ME A SECOND.
......
CREAK
ALICE.
YOU...
YOU WERE TRYING TO OPEN A DOOR, RIGHT?
TO GO SOME-WHERE.
SOME-WHERE AWAY FROM HERE...
AND AWAY FROM ME.
A WORLD...
THAT DOESN'T HAVE ME IN IT.
JUST TELL ME STRAIGHT, OKAY?
DO YOU WANT ME IN YOUR LIFE OR NOT?

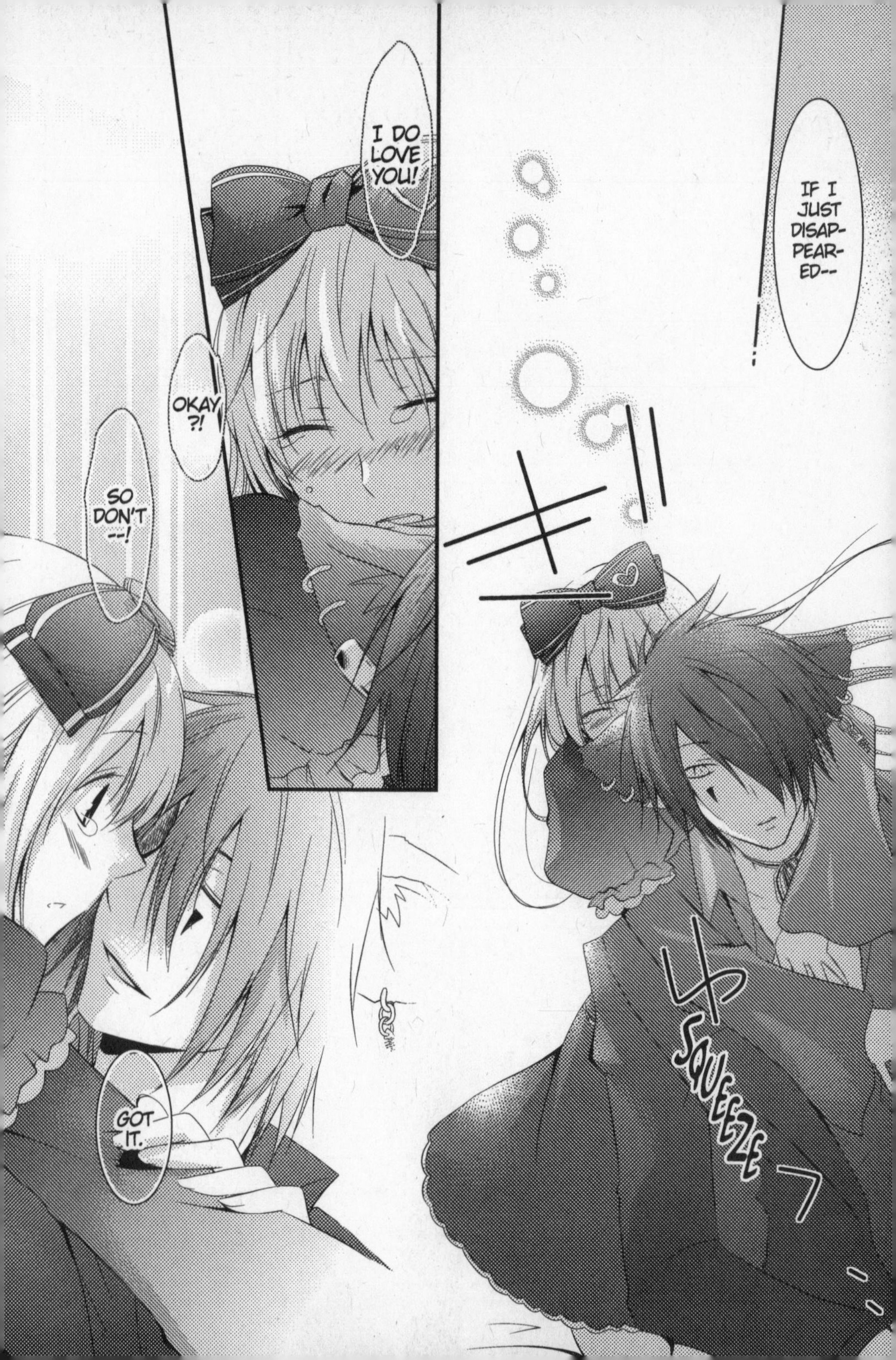
IF I JUST DISAP-PEAR-ED--
I DO LOVE YOU!
OKAY?!
SO DON'T --!
SQUEEZE
GOT IT.

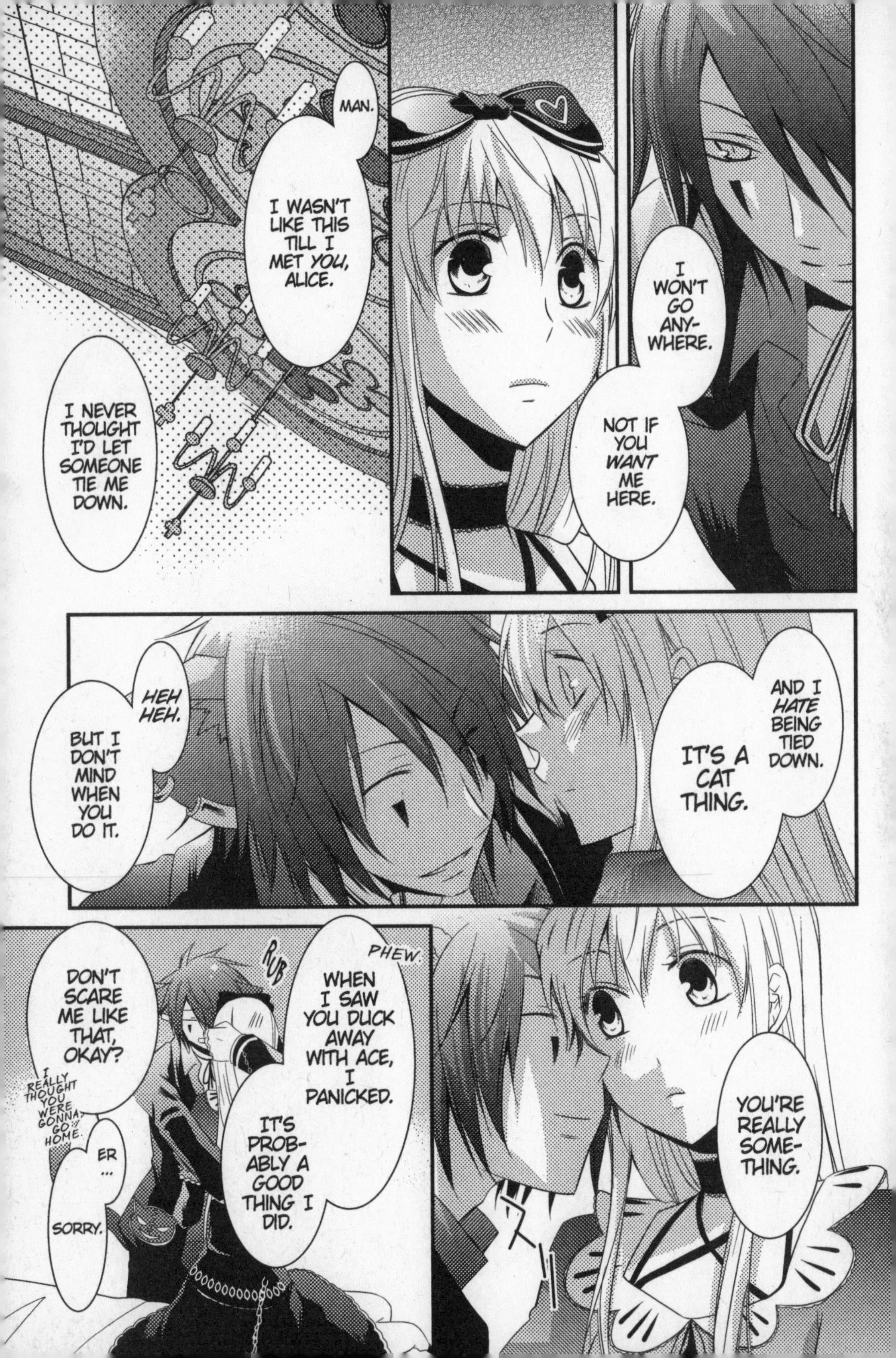
I WON'T GO ANYWHERE.
NOT IF YOU WANT ME HERE.
MAN.
I WASN'T LIKE THIS TILL I MET YOU, ALICE.
I NEVER THOUGHT I'D LET SOMEONE TIE ME DOWN.
AND I HATE BEING TIED DOWN.
IT'S A CAT THING.
HEH HEH.
BUT I DON'T MIND WHEN YOU DO IT.
YOU'RE REALLY SOMETHING.
PHEW.
WHEN I SAW YOU DUCK AWAY WITH ACE, I PANICKED.
IT'S PROBABLY A GOOD THING I DID.
RUB
DON'T SCARE ME LIKE THAT, OKAY?
I REALLY THOUGHT YOU WERE GONNA GO HOME.
ER ...
SORRY.

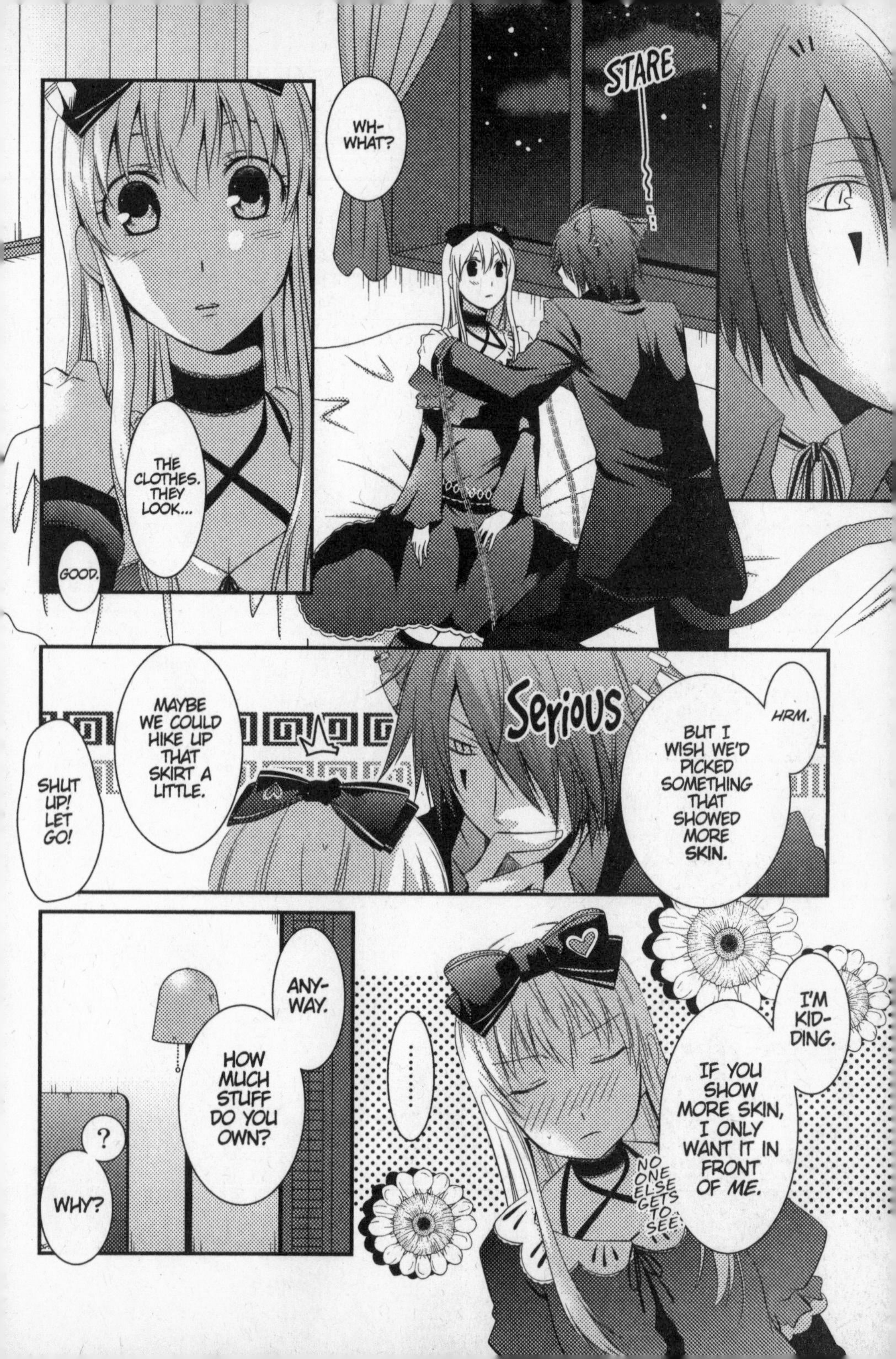
STARE
WH-WHAT?
THE CLOTHES. THEY LOOK...
GOOD.
HRM.
BUT I WISH WE'D PICKED SOMETHING THAT SHOWED MORE SKIN.
Serious
MAYBE WE COULD HIKE UP THAT SKIRT A LITTLE.
SHUT UP! LET GO!
I'M KID-DING.
IF YOU SHOW MORE SKIN, I ONLY WANT IT IN FRONT OF ME.
NO ONE ELSE GETS TO SEE.
......
ANY-WAY.
HOW MUCH STUFF DO YOU OWN?
?
WHY?

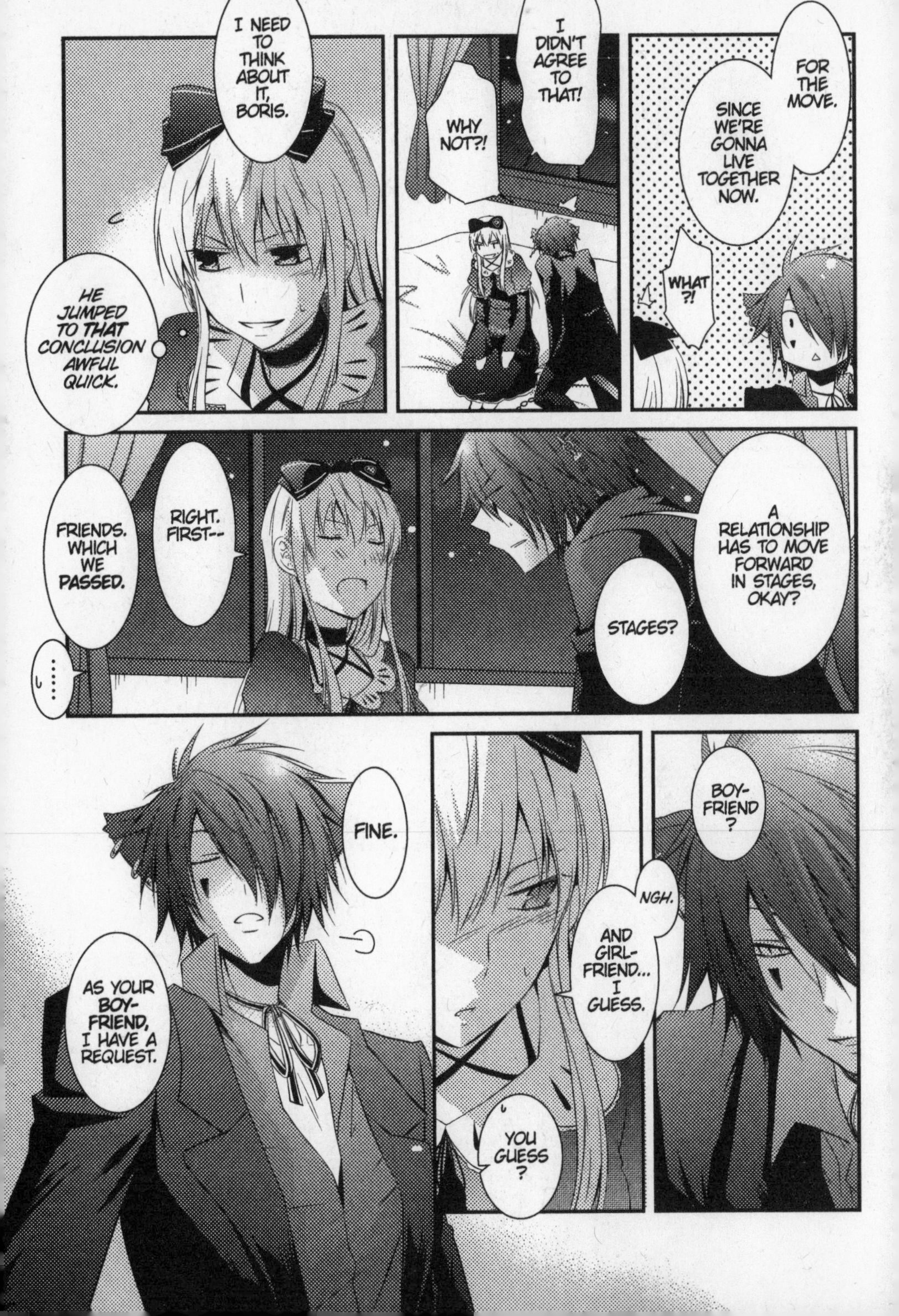
FOR THE MOVE.
SINCE WE'RE GONNA LIVE TOGETHER NOW.
WHAT?!
I DIDN'T AGREE TO THAT!
WHY NOT?!
I NEED TO THINK ABOUT IT, BORIS.
HE JUMPED TO THAT CONCLUSION AWFUL QUICK.
A RELATIONSHIP HAS TO MOVE FORWARD IN STAGES, OKAY?
STAGES?
RIGHT. FIRST--
FRIENDS. WHICH WE PASSED.
......
BOY-FRIEND?
NGH.
AND GIRL-FRIEND... I GUESS.
YOU GUESS?
FINE.
AS YOUR BOY-FRIEND, I HAVE A REQUEST.

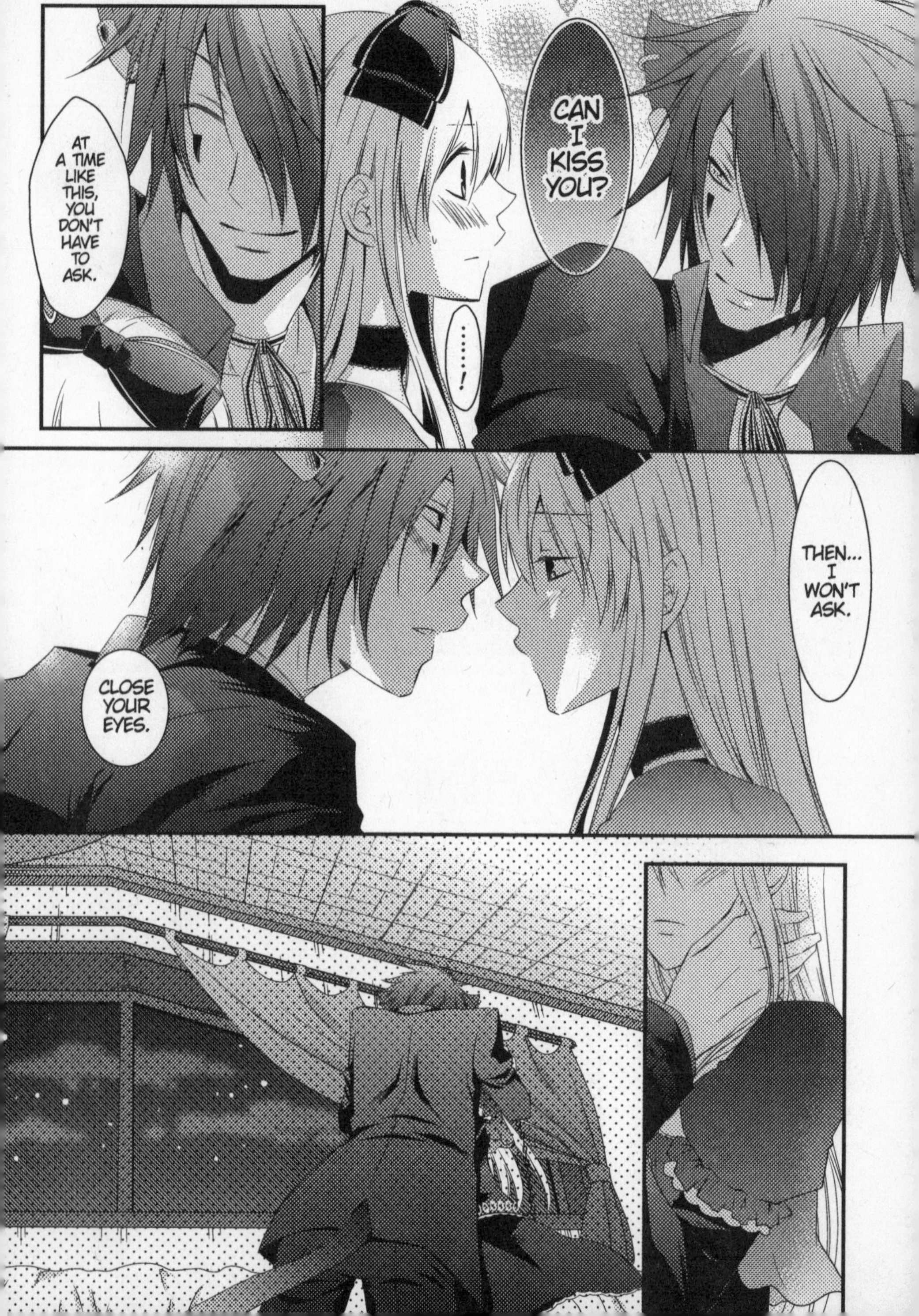
CAN I KISS YOU?
......!
AT A TIME LIKE THIS, YOU DON'T HAVE TO ASK.
THEN... I WON'T ASK.
CLOSE YOUR EYES.

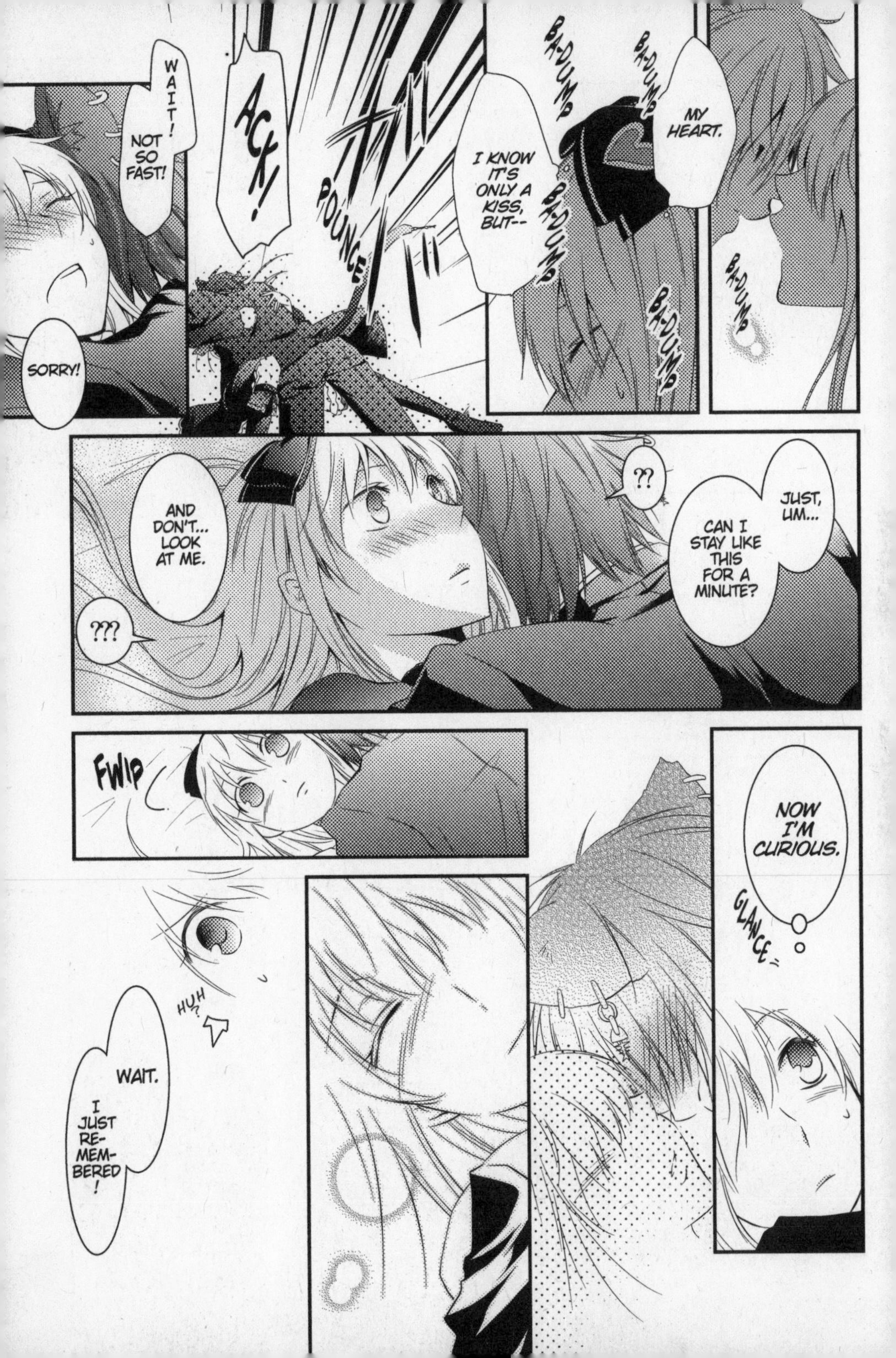
BA-DUMP
BA-DUMP
MY HEART.
BA-DUMP
BA-DUMP
BA-DUMP
BA-DUMP
I KNOW IT'S ONLY A KISS, BUT--
ACK!
POUNCE
WAIT! NOT SO FAST!
SORRY!
JUST, UM... CAN I STAY LIKE THIS FOR A MINUTE?
??
AND DON'T... LOOK AT ME.
???
NOW I'M CURIOUS.
GLANCE
FWIP
HUH?
WAIT. I JUST RE-MEM-BERED!

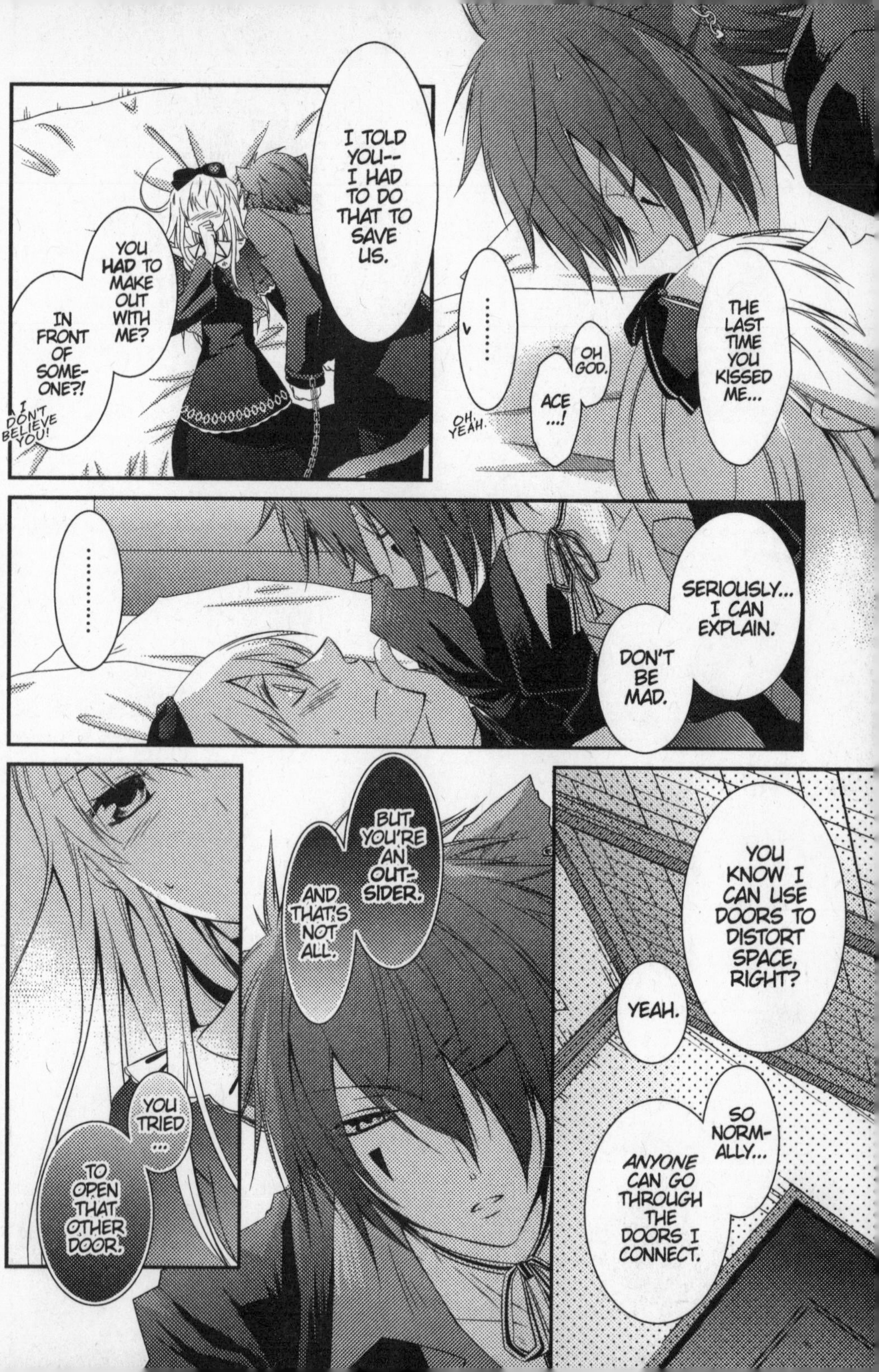
THE LAST TIME YOU KISSED ME...
OH GOD, ACE...!
OH, YEAH.
......?
I TOLD YOU-- I HAD TO DO THAT TO SAVE US.
YOU HAD TO MAKE OUT WITH ME?
IN FRONT OF SOME-ONE?!
I DON'T BELIEVE YOU!
SERIOUSLY... I CAN EXPLAIN.
DON'T BE MAD.
......
YOU KNOW I CAN USE DOORS TO DISTORT SPACE, RIGHT?
YEAH.
SO NORM-ALLY...
ANYONE CAN GO THROUGH THE DOORS I CONNECT.
BUT YOU'RE AN OUT-SIDER.
AND THAT'S NOT ALL.
YOU TRIED...
TO OPEN THAT OTHER DOOR.

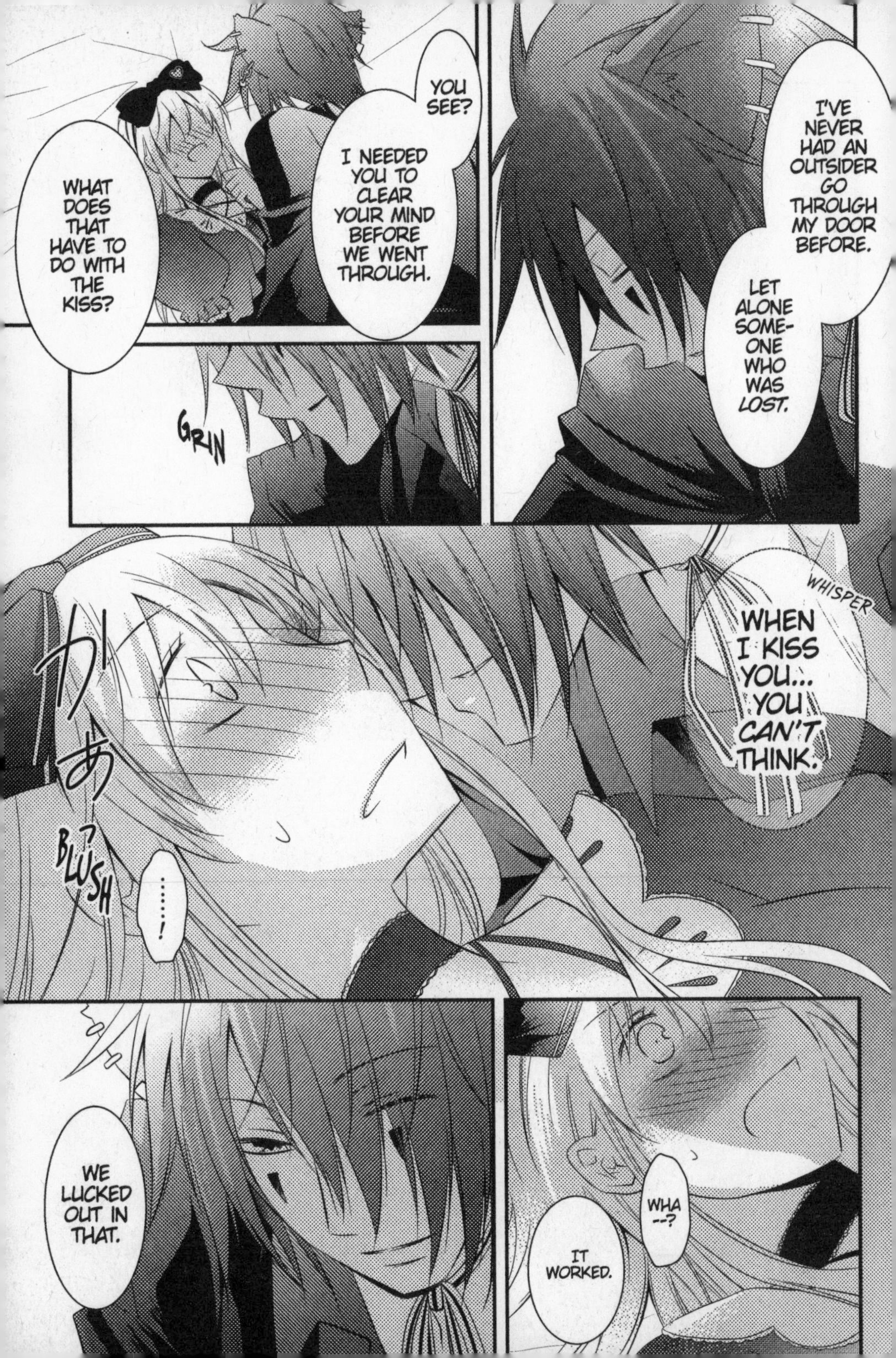
I'VE NEVER HAD AN OUTSIDER GO THROUGH MY DOOR BEFORE.
LET ALONE SOME-ONE WHO WAS LOST.
YOU SEE?
I NEEDED YOU TO CLEAR YOUR MIND BEFORE WE WENT THROUGH.
WHAT DOES THAT HAVE TO DO WITH THE KISS?
GRIN
WHISPER
WHEN I KISS YOU... YOU CAN'T THINK.
かぁ
BLUSH
......!
WHA--?
IT WORKED.
WE LUCKED OUT IN THAT.

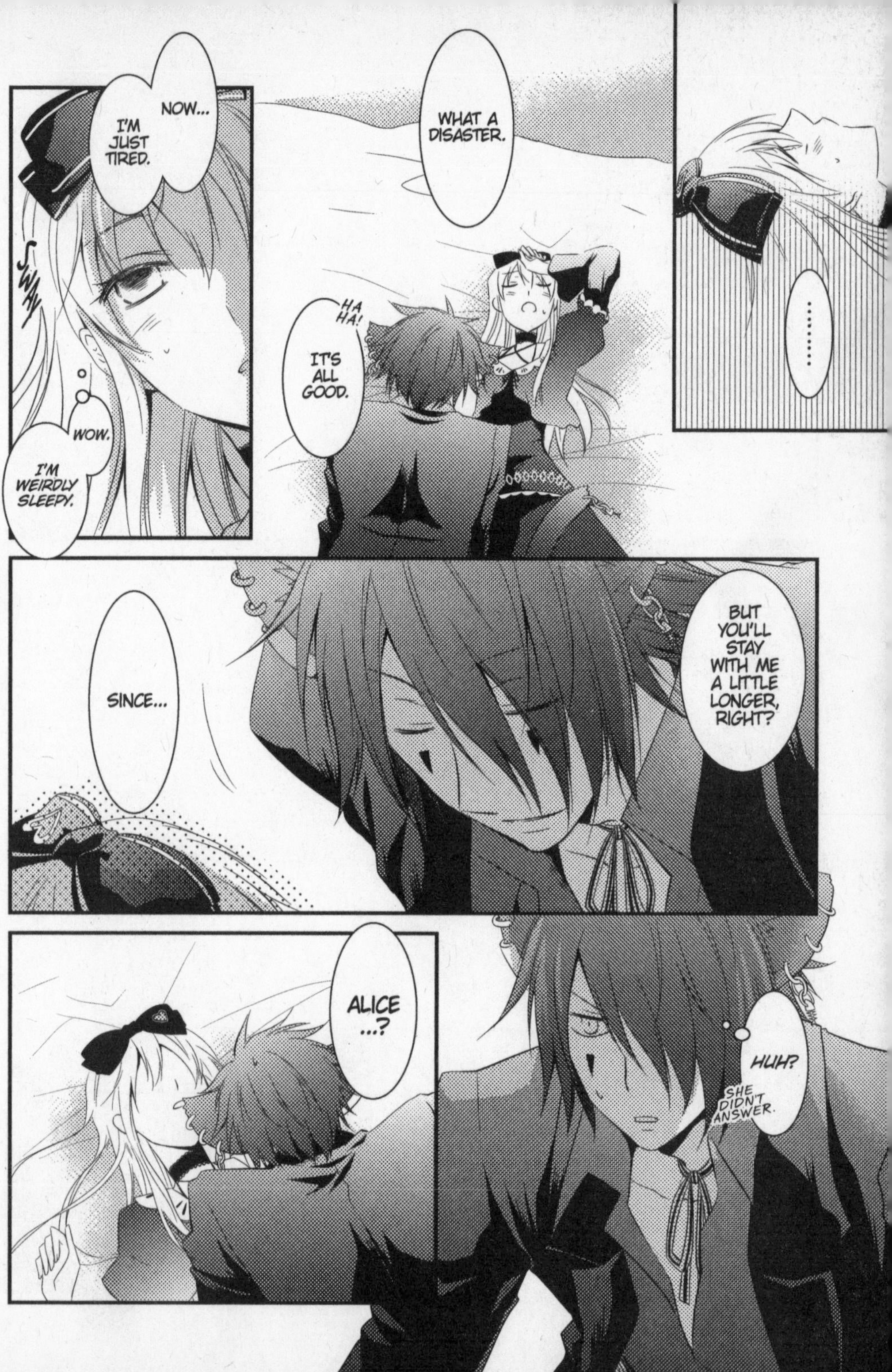
......
WHAT A DISASTER.
HA HA!
IT'S ALL GOOD.
NOW... I'M JUST TIRED.
SWAY
WOW. I'M WEIRDLY SLEEPY.
BUT YOU'LL STAY WITH ME A LITTLE LONGER, RIGHT?
SINCE...
HUH?
SHE DIDN'T ANSWER.
ALICE ...?

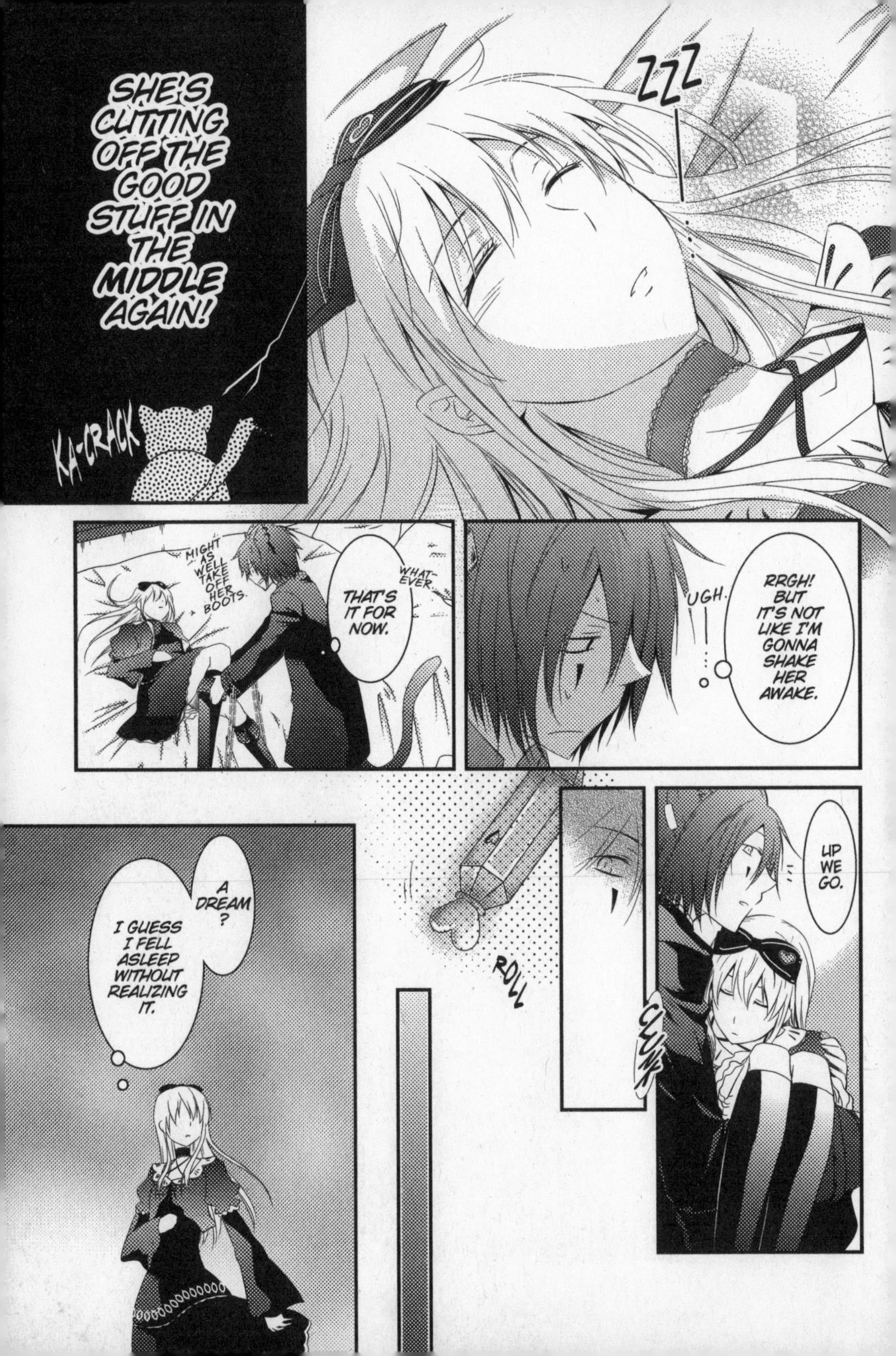
ZZZ
SHE'S CUTTING OFF THE GOOD STUFF IN THE MIDDLE AGAIN!
KA-CRACK
UGH.
RRGH! BUT IT'S NOT LIKE I'M GONNA SHAKE HER AWAKE.
WHATEVER...
THAT'S IT FOR NOW.
MIGHT AS WELL TAKE OFF HER BOOTS.
UP WE GO.
CLUNK
ROLL
A DREAM?
I GUESS I FELL ASLEEP WITHOUT REALIZING IT.

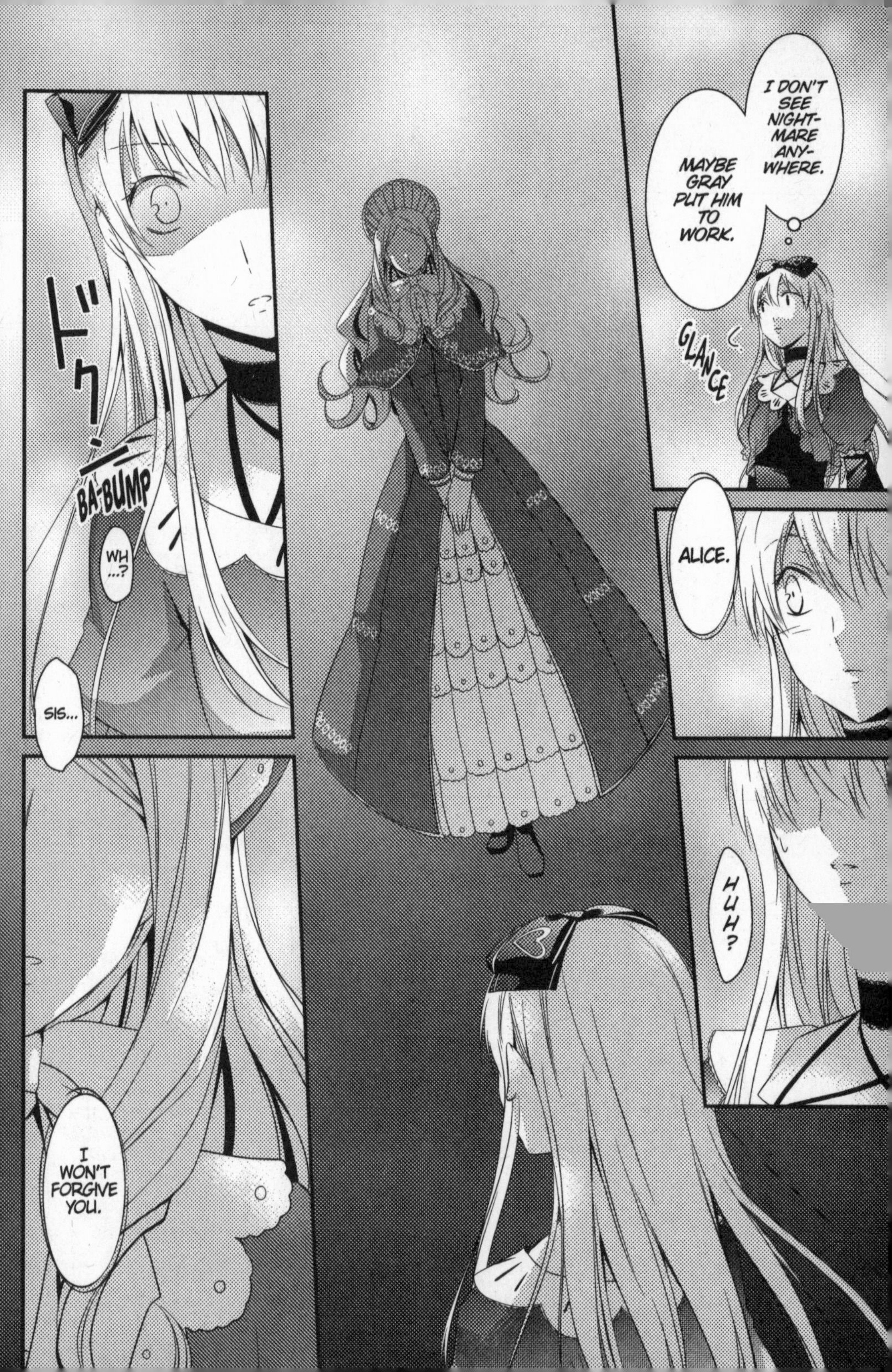
I DON'T SEE NIGHT-MARE ANY-WHERE.
MAYBE GRAY PUT HIM TO WORK.
GLANCE
ALICE.
HUH?
ドク
BA-BUMP
WH...?
SIS...
I WON'T FORGIVE YOU.

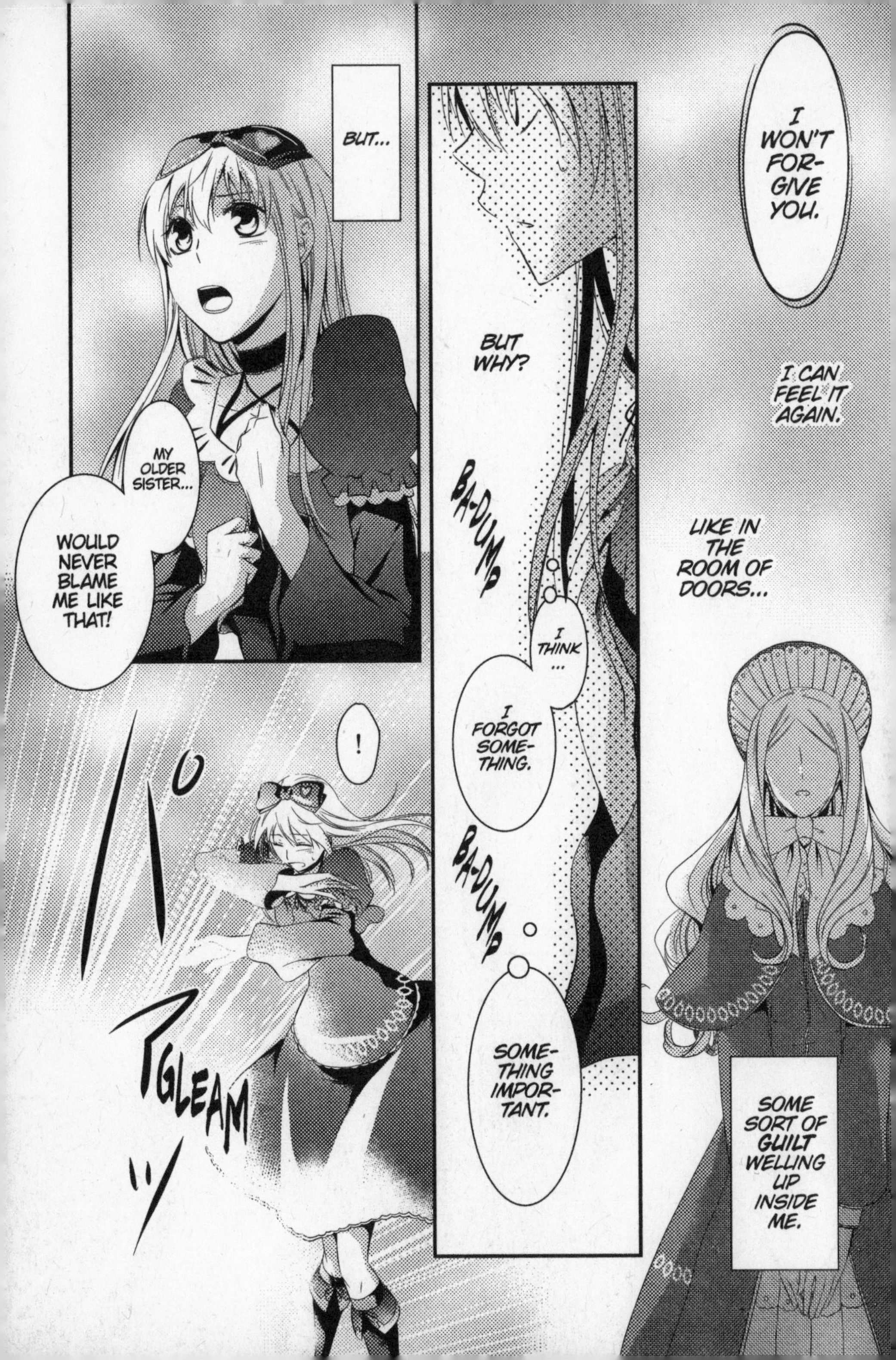
I WON'T FORGIVE YOU.
I CAN FEEL IT AGAIN.
LIKE IN THE ROOM OF DOORS...
SOME SORT OF GUILT WELLING UP INSIDE ME.
BUT WHY?
BA-DUMP
I THINK...
I FORGOT SOMETHING.
BA-DUMP
SOMETHING IMPORTANT.
BUT...
MY OLDER SISTER...
WOULD NEVER BLAME ME LIKE THAT!
!
GLEAM

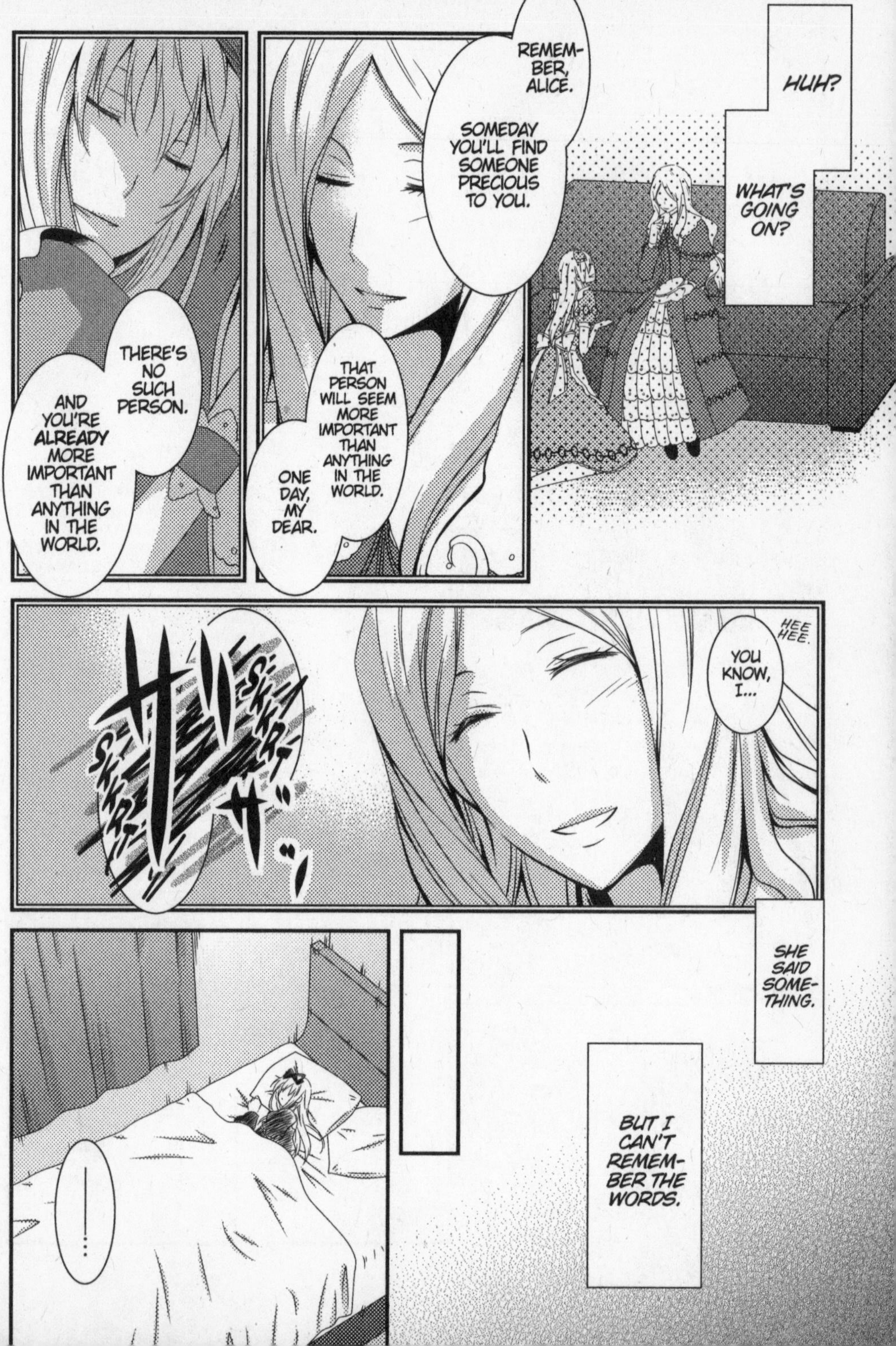
HUH?
WHAT'S GOING ON?
REMEMBER, ALICE.
SOMEDAY YOU'LL FIND SOMEONE PRECIOUS TO YOU.
THAT PERSON WILL SEEM MORE IMPORTANT THAN ANYTHING IN THE WORLD.
ONE DAY, MY DEAR.
THERE'S NO SUCH PERSON.
AND YOU'RE ALREADY MORE IMPORTANT THAN ANYTHING IN THE WORLD.
HEE HEE.
YOU KNOW, I...
SKKRT
SKKRT
SHE SAID SOMETHING.
BUT I CAN'T REMEMBER THE WORDS.
......!

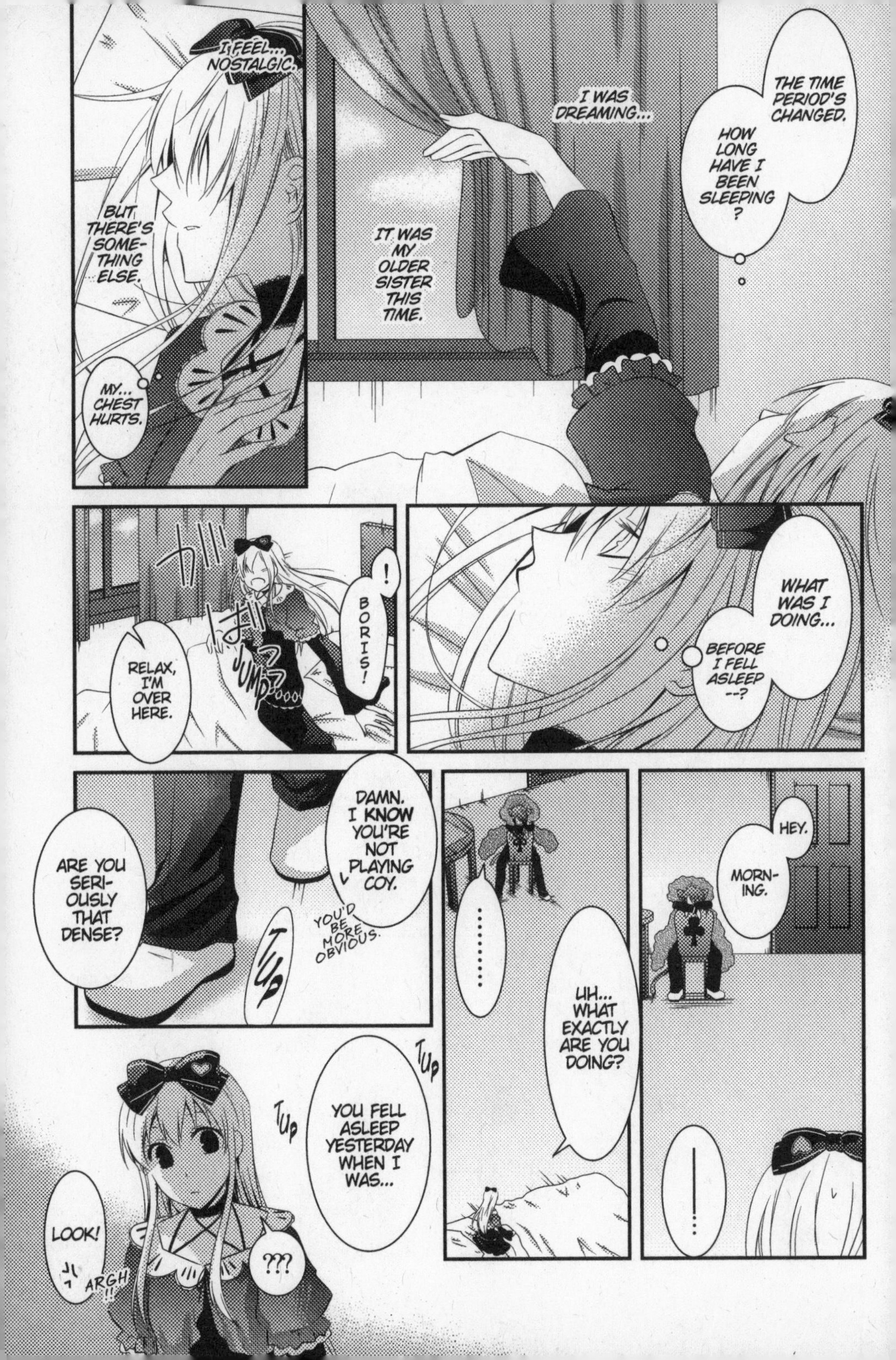
THE TIME PERIOD'S CHANGED.
HOW LONG HAVE I BEEN SLEEPING?
I WAS DREAMING...
IT WAS MY OLDER SISTER THIS TIME.
I FEEL... NOSTALGIC.
BUT THERE'S SOMETHING ELSE.
MY... CHEST HURTS.
WHAT WAS I DOING...
BEFORE I FELL ASLEEP--?
!
BORIS!
JUMP
RELAX, I'M OVER HERE.
HEY.
MORNING.
....
UH... WHAT EXACTLY ARE YOU DOING?
!......
DAMN. I KNOW YOU'RE NOT PLAYING COY.
YOU'D BE MORE OBVIOUS.
ARE YOU SERIOUSLY THAT DENSE?
TUP
TUP
TUP
YOU FELL ASLEEP YESTERDAY WHEN I WAS...
???
LOOK!
ARGH!!

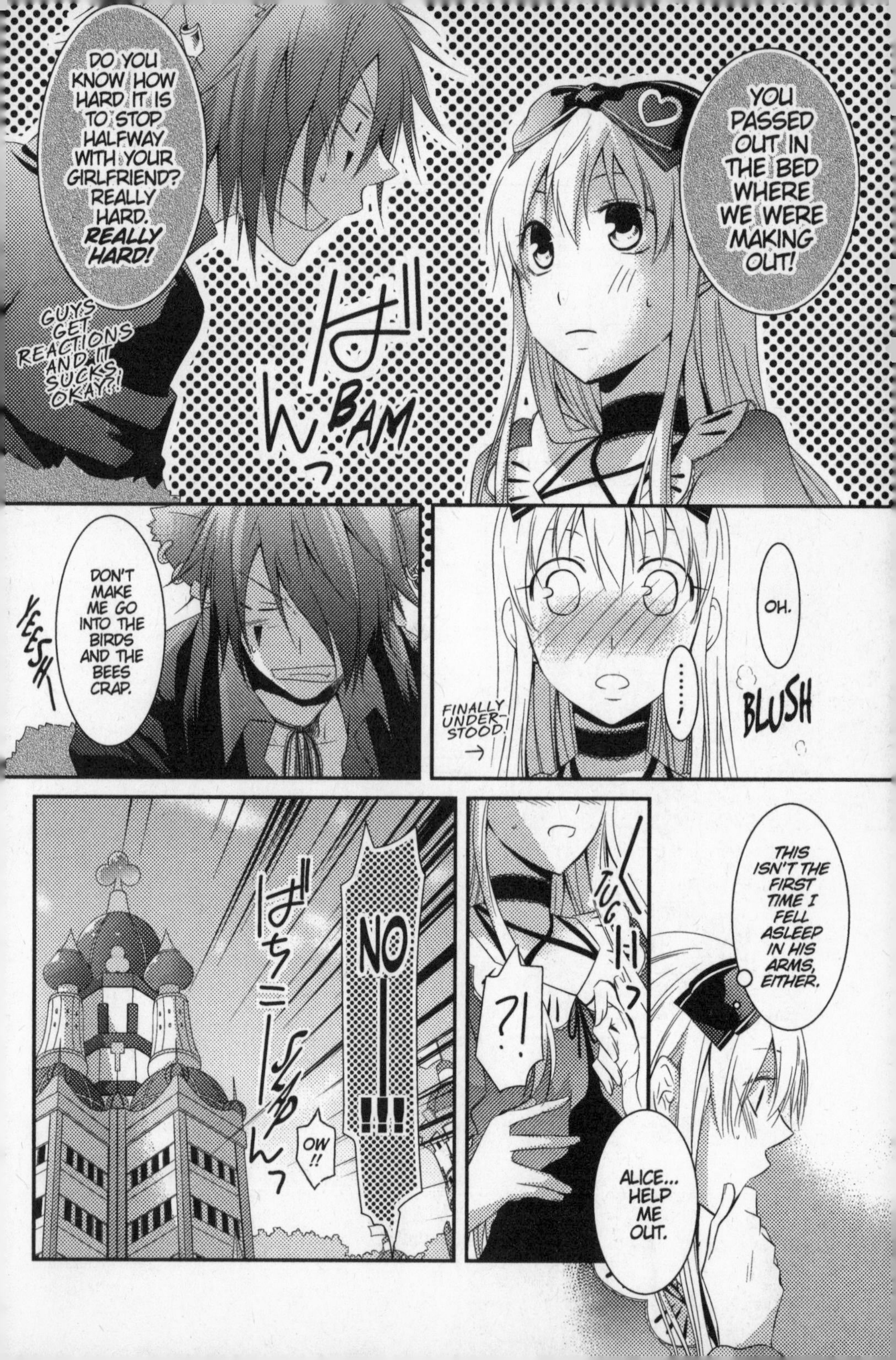
YOU PASSED OUT IN THE BED WHERE WE WERE MAKING OUT!
DO YOU KNOW HOW HARD IT IS TO STOP HALFWAY WITH YOUR GIRLFRIEND? REALLY HARD. REALLY HARD!
GUYS GET REACTIONS AND IT SUCKS, OKAY?!
ばんっ
BAM
OH.
......!
BLUSH
FINALLY UNDER-STOOD!
DON'T MAKE ME GO INTO THE BIRDS AND THE BEES CRAP.
YEESH
THIS ISN'T THE FIRST TIME I FELL ASLEEP IN HIS ARMS, EITHER.
TUG
?!
ALICE... HELP ME OUT.
NO—!!!
ばちーんっ
SLAP
OW!!

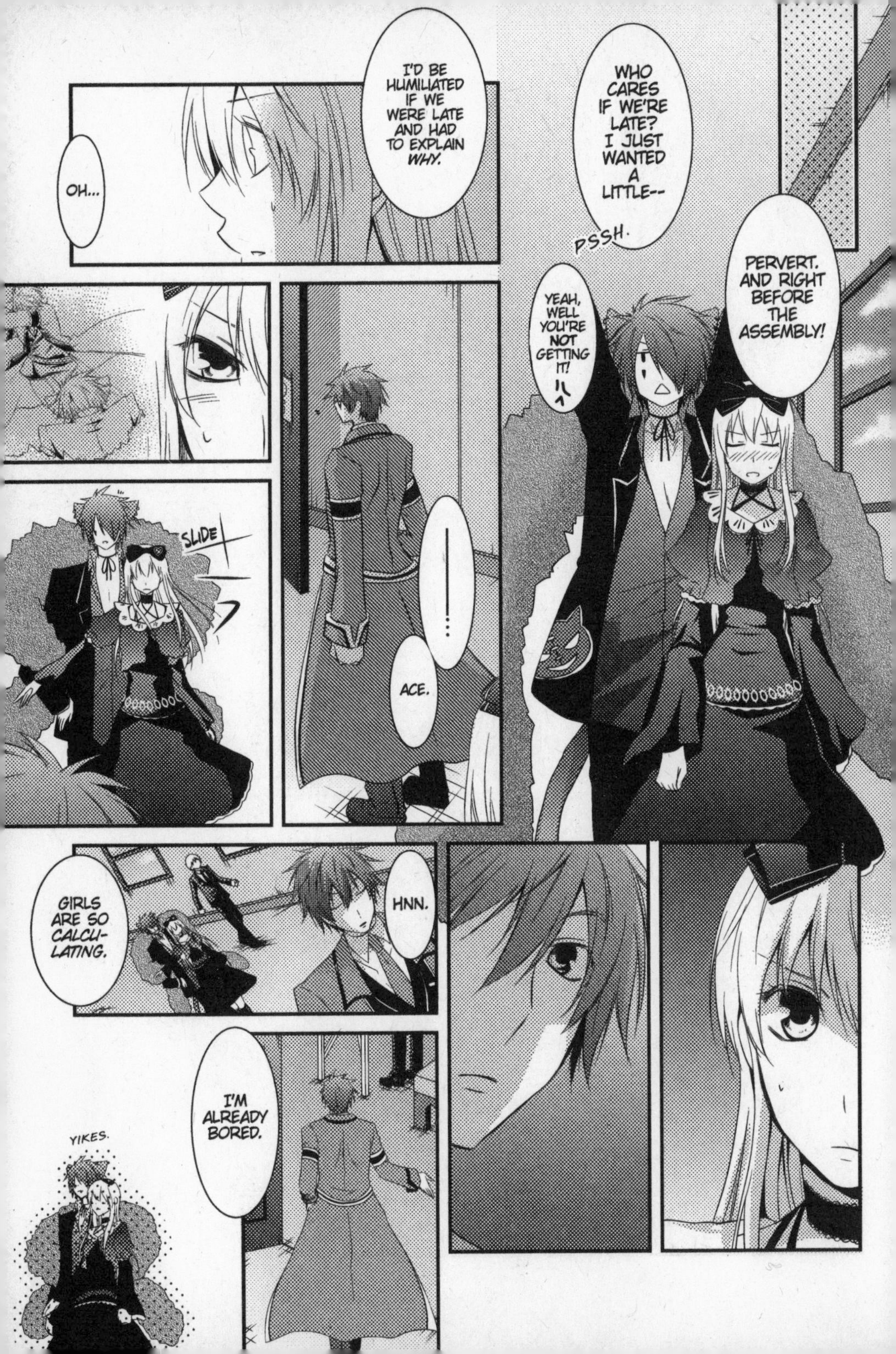
WHO CARES IF WE'RE LATE? I JUST WANTED A LITTLE--
PSSH.
PERVERT. AND RIGHT BEFORE THE ASSEMBLY!
YEAH, WELL YOU'RE NOT GETTING IT!
I'D BE HUMILIATED IF WE WERE LATE AND HAD TO EXPLAIN WHY.
OH...
......
ACE.
SLIDE
HNN.
GIRLS ARE SO CALCULATING.
I'M ALREADY BORED.
YIKES.

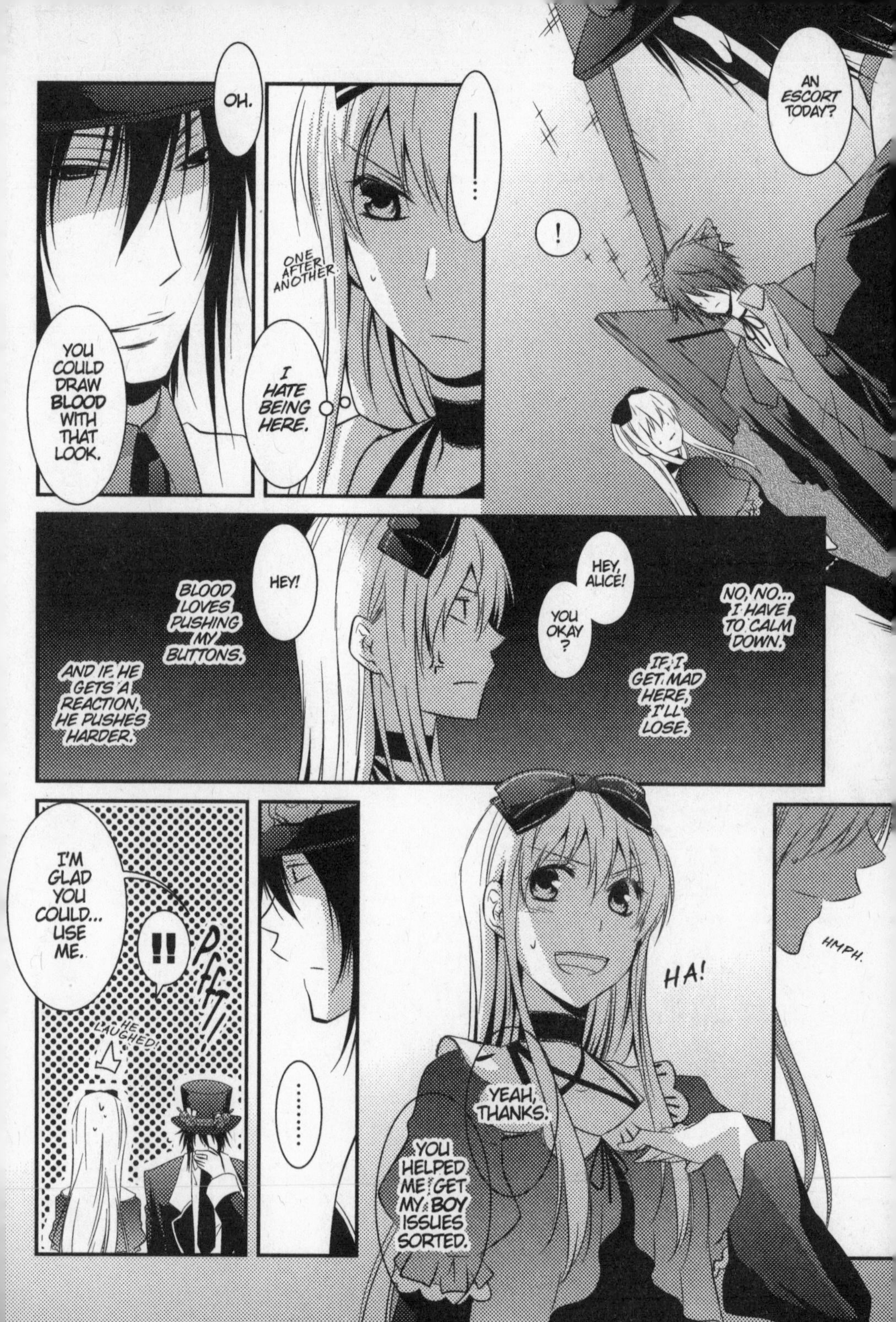
AN ESCORT TODAY?
!
!......
ONE AFTER ANOTHER
I HATE BEING HERE.
OH.
YOU COULD DRAW BLOOD WITH THAT LOOK.
NO, NO... I HAVE TO CALM DOWN.
IF I GET MAD HERE, I'LL LOSE.
HEY, ALICE!
YOU OKAY?
HEY!
BLOOD LOVES PUSHING MY BUTTONS.
AND IF HE GETS A REACTION, HE PUSHES HARDER.
HMPH.
HA!
YEAH, THANKS.
YOU HELPED ME GET MY BOY ISSUES SORTED.
......
I'M GLAD YOU COULD... USE ME.
!!
PFFT!
HE LAUGHED!

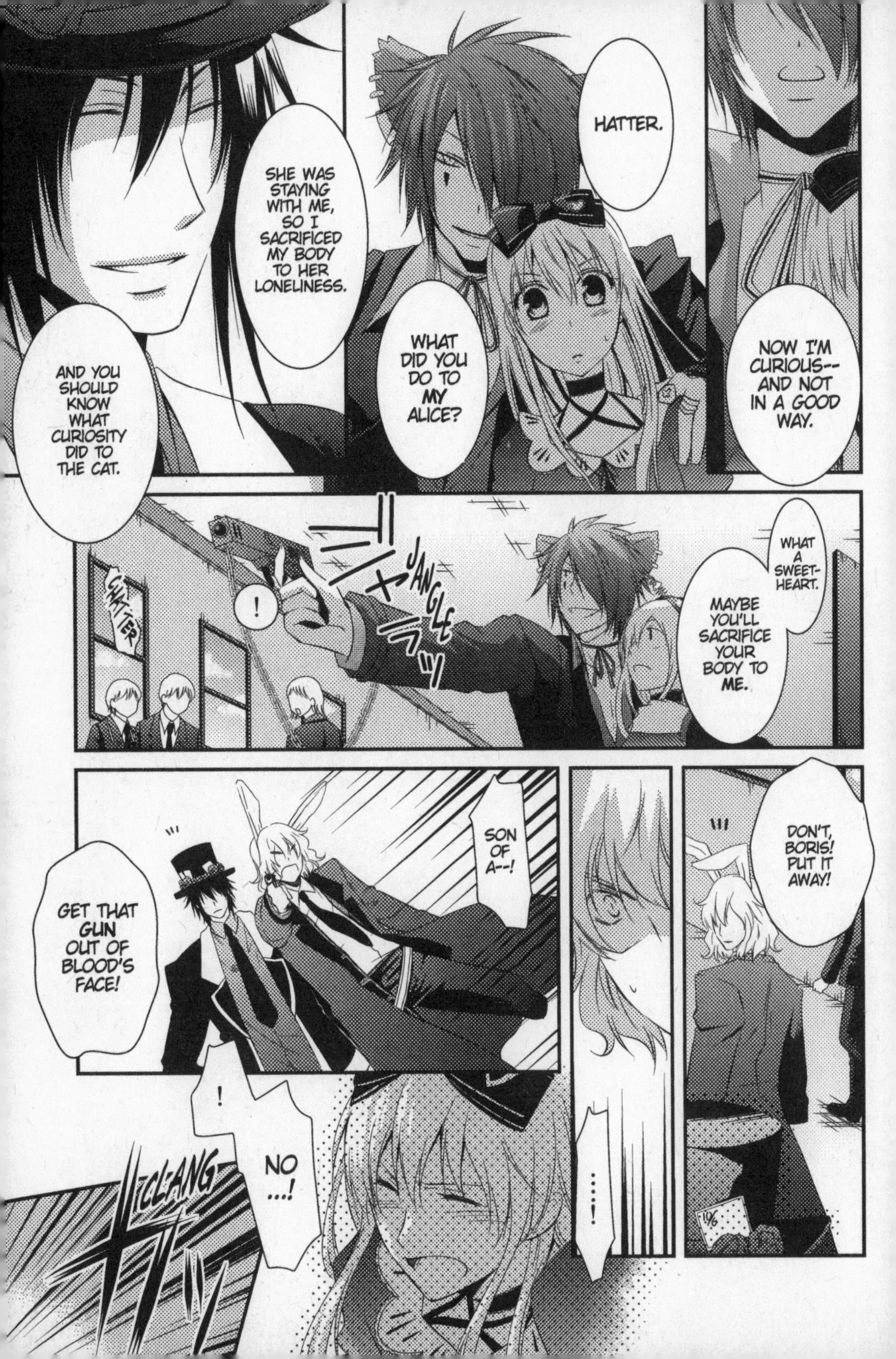
HATTER.
SHE WAS STAYING WITH ME, SO I SACRIFICED MY BODY TO HER LONELINESS.
WHAT DID YOU DO TO MY ALICE?
NOW I'M CURIOUS-- AND NOT IN A GOOD WAY.
AND YOU SHOULD KNOW WHAT CURIOSITY DID TO THE CAT.
WHAT A SWEET-HEART.
MAYBE YOU'LL SACRIFICE YOUR BODY TO ME.
JANGLE
!
CHATTER
DON'T, BORIS! PUT IT AWAY!
SON OF A--!
GET THAT GUN OUT OF BLOOD'S FACE!
...!
NO ...!
!
CLANG

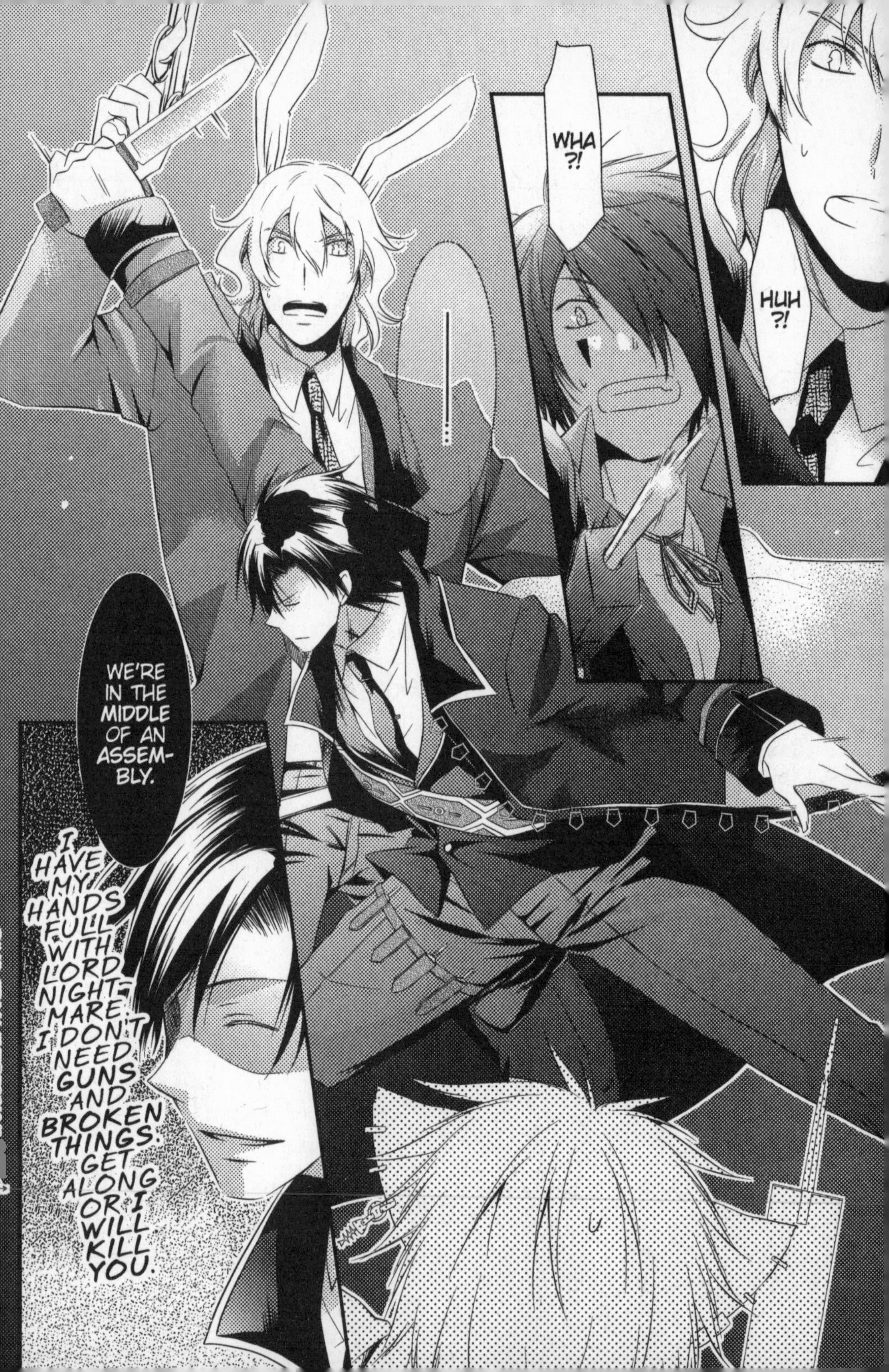
HUH?!
WHA?!
WE'RE IN THE MIDDLE OF AN ASSEMBLY.
I HAVE MY HANDS FULL WITH LORD NIGHTMARE. I DON'T NEED GUNS AND BROKEN THINGS. GET ALONG OR I WILL KILL YOU.

READ FROM EXPRESSION!

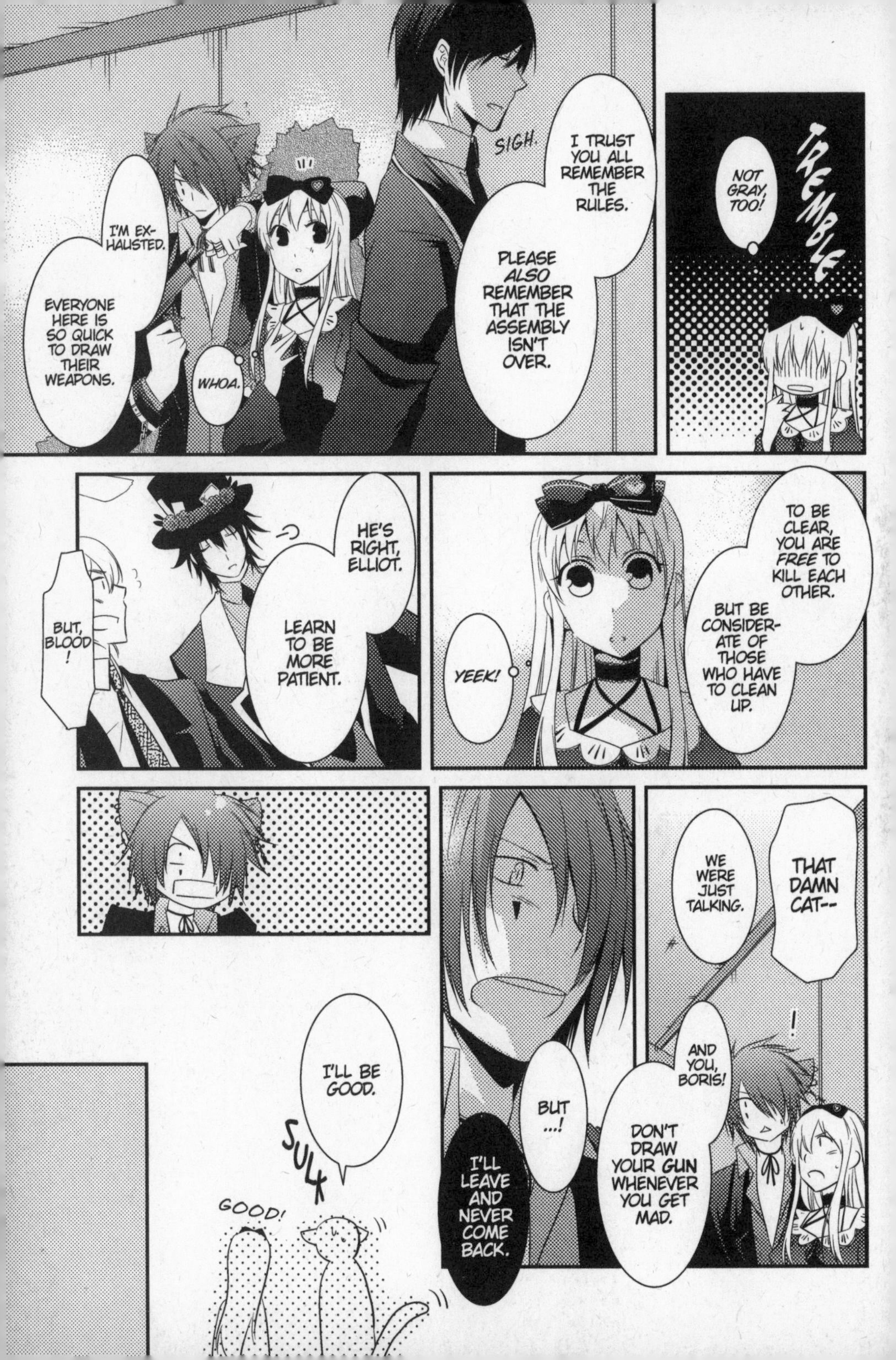
SIGH.
I TRUST YOU ALL REMEMBER THE RULES.
PLEASE *ALSO* REMEMBER THAT THE ASSEMBLY ISN'T OVER.
WHOA.
I'M EX-HAUSTED.
EVERYONE HERE IS SO QUICK TO DRAW THEIR WEAPONS.
NOT GRAY, TOO!
TREMBLE
TO BE CLEAR, YOU ARE *FREE* TO KILL EACH OTHER.
BUT BE CONSIDER-ATE OF THOSE WHO HAVE TO CLEAN UP.
YEEK!
HE'S RIGHT, ELLIOT.
LEARN TO BE MORE PATIENT.
BUT, BLOOD!
THAT DAMN CAT--
WE WERE JUST TALKING.
!
AND YOU, BORIS!
DON'T DRAW YOUR GUN WHENEVER YOU GET MAD.
BUT ...!
I'LL LEAVE AND NEVER COME BACK.
I'LL BE GOOD.
SULK
GOOD!

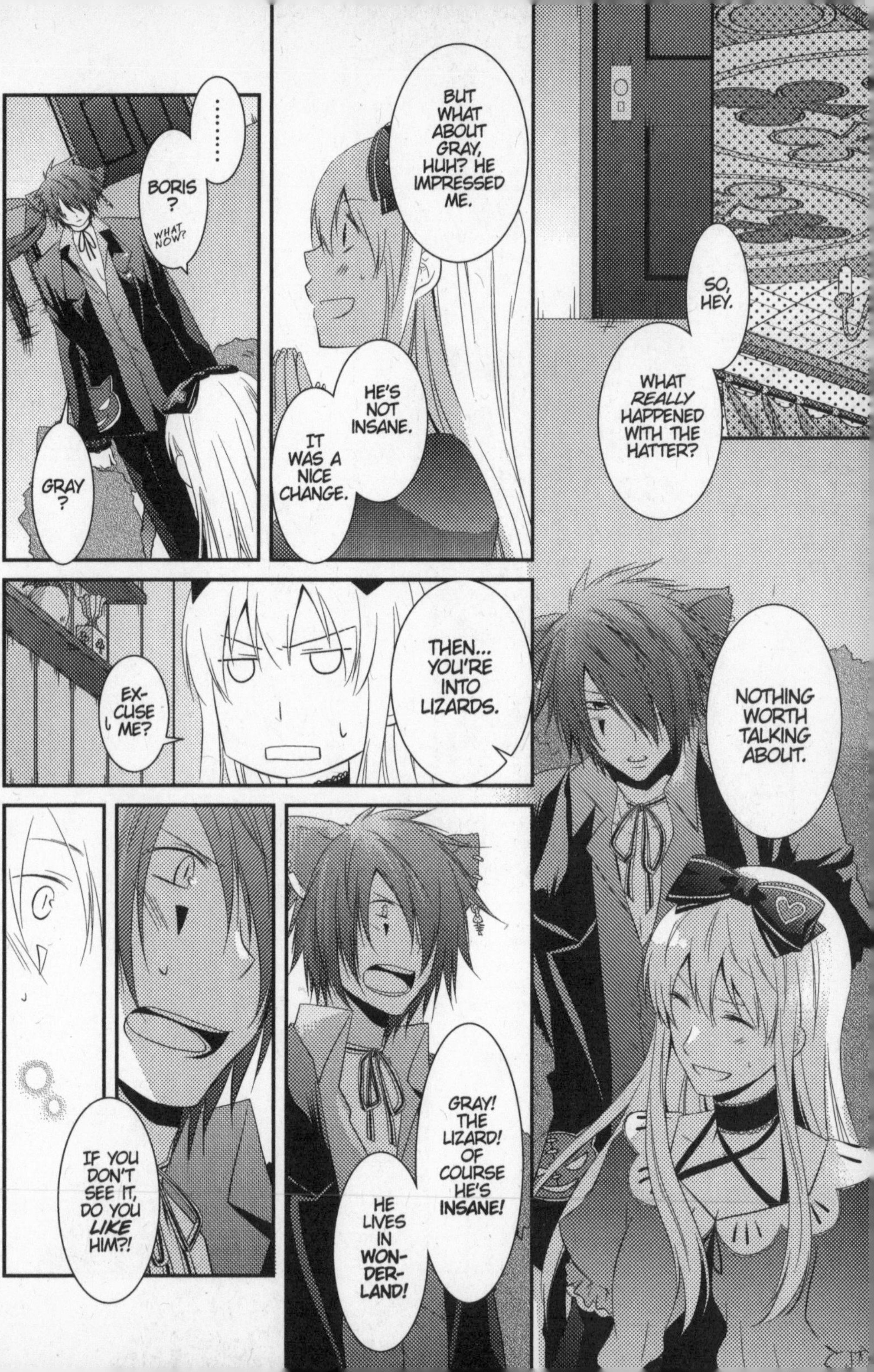
SO, HEY.
WHAT *REALLY* HAPPENED WITH THE HATTER?
NOTHING WORTH TALKING ABOUT.
BUT WHAT ABOUT GRAY, HUH? HE IMPRESSED ME.
HE'S NOT INSANE.
IT WAS A NICE CHANGE.
......
BORIS?
WHAT NOW?
GRAY?
THEN... YOU'RE INTO LIZARDS.
EX-CUSE ME?
GRAY! THE LIZARD! OF COURSE HE'S INSANE!
HE LIVES IN WON-DER-LAND!
IF YOU DON'T SEE IT, DO YOU *LIKE* HIM?!

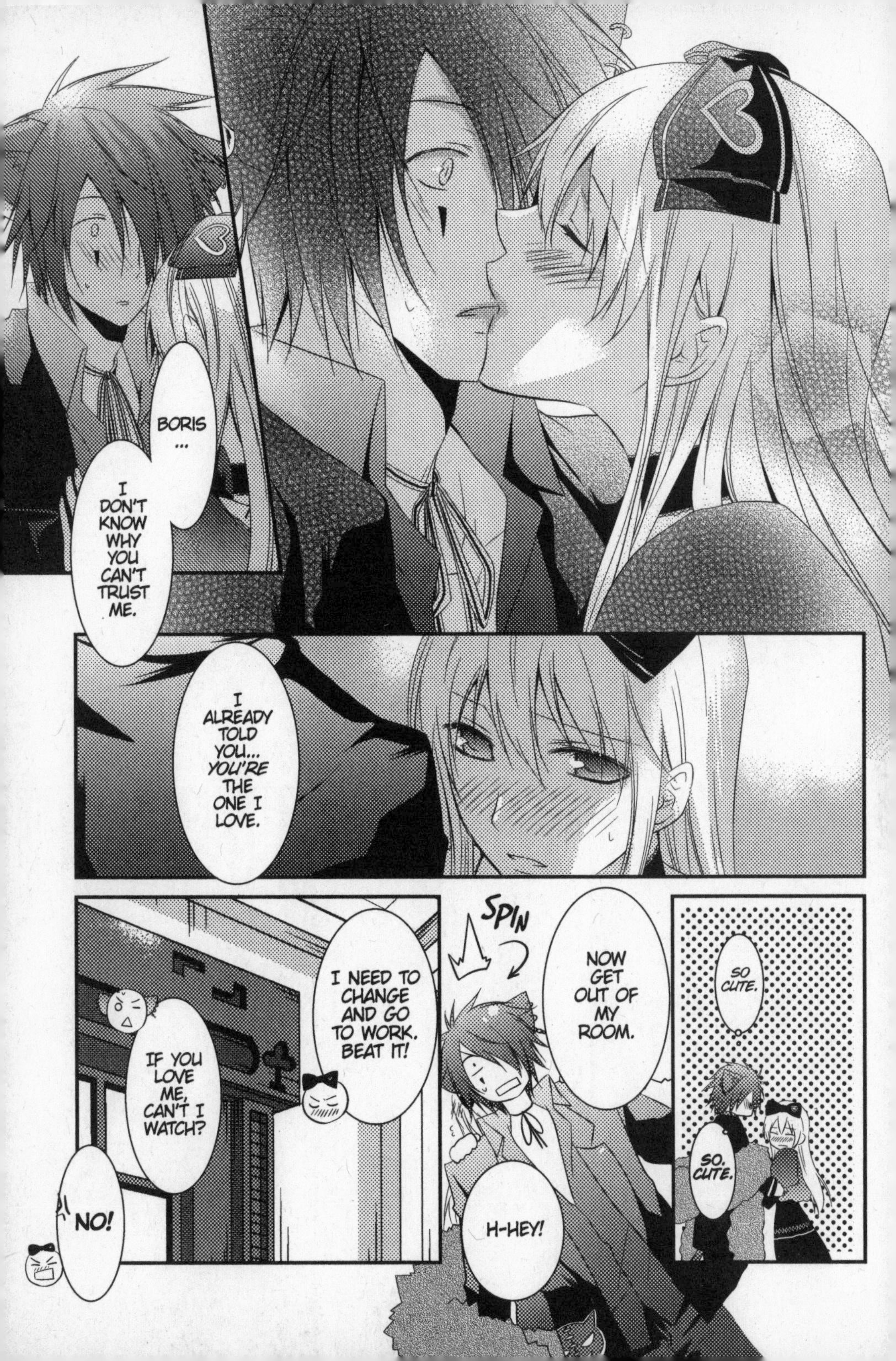
BORIS...
I DON'T KNOW WHY YOU CAN'T TRUST ME.
I ALREADY TOLD YOU... YOU'RE THE ONE I LOVE.
SO CUTE.
SO. CUTE.
NOW GET OUT OF MY ROOM.
SPIN
H-HEY!
I NEED TO CHANGE AND GO TO WORK. BEAT IT!
IF YOU LOVE ME, CAN'T I WATCH?
NO!

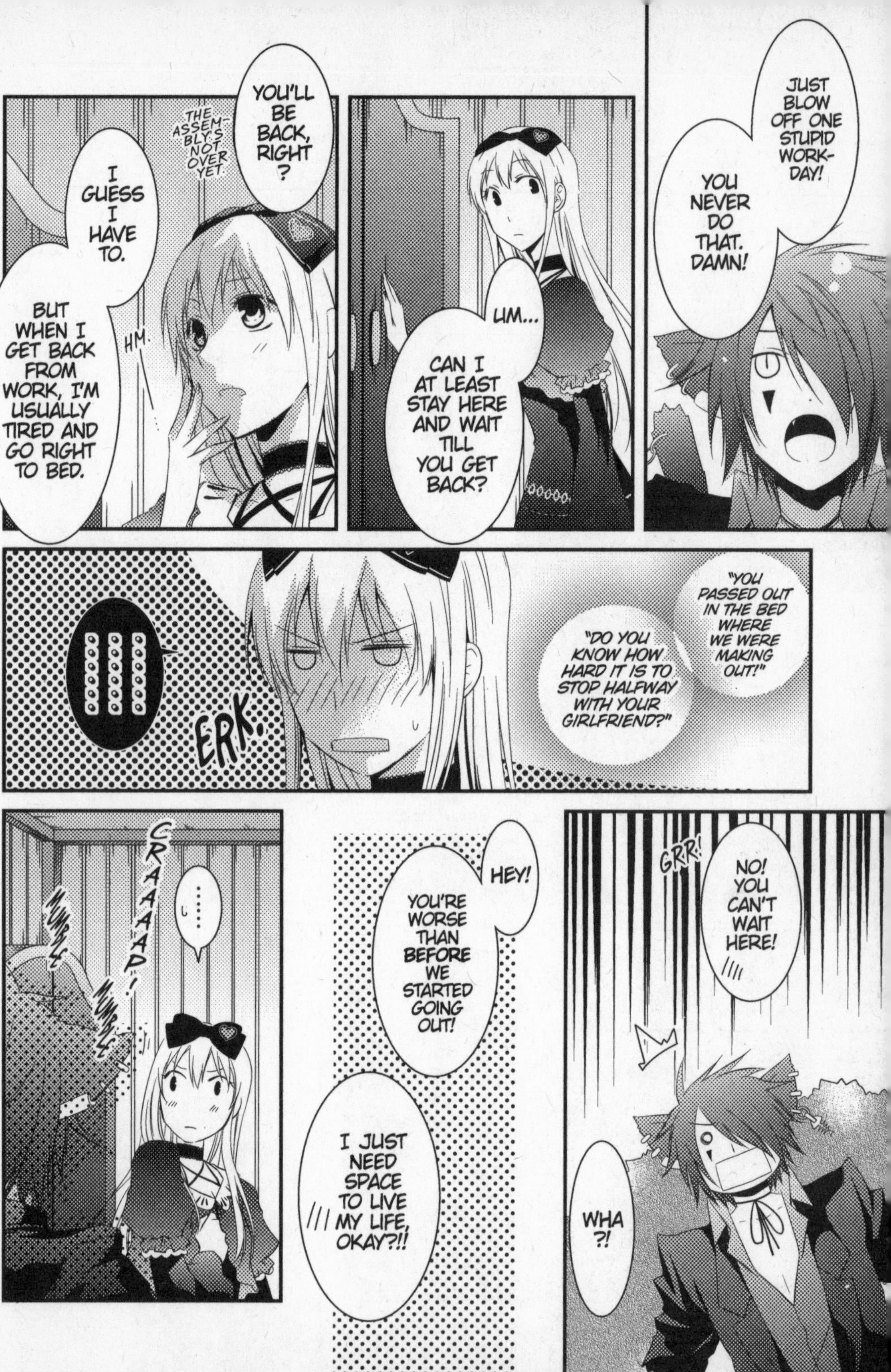
JUST BLOW OFF ONE STUPID WORK-DAY!
YOU NEVER DO THAT. DAMN!
UM...
CAN I AT LEAST STAY HERE AND WAIT TILL YOU GET BACK?
YOU'LL BE BACK, RIGHT?
THE ASSEMBLY'S NOT OVER YET.
I GUESS I HAVE TO.
HM.
BUT WHEN I GET BACK FROM WORK, I'M USUALLY TIRED AND GO RIGHT TO BED.
"YOU PASSED OUT IN THE BED WHERE WE WERE MAKING OUT!"
"DO YOU KNOW HOW HARD IT IS TO STOP HALFWAY WITH YOUR GIRLFRIEND?"
ERK.
!!!
GRR!
NO! YOU CAN'T WAIT HERE!
WHA?!
HEY!
YOU'RE WORSE THAN BEFORE WE STARTED GOING OUT!
I JUST NEED SPACE TO LIVE MY LIFE, OKAY?!!
CRAAAAP!
MUMBLE MUMBLE
......

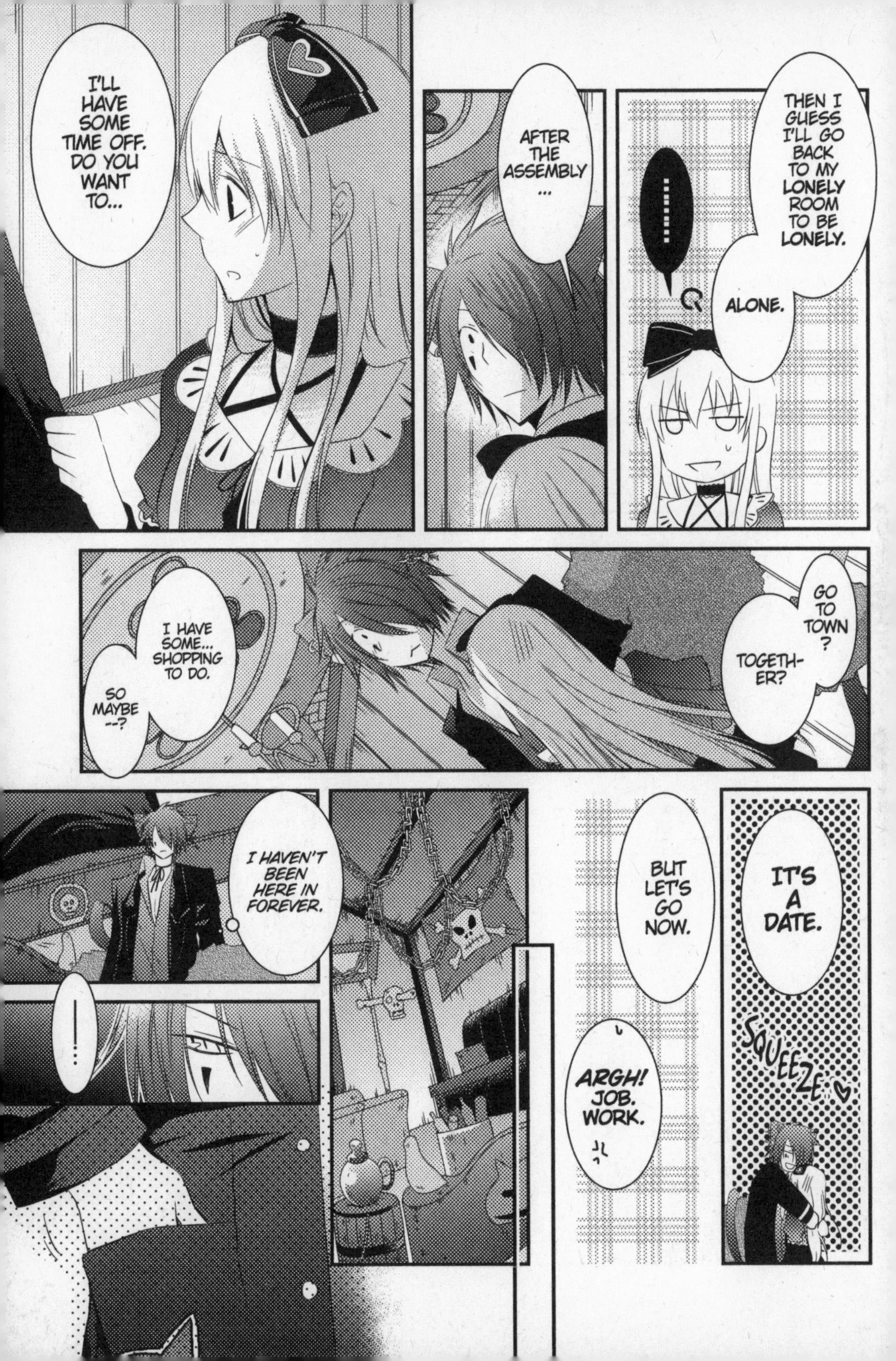
THEN I GUESS I'LL GO BACK TO MY LONELY ROOM TO BE LONELY.
......
ALONE.
AFTER THE ASSEMBLY ...
I'LL HAVE SOME TIME OFF. DO YOU WANT TO...
GO TO TOWN?
TOGETH-ER?
I HAVE SOME... SHOPPING TO DO.
SO MAYBE --?
IT'S A DATE.
SQUEEZE
BUT LET'S GO NOW.
ARGH! JOB. WORK.
I HAVEN'T BEEN HERE IN FOREVER.

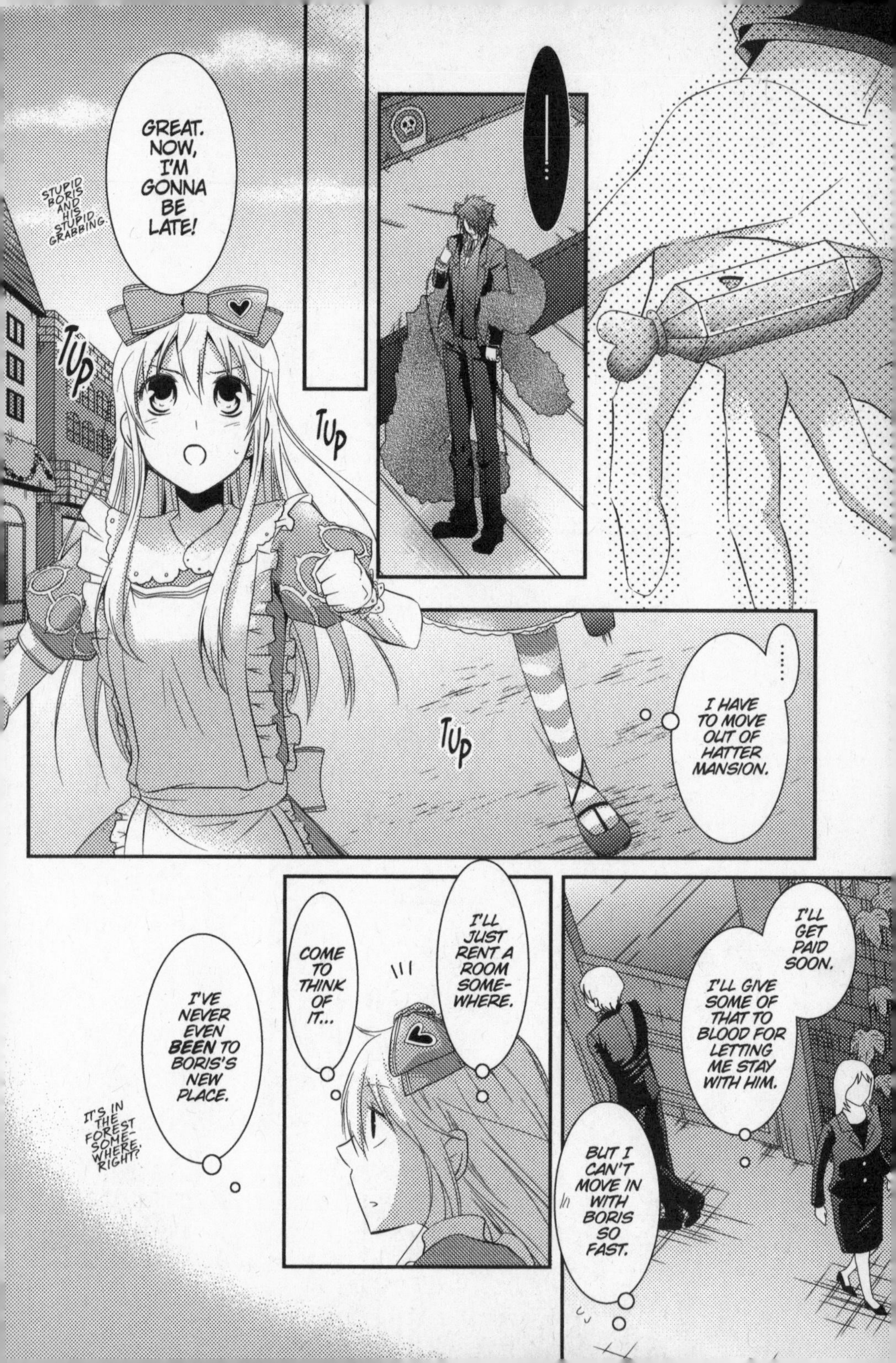

!...
GREAT. NOW, I'M GONNA BE LATE!
STUPID BORIS AND HIS STUPID GRABBING.
TUP
TUP
...
I HAVE TO MOVE OUT OF HATTER MANSION.
TUP
I'LL GET PAID SOON.
I'LL GIVE SOME OF THAT TO BLOOD FOR LETTING ME STAY WITH HIM.
BUT I CAN'T MOVE IN WITH BORIS SO FAST.
I'LL JUST RENT A ROOM SOME-WHERE.
COME TO THINK OF IT...
I'VE NEVER EVEN BEEN TO BORIS'S NEW PLACE.
IT'S IN THE FOREST SOME-WHERE, RIGHT?

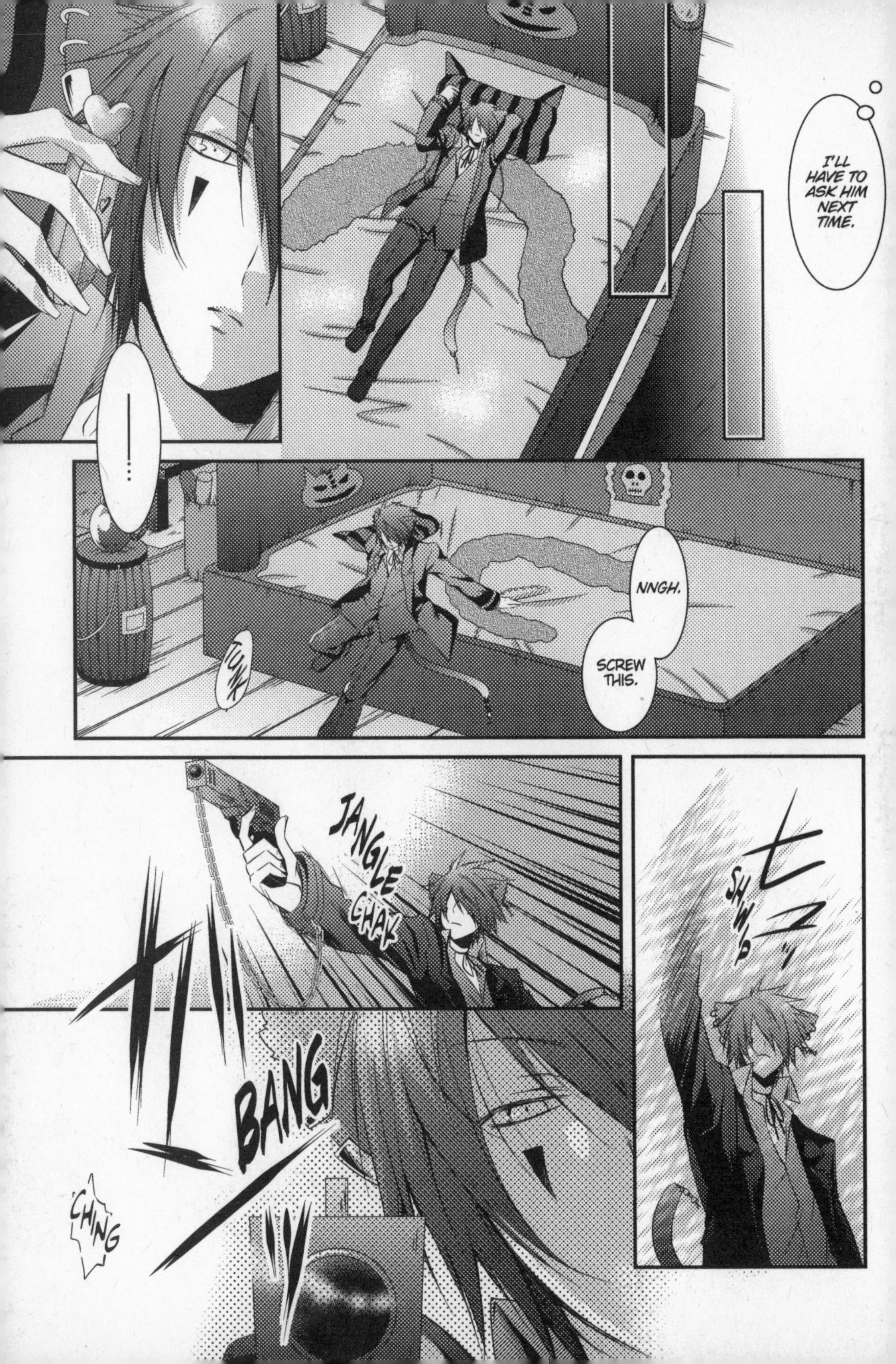
I'LL HAVE TO ASK HIM NEXT TIME.
......
NNGH.
SCREW THIS.
TUNK
SHWIP
JANGLE
CHAK
BANG
CHING

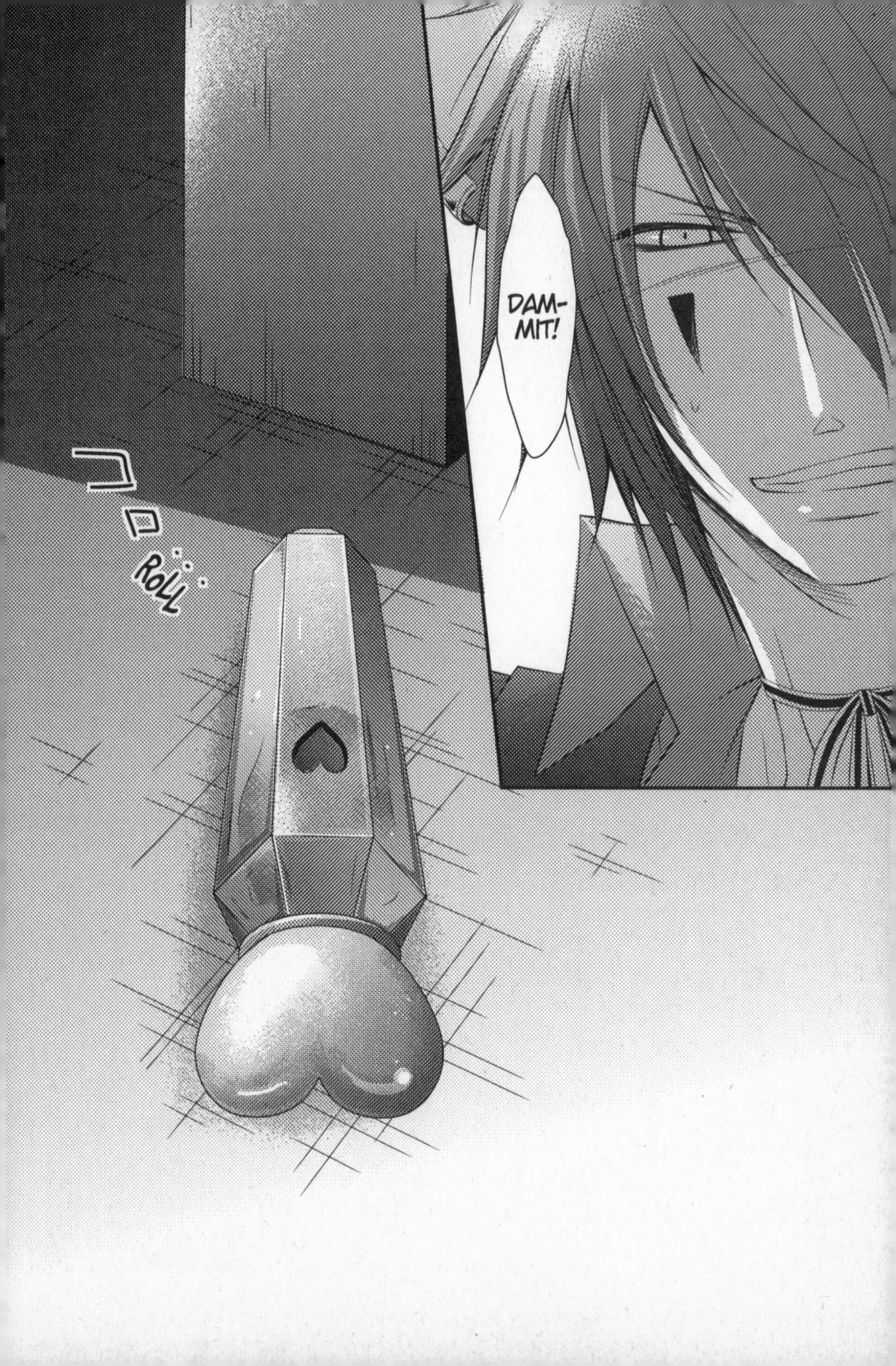
DAM-MIT!
コロ
ROLL

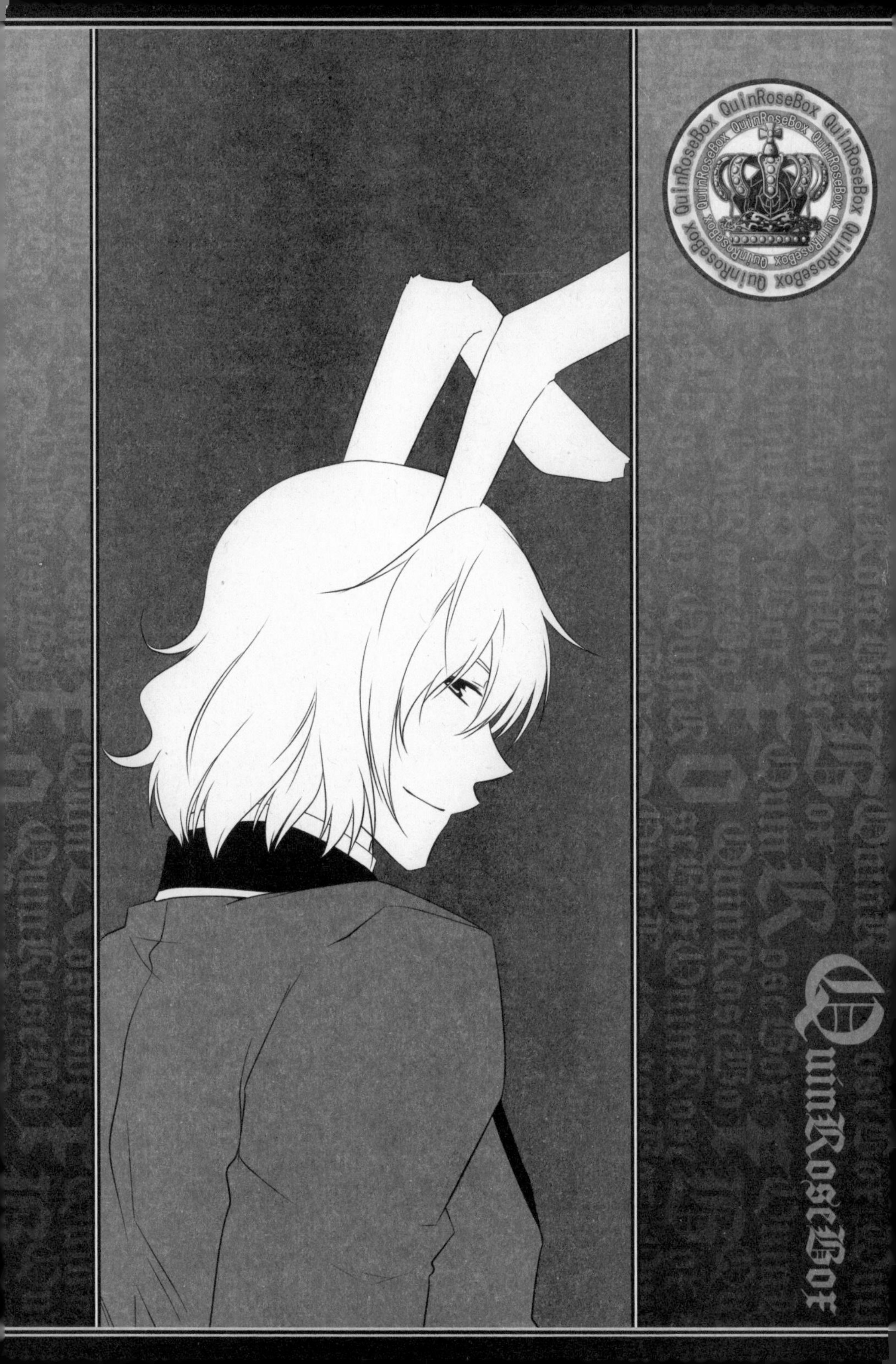
QuinRoseBox

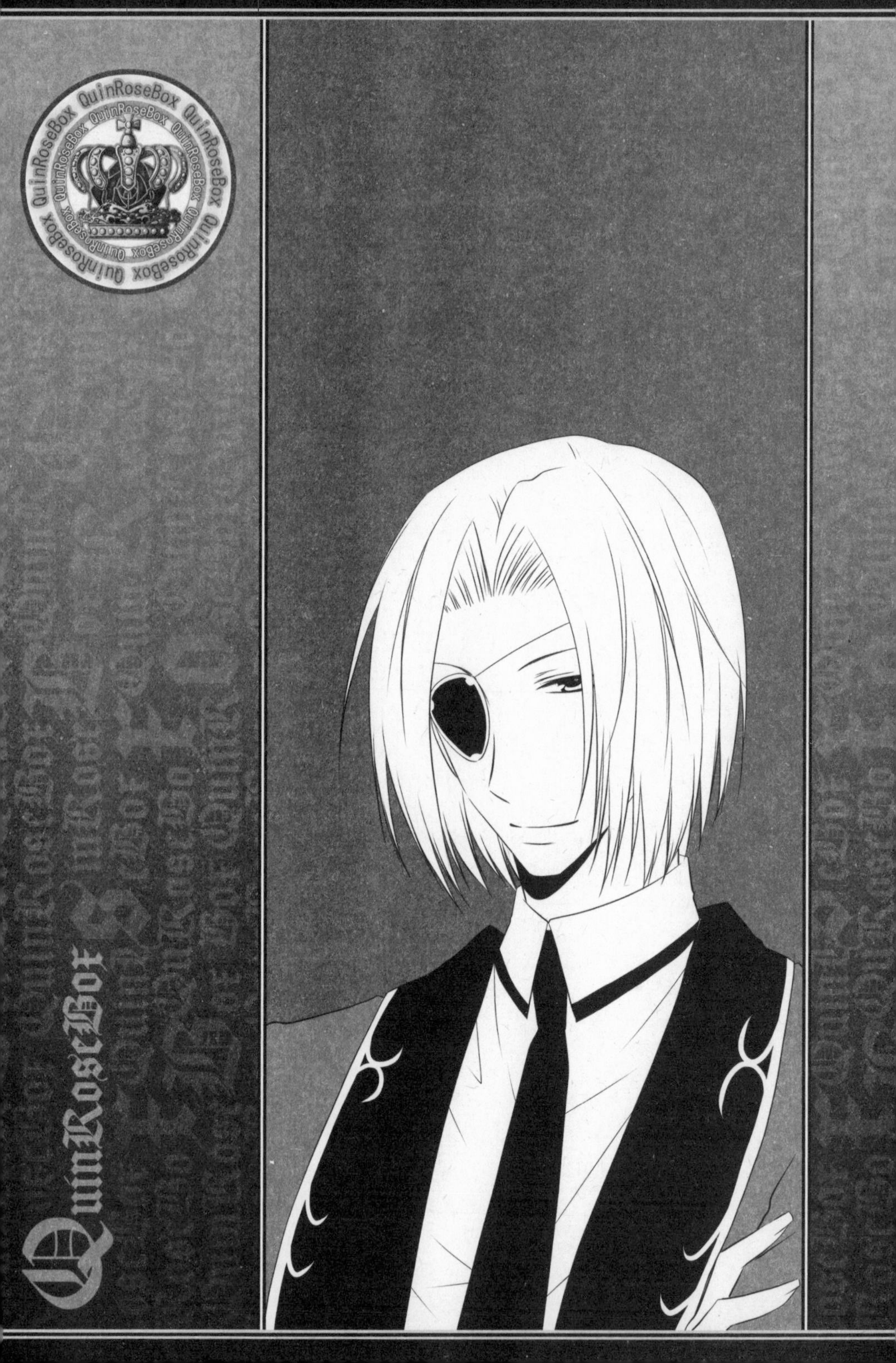
QuinRoseBox

Chapter 6

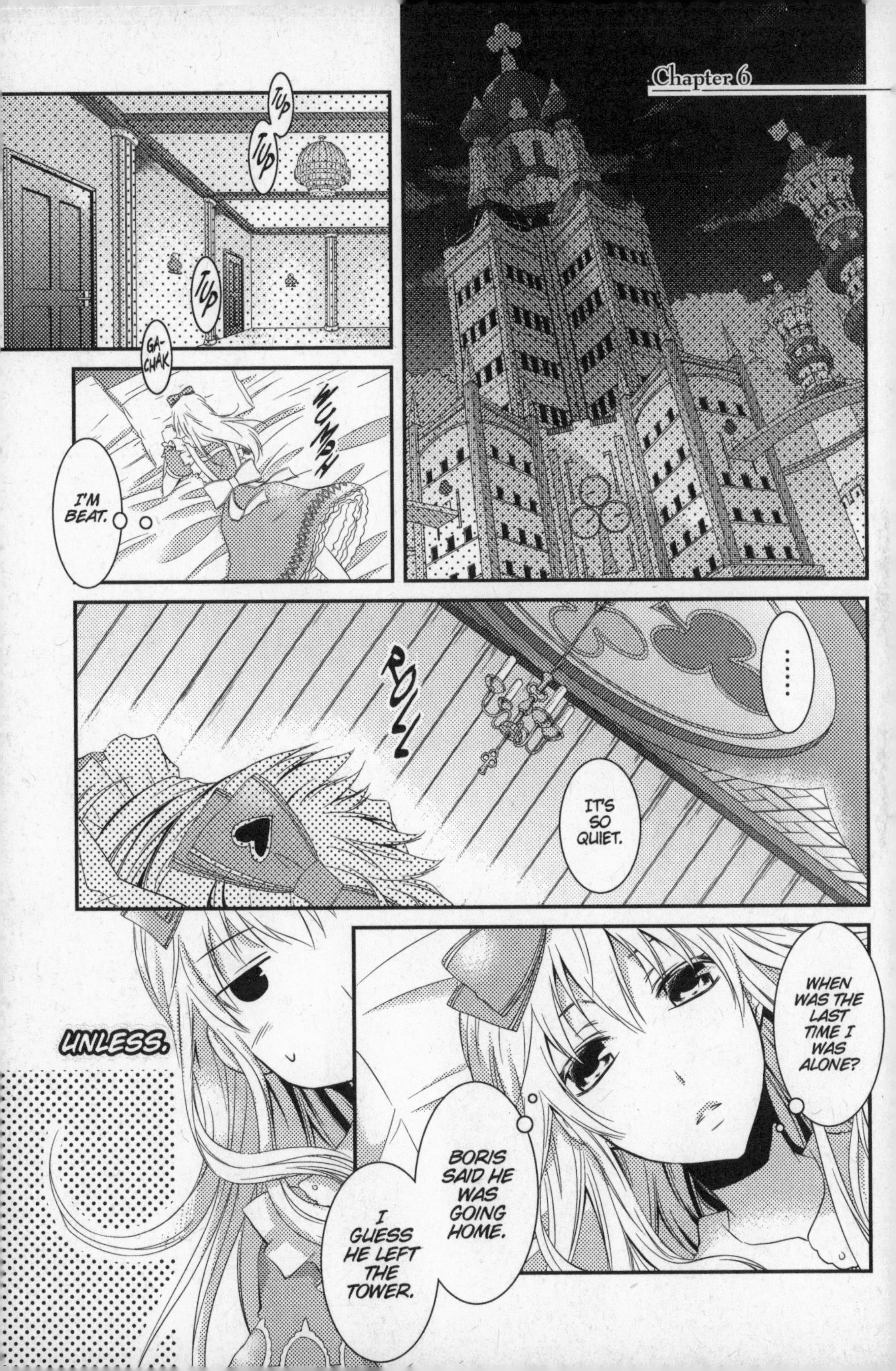
TUP
TUP
TUP
GA-CHAK
WUMPH
I'M BEAT.
......
ROLL
IT'S SO QUIET.
WHEN WAS THE LAST TIME I WAS ALONE?
BORIS SAID HE WAS GOING HOME.
I GUESS HE LEFT THE TOWER.
UNLESS.

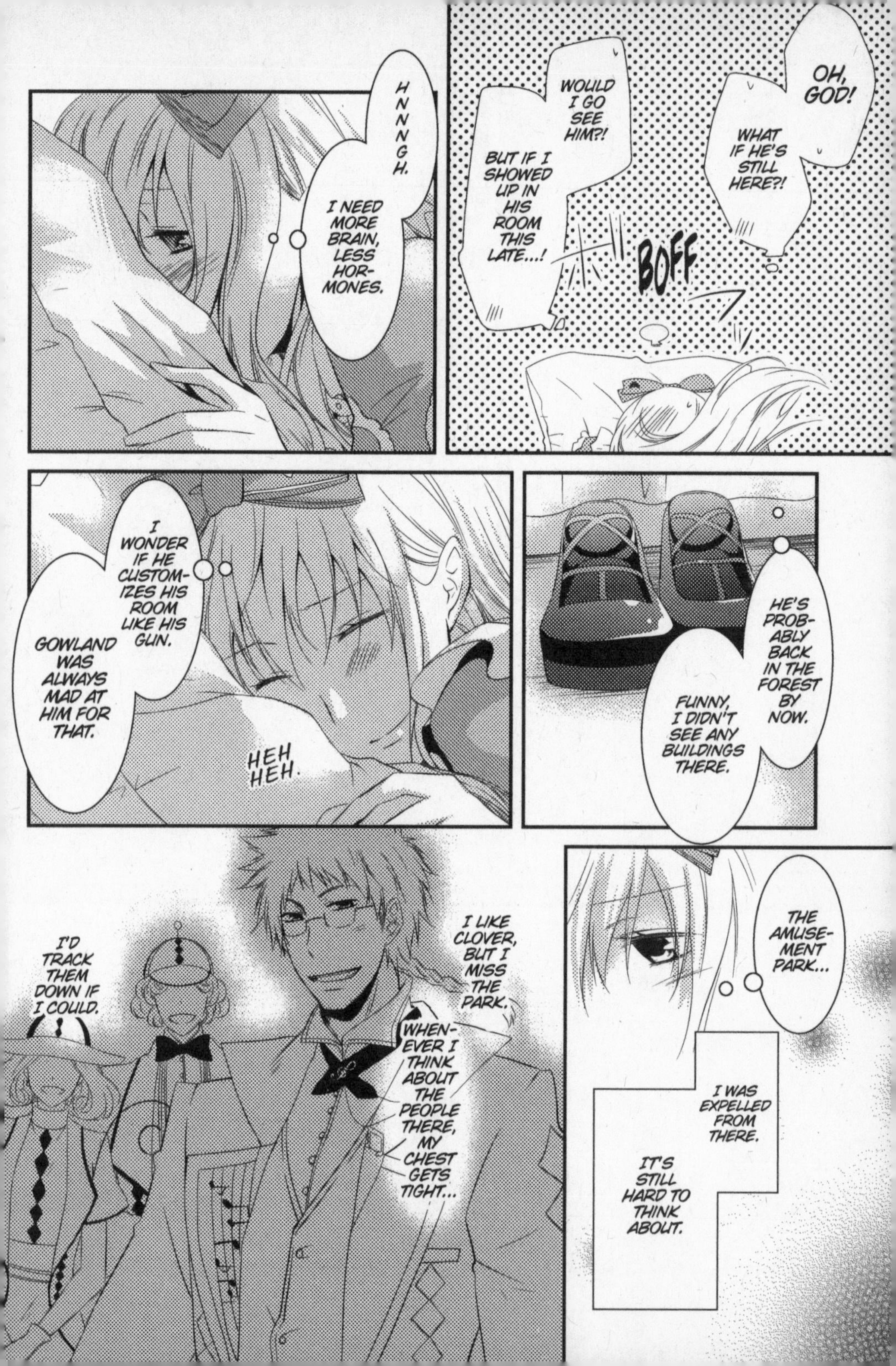
OH, GOD!
WHAT IF HE'S STILL HERE?!
WOULD I GO SEE HIM?!
BUT IF I SHOWED UP IN HIS ROOM THIS LATE...!
BOFF
HNNNNGH.
I NEED MORE BRAIN, LESS HOR-MONES.
HE'S PROB-ABLY BACK IN THE FOREST BY NOW.
FUNNY, I DIDN'T SEE ANY BUILDINGS THERE.
I WONDER IF HE CUSTOM-IZES HIS ROOM LIKE HIS GUN.
GOWLAND WAS ALWAYS MAD AT HIM FOR THAT.
HEH HEH.
THE AMUSE-MENT PARK...
I WAS EXPELLED FROM THERE.
IT'S STILL HARD TO THINK ABOUT.
I LIKE CLOVER, BUT I MISS THE PARK.
WHEN-EVER I THINK ABOUT THE PEOPLE THERE, MY CHEST GETS TIGHT...
I'D TRACK THEM DOWN IF I COULD.

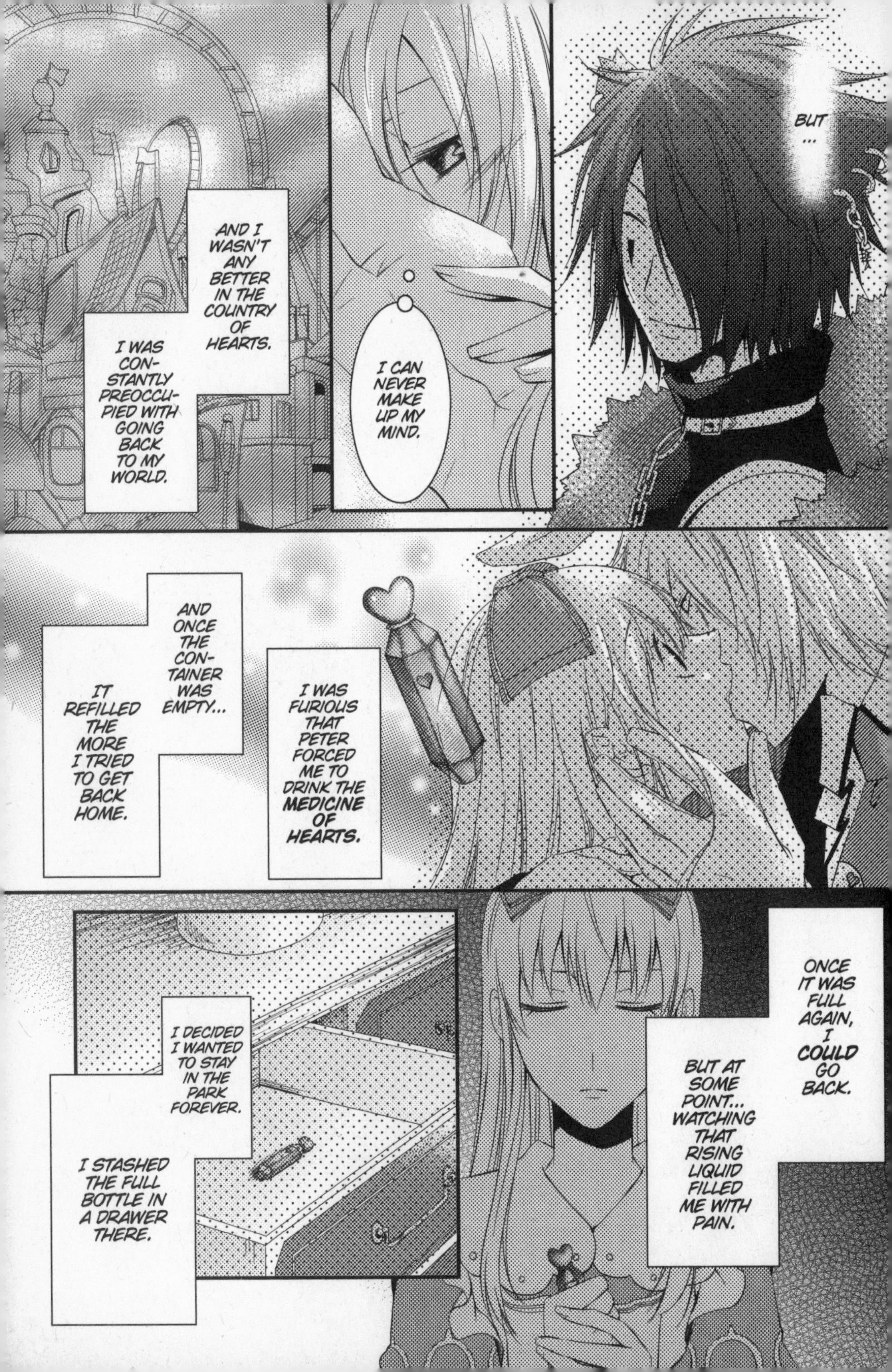

BUT ...
I CAN NEVER MAKE UP MY MIND.
AND I WASN'T ANY BETTER IN THE COUNTRY OF HEARTS.
I WAS CONSTANTLY PREOCCUPIED WITH GOING BACK TO MY WORLD.
I WAS FURIOUS THAT PETER FORCED ME TO DRINK THE **MEDICINE OF HEARTS.**
AND ONCE THE CONTAINER WAS EMPTY...
IT REFILLED THE MORE I TRIED TO GET BACK HOME.
ONCE IT WAS FULL AGAIN, I **COULD** GO BACK.
BUT AT SOME POINT... WATCHING THAT RISING LIQUID FILLED ME WITH PAIN.
I DECIDED I WANTED TO STAY IN THE PARK FOREVER.
I STASHED THE FULL BOTTLE IN A DRAWER THERE.

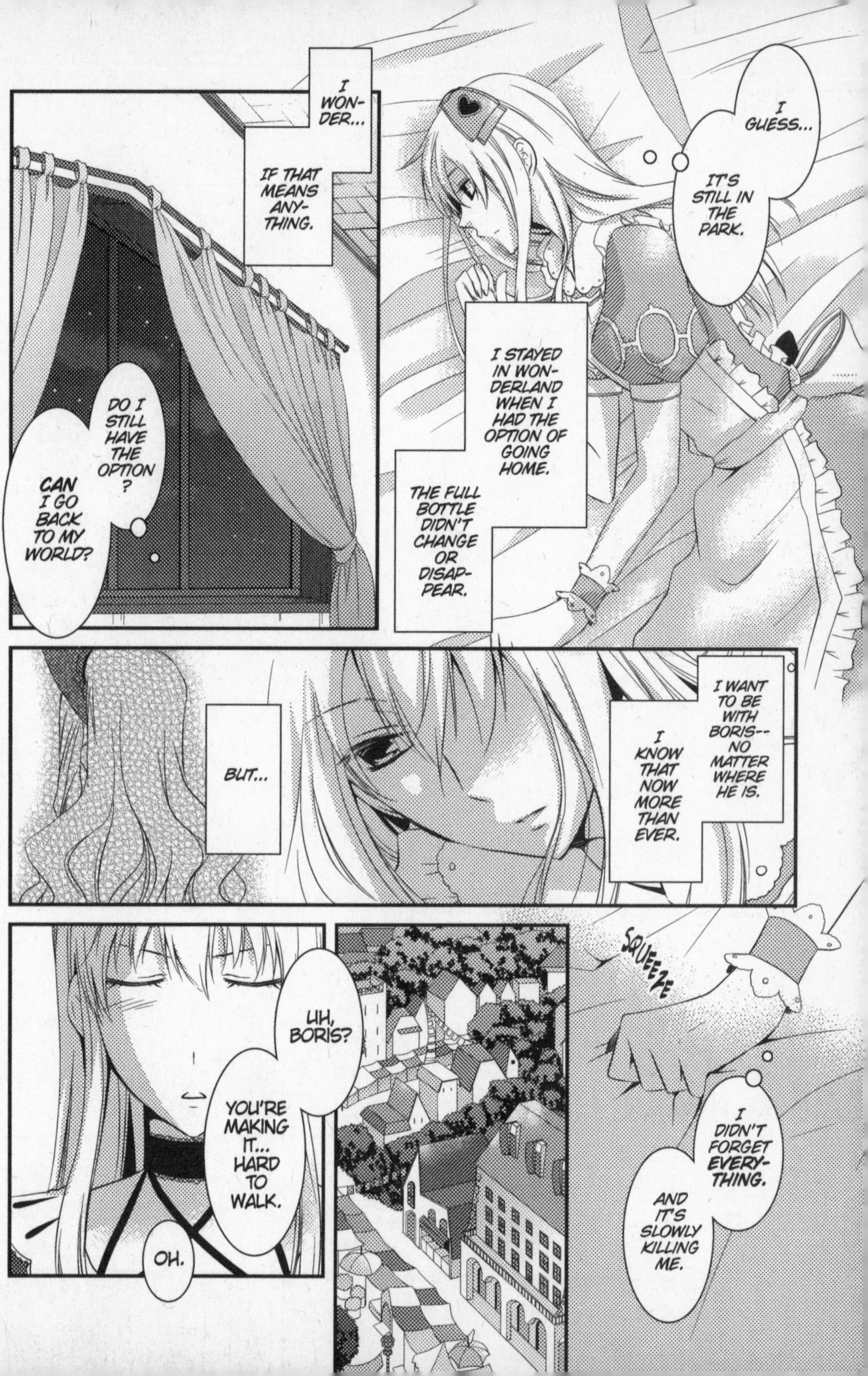
I GUESS...
IT'S STILL IN THE PARK.
I STAYED IN WONDERLAND WHEN I HAD THE OPTION OF GOING HOME.
THE FULL BOTTLE DIDN'T CHANGE OR DISAPPEAR.
I WONDER...
IF THAT MEANS ANYTHING.
DO I STILL HAVE THE OPTION?
CAN I GO BACK TO MY WORLD?
I WANT TO BE WITH BORIS--NO MATTER WHERE HE IS.
I KNOW THAT NOW MORE THAN EVER.
BUT...
SQUEEZE
I DIDN'T FORGET EVERYTHING.
AND IT'S SLOWLY KILLING ME.
UH, BORIS?
YOU'RE MAKING IT... HARD TO WALK.
OH.

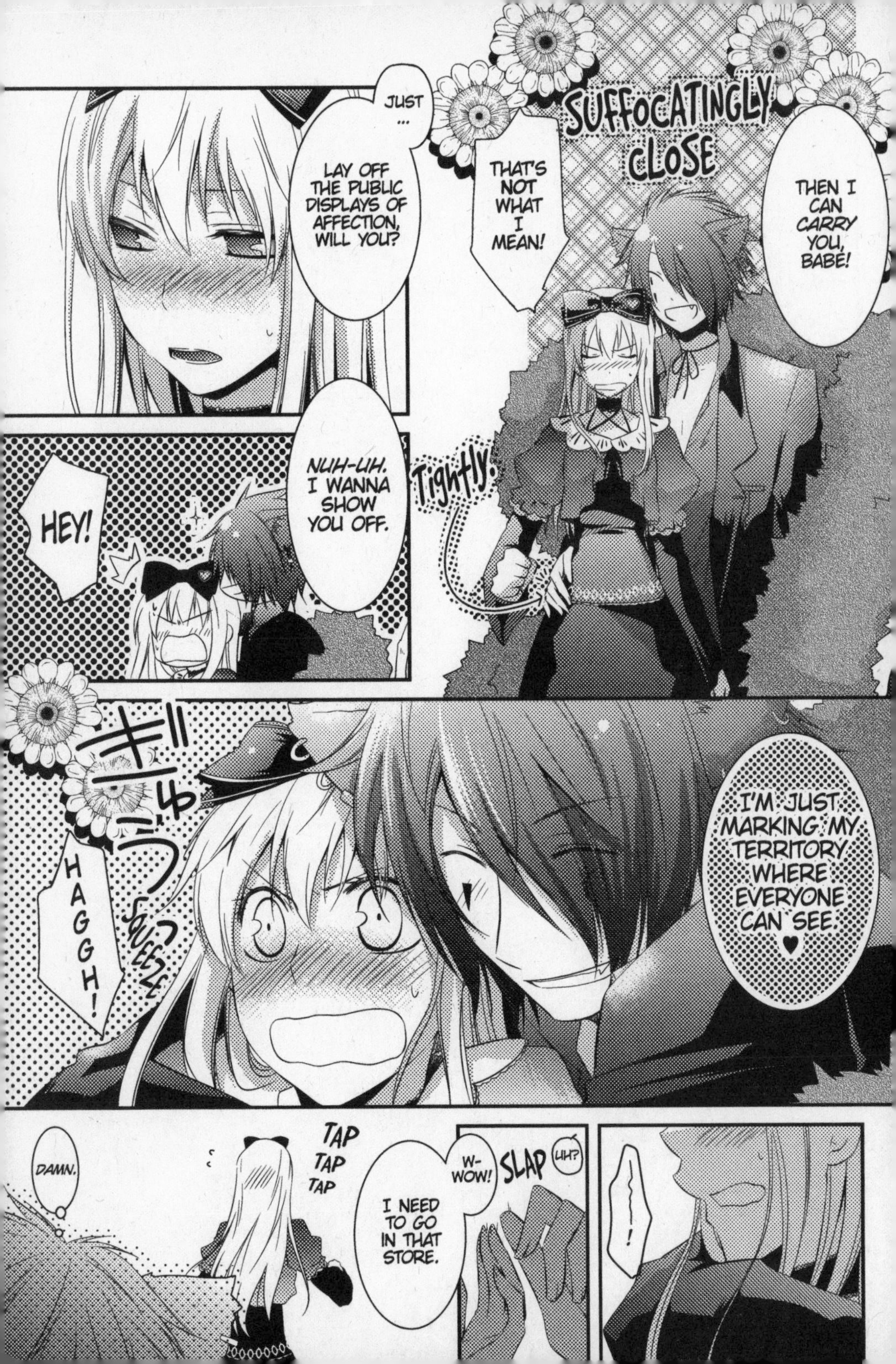
THEN I CAN CARRY YOU, BABE!
SUFFOCATINGLY CLOSE
THAT'S NOT WHAT I MEAN!
Tightly.
JUST ...
LAY OFF THE PUBLIC DISPLAYS OF AFFECTION, WILL YOU?
NUH-UH. I WANNA SHOW YOU OFF.
HEY!
I'M JUST MARKING MY TERRITORY WHERE EVERYONE CAN SEE. ♥
SQUEEZE
HAGGH!
...!
UH?
SLAP
W-WOW!
I NEED TO GO IN THAT STORE.
TAP TAP TAP
DAMN.

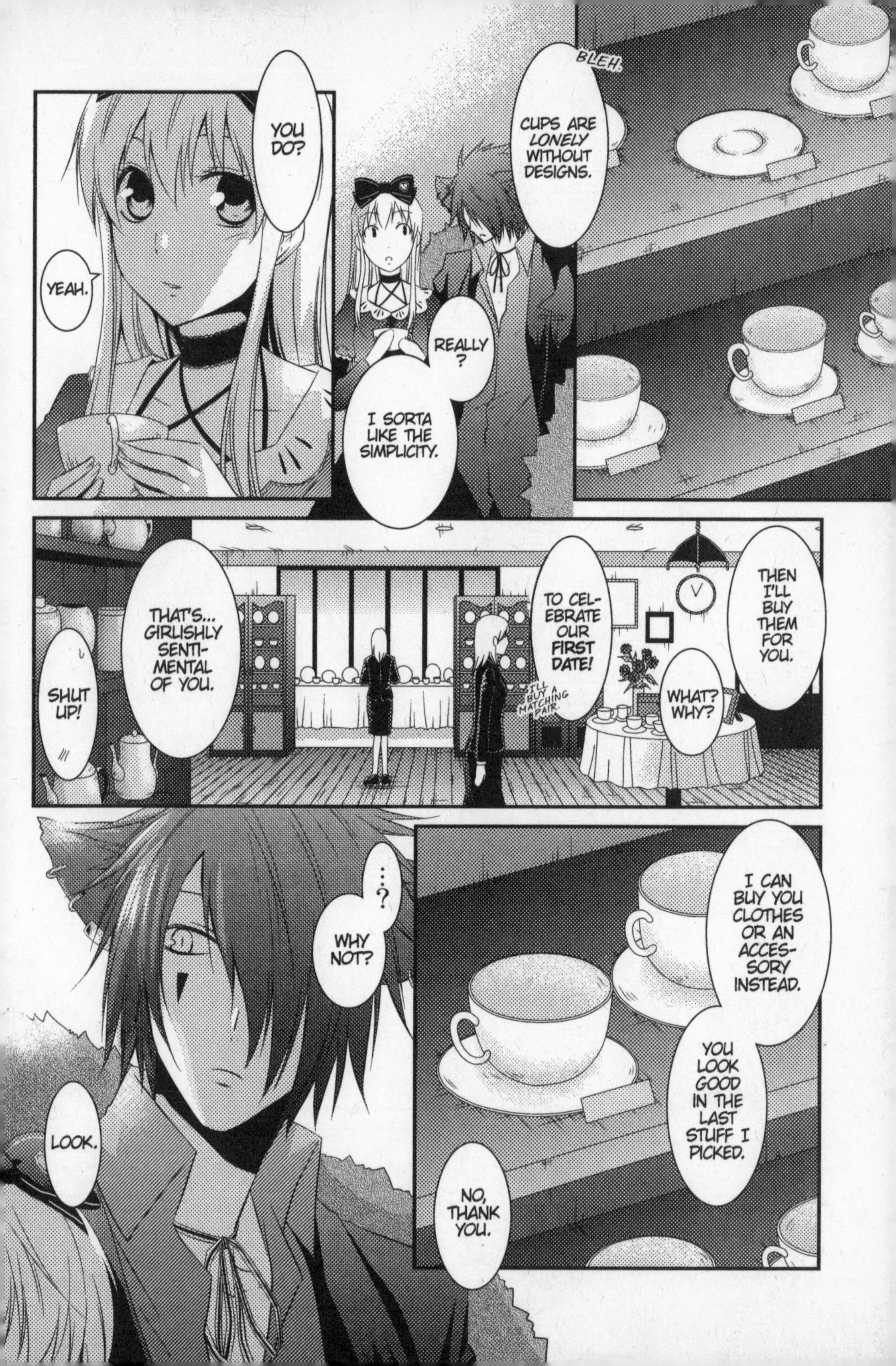
BLEH.
CUPS ARE LONELY WITHOUT DESIGNS.
REALLY?
I SORTA LIKE THE SIMPLICITY.
YOU DO?
YEAH.
THEN I'LL BUY THEM FOR YOU.
WHAT? WHY?
TO CELEBRATE OUR FIRST DATE!
I'LL BUY A MATCHING PAIR.
THAT'S... GIRLISHLY SENTIMENTAL OF YOU.
SHUT UP!
I CAN BUY YOU CLOTHES OR AN ACCES-SORY INSTEAD.
YOU LOOK GOOD IN THE LAST STUFF I PICKED.
NO, THANK YOU.
...?
WHY NOT?
LOOK.

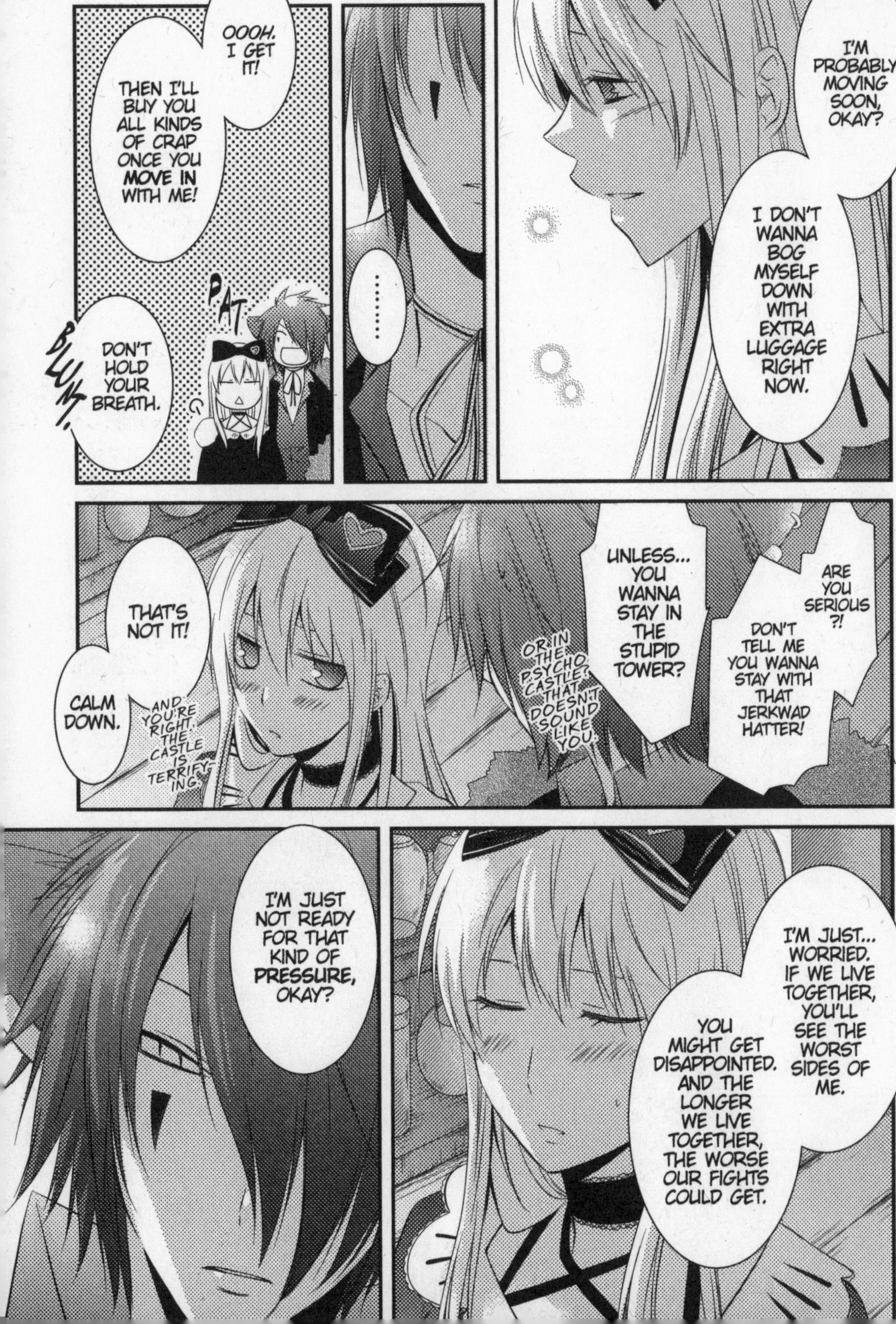
I'M PROBABLY MOVING SOON, OKAY?
I DON'T WANNA BOG MYSELF DOWN WITH EXTRA LUGGAGE RIGHT NOW.
......
OOOH. I GET IT!
THEN I'LL BUY YOU ALL KINDS OF CRAP ONCE YOU MOVE IN WITH ME!
PAT
BLUM!
DON'T HOLD YOUR BREATH.
ARE YOU SERIOUS?!
DON'T TELL ME YOU WANNA STAY WITH THAT JERKWAD HATTER!
UNLESS... YOU WANNA STAY IN THE STUPID TOWER?
OR IN THE PSYCHO CASTLE? THAT DOESN'T SOUND LIKE YOU.
THAT'S NOT IT!
CALM DOWN.
AND YOU'RE RIGHT, THE CASTLE IS TERRIFYING.
I'M JUST... WORRIED. IF WE LIVE TOGETHER, YOU'LL SEE THE WORST SIDES OF ME.
YOU MIGHT GET DISAPPOINTED. AND THE LONGER WE LIVE TOGETHER, THE WORSE OUR FIGHTS COULD GET.
I'M JUST NOT READY FOR THAT KIND OF PRESSURE, OKAY?

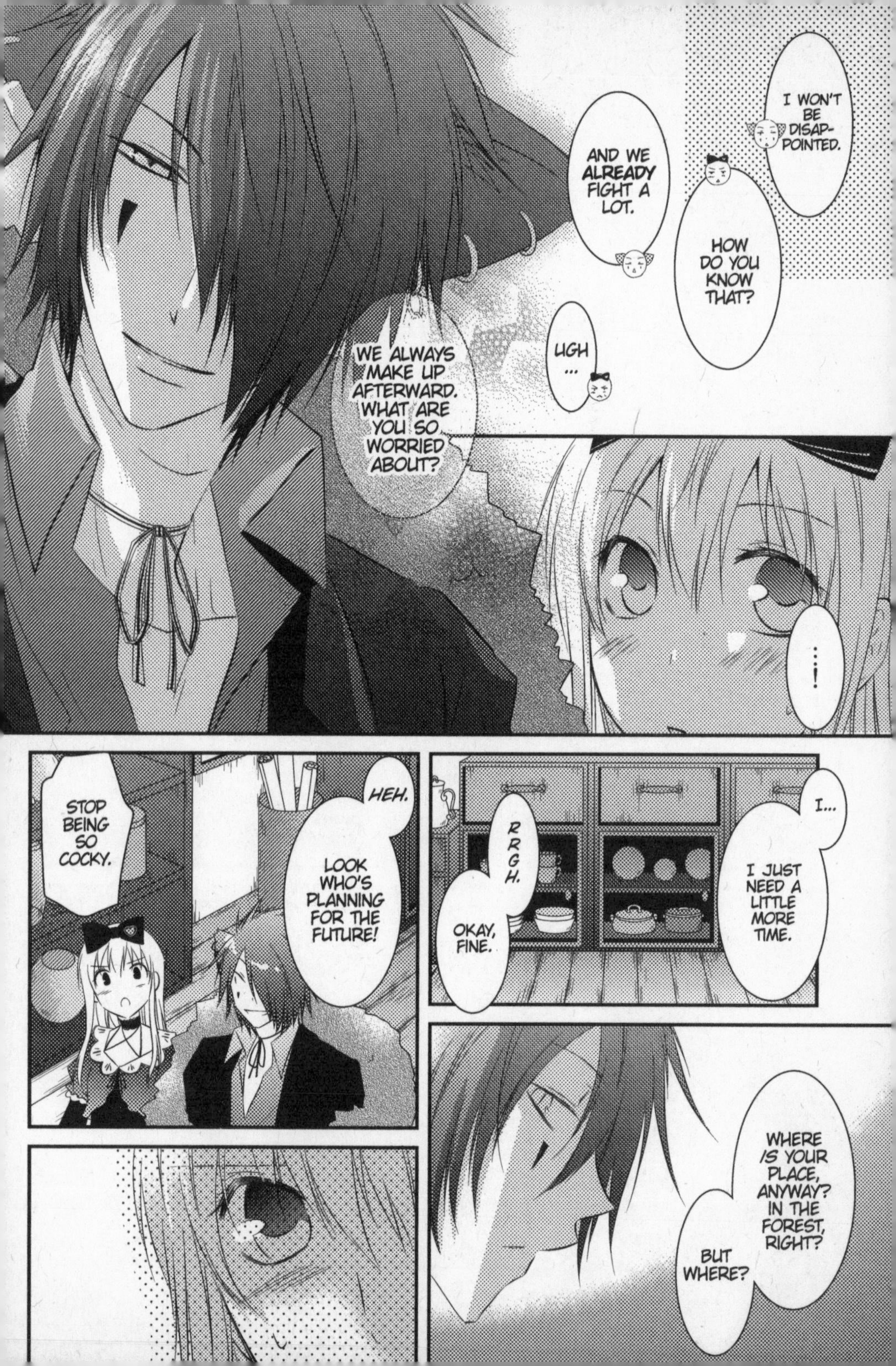
I WON'T BE DISAPPOINTED.
HOW DO YOU KNOW THAT?
AND WE ALREADY FIGHT A LOT.
UGH ...
WE ALWAYS MAKE UP AFTERWARD. WHAT ARE YOU SO WORRIED ABOUT?
...!
I...
I JUST NEED A LITTLE MORE TIME.
RRGH.
OKAY, FINE.
HEH.
LOOK WHO'S PLANNING FOR THE FUTURE!
STOP BEING SO COCKY.
WHERE *IS* YOUR PLACE, ANYWAY? IN THE FOREST, RIGHT?
BUT WHERE?

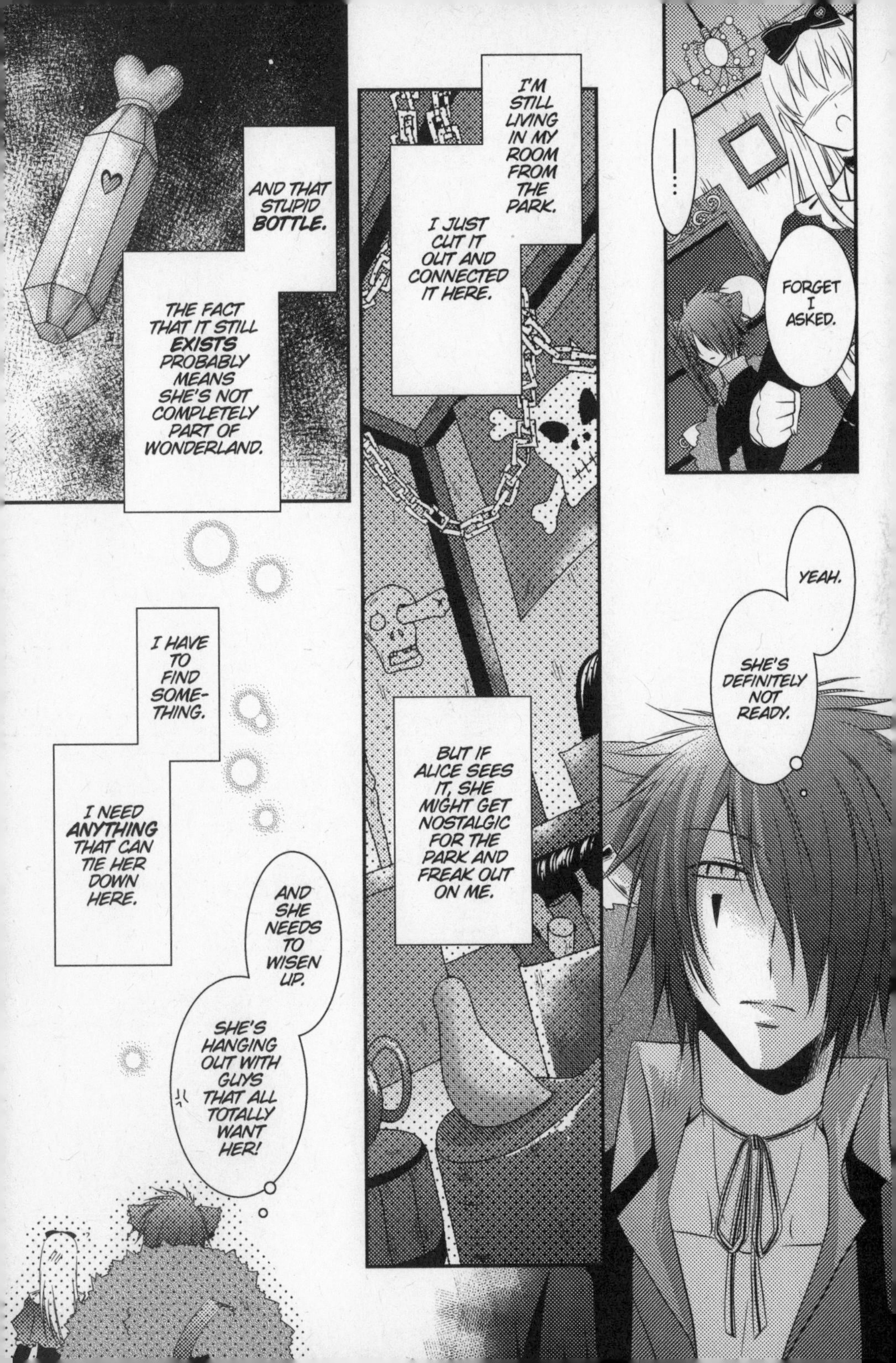
......!
FORGET I ASKED.
YEAH.
SHE'S DEFINITELY NOT READY.
I'M STILL LIVING IN MY ROOM FROM THE PARK.
I JUST CUT IT OUT AND CONNECTED IT HERE.
BUT IF ALICE SEES IT, SHE MIGHT GET NOSTALGIC FOR THE PARK AND FREAK OUT ON ME.
AND THAT STUPID BOTTLE.
THE FACT THAT IT STILL EXISTS PROBABLY MEANS SHE'S NOT COMPLETELY PART OF WONDERLAND.
I HAVE TO FIND SOME-THING.
I NEED ANYTHING THAT CAN TIE HER DOWN HERE.
AND SHE NEEDS TO WISEN UP.
SHE'S HANGING OUT WITH GUYS THAT ALL TOTALLY WANT HER!

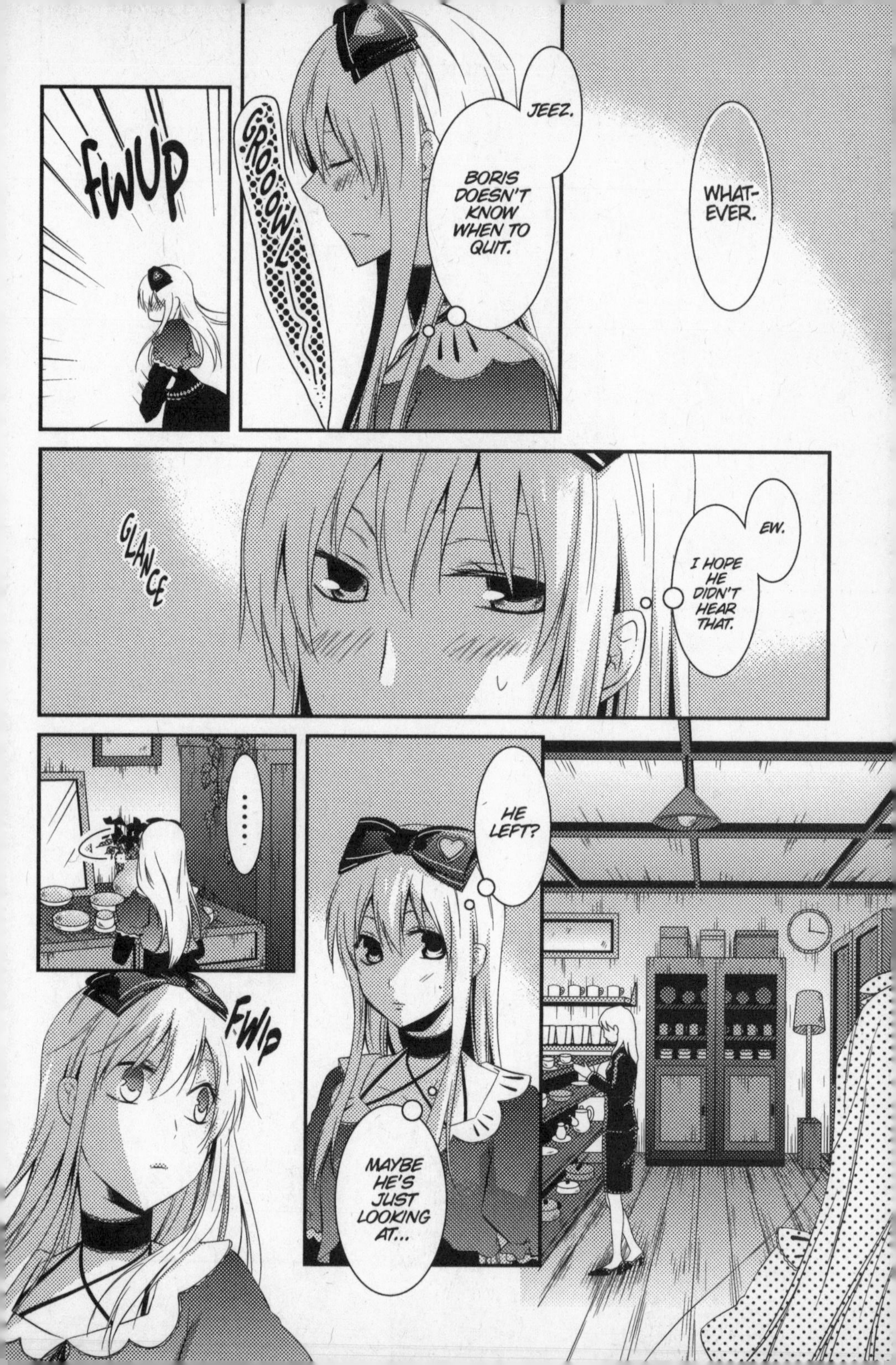
WHAT-EVER.
JEEZ.
BORIS DOESN'T KNOW WHEN TO QUIT.
GROOOWL
FWUP
EW.
I HOPE HE DIDN'T HEAR THAT.
GLANCE
HE LEFT?
MAYBE HE'S JUST LOOKING AT...
......
FWIP

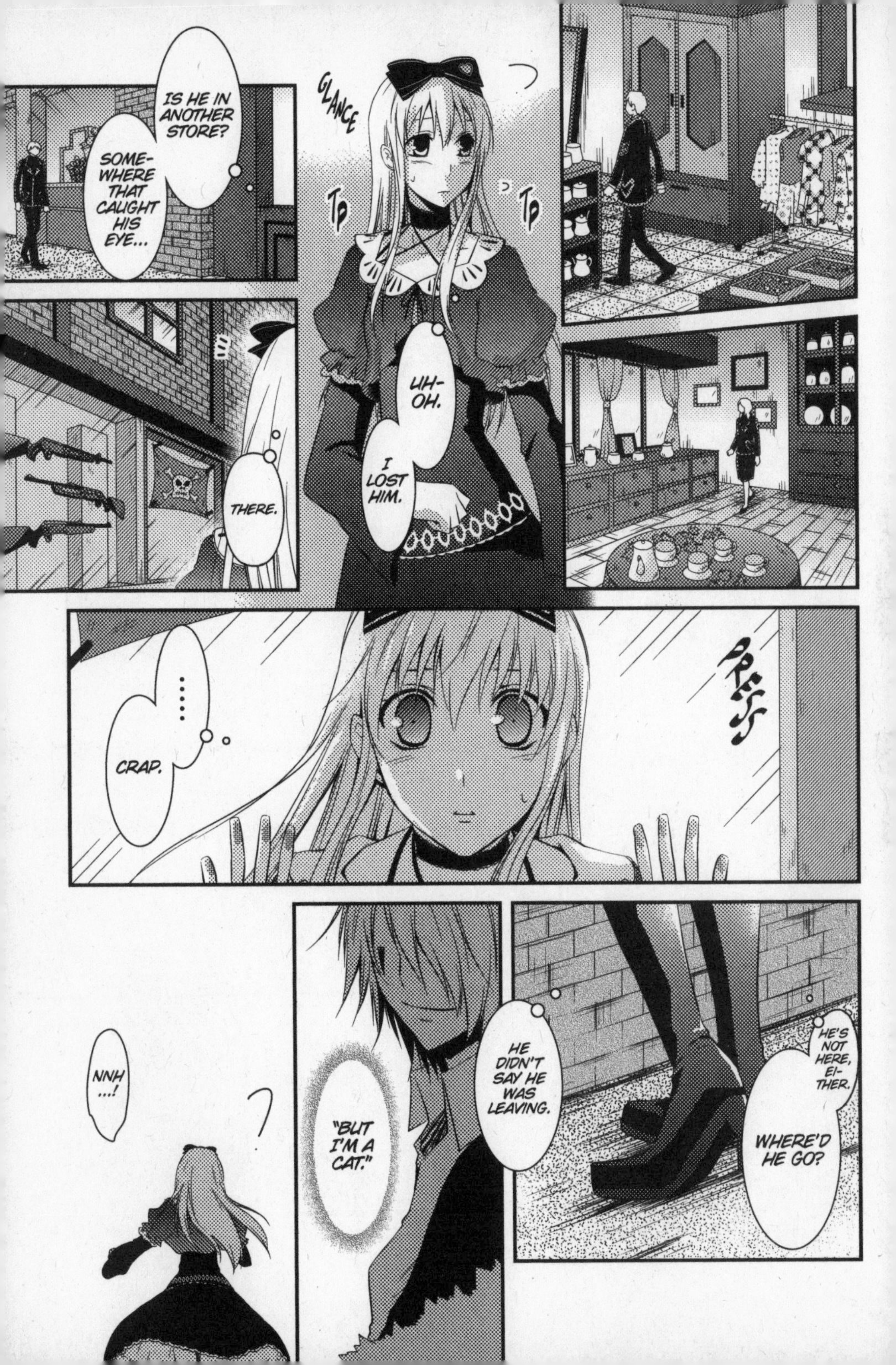
GLANCE
TP
TP
UH-OH.
I LOST HIM.
IS HE IN ANOTHER STORE?
SOMEWHERE THAT CAUGHT HIS EYE...
THERE.
PRESS
......
CRAP.
HE'S NOT HERE, EITHER.
WHERE'D HE GO?
HE DIDN'T SAY HE WAS LEAVING.
"BUT I'M A CAT."
NNH ...!

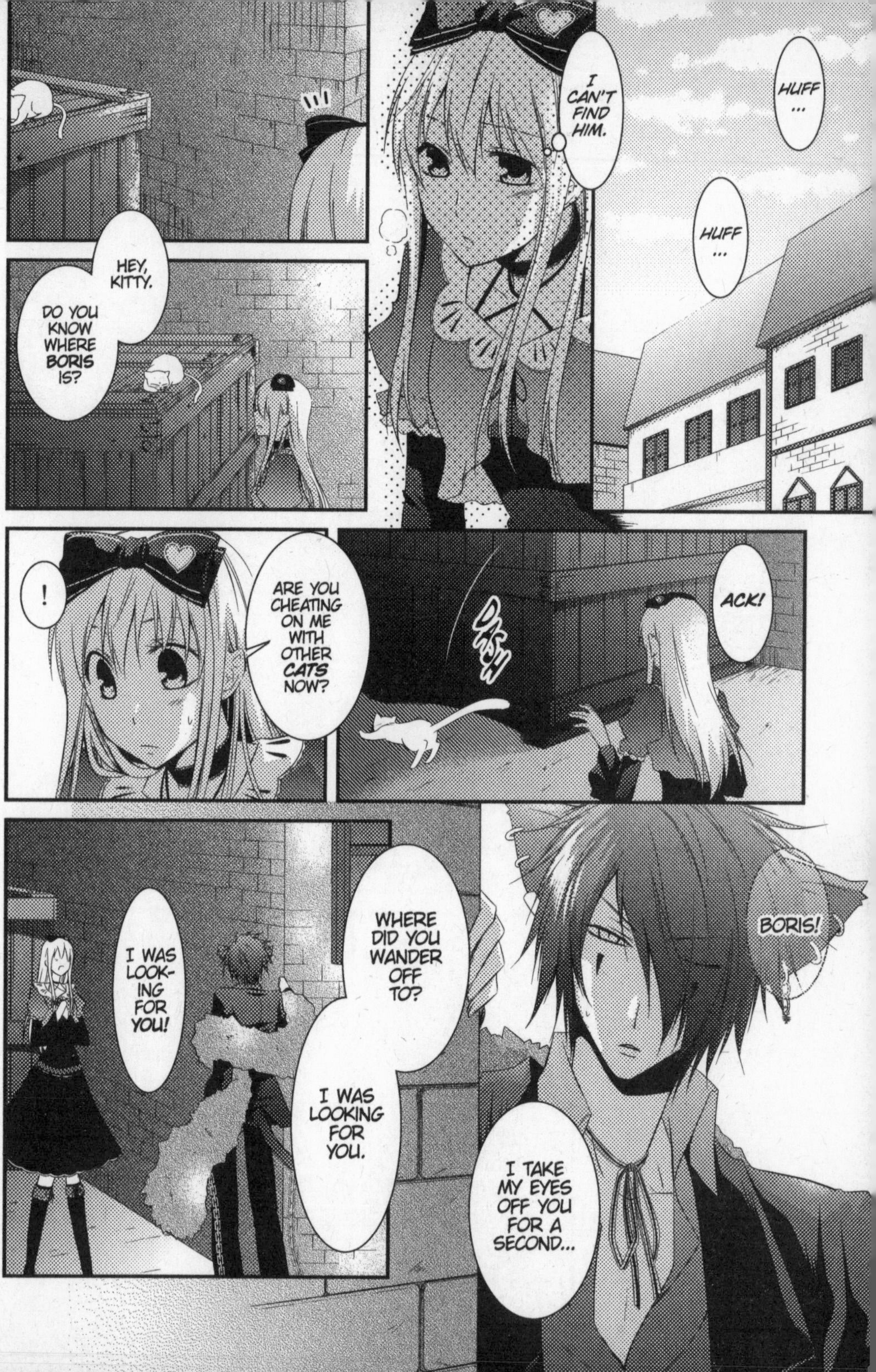
HUFF...
HUFF...
I CAN'T FIND HIM.
HEY, KITTY.
DO YOU KNOW WHERE BORIS IS?
ACK!
DASH
ARE YOU CHEATING ON ME WITH OTHER *CATS* NOW?
!
BORIS!
I TAKE MY EYES OFF YOU FOR A SECOND...
WHERE DID YOU WANDER OFF TO?
I WAS LOOKING FOR YOU.
I WAS LOOKING FOR YOU!

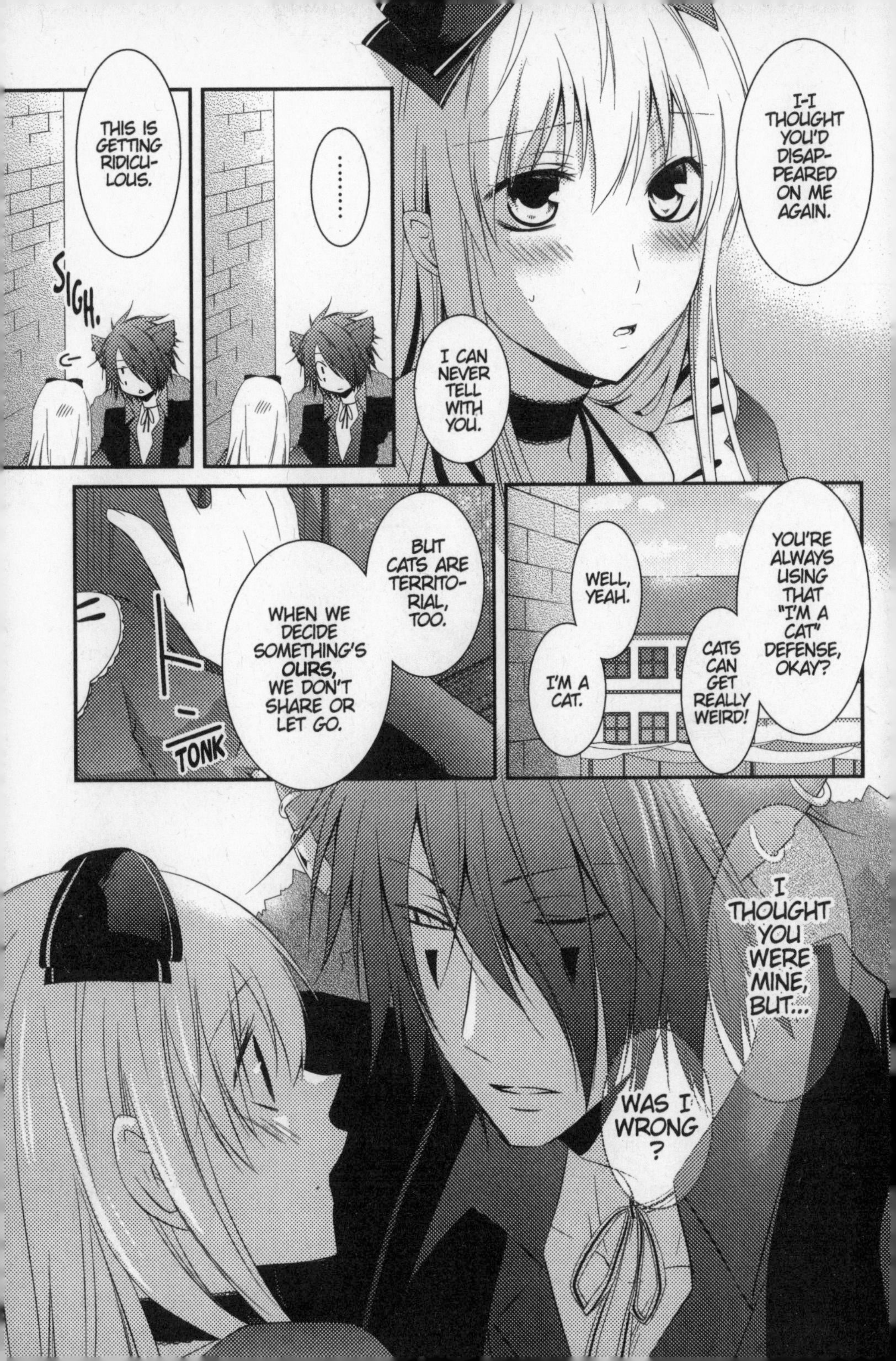
I-I THOUGHT YOU'D DISAPPEARED ON ME AGAIN.
I CAN NEVER TELL WITH YOU.
....
THIS IS GETTING RIDICULOUS.
SIGH.
YOU'RE ALWAYS USING THAT "I'M A CAT" DEFENSE, OKAY?
CATS CAN GET REALLY WEIRD!
WELL, YEAH.
I'M A CAT.
BUT CATS ARE TERRITORIAL, TOO.
WHEN WE DECIDE SOMETHING'S OURS, WE DON'T SHARE OR LET GO.
TONK
I THOUGHT YOU WERE MINE, BUT...
WAS I WRONG?

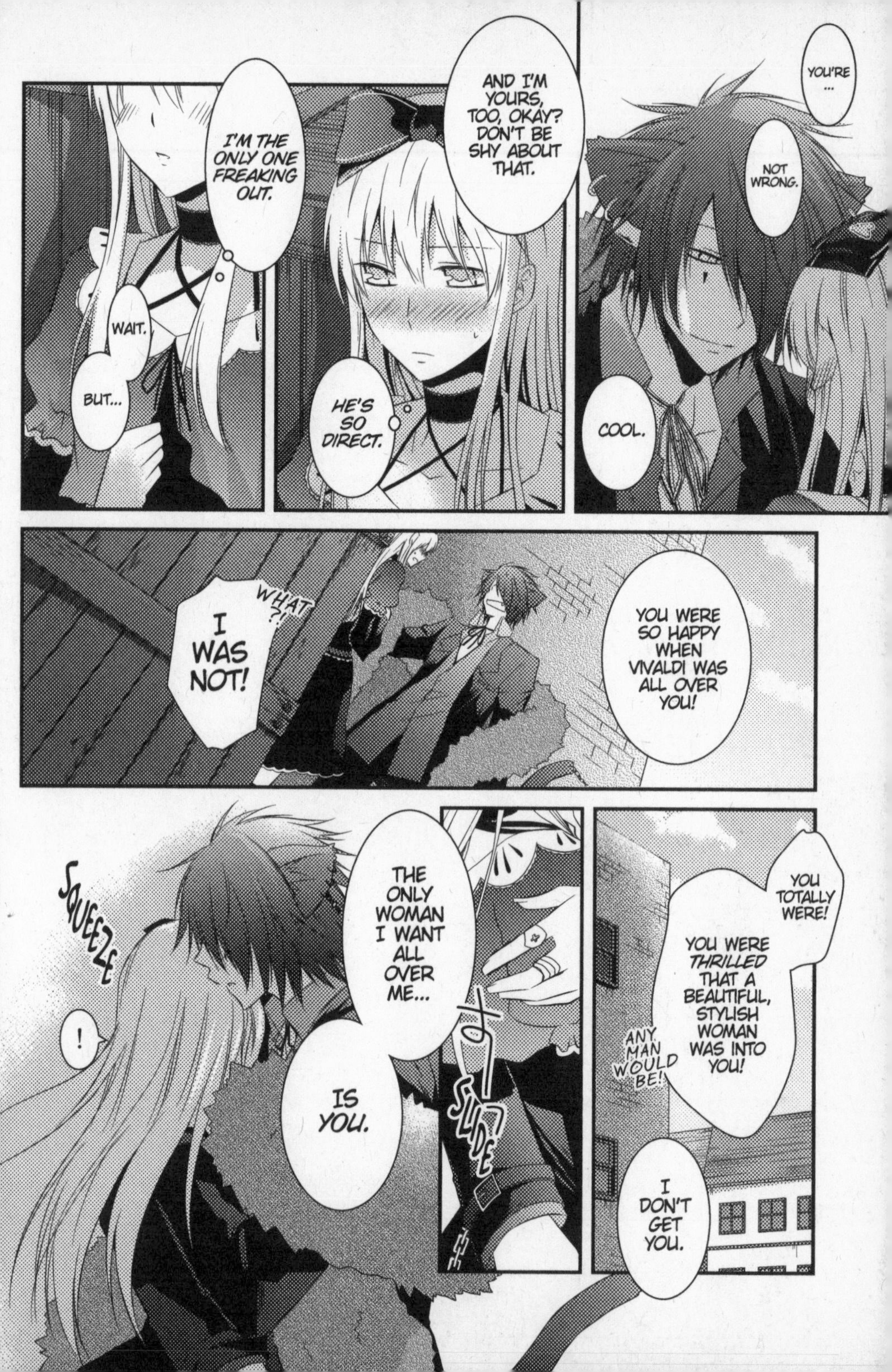
YOU'RE ...
NOT WRONG.
COOL.
AND I'M YOURS, TOO, OKAY? DON'T BE SHY ABOUT THAT.
HE'S SO DIRECT.
I'M THE ONLY ONE FREAKING OUT.
WAIT.
BUT...
YOU WERE SO HAPPY WHEN VIVALDI WAS ALL OVER YOU!
WHAT?!
I WAS NOT!
YOU TOTALLY WERE!
YOU WERE *THRILLED* THAT A BEAUTIFUL, STYLISH WOMAN WAS INTO YOU!
ANY MAN WOULD BE!
I DON'T GET YOU.
SLIDE
THE ONLY WOMAN I WANT ALL OVER ME...
IS YOU.
SQUEEZE
!

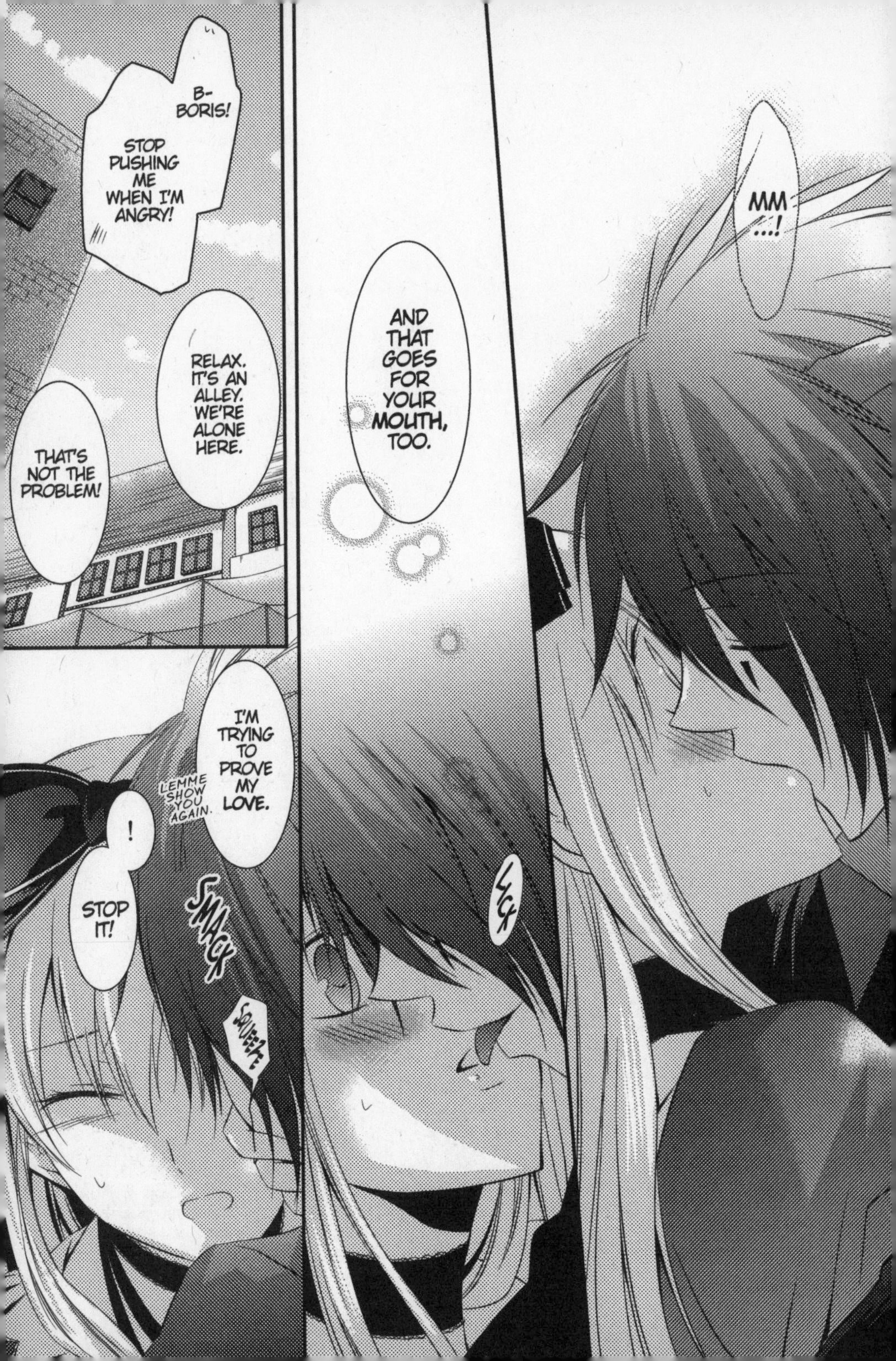
MM ...!
AND THAT GOES FOR YOUR MOUTH, TOO.
LICK
B-BORIS!
STOP PUSHING ME WHEN I'M ANGRY!
RELAX. IT'S AN ALLEY. WE'RE ALONE HERE.
THAT'S NOT THE PROBLEM!
I'M TRYING TO PROVE MY LOVE.
LEMME SHOW YOU AGAIN.
!
STOP IT!
SMACK
SQUEEZE

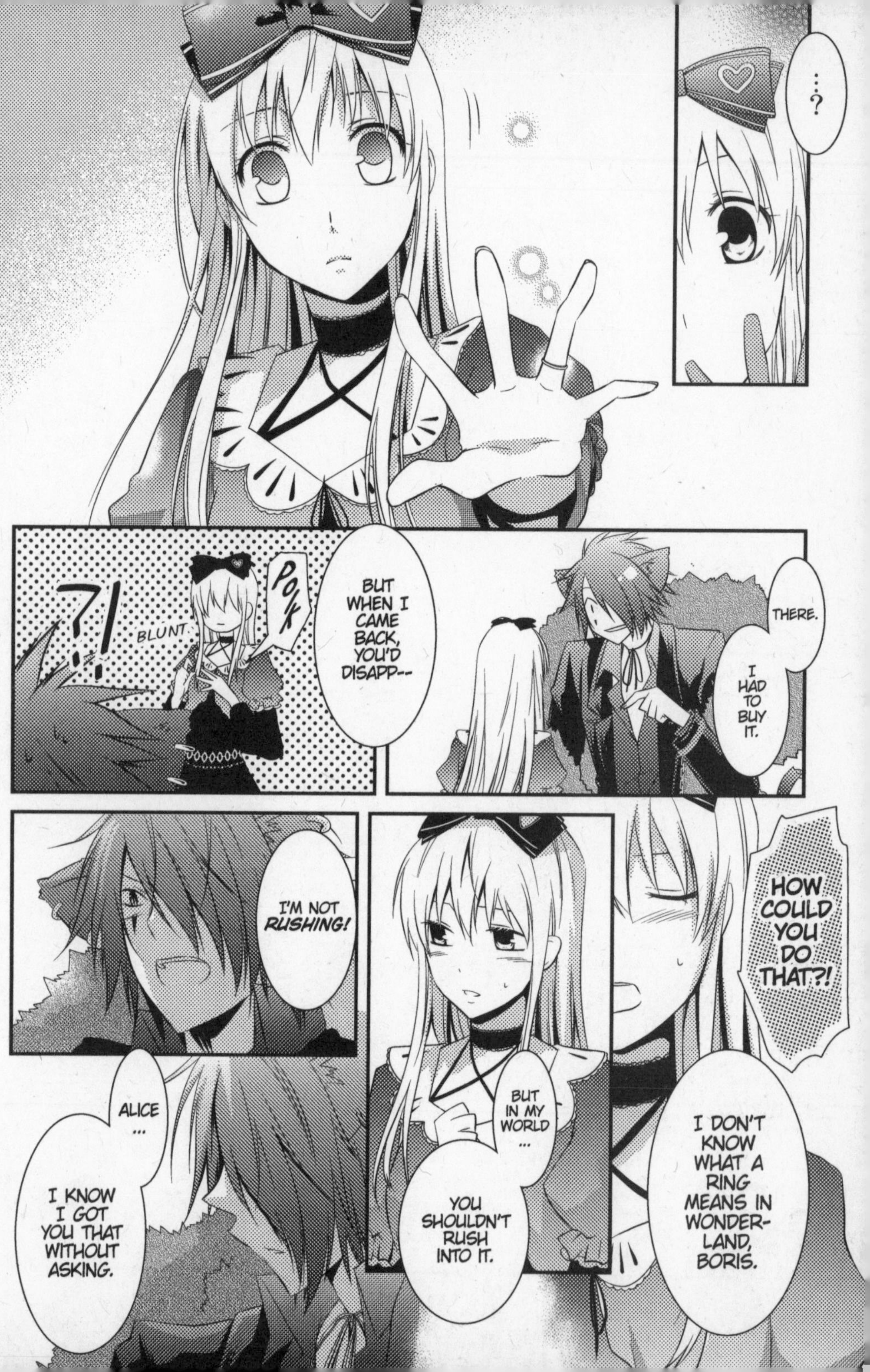
...?
THERE.
I HAD TO BUY IT.
BUT WHEN I CAME BACK, YOU'D DISAPP--
POK
BLUNT
?!
HOW COULD YOU DO THAT?!
I DON'T KNOW WHAT A RING MEANS IN WONDER-LAND, BORIS.
BUT IN MY WORLD...
YOU SHOULDN'T RUSH INTO IT.
I'M NOT RUSHING!
ALICE...
I KNOW I GOT YOU THAT WITHOUT ASKING.

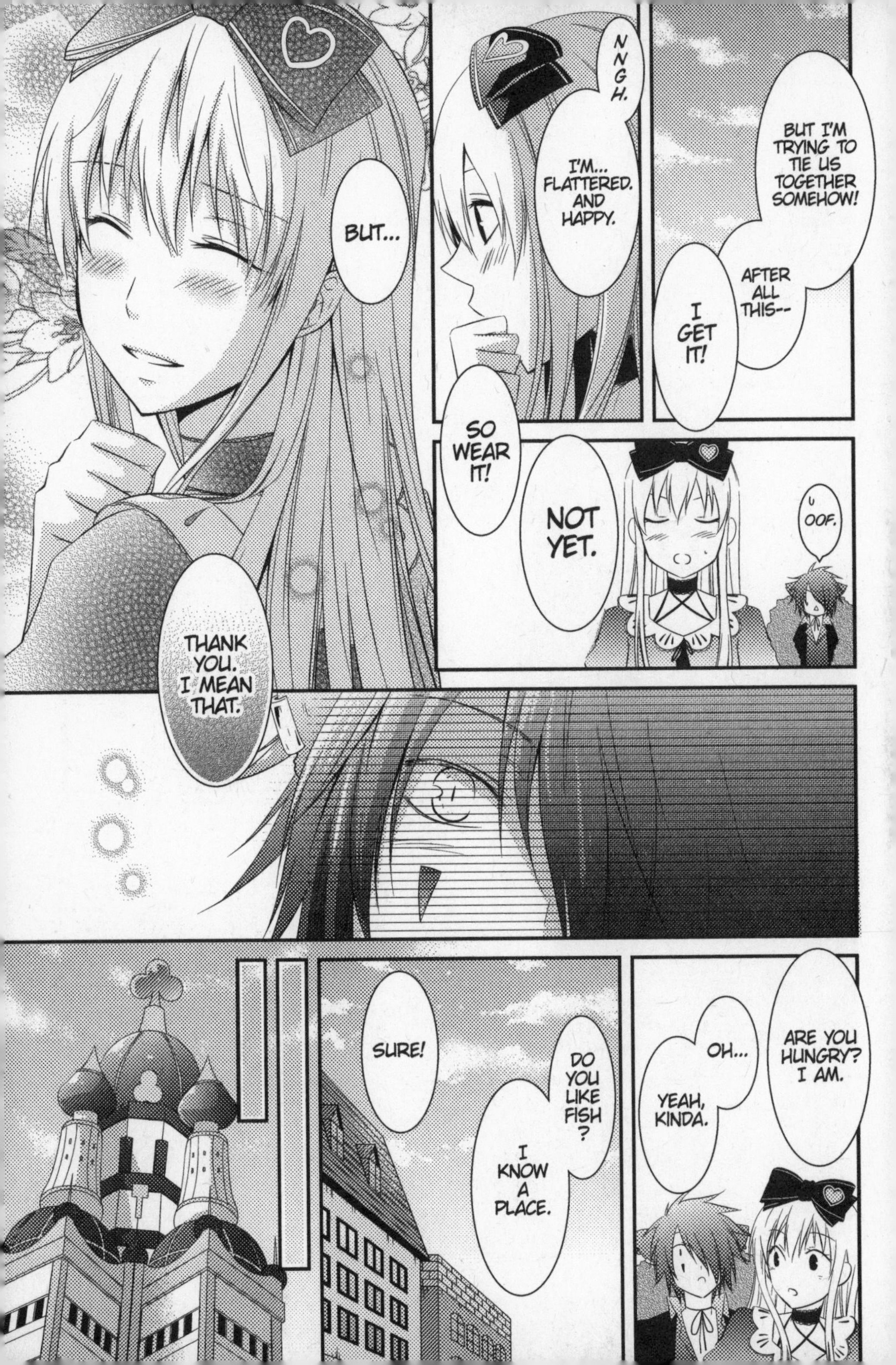
BUT I'M TRYING TO TIE US TOGETHER SOMEHOW!
AFTER ALL THIS--
I GET IT!
NNGH.
I'M... FLATTERED. AND HAPPY.
BUT...
SO WEAR IT!
NOT YET.
OOF.
THANK YOU. I MEAN THAT.
ARE YOU HUNGRY? I AM.
OH...
YEAH, KINDA.
DO YOU LIKE FISH?
I KNOW A PLACE.
SURE!

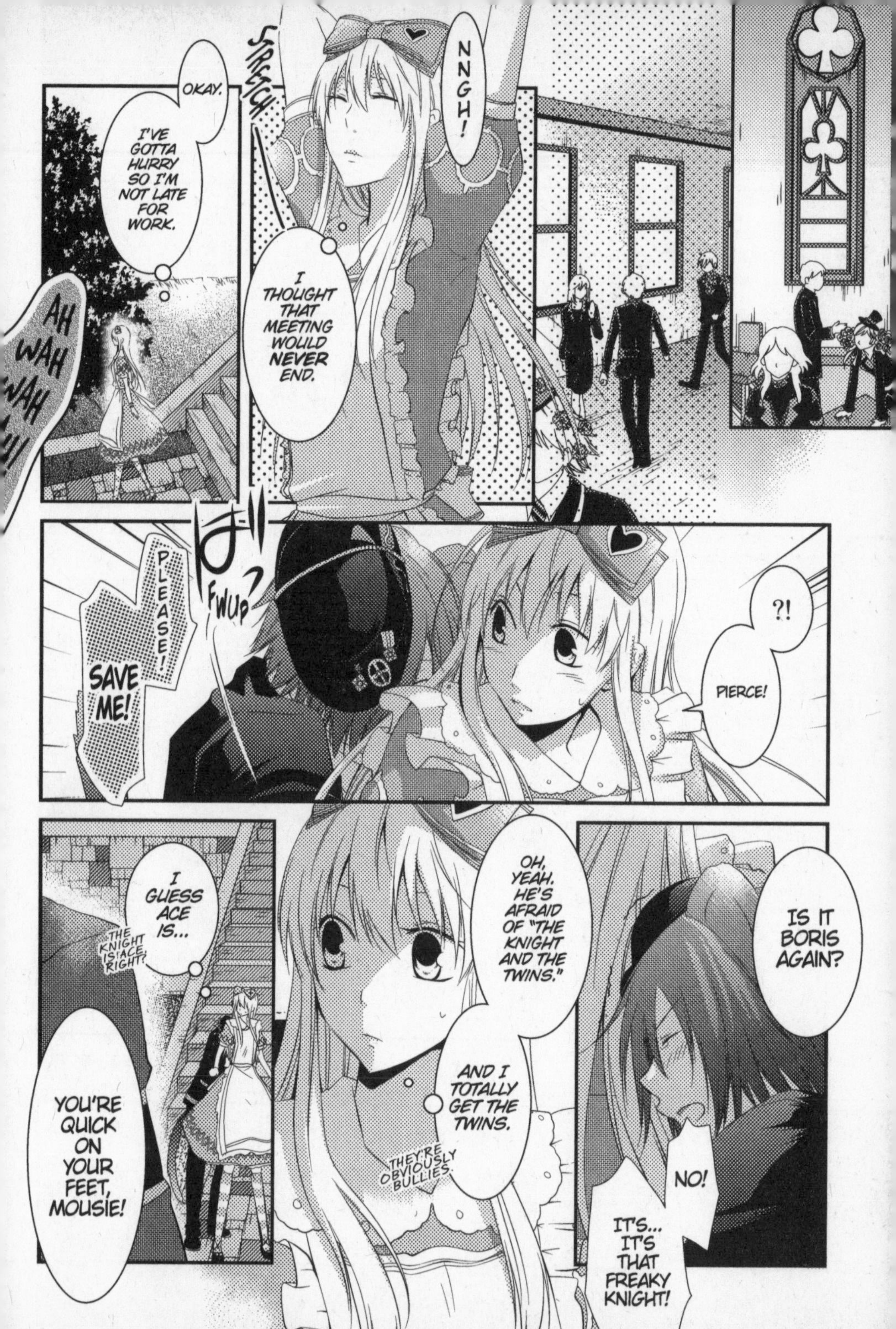
NNGH!
STRETCH
I THOUGHT THAT MEETING WOULD NEVER END.
OKAY.
I'VE GOTTA HURRY SO I'M NOT LATE FOR WORK.
AH WAH WAH WAH
?!
PIERCE!
FWUP
PLEASE!
SAVE ME!
IS IT BORIS AGAIN?
NO!
IT'S... IT'S THAT FREAKY KNIGHT!
OH, YEAH. HE'S AFRAID OF "THE KNIGHT AND THE TWINS."
AND I TOTALLY GET THE TWINS.
THEY'RE OBVIOUSLY BULLIES.
I GUESS ACE IS...
THE KNIGHT IS ACE, RIGHT?
YOU'RE QUICK ON YOUR FEET, MOUSIE!

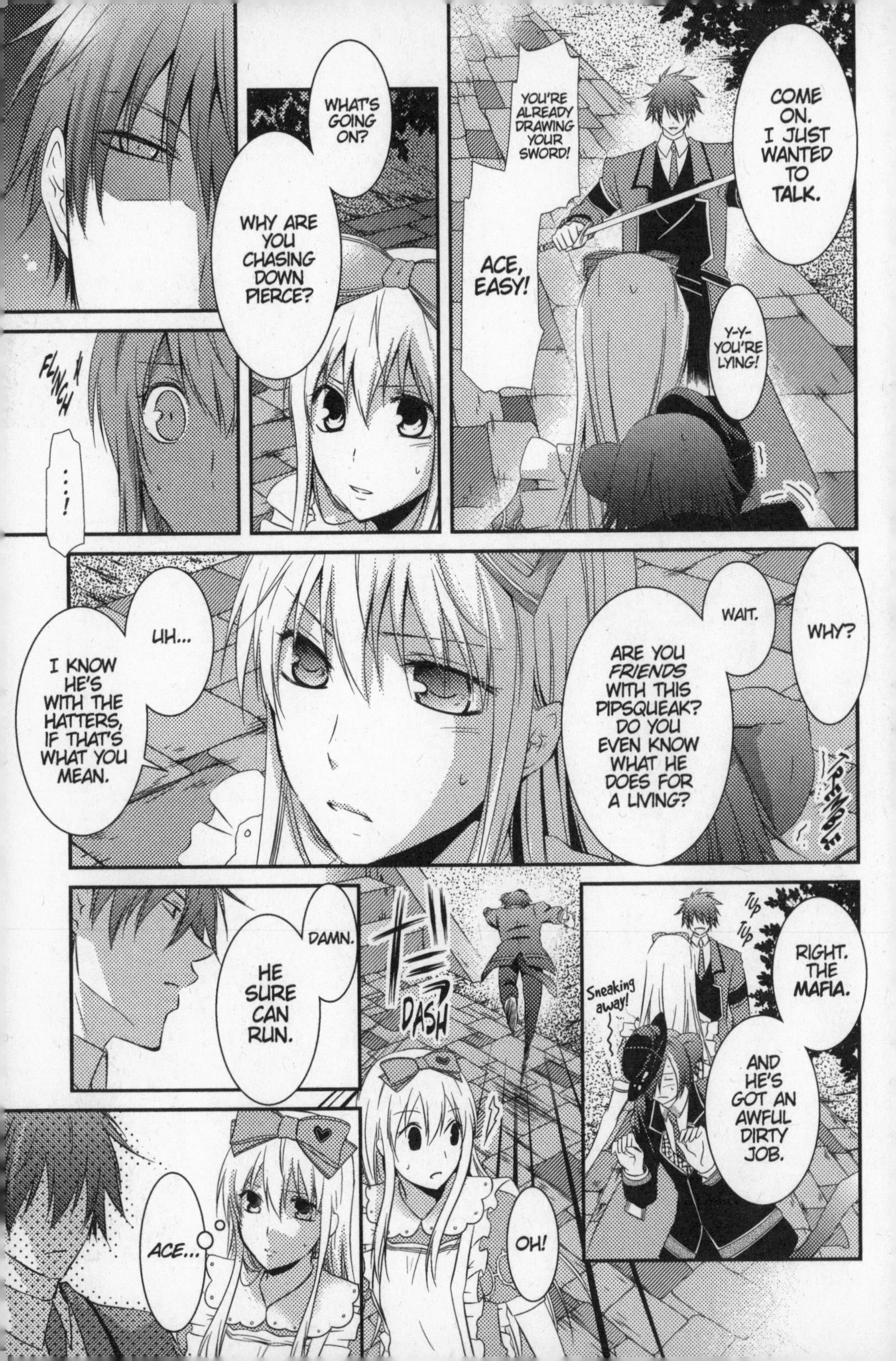
COME ON. I JUST WANTED TO TALK.
YOU'RE ALREADY DRAWING YOUR SWORD!
ACE, EASY!
Y-Y-YOU'RE LYING!
WHAT'S GOING ON?
WHY ARE YOU CHASING DOWN PIERCE?
FLINCH
...!
WHY?
WAIT.
ARE YOU *FRIENDS* WITH THIS PIPSQUEAK? DO YOU EVEN KNOW WHAT HE DOES FOR A LIVING?
TREMBLE
UH...
I KNOW HE'S WITH THE HATTERS, IF THAT'S WHAT YOU MEAN.
TUP TUP
RIGHT. THE MAFIA.
AND HE'S GOT AN AWFUL DIRTY JOB.
Sneaking away!
DASH
DAMN.
HE SURE CAN RUN.
OH!
ACE...

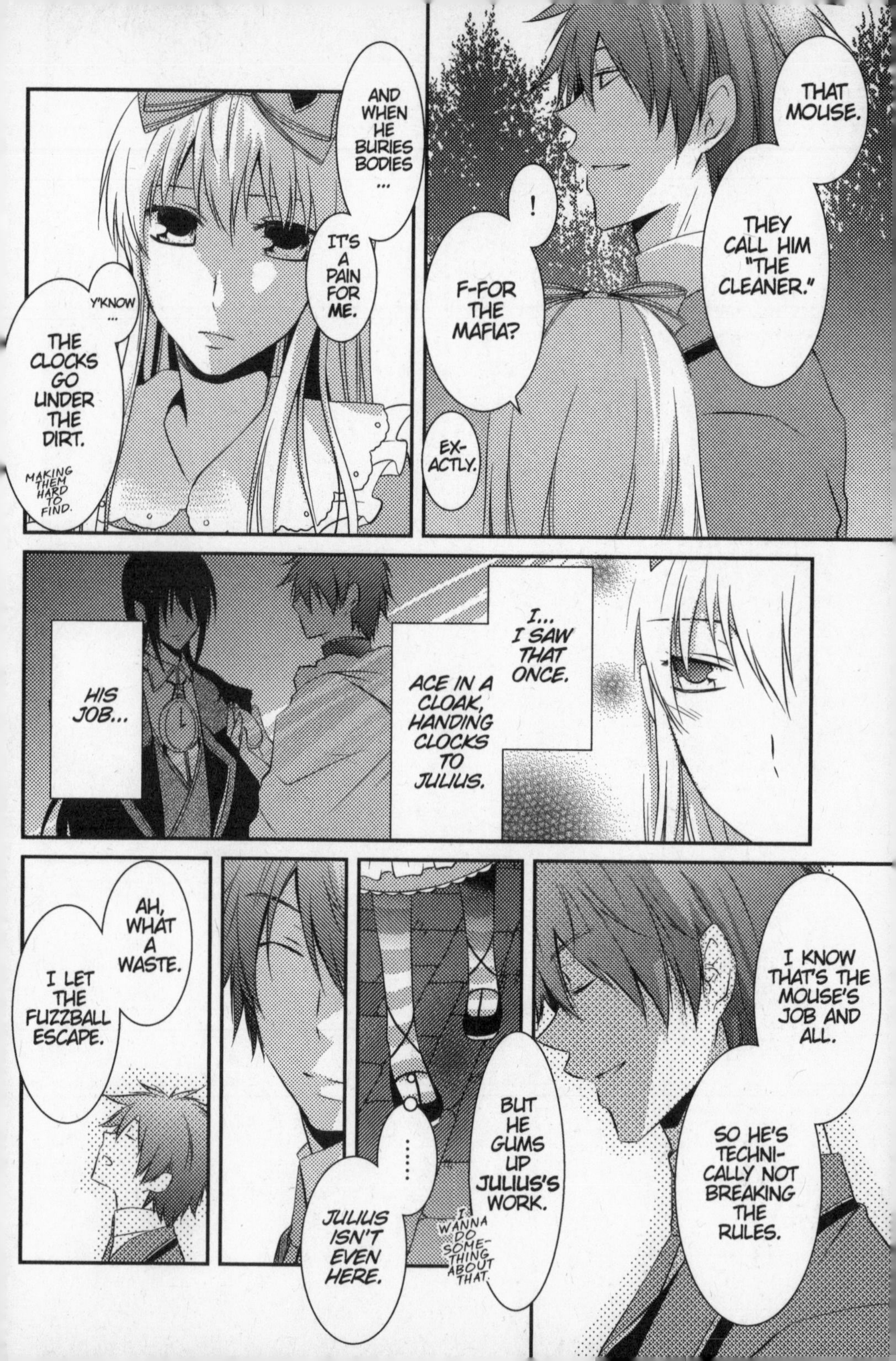
THAT MOUSE.
THEY CALL HIM "THE CLEANER."
!
F-FOR THE MAFIA?
EX-ACTLY.
AND WHEN HE BURIES BODIES ...
IT'S A PAIN FOR ME.
Y'KNOW ...
THE CLOCKS GO UNDER THE DIRT.
MAKING THEM HARD TO FIND.
I... I SAW THAT ONCE.
ACE IN A CLOAK, HANDING CLOCKS TO JULIUS.
HIS JOB...
I KNOW THAT'S THE MOUSE'S JOB AND ALL.
SO HE'S TECHNI-CALLY NOT BREAKING THE RULES.
BUT HE GUMS UP JULIUS'S WORK.
I WANNA DO SOME-THING ABOUT THAT.
......
JULIUS ISN'T EVEN HERE.
AH, WHAT A WASTE.
I LET THE FUZZBALL ESCAPE.

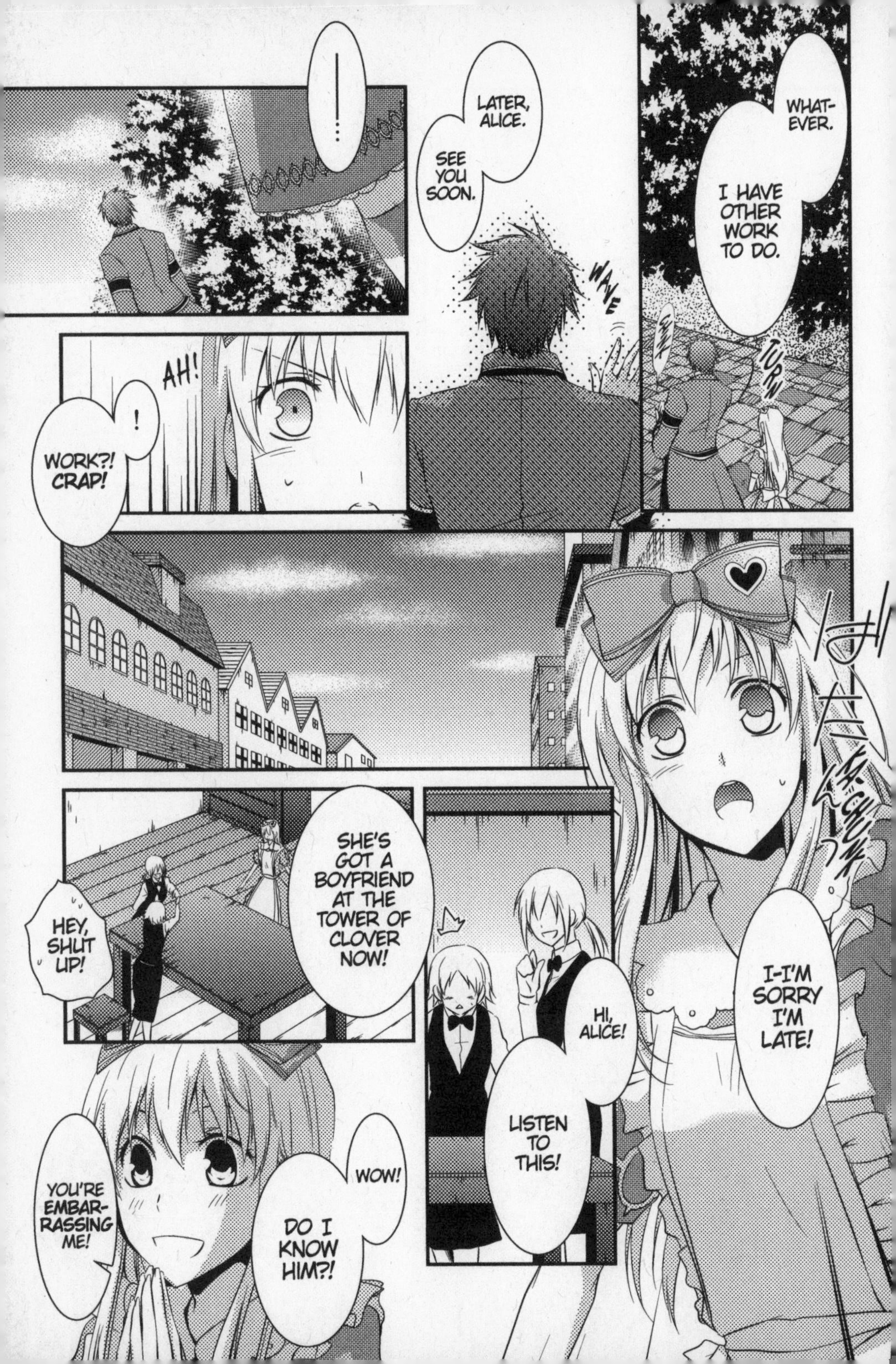

WHAT-EVER.
I HAVE OTHER WORK TO DO.
TURN
LATER, ALICE.
SEE YOU SOON.
WAVE
—......
AH!
!
WORK?! CRAP!
KA-CHUNK
I-I'M SORRY I'M LATE!
HI, ALICE!
LISTEN TO THIS!
SHE'S GOT A BOYFRIEND AT THE TOWER OF CLOVER NOW!
HEY, SHUT UP!
WOW!
DO I KNOW HIM?!
YOU'RE EMBARRASSING ME!

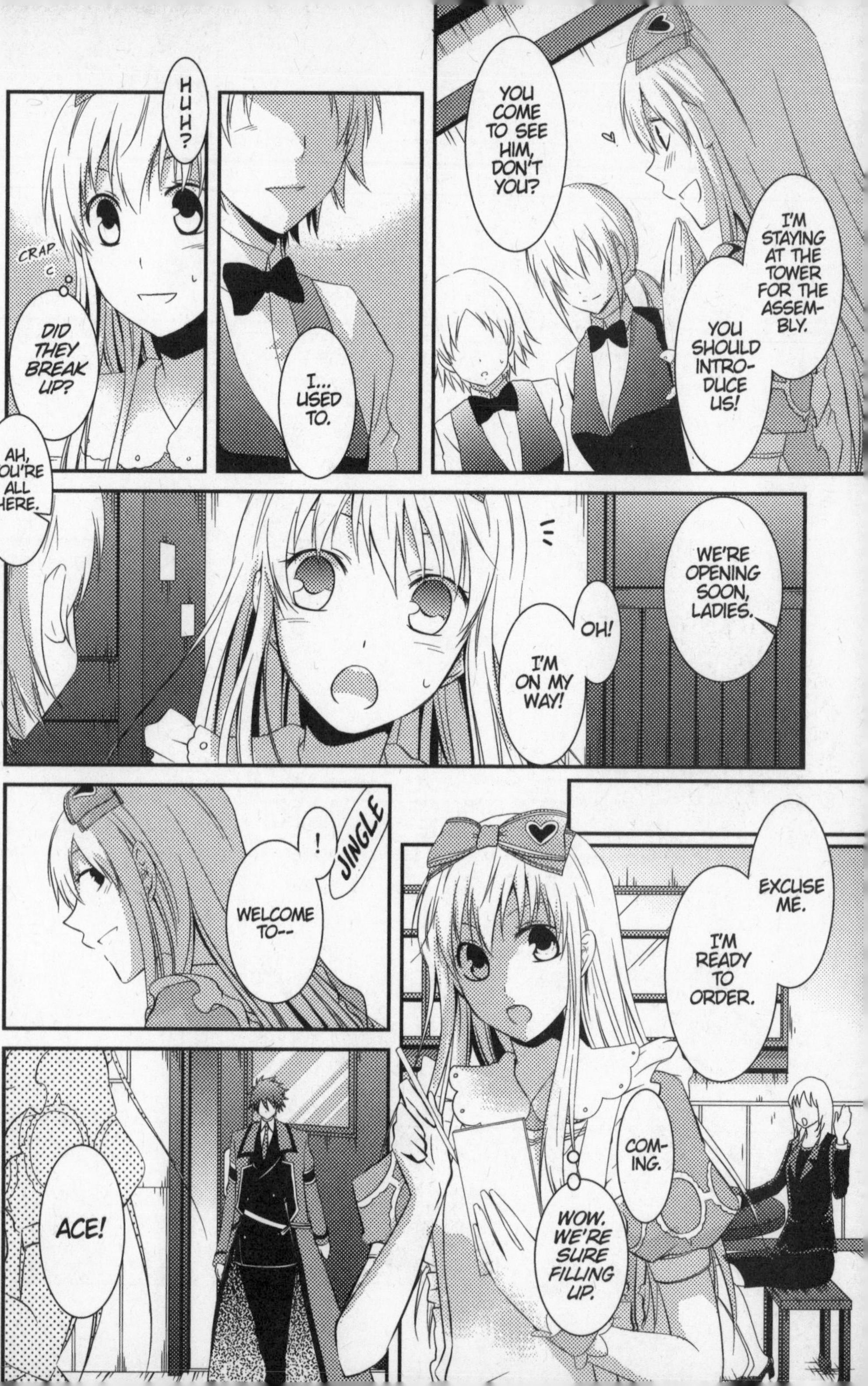
YOU COME TO SEE HIM, DON'T YOU?
I'M STAYING AT THE TOWER FOR THE ASSEMBLY.
YOU SHOULD INTRODUCE US!
HUH?
I... USED TO.
CRAP.
DID THEY BREAK UP?
WE'RE OPENING SOON, LADIES.
OH!
I'M ON MY WAY!
AH, YOU'RE ALL HERE.
EXCUSE ME.
I'M READY TO ORDER.
COMING.
WOW. WE'RE SURE FILLING UP.
JINGLE
!
WELCOME TO--
ACE!

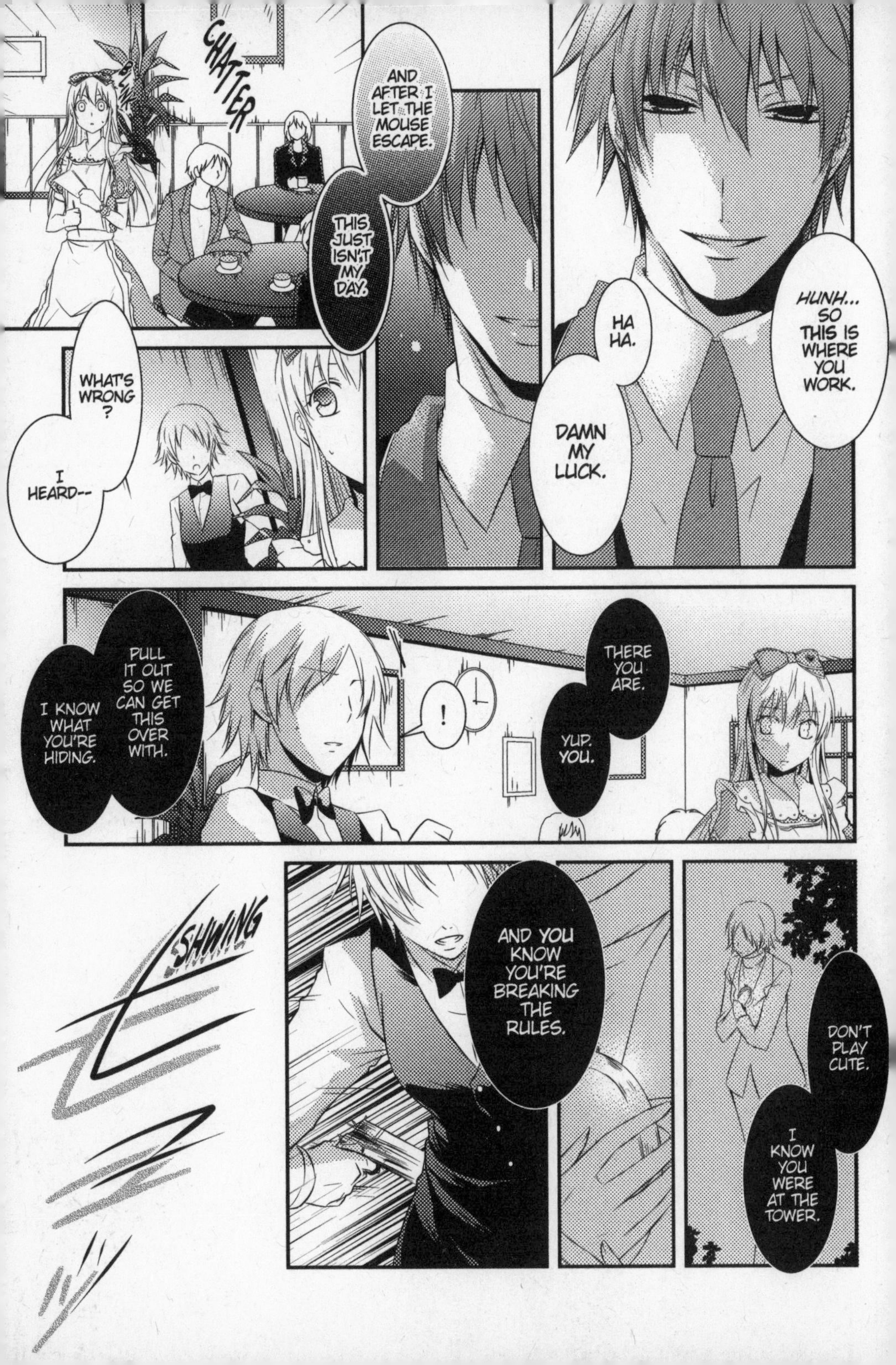
HUNH... SO THIS IS WHERE YOU WORK.
HA HA.
DAMN MY LUCK.
AND AFTER I LET THE MOUSE ESCAPE.
THIS JUST ISN'T MY DAY.
CHATTER
WHAT'S WRONG?
I HEARD--
THERE YOU ARE.
YUP. YOU.
!
PULL IT OUT SO WE CAN GET THIS OVER WITH.
I KNOW WHAT YOU'RE HIDING.
DON'T PLAY CUTE.
I KNOW YOU WERE AT THE TOWER.
AND YOU KNOW YOU'RE BREAKING THE RULES.
SHWING

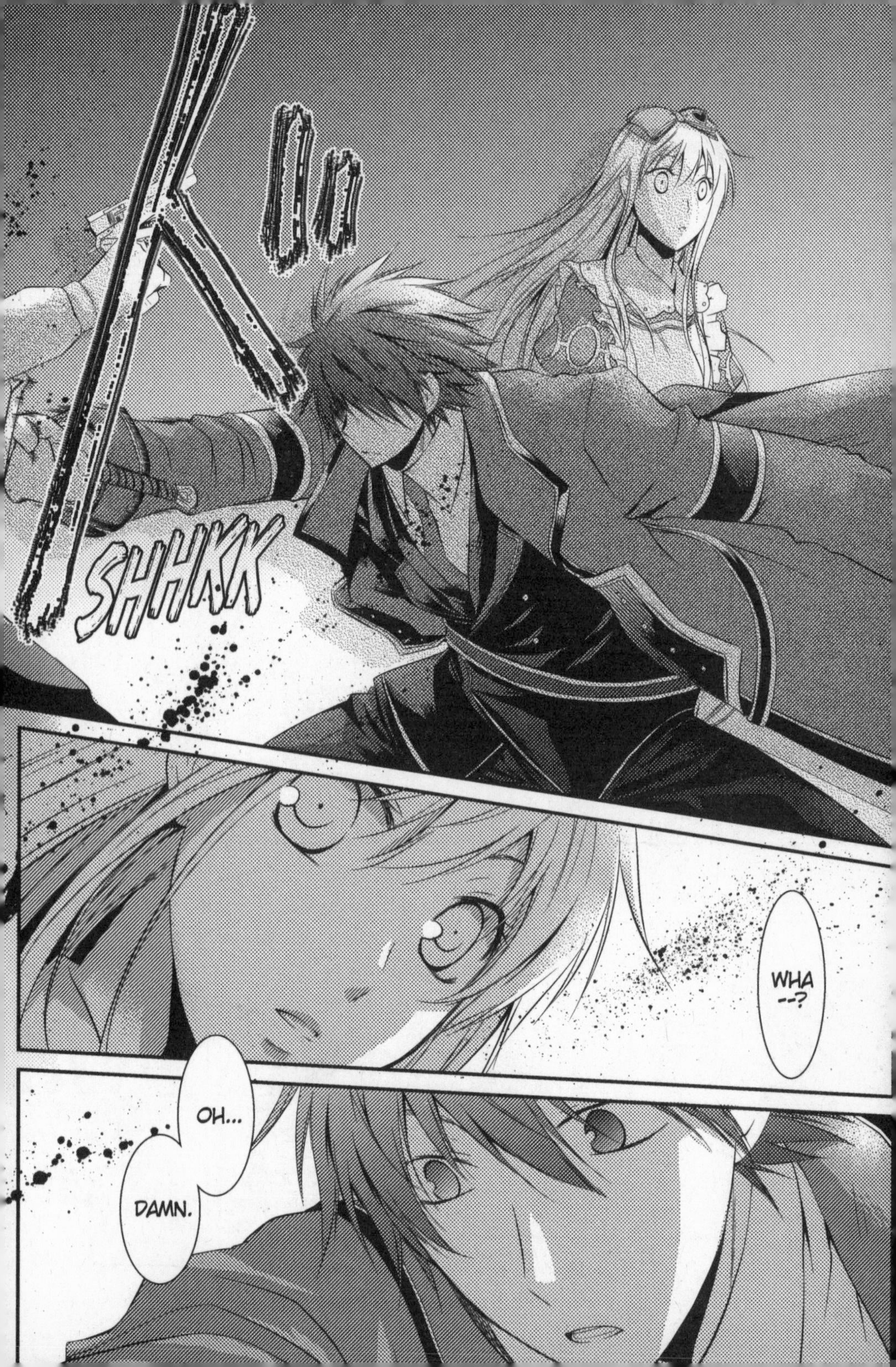
SHHKK
WHA --?
OH...
DAMN.

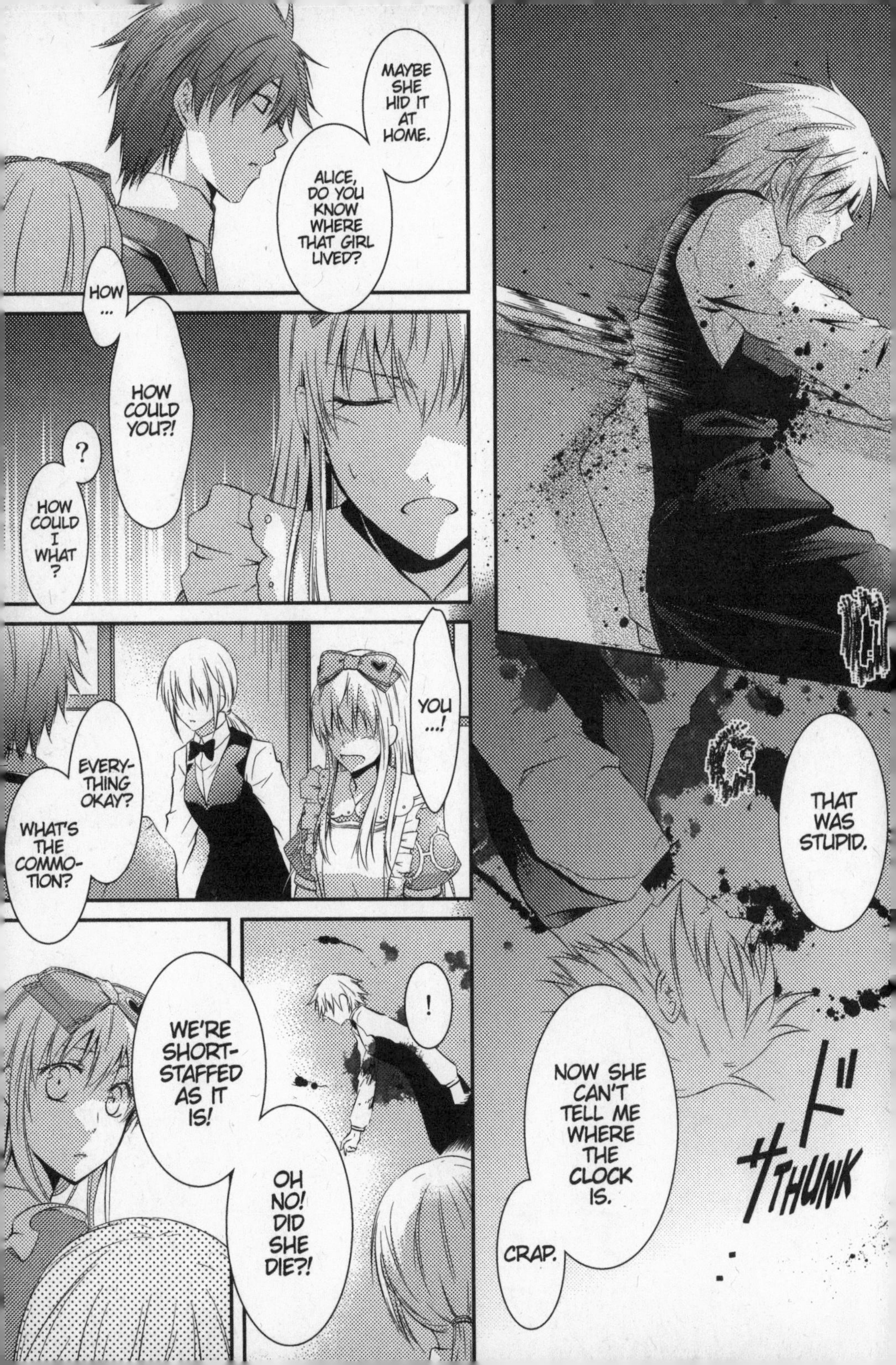

THUNK
THAT WAS STUPID.
NOW SHE CAN'T TELL ME WHERE THE CLOCK IS.
CRAP.
MAYBE SHE HID IT AT HOME.
ALICE, DO YOU KNOW WHERE THAT GIRL LIVED?
HOW ...
HOW COULD YOU?!
?
HOW COULD I WHAT?
YOU ...!
EVERY-THING OKAY?
WHAT'S THE COMMO-TION?
!
OH NO! DID SHE DIE?!
WE'RE SHORT-STAFFED AS IT IS!

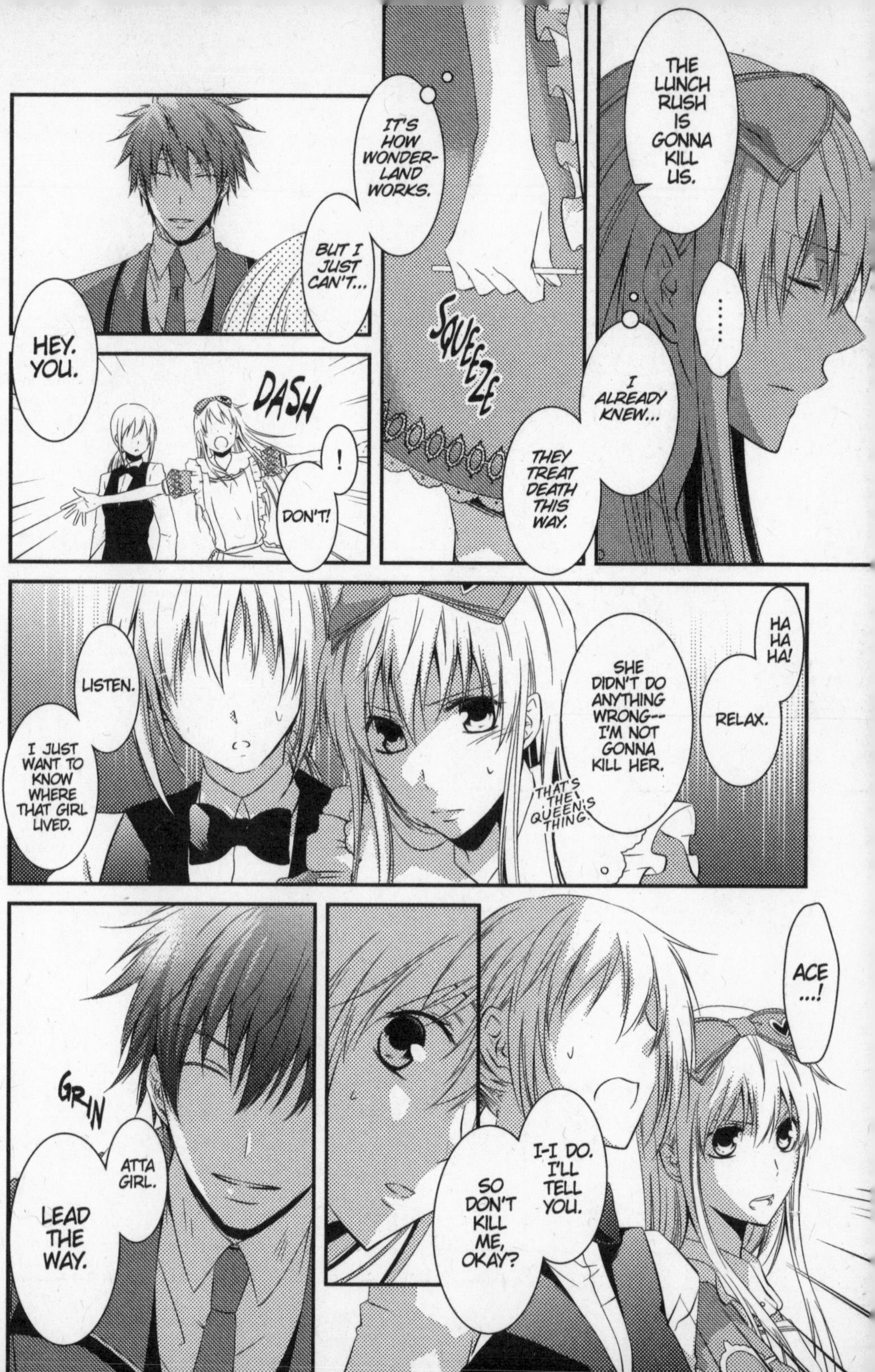
THE LUNCH RUSH IS GONNA KILL US.
......
I ALREADY KNEW...
THEY TREAT DEATH THIS WAY.
IT'S HOW WONDERLAND WORKS.
BUT I JUST CAN'T...
SQUEEZE
HEY. YOU.
DASH
!
DON'T!
HA HA HA!
RELAX.
SHE DIDN'T DO ANYTHING WRONG-- I'M NOT GONNA KILL HER.
THAT'S THE QUEEN'S THING.
LISTEN.
I JUST WANT TO KNOW WHERE THAT GIRL LIVED.
ACE ...!
I-I DO. I'LL TELL YOU.
SO DON'T KILL ME, OKAY?
GRIN
ATTA GIRL.
LEAD THE WAY.

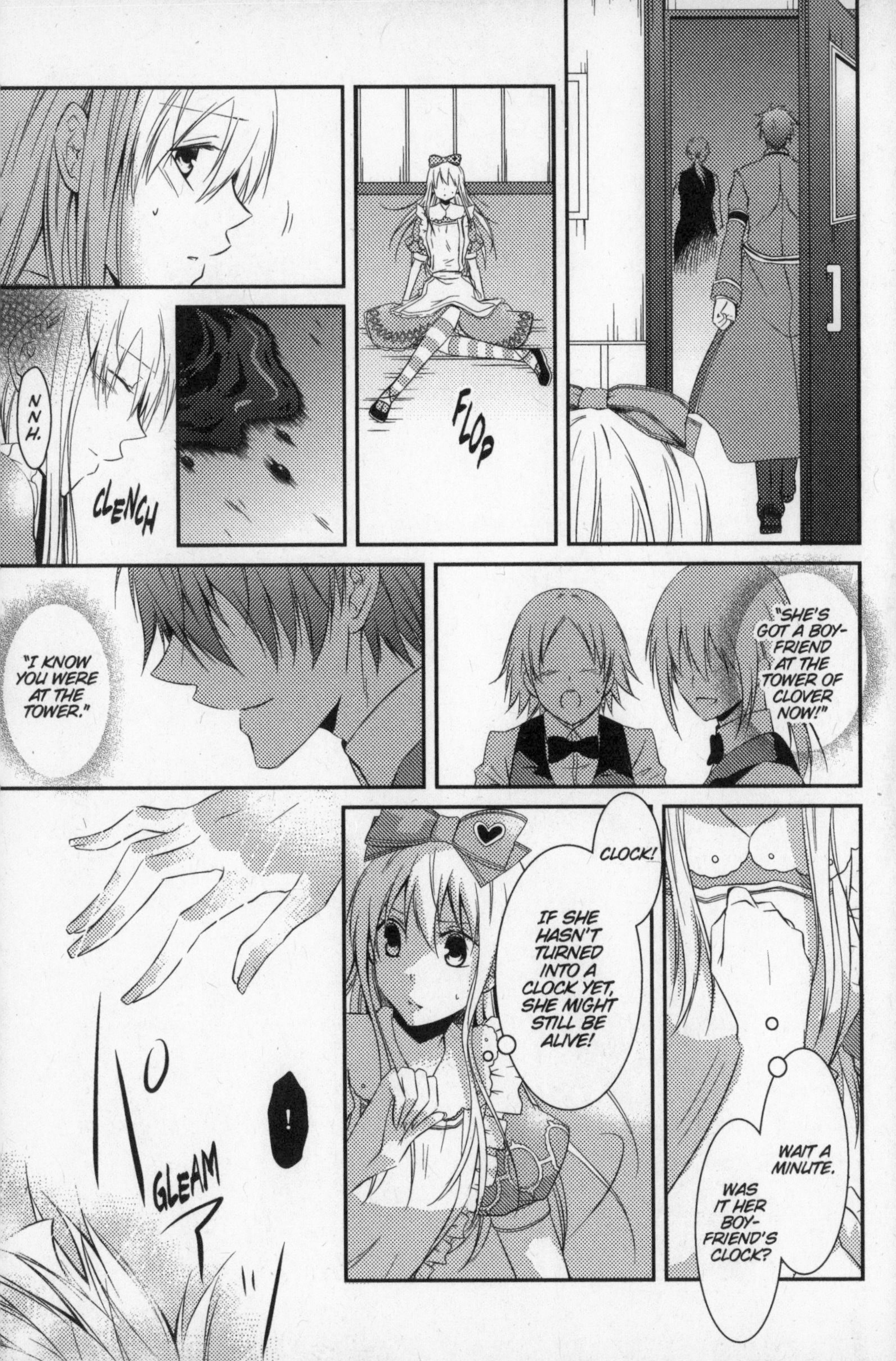
FLOP
NNH.
CLENCH
"SHE'S GOT A BOY-FRIEND AT THE TOWER OF CLOVER NOW!"
"I KNOW YOU WERE AT THE TOWER."
WAIT A MINUTE.
WAS IT HER BOY-FRIEND'S CLOCK?
CLOCK!
IF SHE HASN'T TURNED INTO A CLOCK YET, SHE MIGHT STILL BE ALIVE!
!
GLEAM

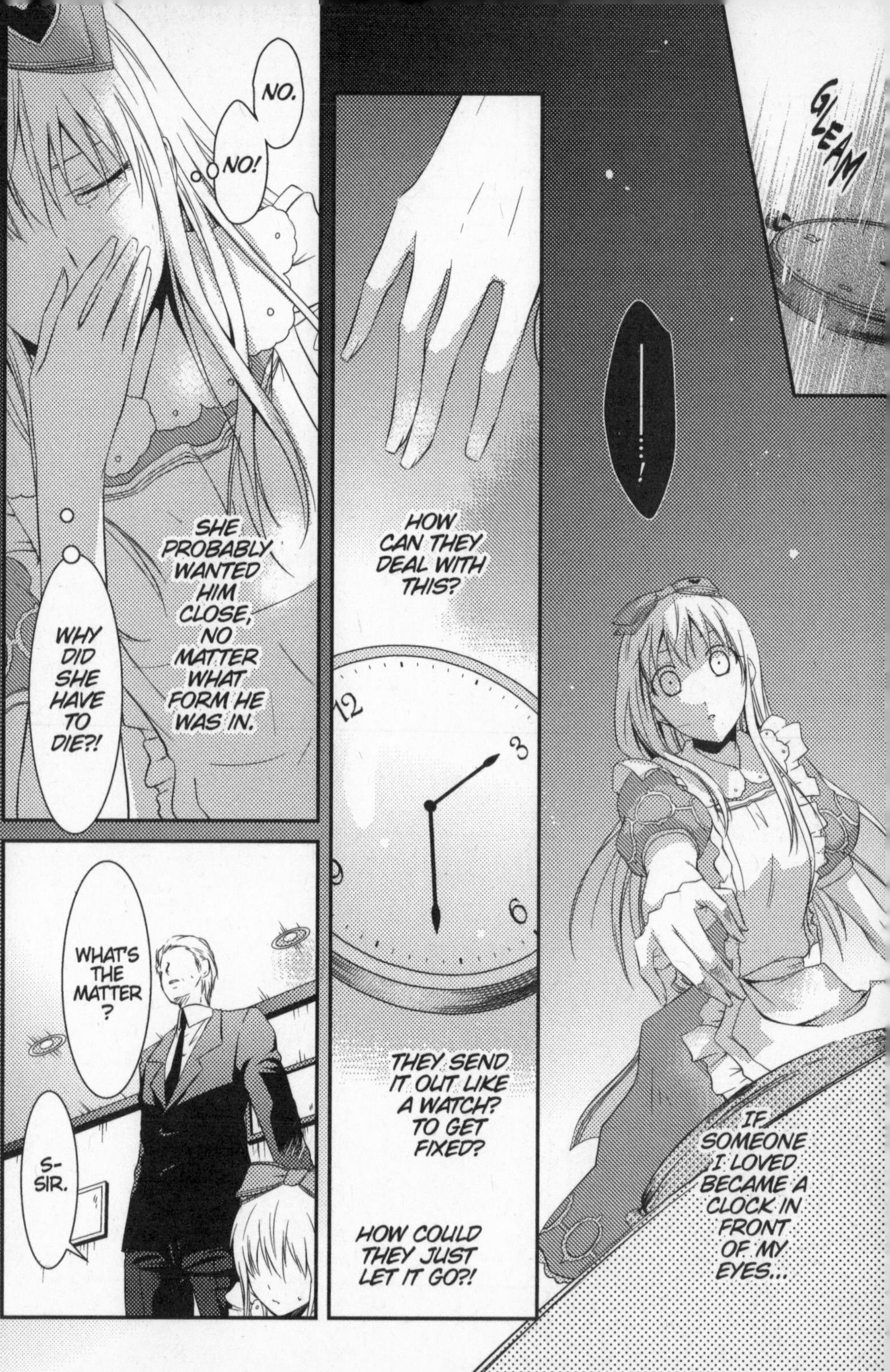
GLEAM
...!
IF SOMEONE I LOVED BECAME A CLOCK IN FRONT OF MY EYES...
HOW CAN THEY DEAL WITH THIS?
THEY SEND IT OUT LIKE A WATCH? TO GET FIXED?
HOW COULD THEY JUST LET IT GO?!
NO.
NO!
SHE PROBABLY WANTED HIM CLOSE, NO MATTER WHAT FORM HE WAS IN.
WHY DID SHE HAVE TO DIE?!
WHAT'S THE MATTER?
S-SIR.

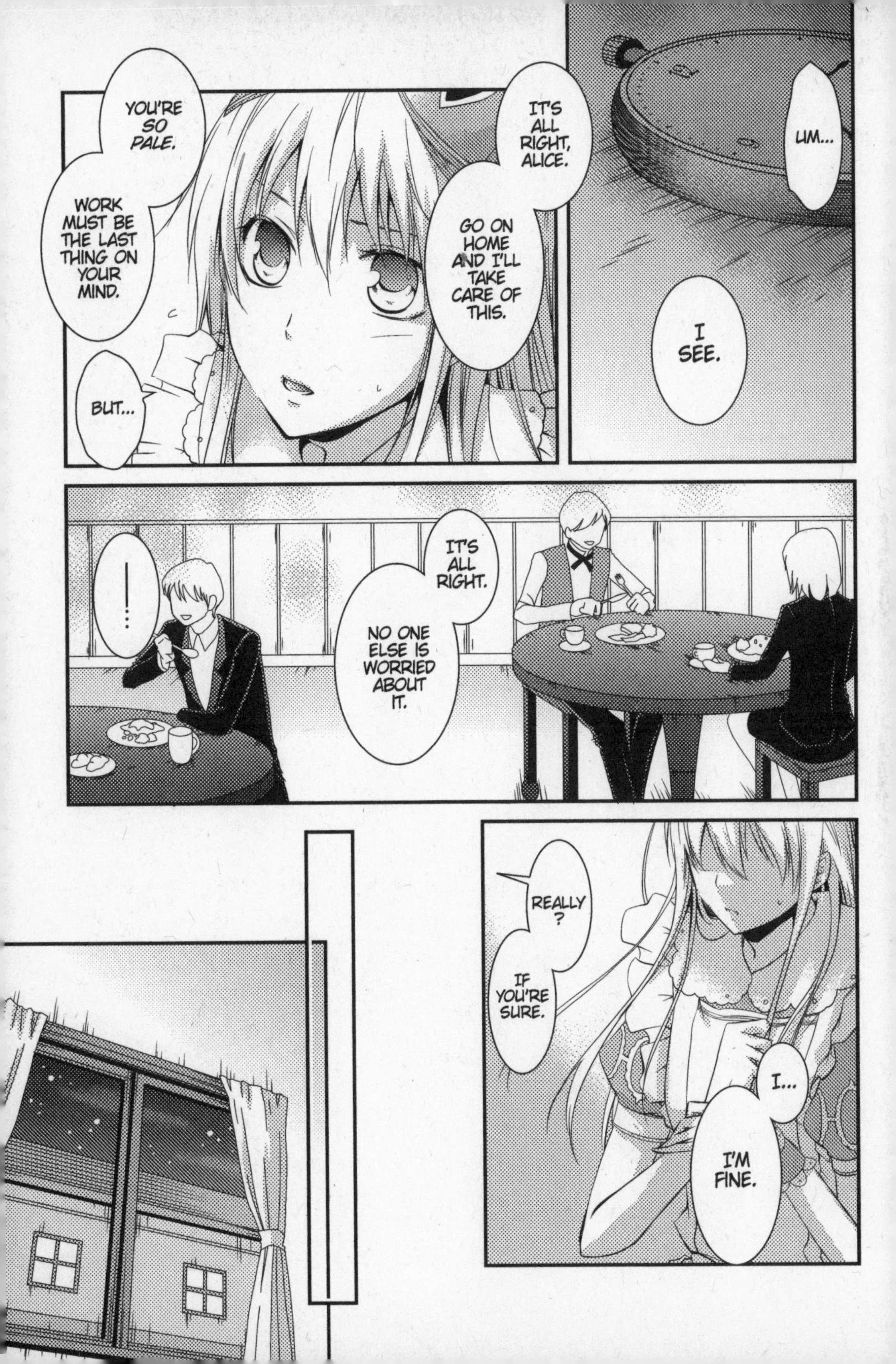
UM...
I SEE.
IT'S ALL RIGHT, ALICE.
GO ON HOME AND I'LL TAKE CARE OF THIS.
YOU'RE SO PALE.
WORK MUST BE THE LAST THING ON YOUR MIND.
BUT...
IT'S ALL RIGHT.
NO ONE ELSE IS WORRIED ABOUT IT.
!......
I...
I'M FINE.
REALLY?
IF YOU'RE SURE.

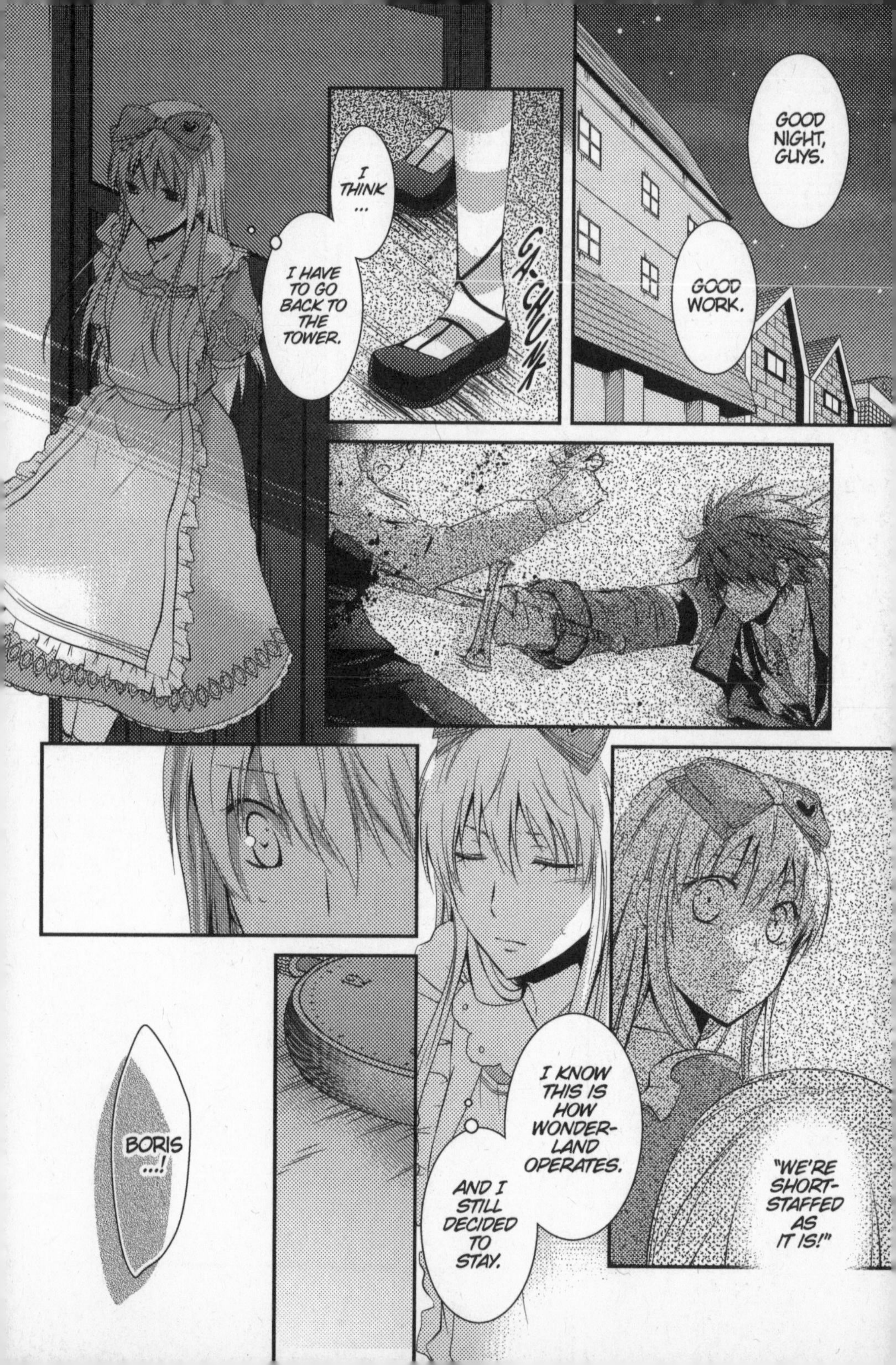
GOOD NIGHT, GUYS.
GOOD WORK.
GA-CHUNK
I THINK ...
I HAVE TO GO BACK TO THE TOWER.
"WE'RE SHORT-STAFFED AS IT IS!"
I KNOW THIS IS HOW WONDER-LAND OPERATES.
AND I STILL DECIDED TO STAY.
BORIS ...!

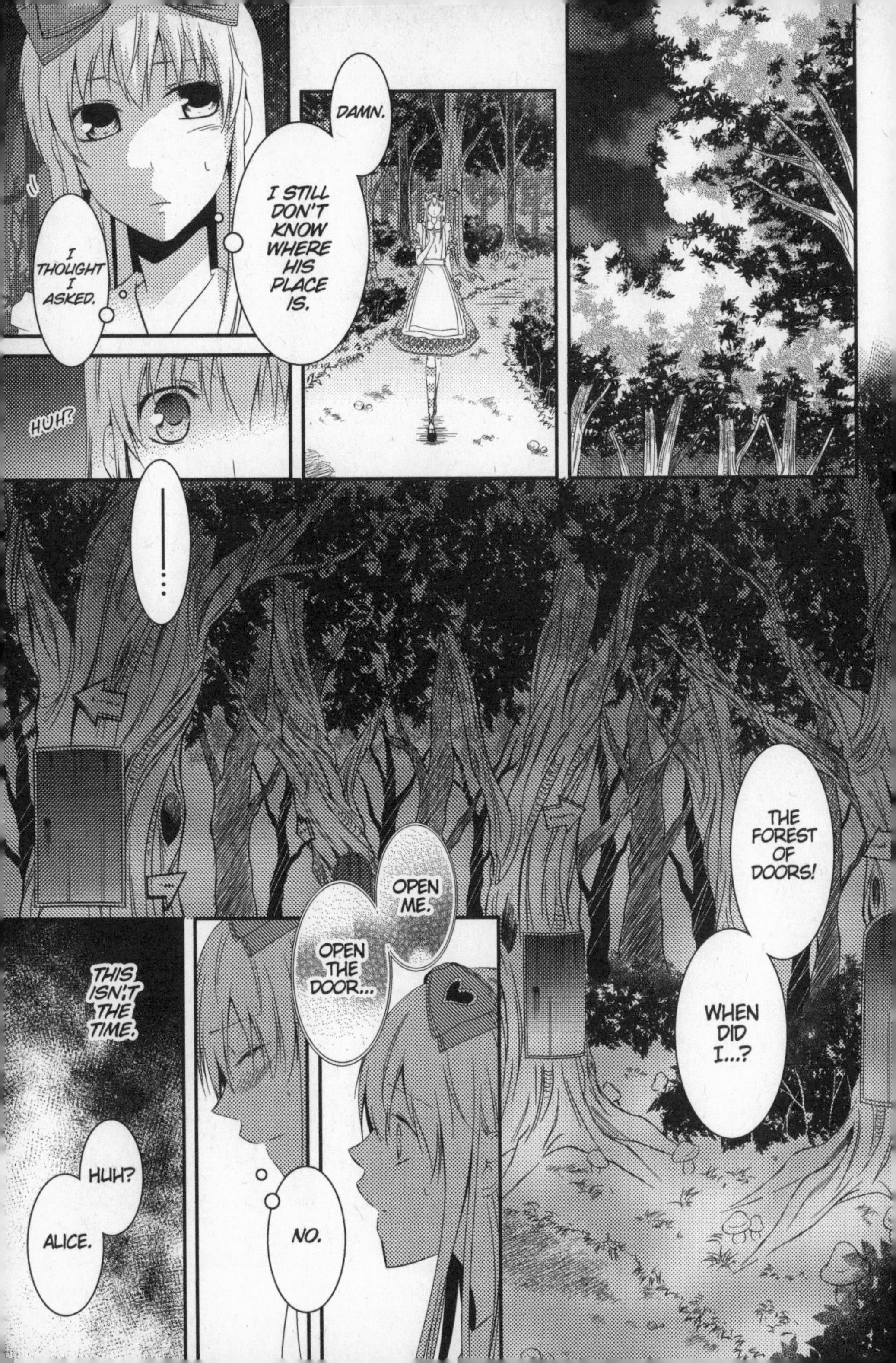
DAMN.
I STILL DON'T KNOW WHERE HIS PLACE IS.
I THOUGHT I ASKED.
HUH?
—…
THE FOREST OF DOORS!
WHEN DID I...?
OPEN ME.
OPEN THE DOOR...
NO.
THIS ISN'T THE TIME.
HUH?
ALICE.

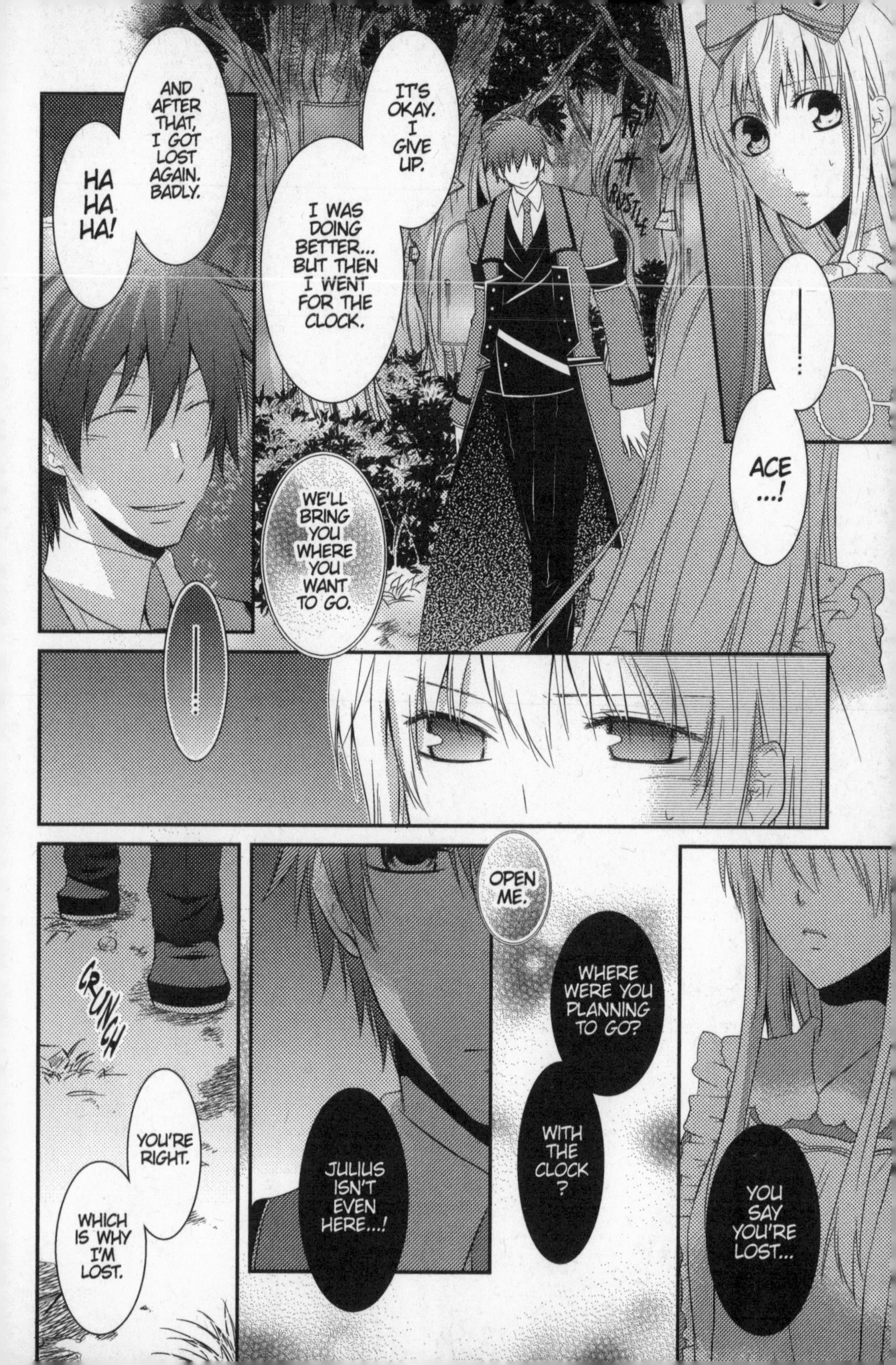
…!
ACE …!
IT'S OKAY. I GIVE UP.
I WAS DOING BETTER… BUT THEN I WENT FOR THE CLOCK.
RUSTLE
WE'LL BRING YOU WHERE YOU WANT TO GO.
AND AFTER THAT, I GOT LOST AGAIN. BADLY.
HA HA HA!
…!
YOU SAY YOU'RE LOST…
OPEN ME.
WHERE WERE YOU PLANNING TO GO?
WITH THE CLOCK?
JULIUS ISN'T EVEN HERE…!
CRUNCH
YOU'RE RIGHT.
WHICH IS WHY I'M LOST.

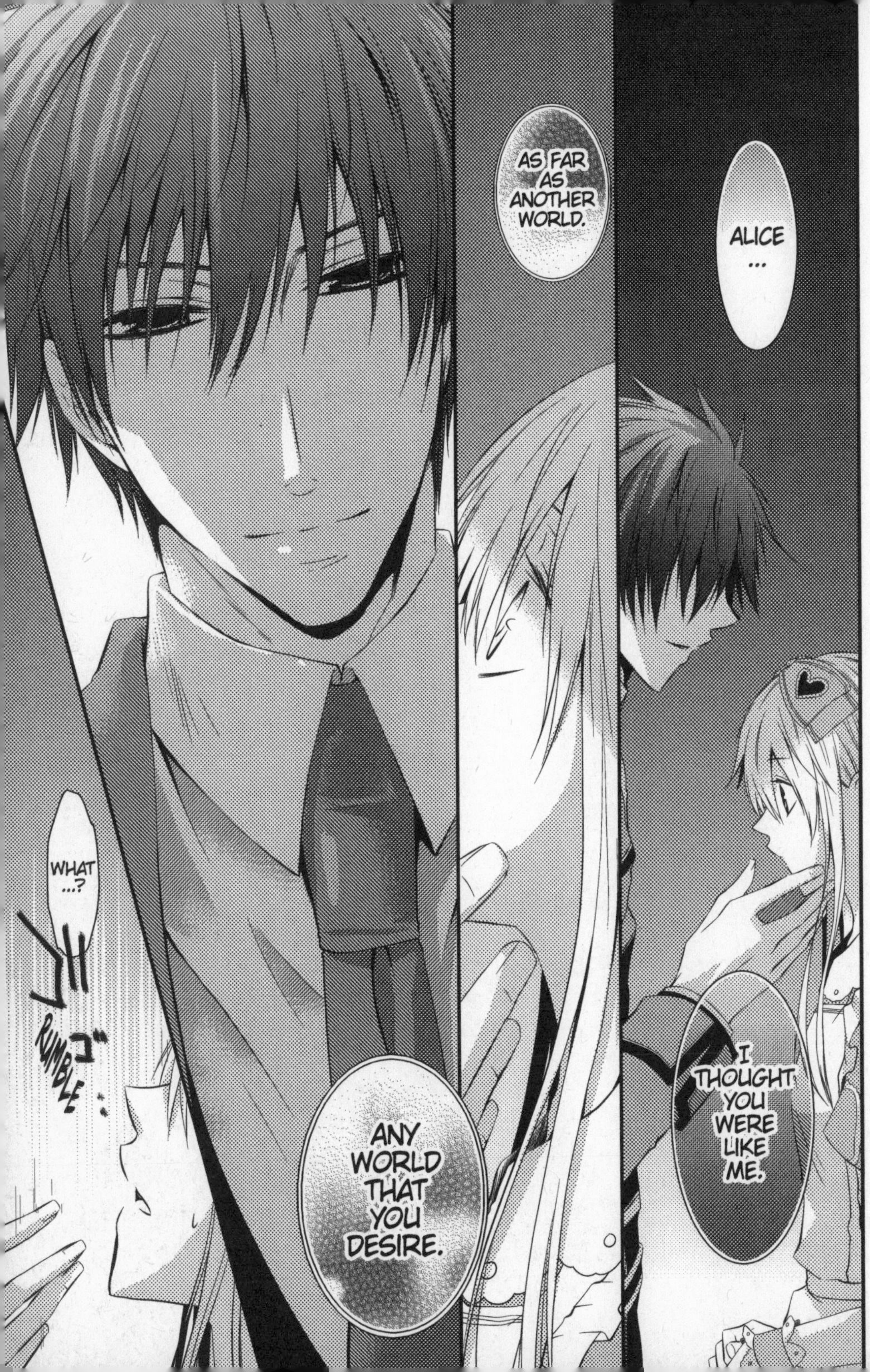
ALICE ...
I THOUGHT YOU WERE LIKE ME.
AS FAR AS ANOTHER WORLD.
ANY WORLD THAT YOU DESIRE.
WHAT ...?
RUMBLE

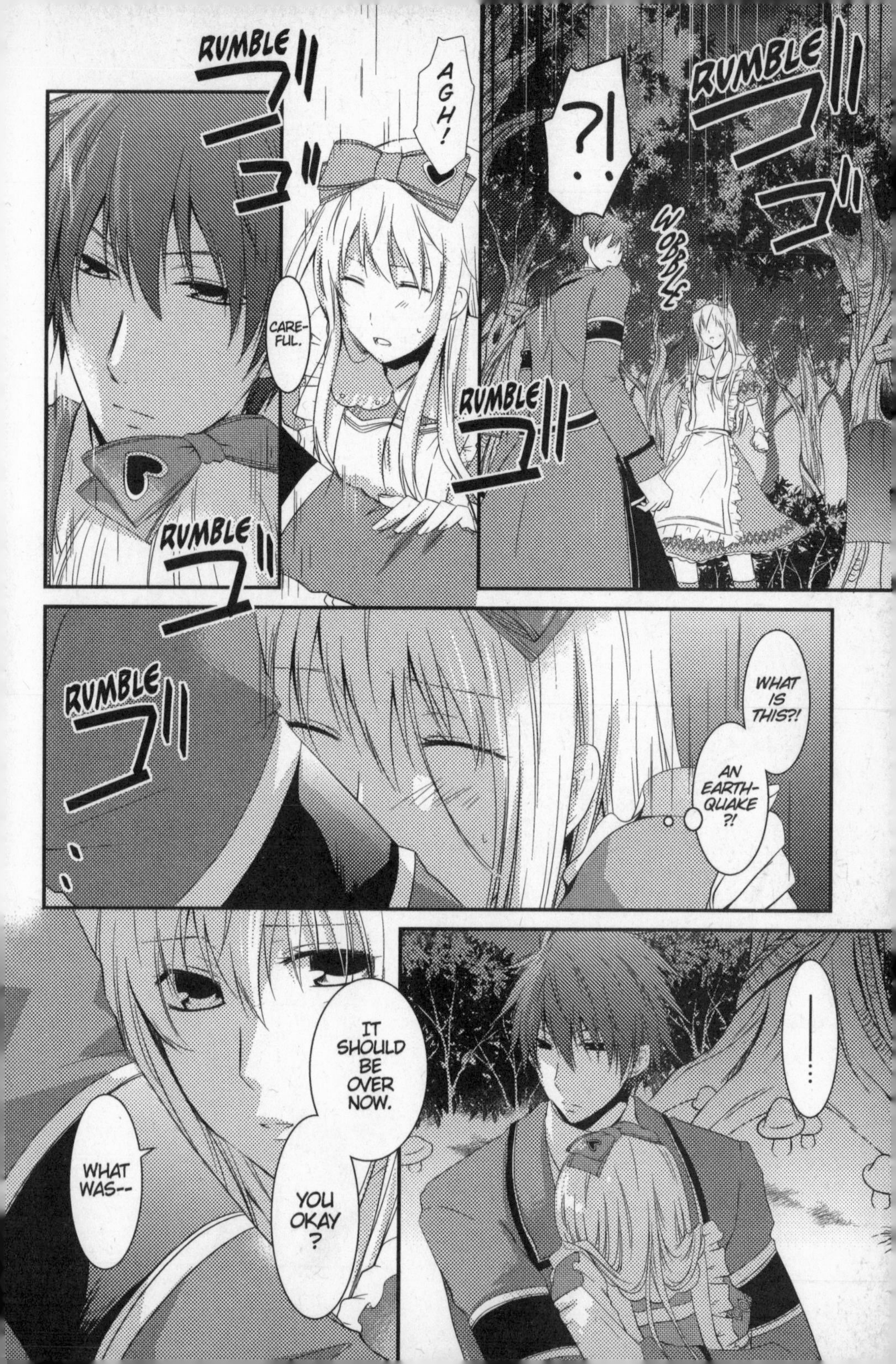
RUMBLE
?!
WOBBLE
RUMBLE
AGH!
CARE-FUL.
RUMBLE
RUMBLE
WHAT IS THIS?!
AN EARTH-QUAKE?!
RUMBLE
—...
IT SHOULD BE OVER NOW.
YOU OKAY?
WHAT WAS--

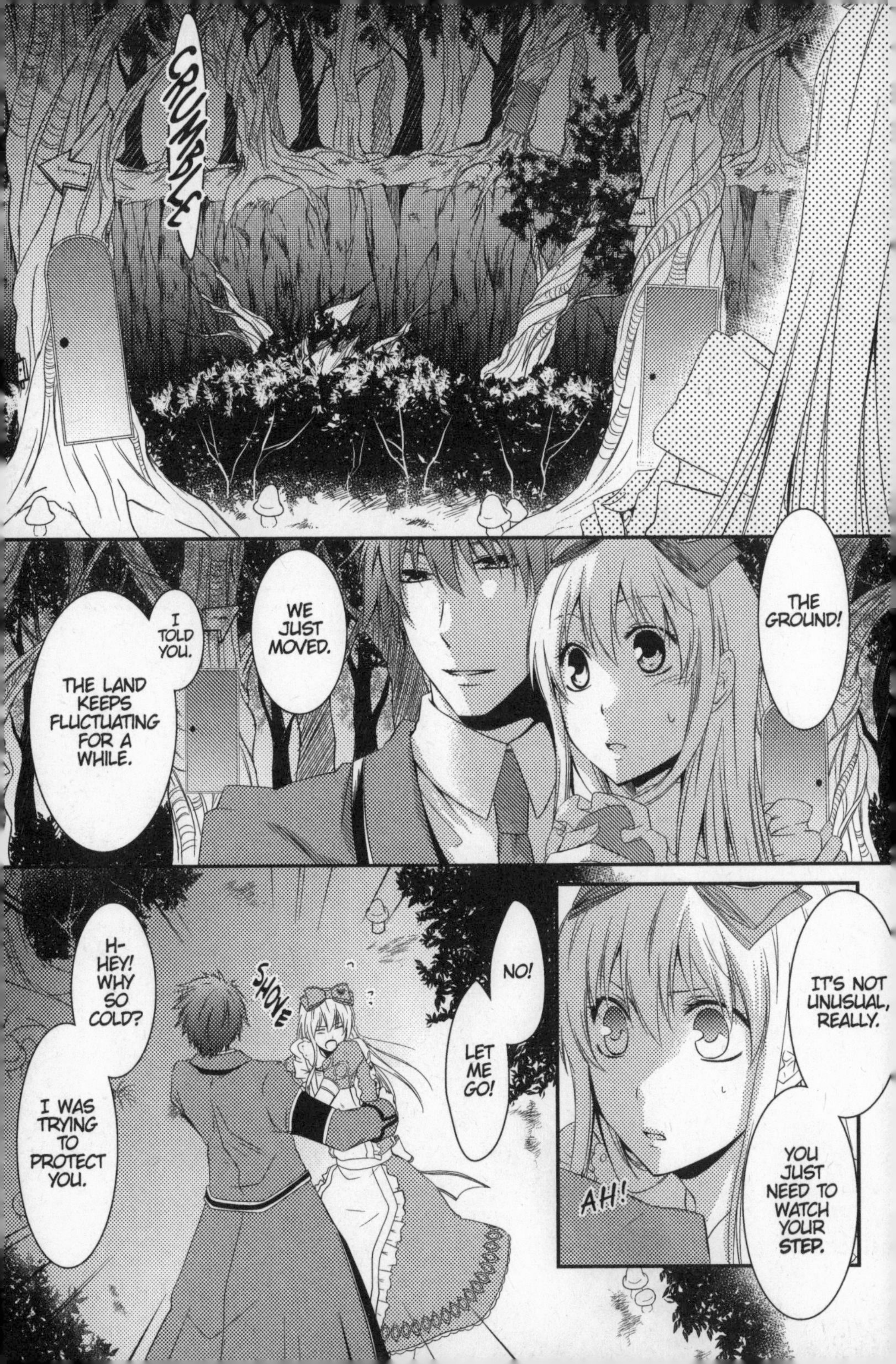
CRUMBLE
THE GROUND!
WE JUST MOVED.
I TOLD YOU.
THE LAND KEEPS FLUCTUATING FOR A WHILE.
IT'S NOT UNUSUAL, REALLY.
YOU JUST NEED TO WATCH YOUR STEP.
AH!
NO!
LET ME GO!
SHOVE
H-HEY! WHY SO COLD?
I WAS TRYING TO PROTECT YOU.

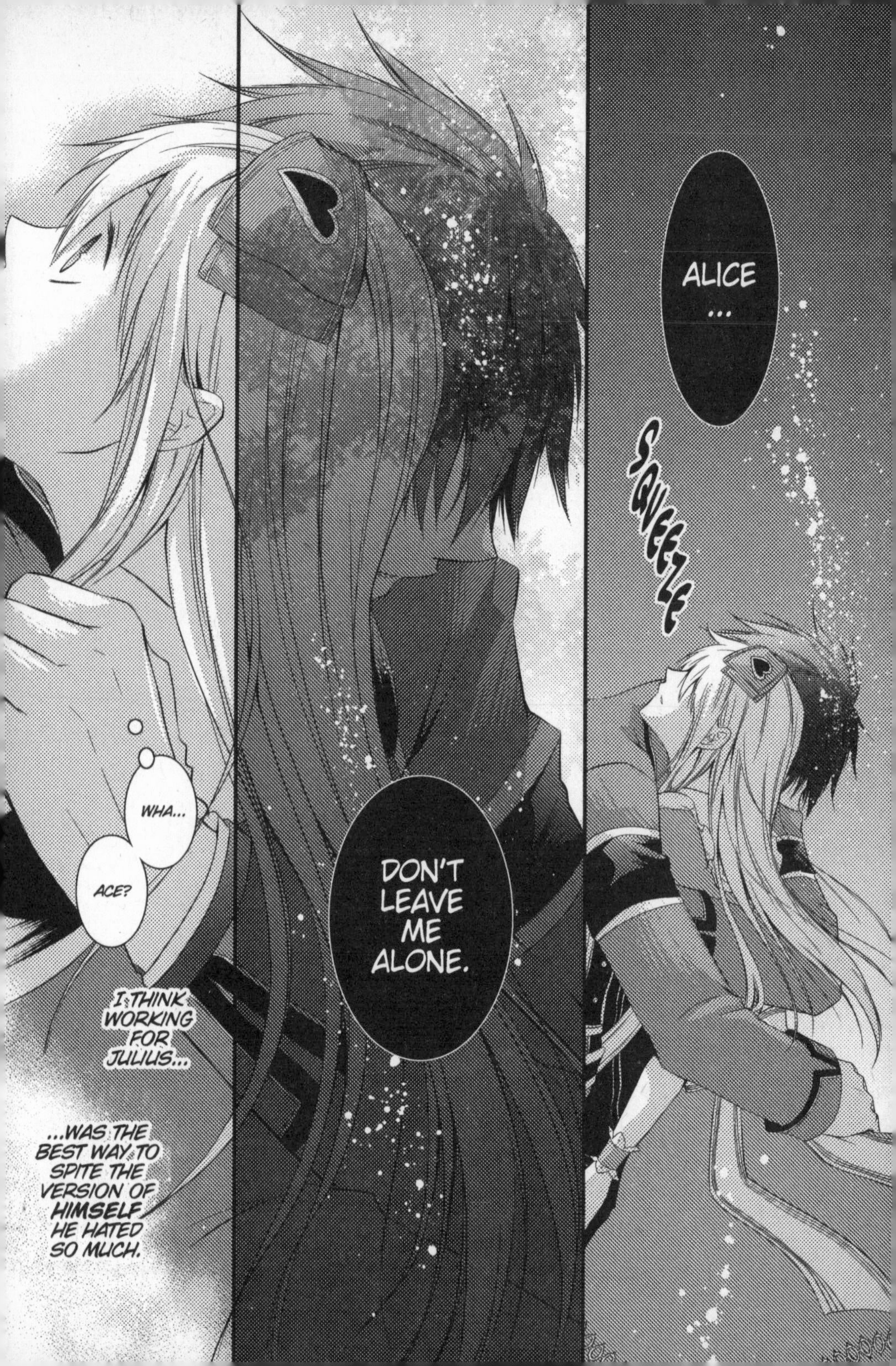
ALICE ...
SQUEEZE
DON'T LEAVE ME ALONE.
WHA...
ACE?
I THINK WORKING FOR JULIUS...
...WAS THE BEST WAY TO SPITE THE VERSION OF HIMSELF HE HATED SO MUCH.

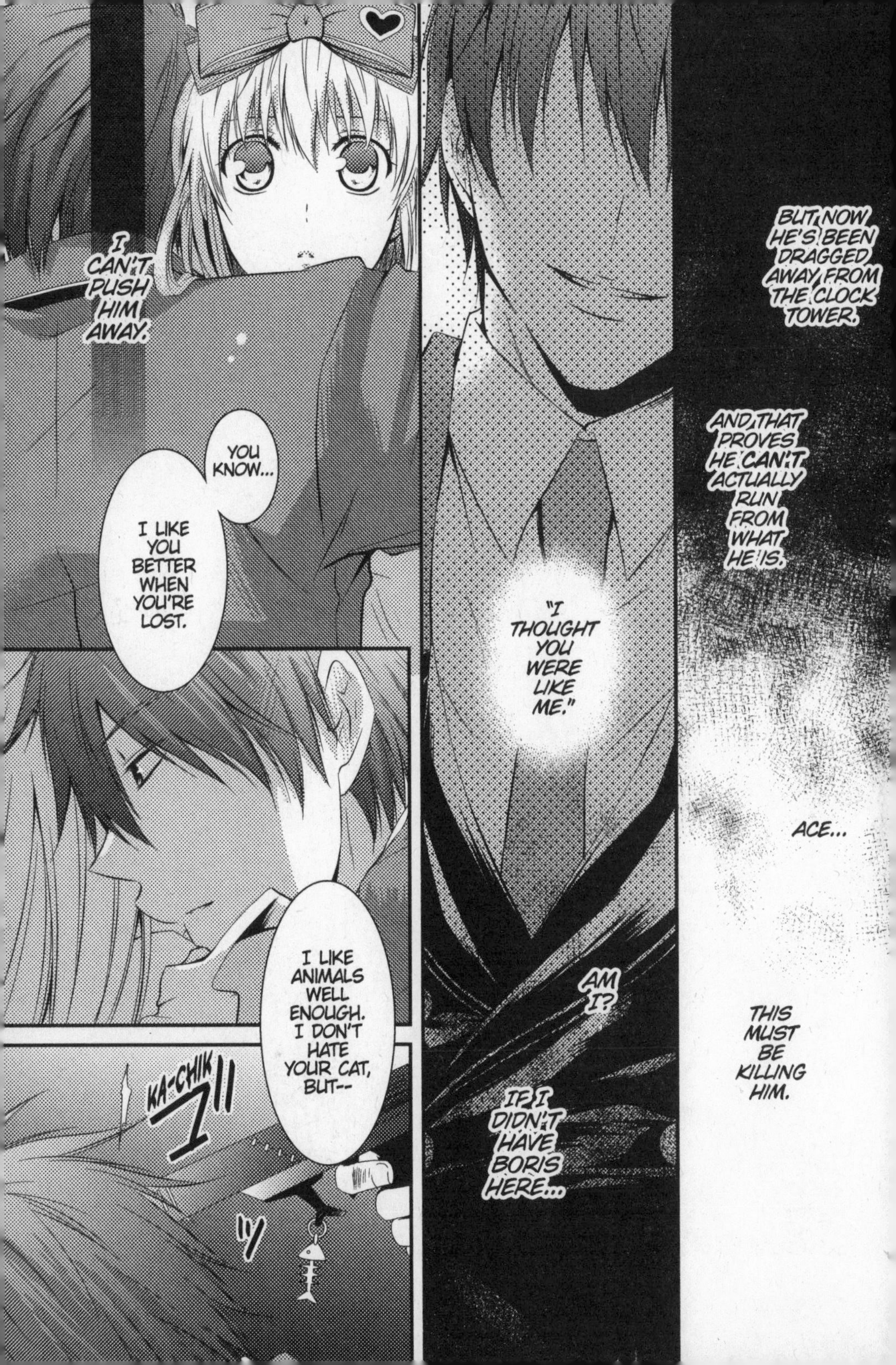
BUT NOW HE'S BEEN DRAGGED AWAY FROM THE CLOCK TOWER.
AND THAT PROVES HE CAN'T ACTUALLY RUN FROM WHAT HE IS.
"I THOUGHT YOU WERE LIKE ME."
ACE...
THIS MUST BE KILLING HIM.
AM I?
IF I DIDN'T HAVE BORIS HERE...
I CAN'T PUSH HIM AWAY.
YOU KNOW...
I LIKE YOU BETTER WHEN YOU'RE LOST.
I LIKE ANIMALS WELL ENOUGH. I DON'T HATE YOUR CAT, BUT--
KA-CHIK

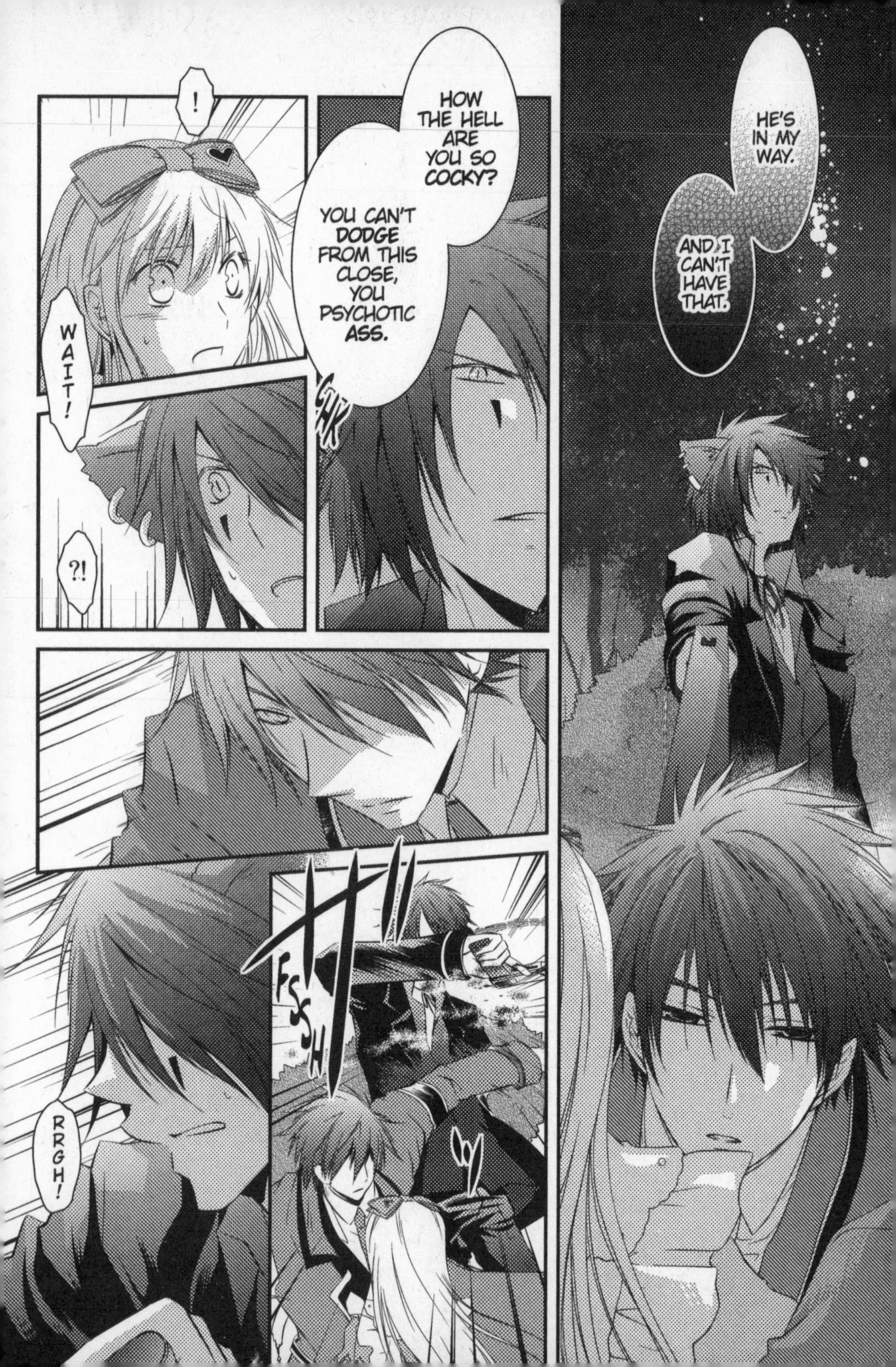
HE'S IN MY WAY.
AND I CAN'T HAVE THAT.
HOW THE HELL ARE YOU SO COCKY?
YOU CAN'T DODGE FROM THIS CLOSE, YOU PSYCHOTIC ASS.
SHK
!
WAIT!
?!
FSSH
RRGH!

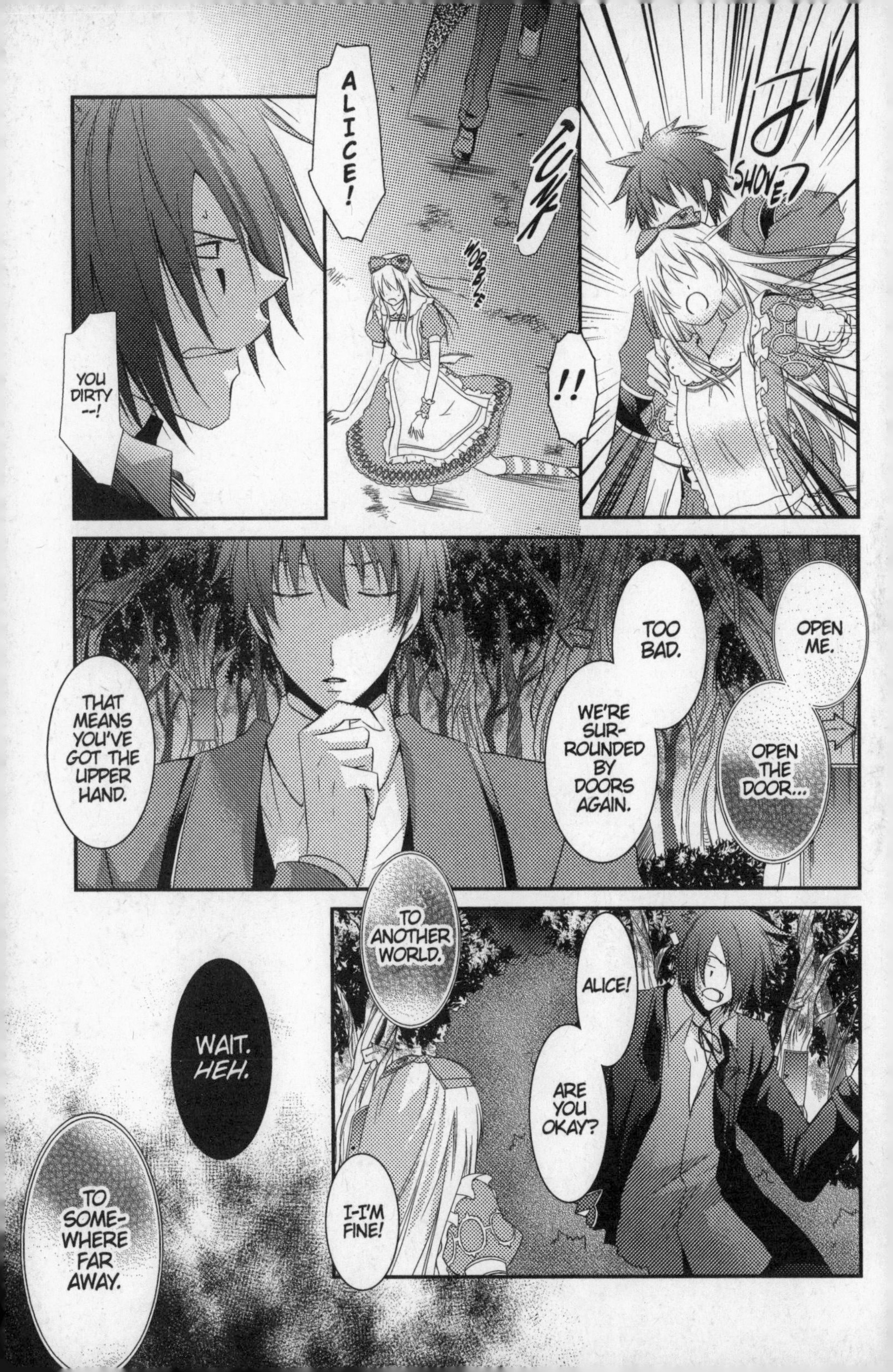

SHOVE
!!
ALICE!
TUNK
WOBBLE
YOU DIRTY --!
OPEN ME.
OPEN THE DOOR...
TOO BAD.
WE'RE SUR-ROUNDED BY DOORS AGAIN.
THAT MEANS YOU'VE GOT THE UPPER HAND.
TO ANOTHER WORLD.
ALICE!
ARE YOU OKAY?
I-I'M FINE!
WAIT. *HEH.*
TO SOME-WHERE FAR AWAY.

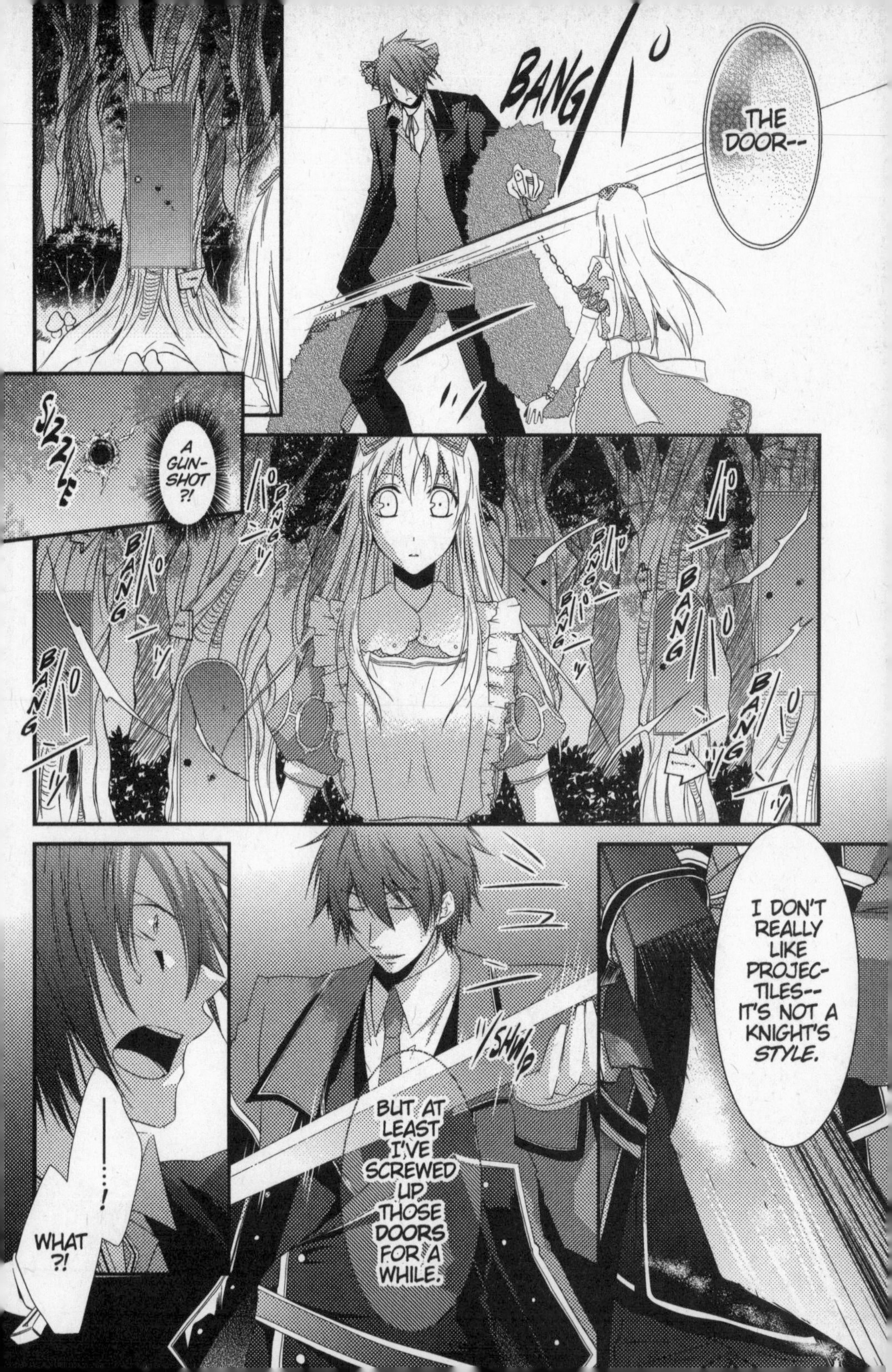

BANG
THE DOOR--
SIZZLE
A GUN-SHOT?!
BANG
BANG
BANG
BANG
BANG
BANG
BANG
BANG
I DON'T REALLY LIKE PROJEC-TILES-- IT'S NOT A KNIGHT'S *STYLE*.
SHWIP
BUT AT LEAST I'VE SCREWED UP THOSE DOORS FOR A WHILE.
......!
WHAT?!

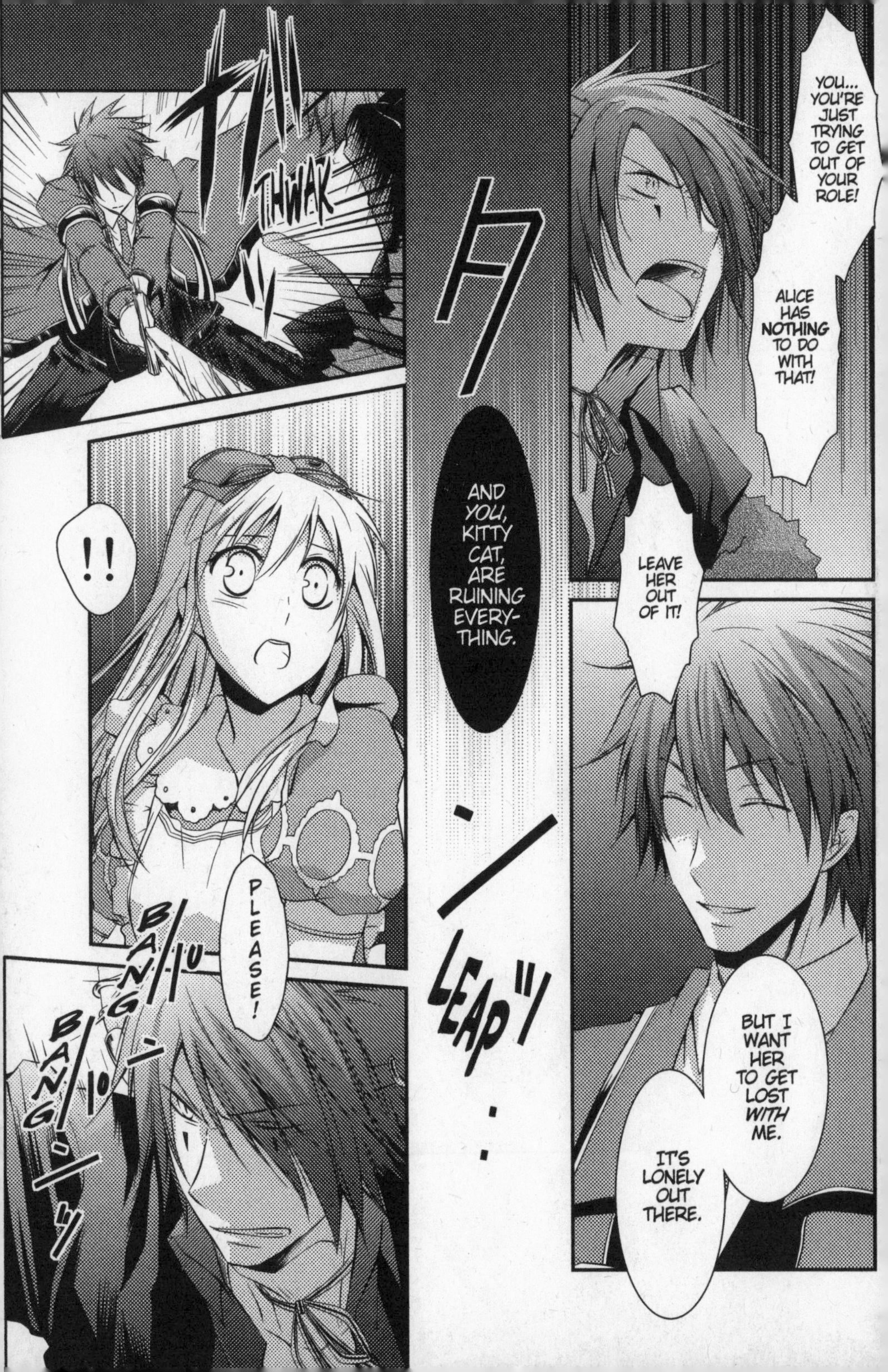
YOU... YOU'RE JUST TRYING TO GET OUT OF YOUR ROLE!
ALICE HAS NOTHING TO DO WITH THAT!
LEAVE HER OUT OF IT!
BUT I WANT HER TO GET LOST WITH ME.
IT'S LONELY OUT THERE.
AND YOU, KITTY CAT, ARE RUINING EVERYTHING.
LEAP
THWAK
!!
PLEASE!
BANG
BANG

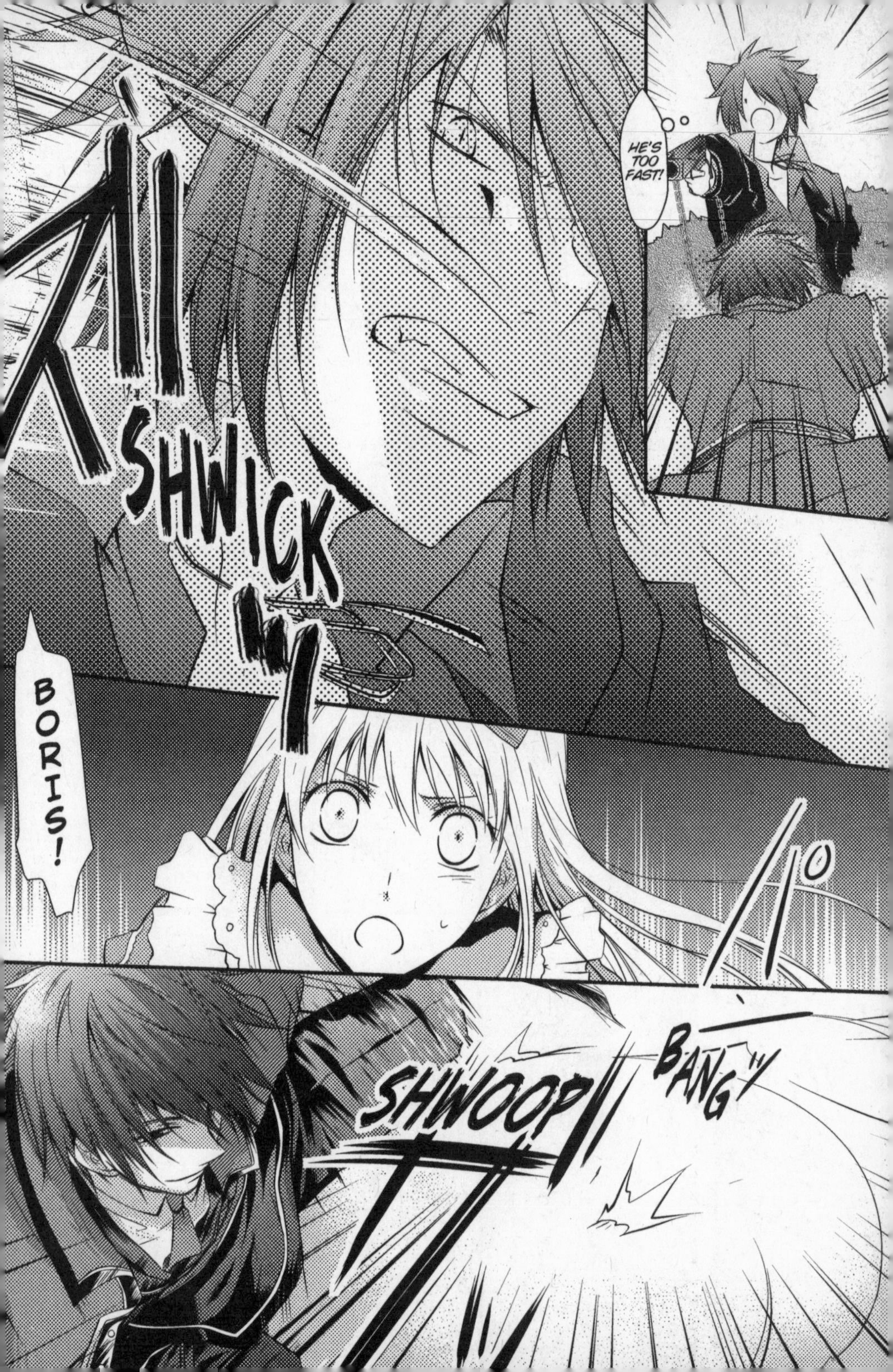
HE'S TOO FAST!
SHWICK
BORIS!
BANG
SHWOOP

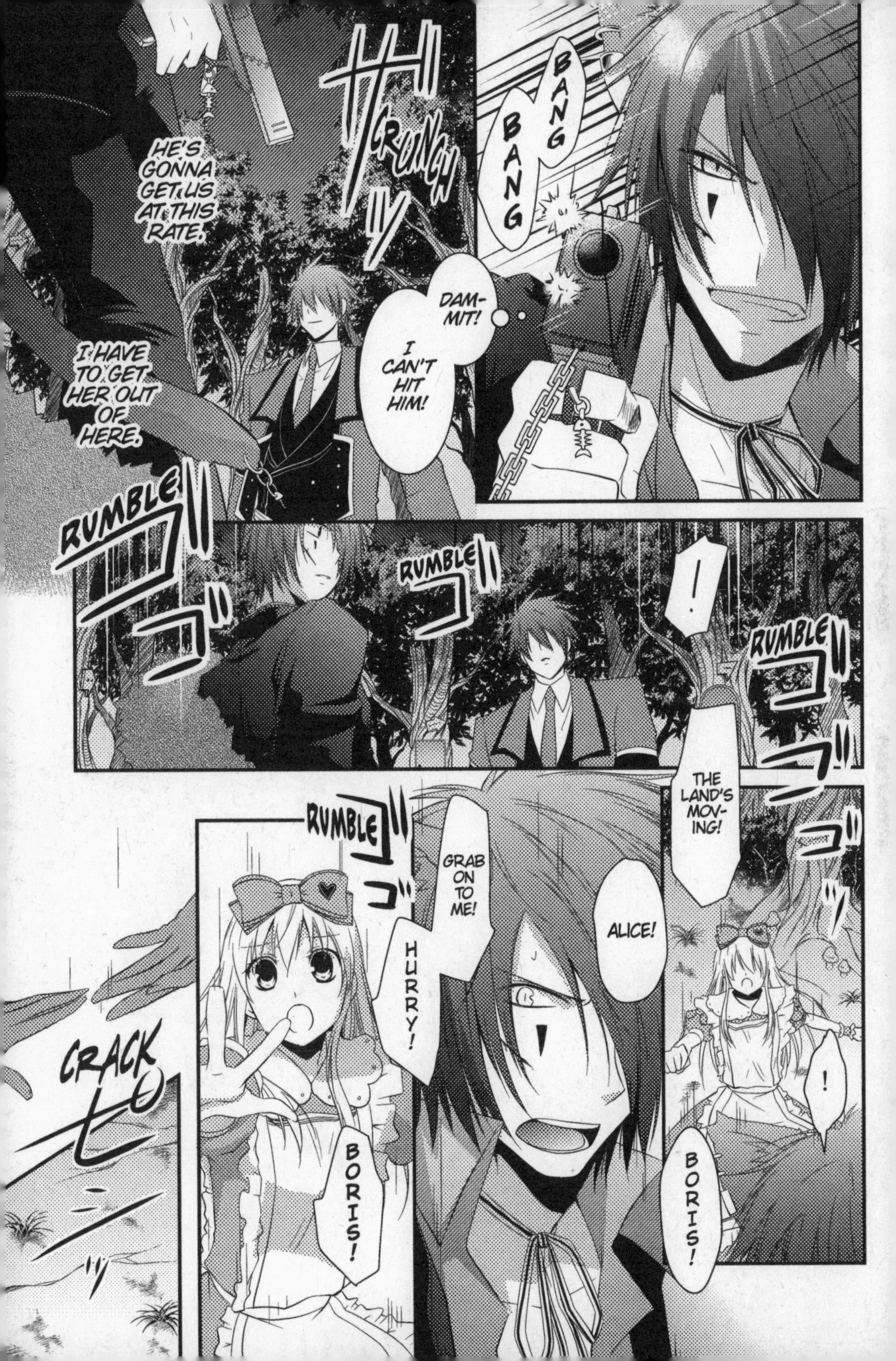

BANG
BANG
BANG
DAM-MIT!
I CAN'T HIT HIM!
CRUNCH
HE'S GONNA GET US AT THIS RATE.
I HAVE TO GET HER OUT OF HERE.
!
RUMBLE
RUMBLE
RUMBLE
THE LAND'S MOV-ING!
!
BORIS!
ALICE!
GRAB ON TO ME!
HURRY!
RUMBLE
CRACK
BORIS!

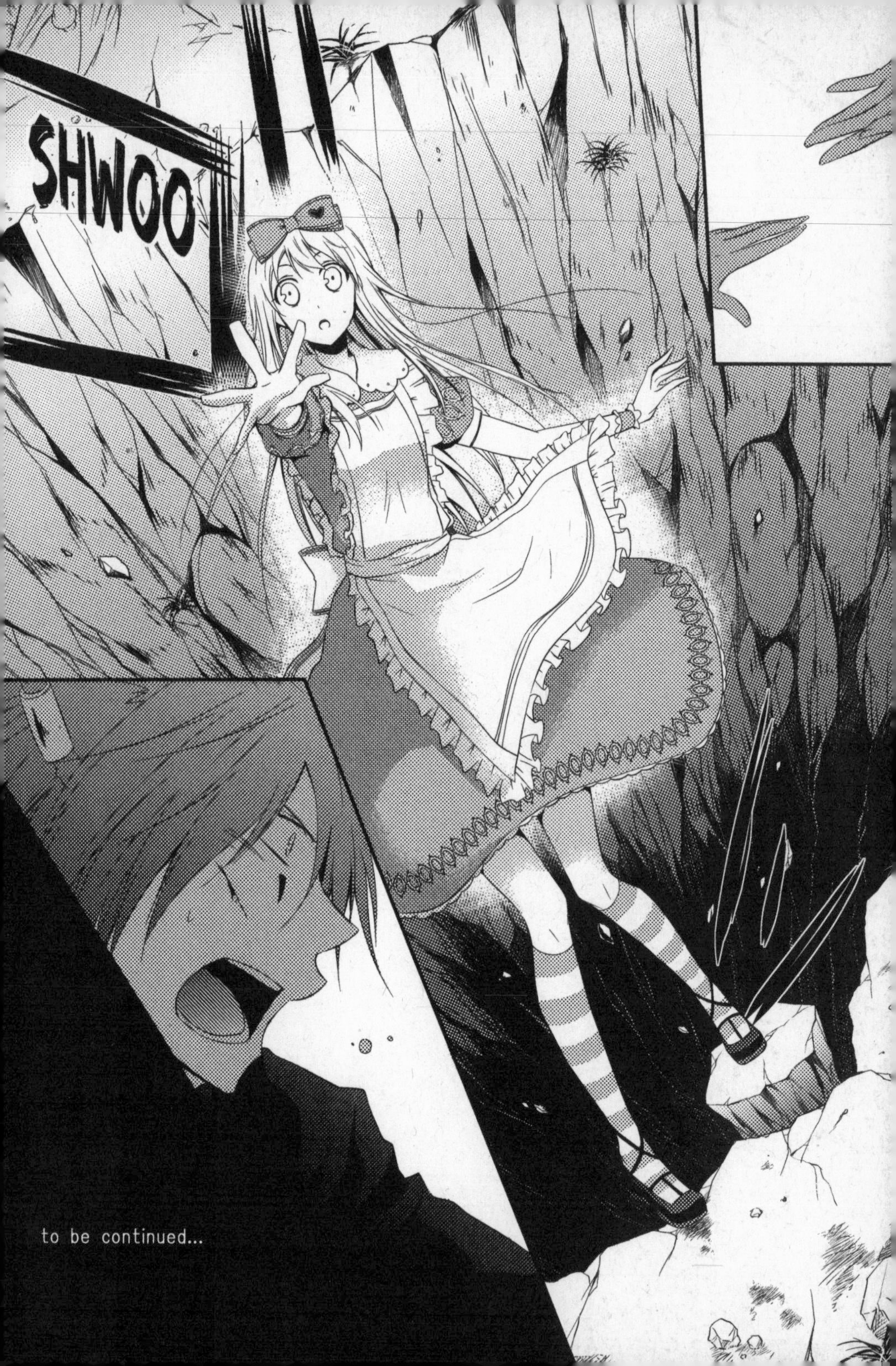
SHWOO
to be continued...

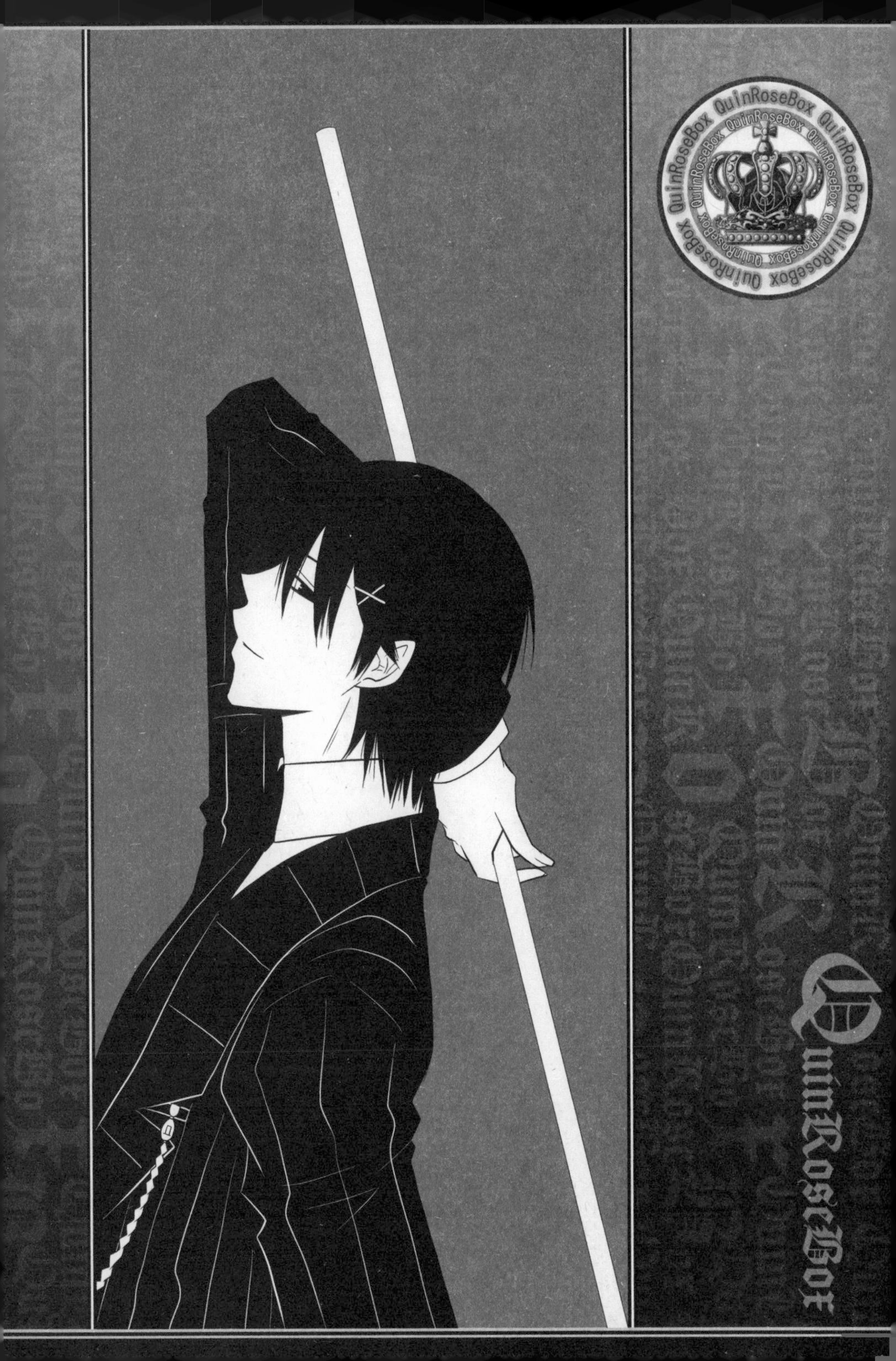
QuinRoseBox
QuinRoseBox

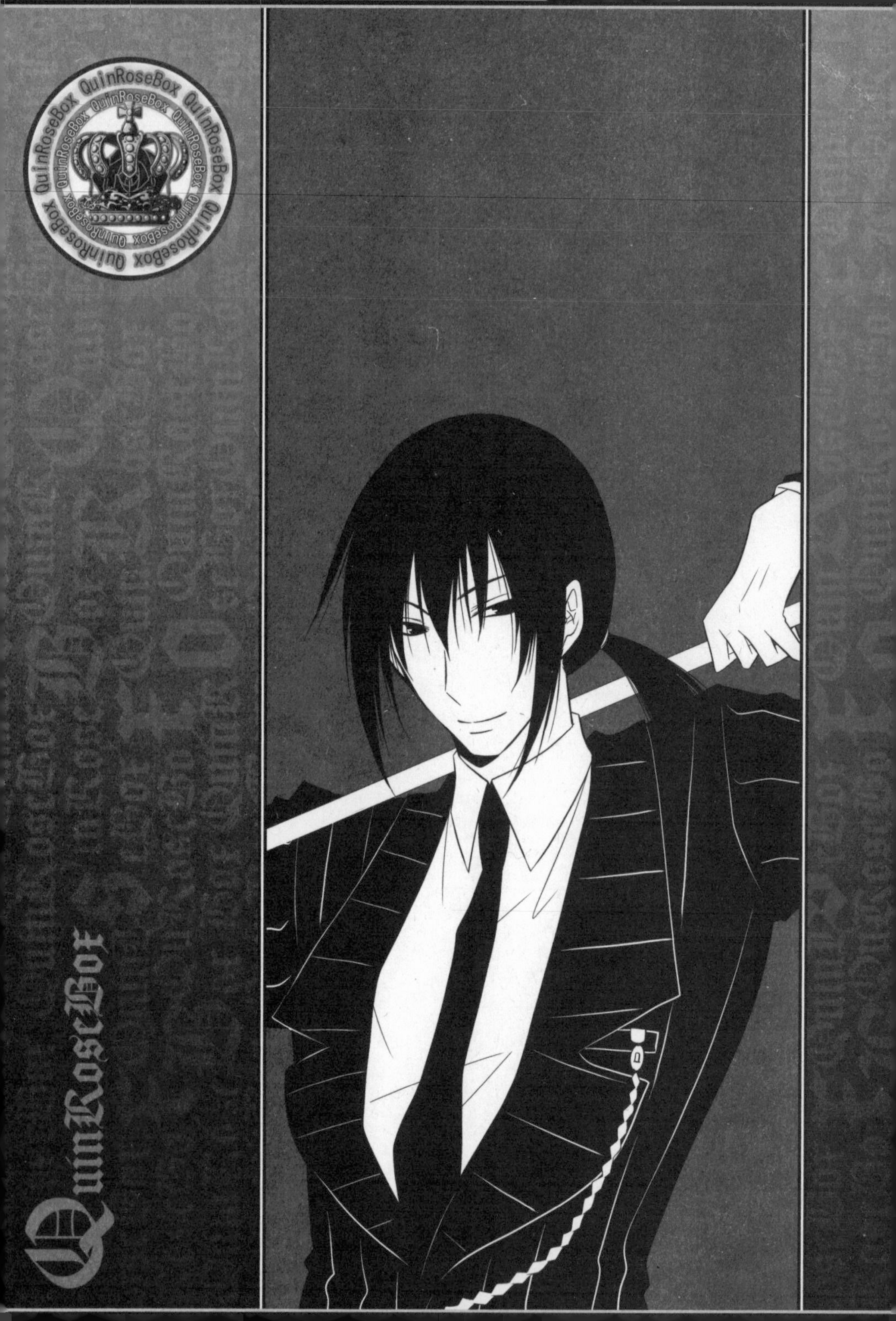
QuinRoseBox

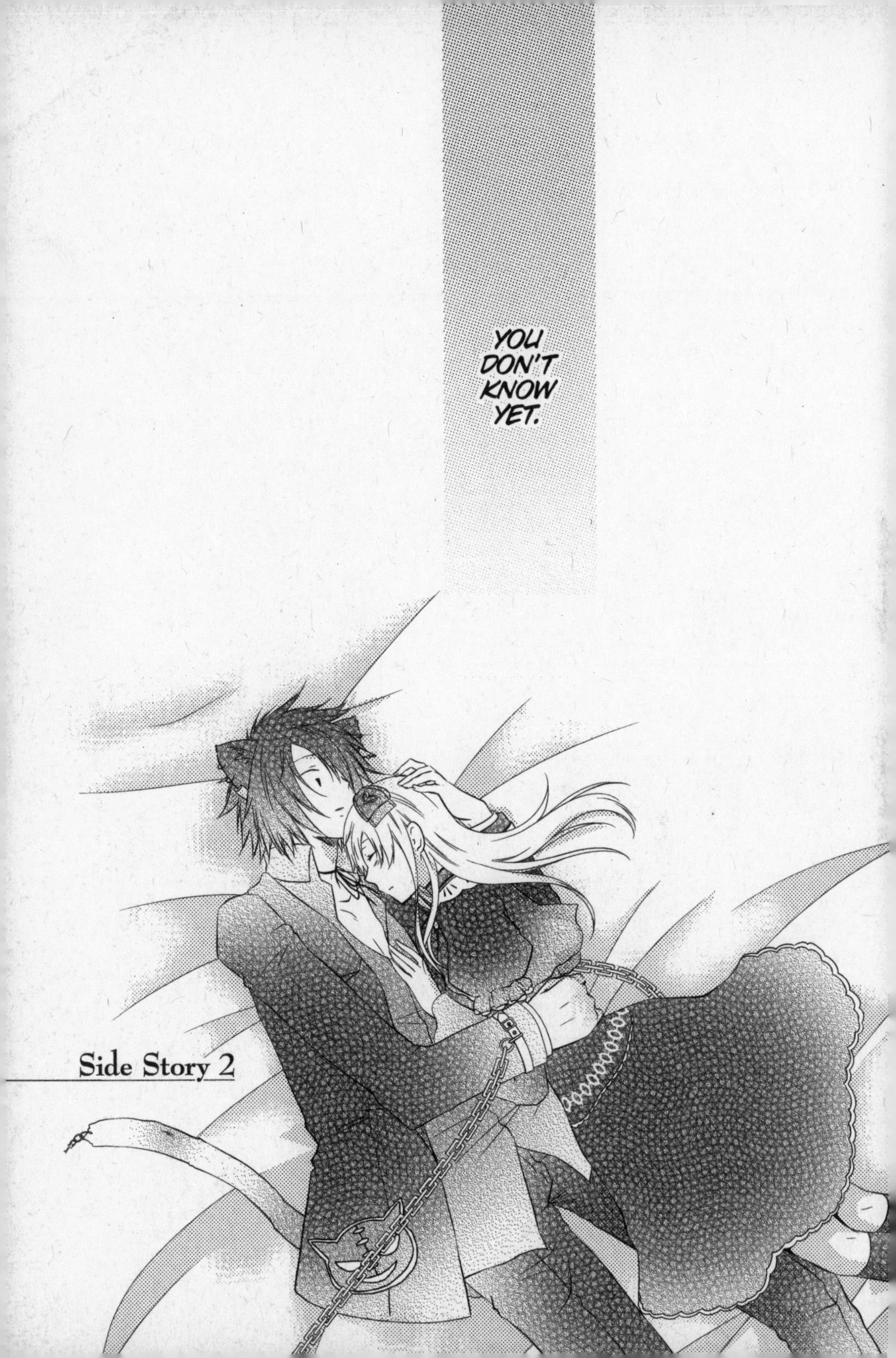
YOU DON'T KNOW YET.

Side Story 2

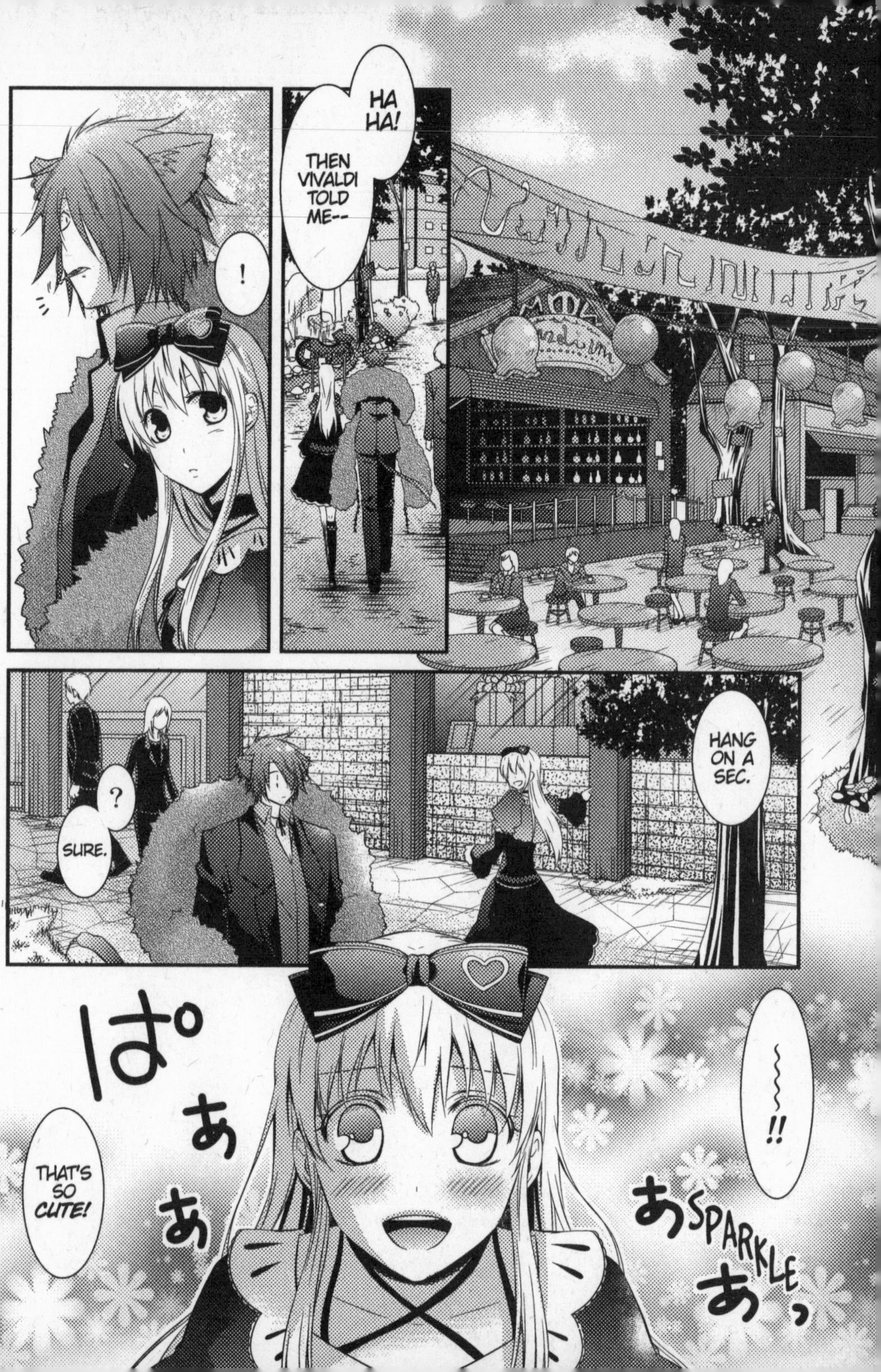
HA HA!
THEN VIVALDI TOLD ME--
!
HANG ON A SEC.
?
SURE.
~~~~!!
あSPARKLEあっ
ぱぁぁ
THAT'S SO CUTE!
~~~~

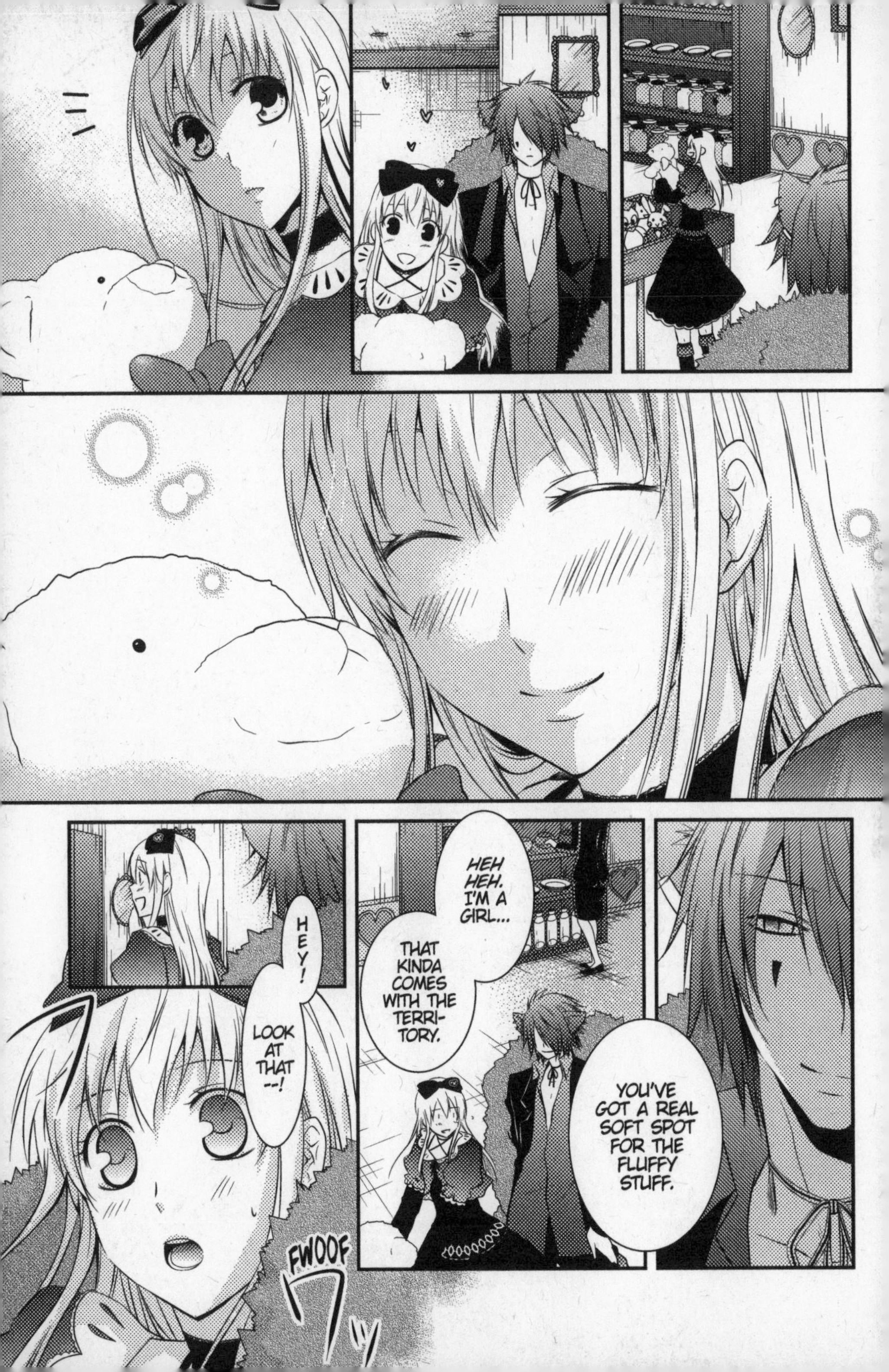
YOU'VE GOT A REAL SOFT SPOT FOR THE FLUFFY STUFF.
HEH HEH. I'M A GIRL...
THAT KINDA COMES WITH THE TERRITORY.
HEY!
LOOK AT THAT --!
FWOOF

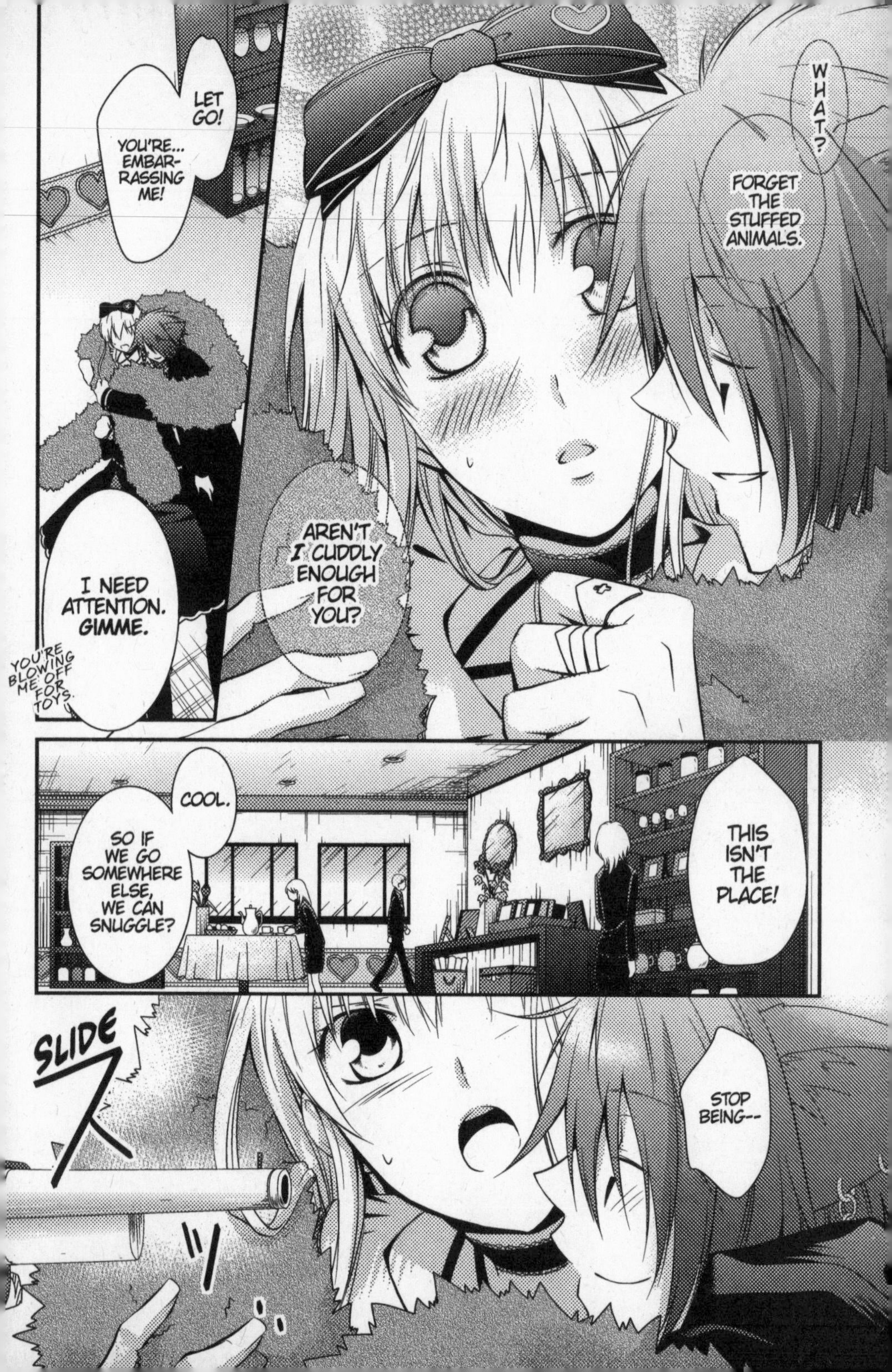

WHAT?
FORGET THE STUFFED ANIMALS.
AREN'T *I* CUDDLY ENOUGH FOR YOU?
LET GO!
YOU'RE... EMBARRASSING ME!
I NEED ATTENTION. GIMME.
YOU'RE BLOWING ME OFF FOR TOYS.
THIS ISN'T THE PLACE!
COOL.
SO IF WE GO SOMEWHERE ELSE, WE CAN SNUGGLE?
STOP BEING--
SLIDE

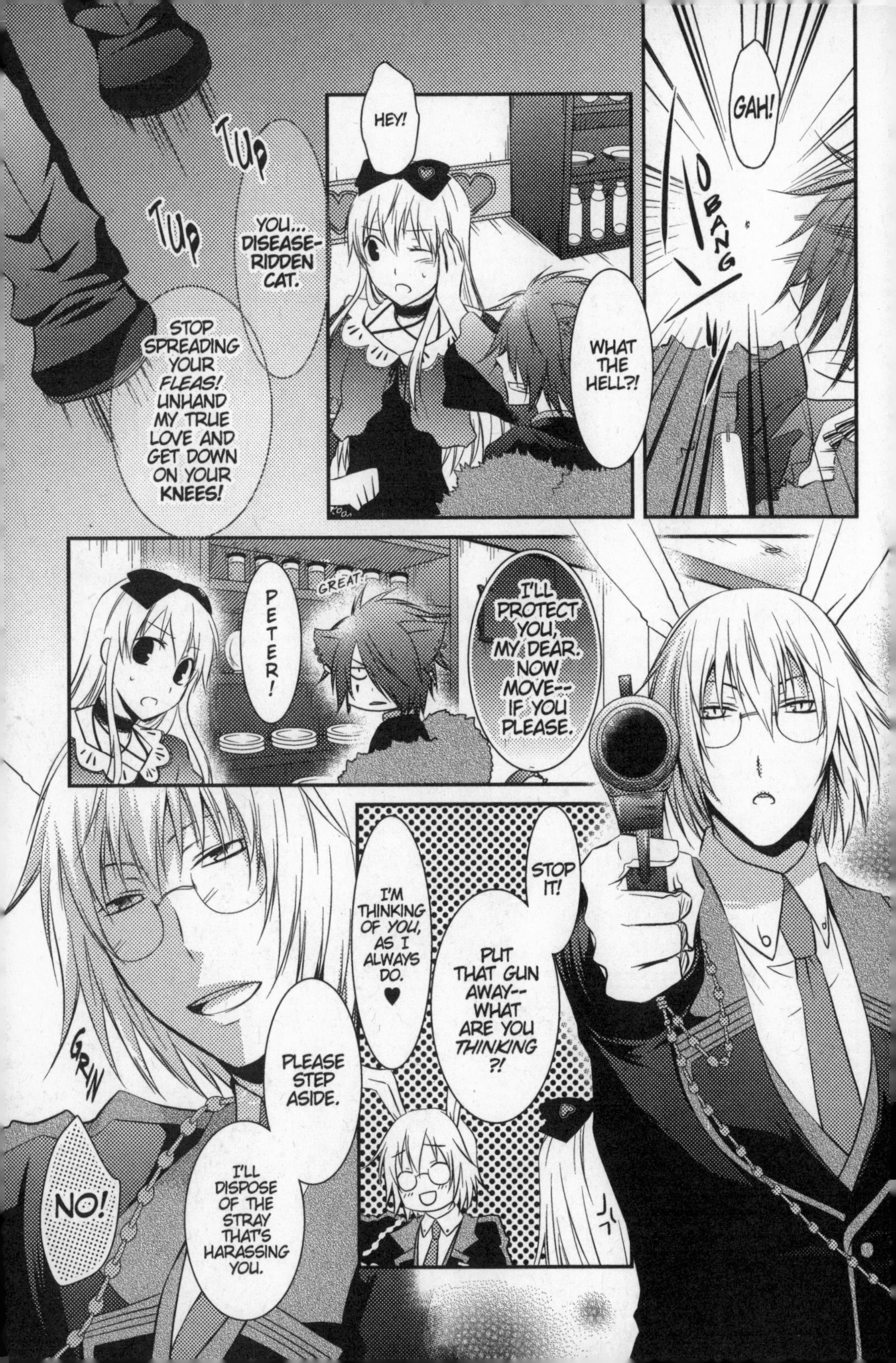
GAH!
BANG
HEY!
WHAT THE HELL?!
TUP
TUP
YOU... DISEASE-RIDDEN CAT.
STOP SPREADING YOUR *FLEAS!* UNHAND MY TRUE LOVE AND GET DOWN ON YOUR KNEES!
I'LL PROTECT YOU, MY DEAR. NOW MOVE--IF YOU PLEASE.
PETER!
GREAT.
STOP IT!
PUT THAT GUN AWAY--WHAT ARE YOU *THINKING*?!
I'M THINKING OF *YOU*, AS I ALWAYS DO. ♥
PLEASE STEP ASIDE.
I'LL DISPOSE OF THE STRAY THAT'S HARASSING YOU.
GRIN
NO!

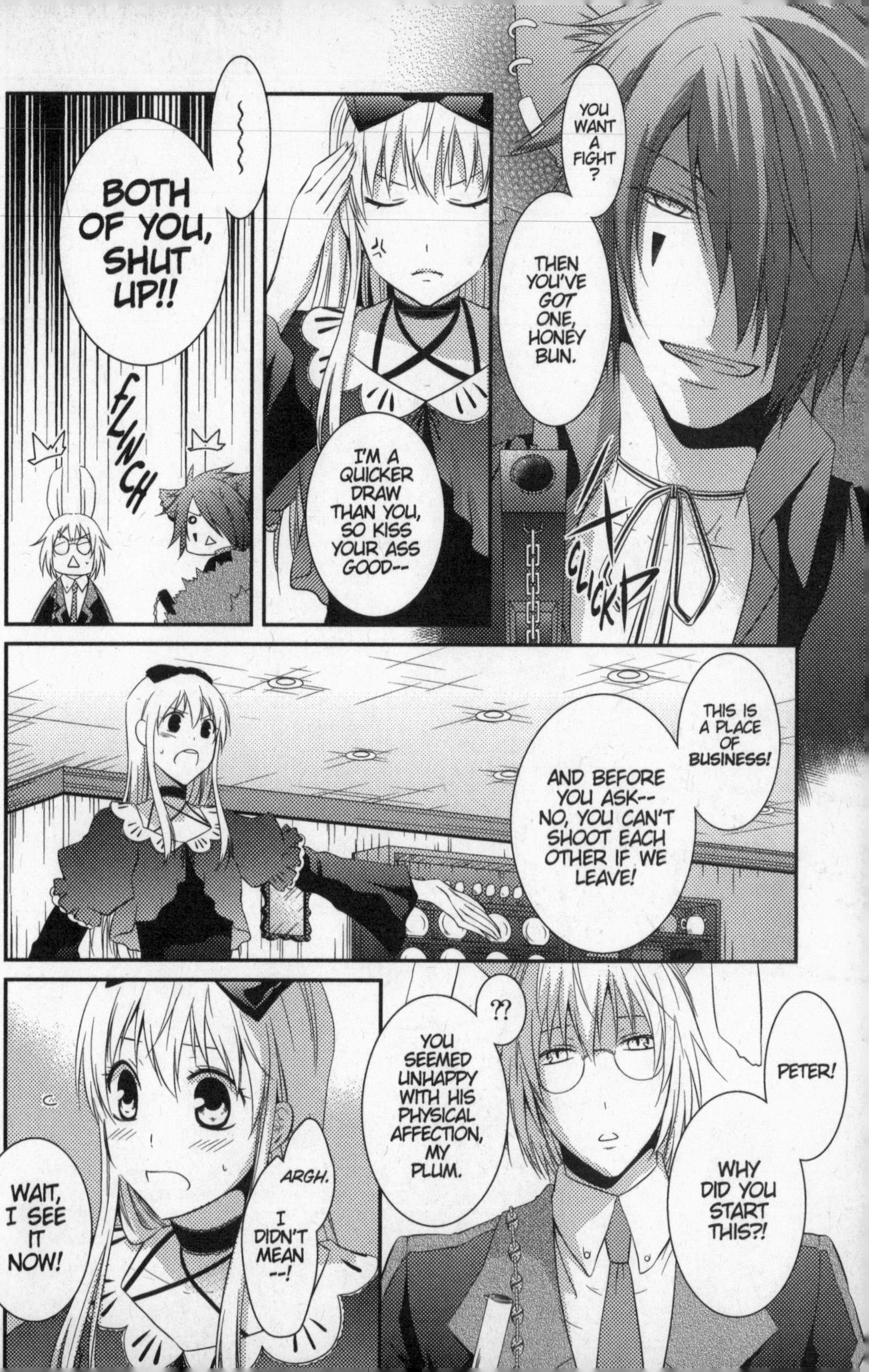
YOU WANT A FIGHT?
THEN YOU'VE GOT ONE, HONEY BUN.
CLICK
I'M A QUICKER DRAW THAN YOU, SO KISS YOUR ASS GOOD--
......
BOTH OF YOU, SHUT UP!!
FLINCH
THIS IS A PLACE OF BUSINESS!
AND BEFORE YOU ASK-- NO, YOU CAN'T SHOOT EACH OTHER IF WE LEAVE!
PETER!
WHY DID YOU START THIS?!
??
YOU SEEMED UNHAPPY WITH HIS PHYSICAL AFFECTION, MY PLUM.
ARGH.
I DIDN'T MEAN --!
WAIT, I SEE IT NOW!

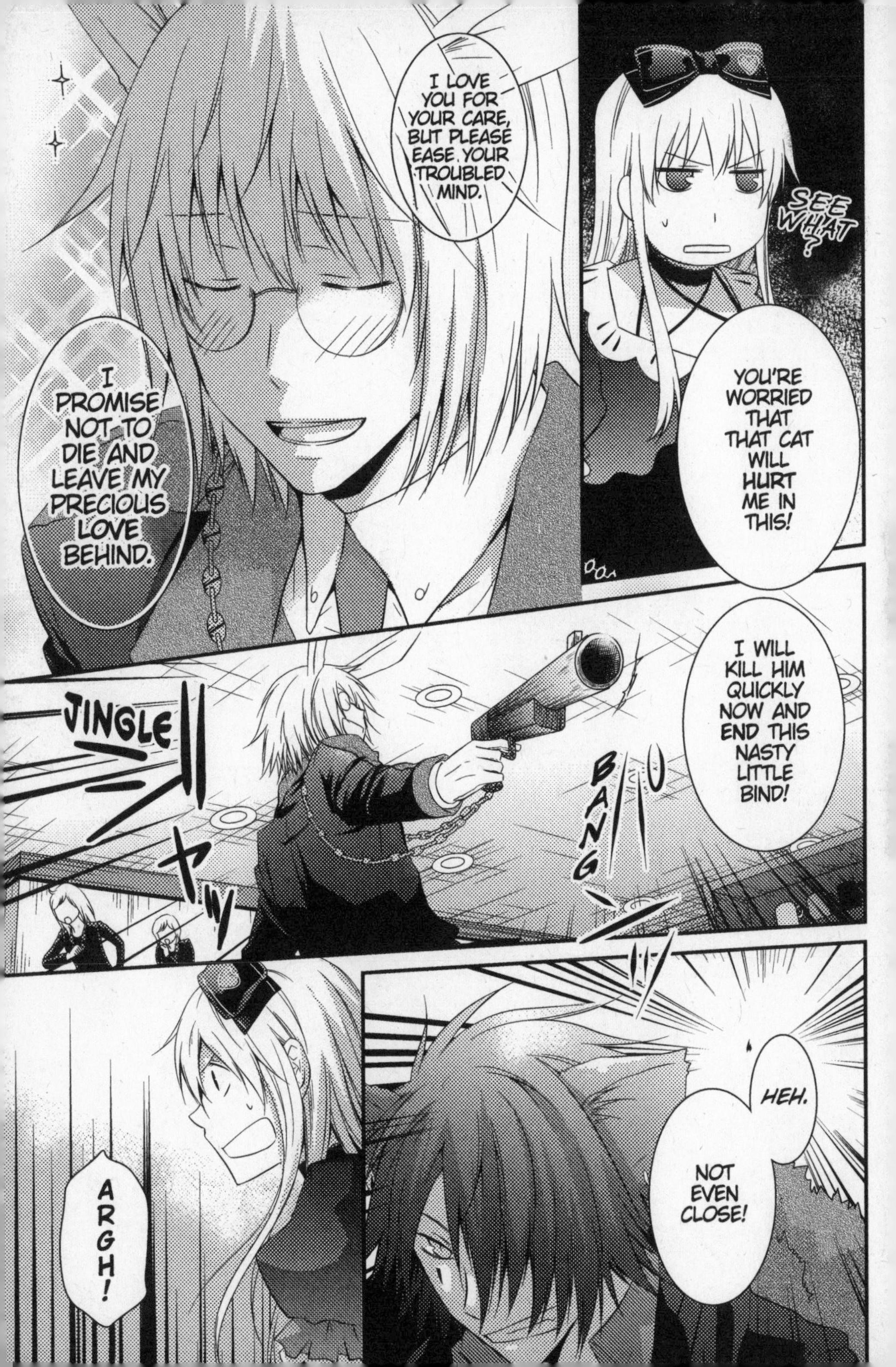
SEE WHAT?
YOU'RE WORRIED THAT THAT CAT WILL HURT ME IN THIS!
I LOVE YOU FOR YOUR CARE, BUT PLEASE EASE YOUR TROUBLED MIND.
I PROMISE NOT TO DIE AND LEAVE MY PRECIOUS LOVE BEHIND.
I WILL KILL HIM QUICKLY NOW AND END THIS NASTY LITTLE BIND!
BANG
JINGLE
HEH.
NOT EVEN CLOSE!
ARGH!

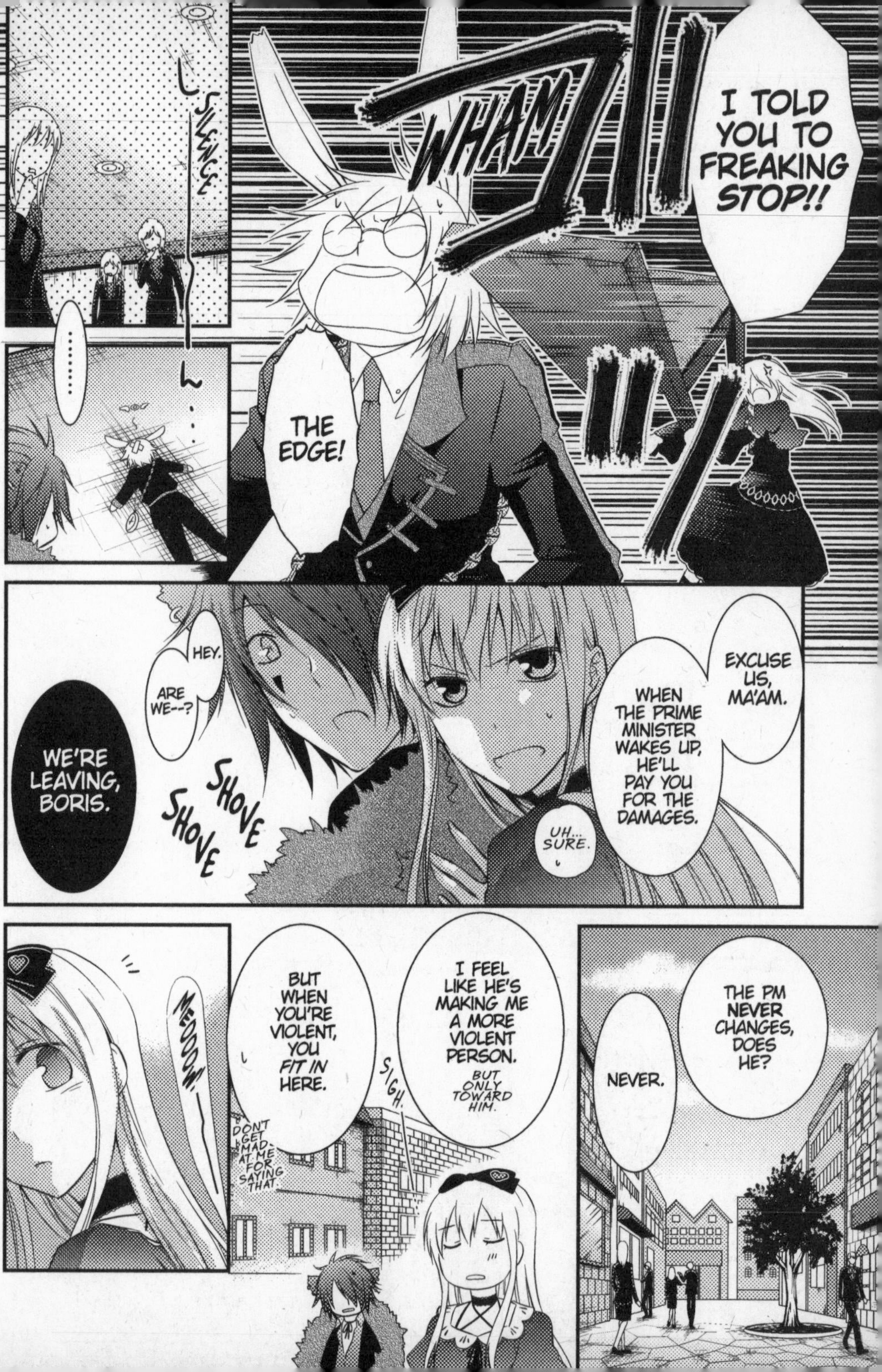
I TOLD YOU TO FREAKING STOP!!
WHAM
THE EDGE!
SILENCE
しーん…
......
EXCUSE US, MA'AM.
WHEN THE PRIME MINISTER WAKES UP, HE'LL PAY YOU FOR THE DAMAGES.
UH... SURE.
HEY.
ARE WE--?
SHOVE SHOVE
WE'RE LEAVING, BORIS.
THE PM NEVER CHANGES, DOES HE?
NEVER.
I FEEL LIKE HE'S MAKING ME A MORE VIOLENT PERSON.
BUT ONLY TOWARD HIM.
SIGH.
BUT WHEN YOU'RE VIOLENT, YOU FIT IN HERE.
DON'T GET MAD AT ME FOR SAYING THAT.
MEOOOW

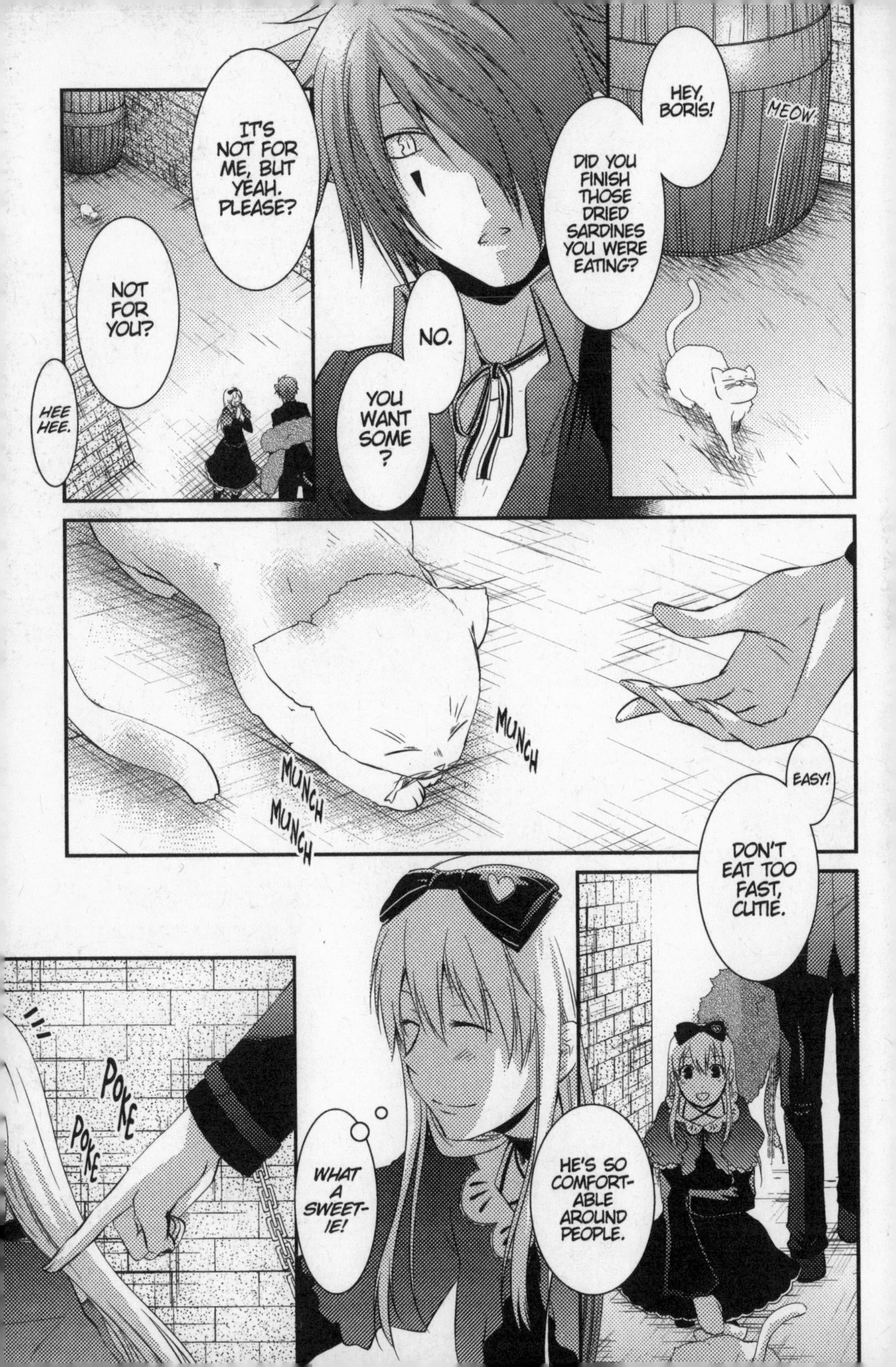
HEY, BORIS!
DID YOU FINISH THOSE DRIED SARDINES YOU WERE EATING?
MEOW.
NO.
YOU WANT SOME?
IT'S NOT FOR ME, BUT YEAH. PLEASE?
NOT FOR YOU?
HEE HEE.
EASY!
DON'T EAT TOO FAST, CUTIE.
MUNCH
MUNCH
MUNCH
HE'S SO COMFORTABLE AROUND PEOPLE.
WHAT A SWEETIE!
POKE
POKE
!!!

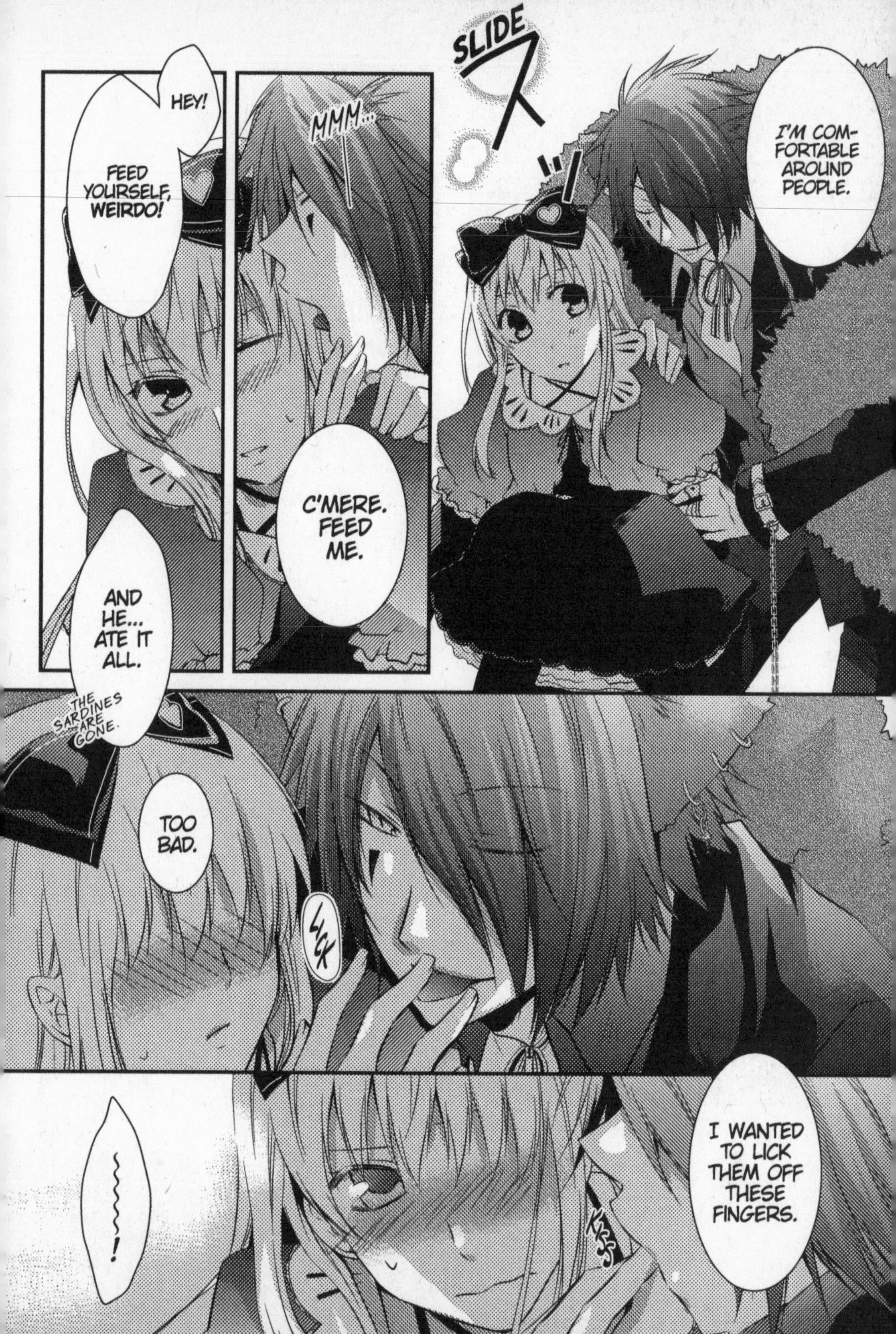
SLIDE
I'M COM-FORTABLE AROUND PEOPLE.
MMM...
C'MERE. FEED ME.
HEY!
FEED YOURSELF, WEIRDO!
AND HE... ATE IT ALL.
THE SARDINES ARE GONE.
TOO BAD.
LICK
I WANTED TO LICK THEM OFF THESE FINGERS.
~~~~!
~~~~

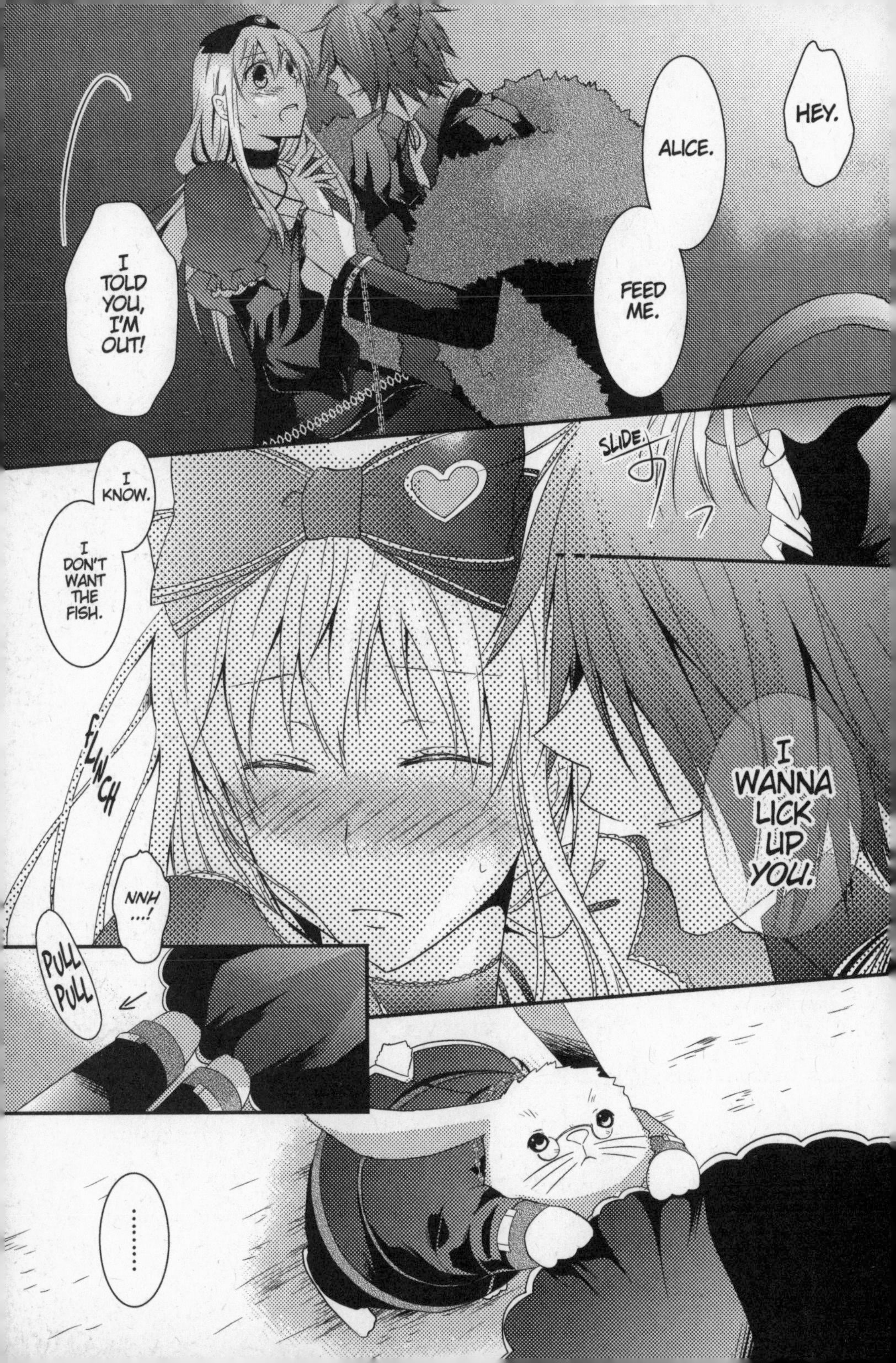
HEY.
ALICE.
FEED ME.
I TOLD YOU, I'M OUT!
SLIDE
I KNOW.
I DON'T WANT THE FISH.
I WANNA LICK UP YOU.
FLINCH
NNH ...!
PULL PULL
......

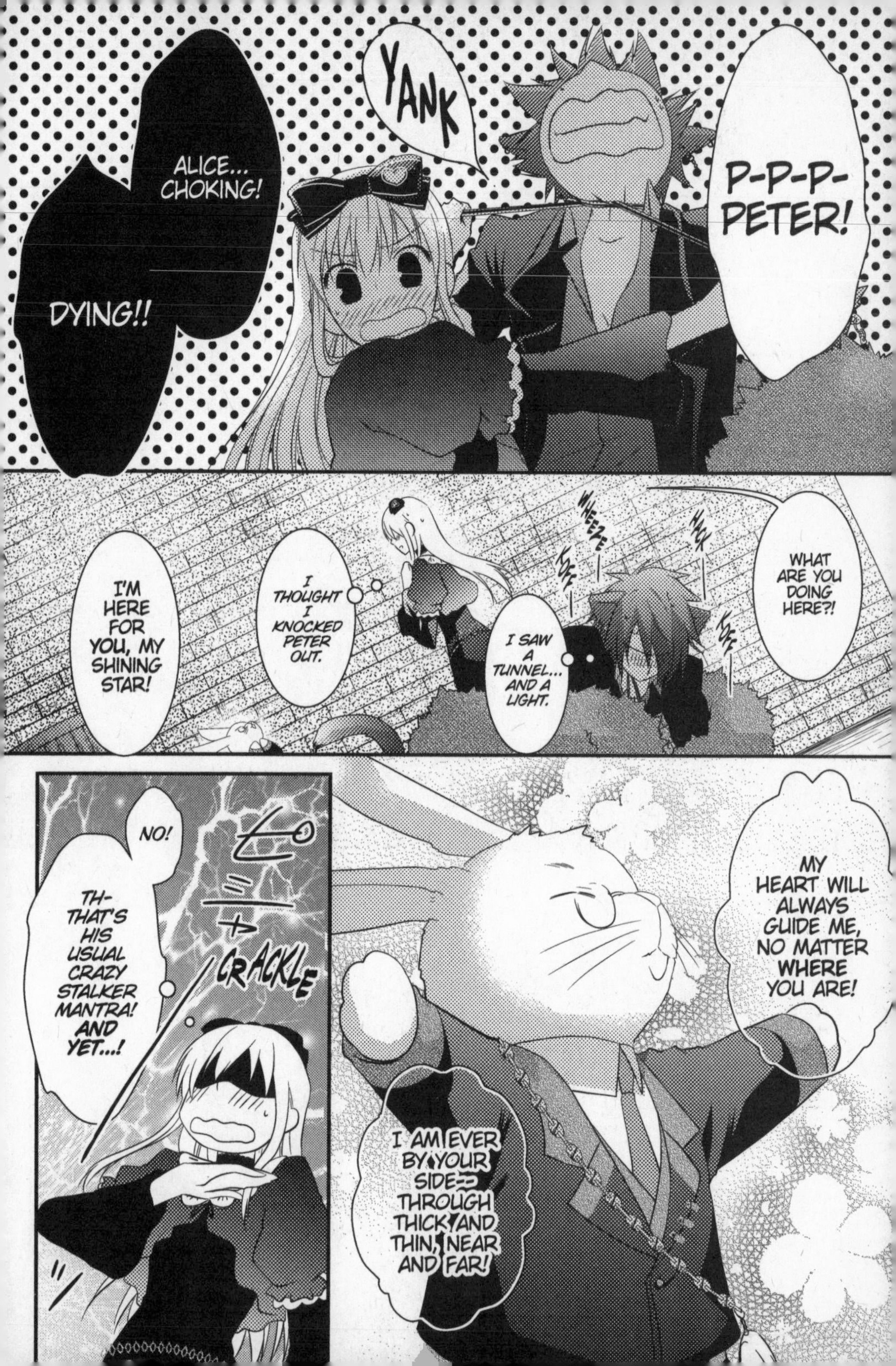
P-P-P-PETER!
YANK
ALICE... CHOKING!
DYING!!
WHAT ARE YOU DOING HERE?!
HACK
WHEEZE
KOFF
KOFF
I SAW A TUNNEL... AND A LIGHT.
I THOUGHT I KNOCKED PETER OUT.
I'M HERE FOR YOU, MY SHINING STAR!
MY HEART WILL ALWAYS GUIDE ME, NO MATTER WHERE YOU ARE!
I AM EVER BY YOUR SIDE-- THROUGH THICK AND THIN, NEAR AND FAR!
NO!
CRACKLE
TH-THAT'S HIS USUAL CRAZY STALKER MANTRA! AND YET...!

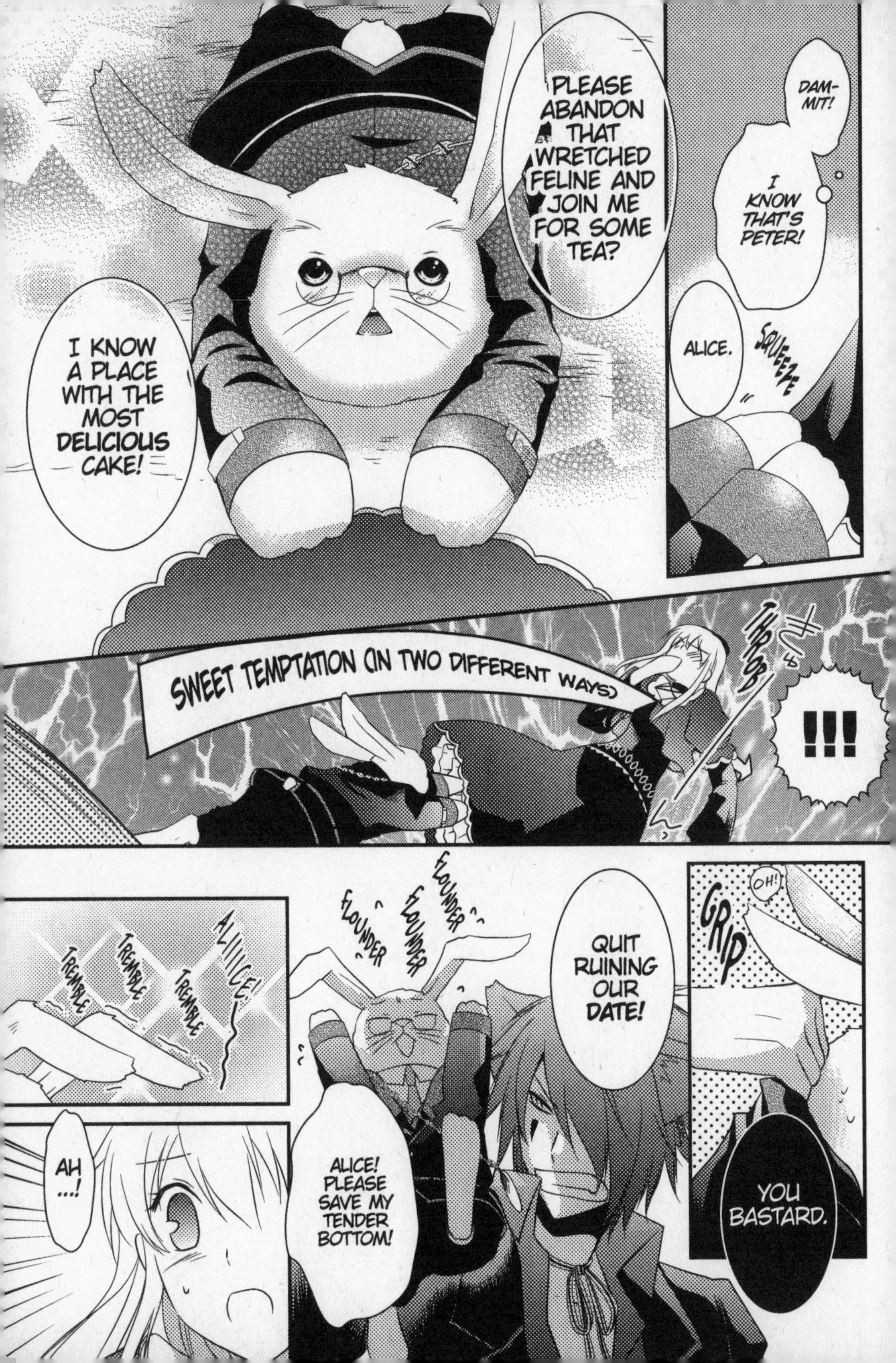
DAM-MIT!
I KNOW THAT'S PETER!
ALICE.
SQUEEZE
PLEASE ABANDON THAT WRETCHED FELINE AND JOIN ME FOR SOME TEA?
I KNOW A PLACE WITH THE MOST DELICIOUS CAKE!
THROB
!!!
SWEET TEMPTATION (IN TWO DIFFERENT WAYS)
GRIP
OH!
YOU BASTARD.
QUIT RUINING OUR DATE!
FLOUNDER
FLOUNDER
FLOUNDER
ALICE! PLEASE SAVE MY TENDER BOTTOM!
ALIIICE!
TREMBLE
TREMBLE
TREMBLE
AH ...!

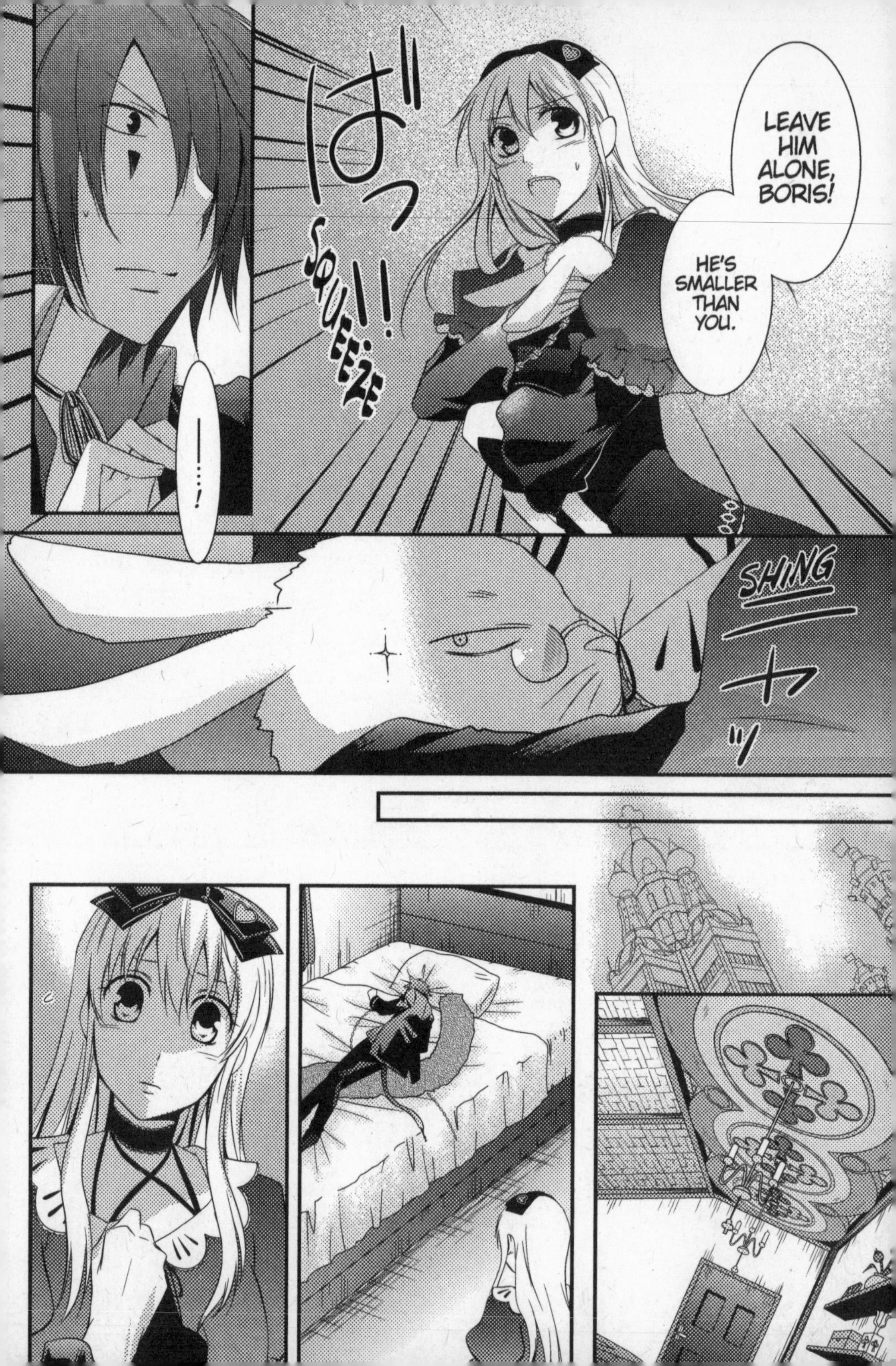
LEAVE HIM ALONE, BORIS!
HE'S SMALLER THAN YOU.
ばっ
SQUEEZE
――…!
SHING
キャッ

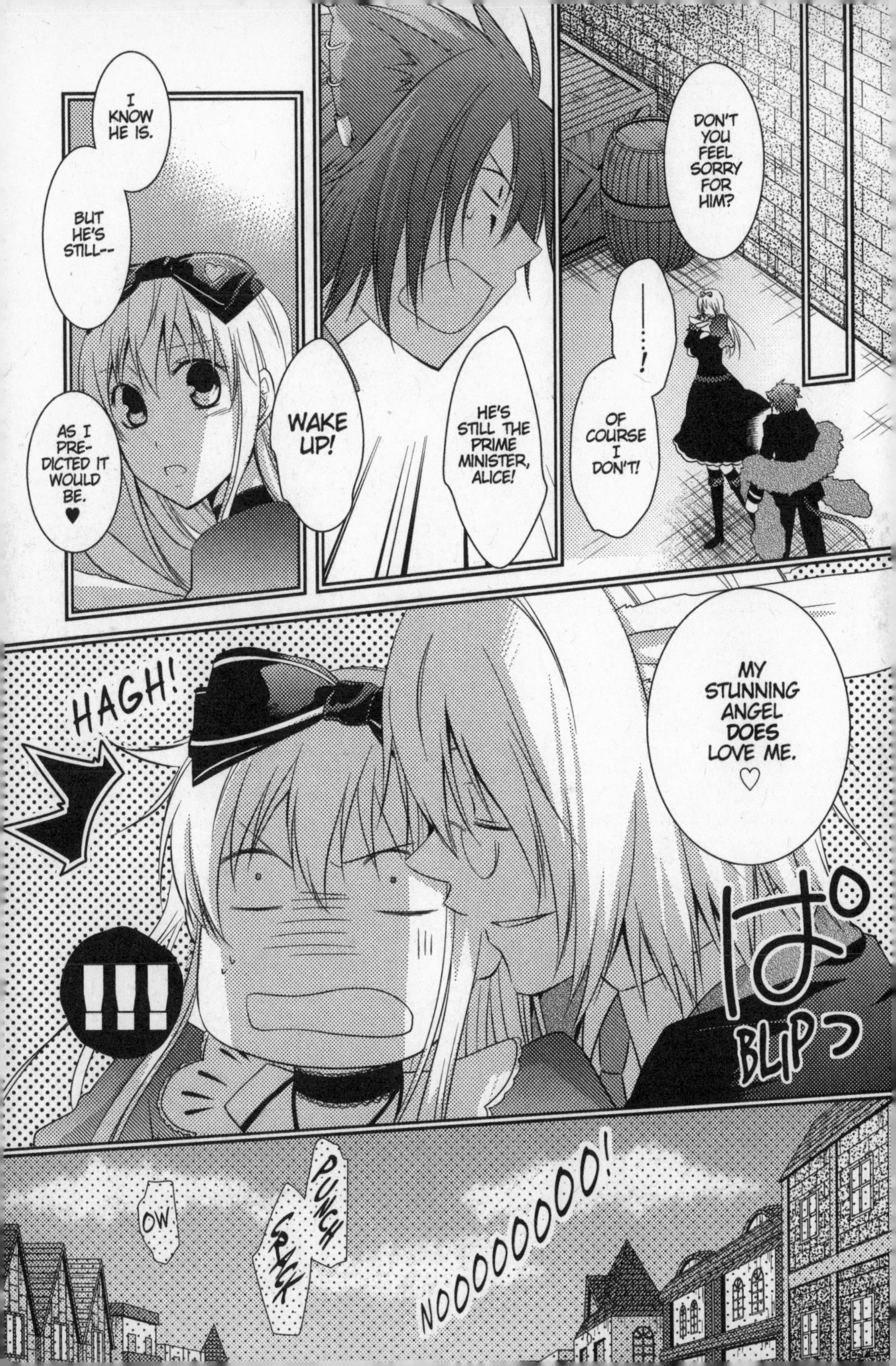
DON'T YOU FEEL SORRY FOR HIM?
...!
OF COURSE I DON'T!
HE'S STILL THE PRIME MINISTER, ALICE!
WAKE UP!
I KNOW HE IS.
BUT HE'S STILL--
AS I PRE-DICTED IT WOULD BE. ♥
MY STUNNING ANGEL DOES LOVE ME. ♡
ぱ
BLIPっ
HAGH!
!!!
NOOOOOOOO!
PUNCH
CRACK
OW

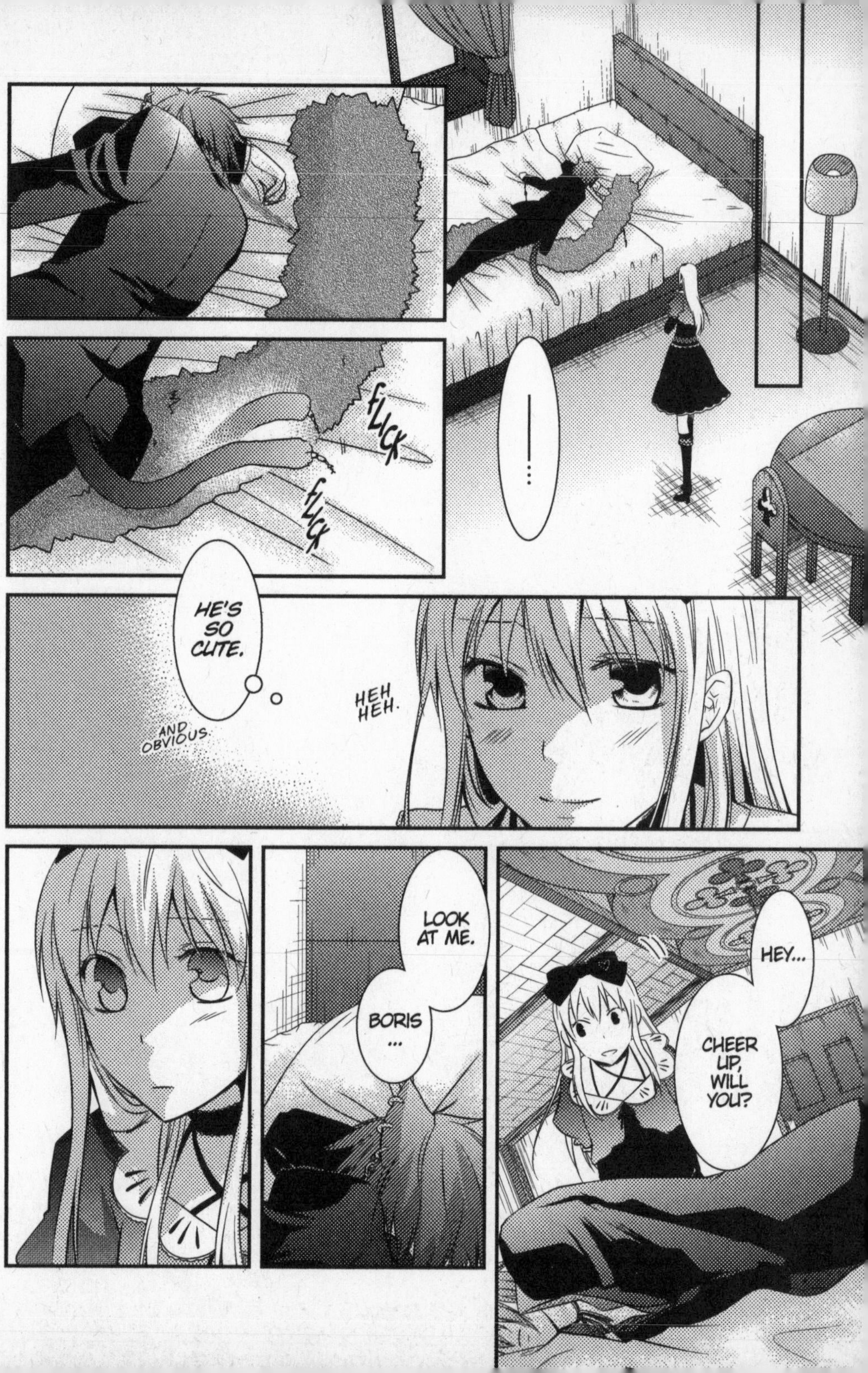

—!...
FLICK
FLICK
HE'S SO CUTE.
HEH HEH.
AND OBVIOUS.
HEY...
CHEER UP, WILL YOU?
LOOK AT ME.
BORIS...

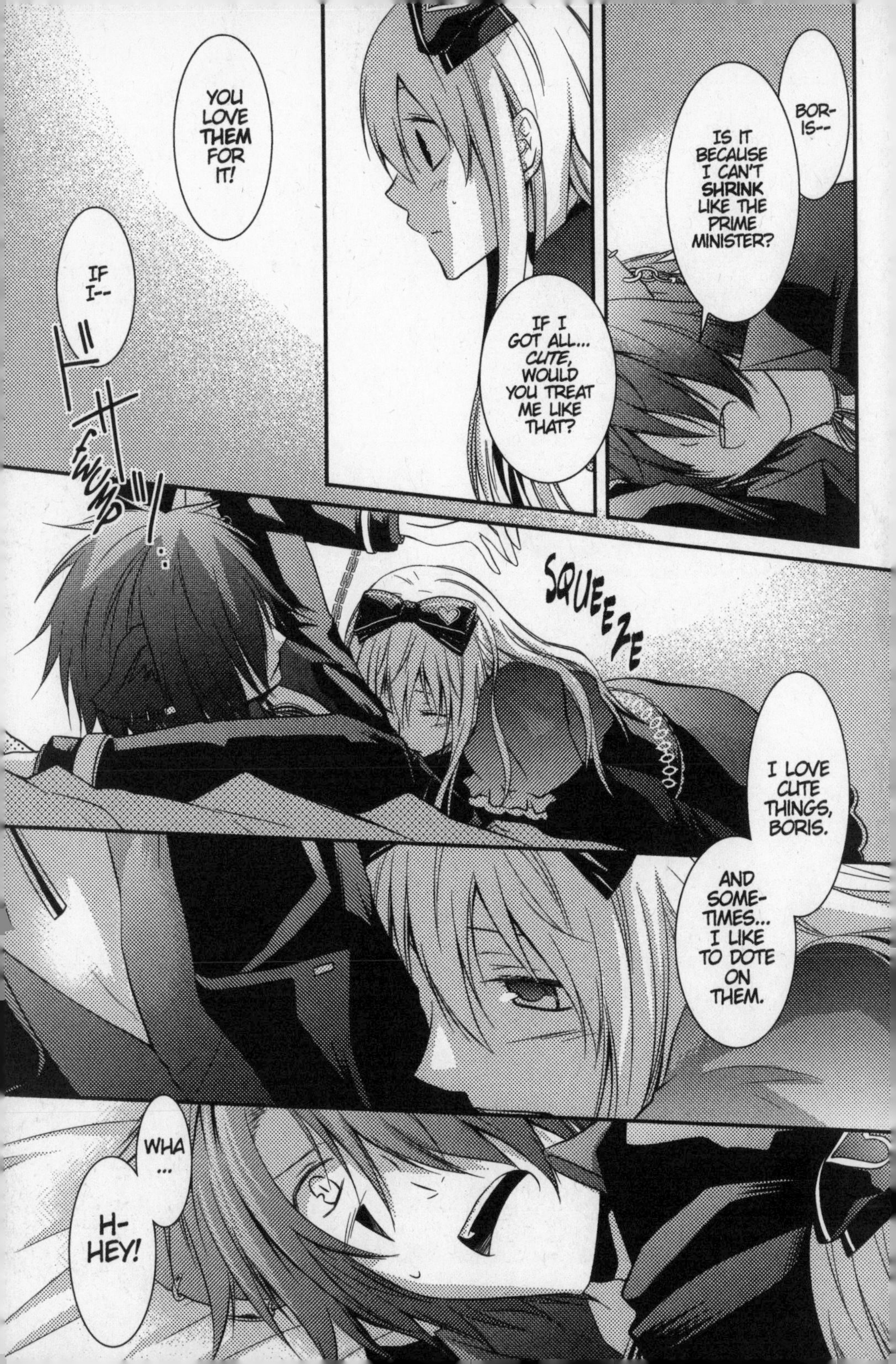
BOR-IS--
IS IT BECAUSE I CAN'T SHRINK LIKE THE PRIME MINISTER?
IF I GOT ALL... CUTE, WOULD YOU TREAT ME LIKE THAT?
YOU LOVE THEM FOR IT!
IF I--
FWUMP
SQUEEZE
I LOVE CUTE THINGS, BORIS.
AND SOMETIMES... I LIKE TO DOTE ON THEM.
WHA...
H-HEY!

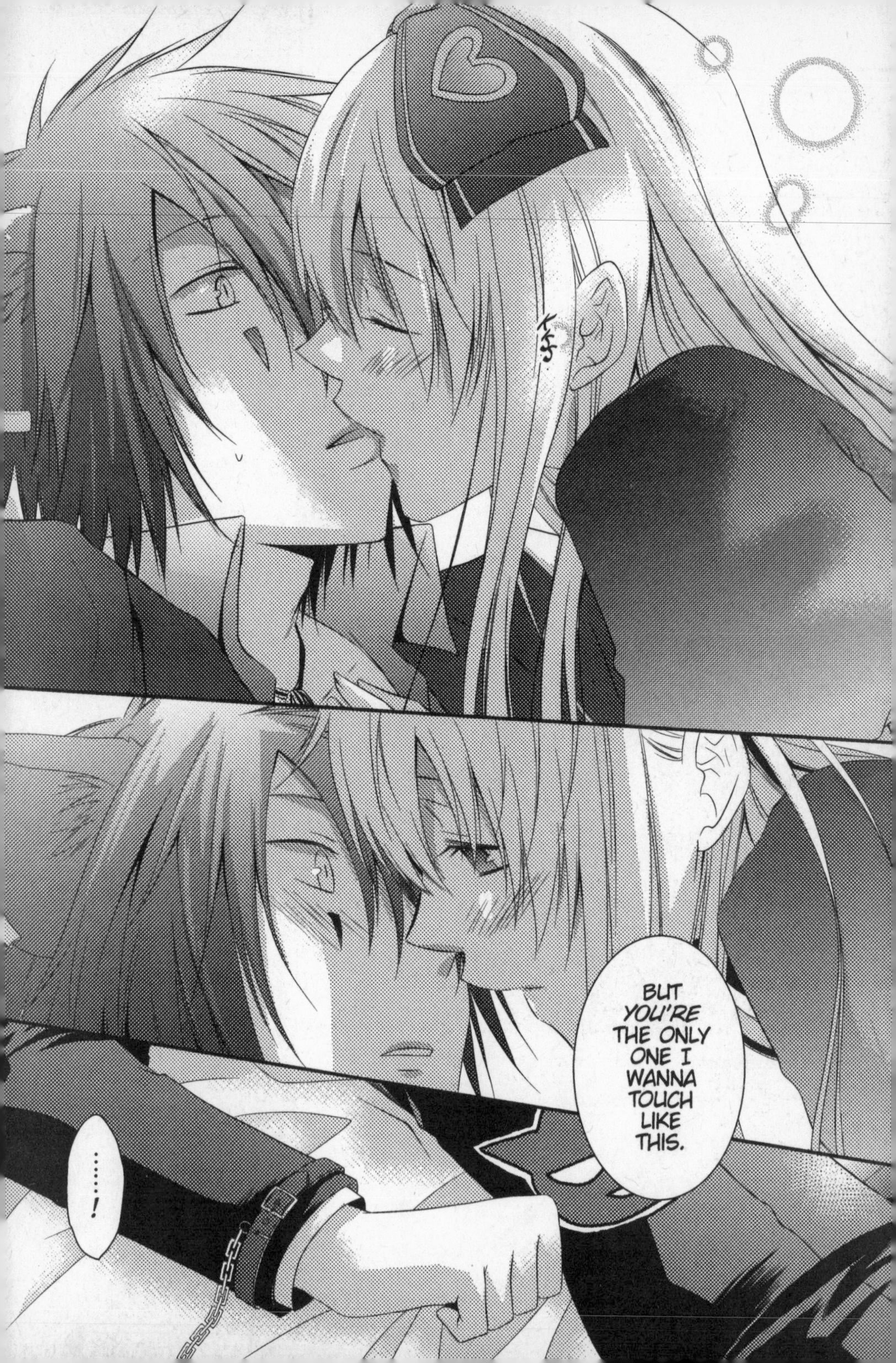
BUT YOU'RE THE ONLY ONE I WANNA TOUCH LIKE THIS.
......!

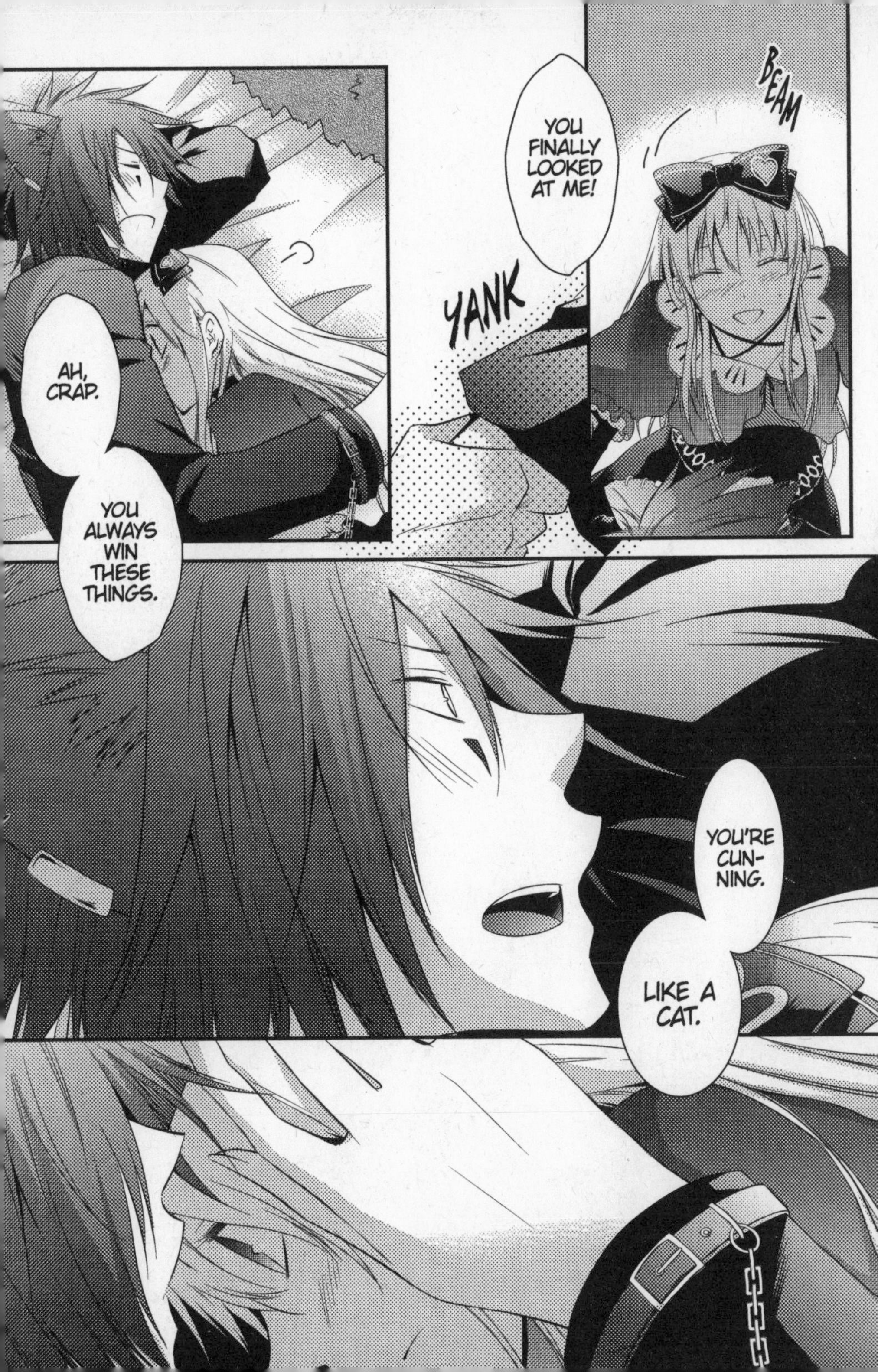
BEAM
YOU FINALLY LOOKED AT ME!
YANK
AH, CRAP.
YOU ALWAYS WIN THESE THINGS.
YOU'RE CUN-NING.
LIKE A CAT.

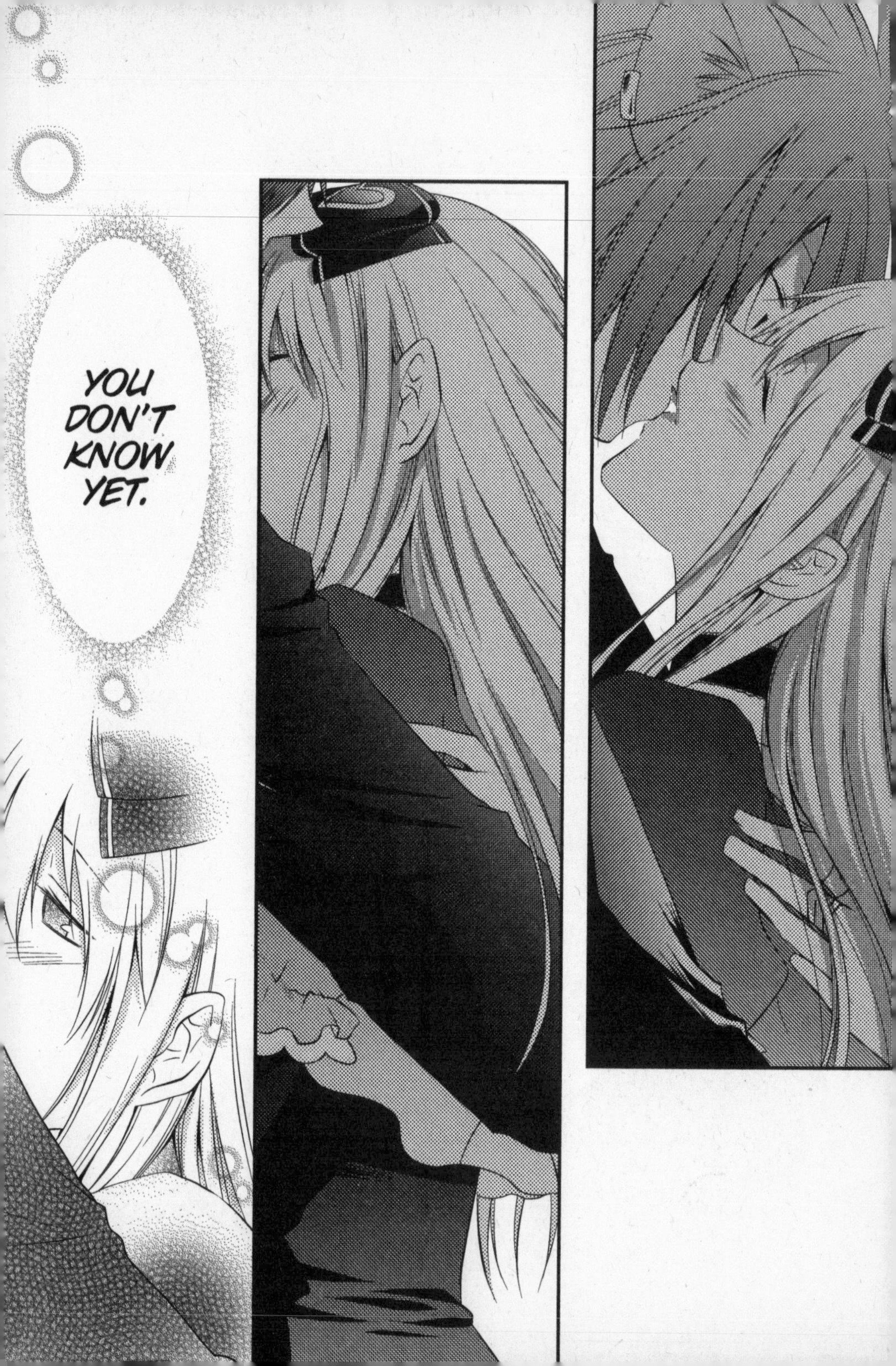
YOU DON'T KNOW YET.

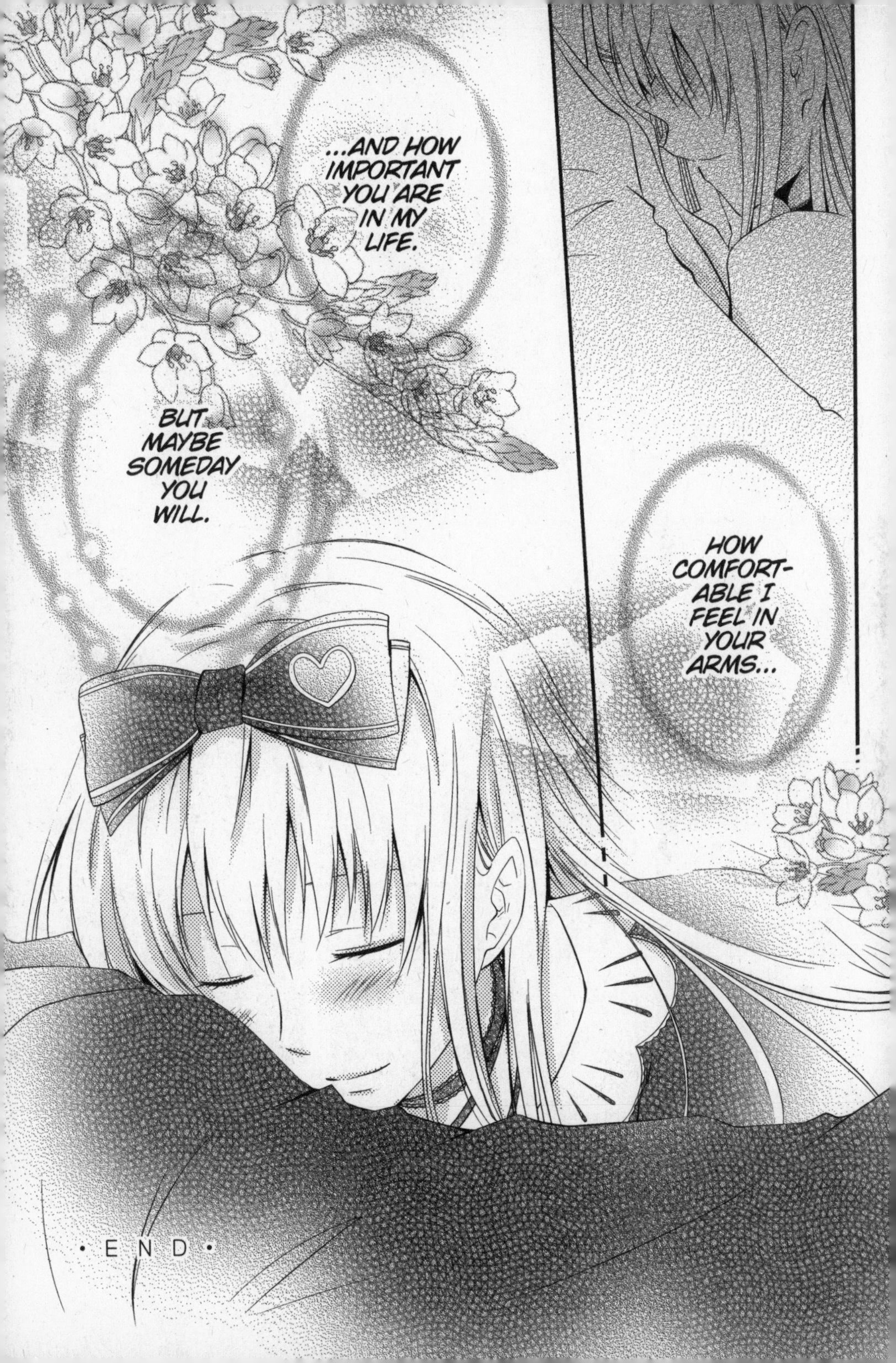
HOW COMFORTABLE I FEEL IN YOUR ARMS...
...AND HOW IMPORTANT YOU ARE IN MY LIFE.
BUT MAYBE SOMEDAY YOU WILL.
• E N D •

• Extra Comic •

Is it canon? You decide!

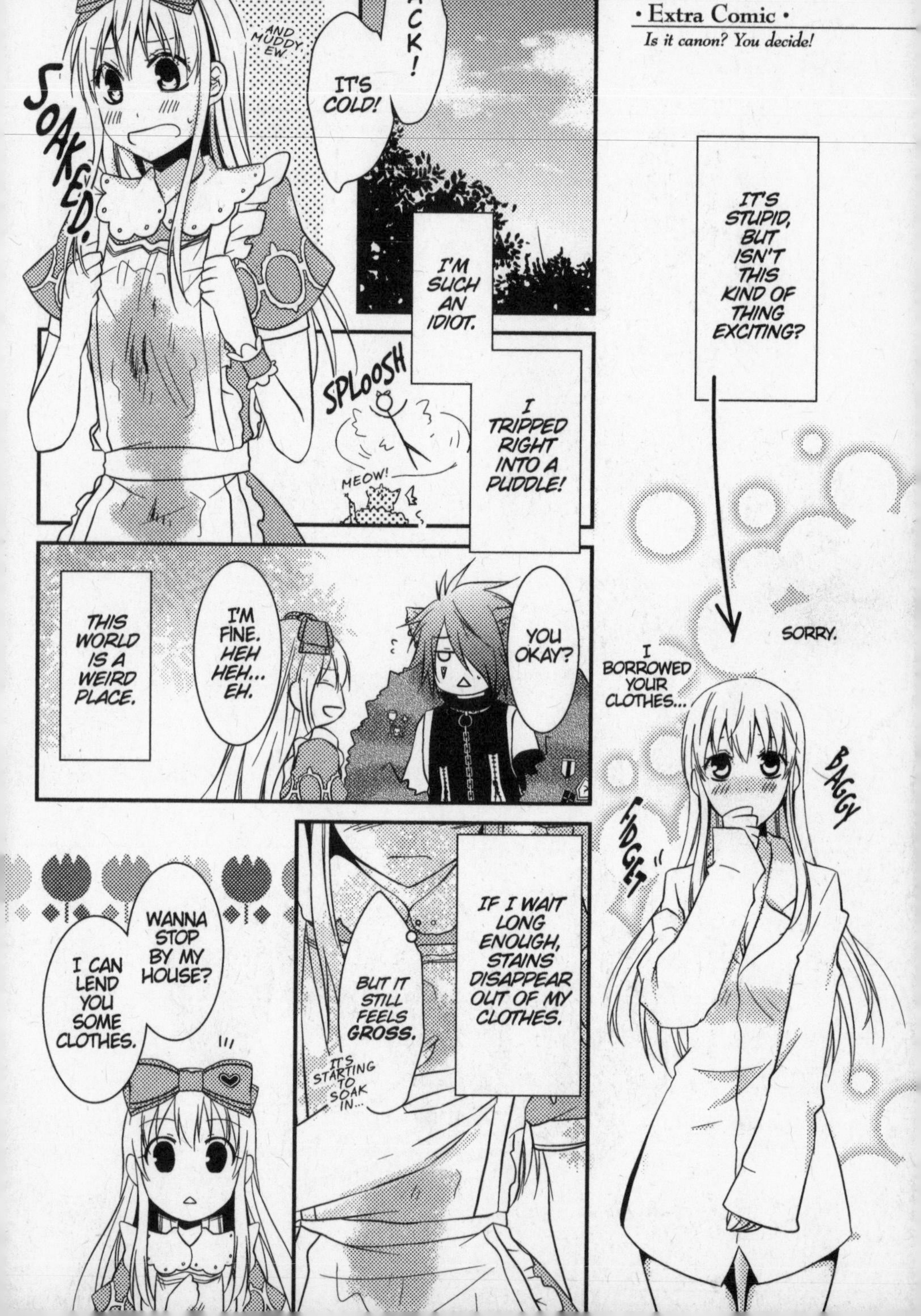

IT'S STUPID, BUT ISN'T THIS KIND OF THING EXCITING?
SORRY.
I BORROWED YOUR CLOTHES...
BAGGY
FIDGET
ACK!
IT'S COLD!
I'M SUCH AN IDIOT.
I TRIPPED RIGHT INTO A PUDDLE!
SPLOOSH
MEOW!
SOAKED.
AND MUDDY, EW.
YOU OKAY?
I'M FINE. HEH HEH... EH.
THIS WORLD IS A WEIRD PLACE.
IF I WAIT LONG ENOUGH, STAINS DISAPPEAR OUT OF MY CLOTHES.
BUT IT STILL FEELS GROSS.
IT'S STARTING TO SOAK IN...
WANNA STOP BY MY HOUSE?
I CAN LEND YOU SOME CLOTHES.

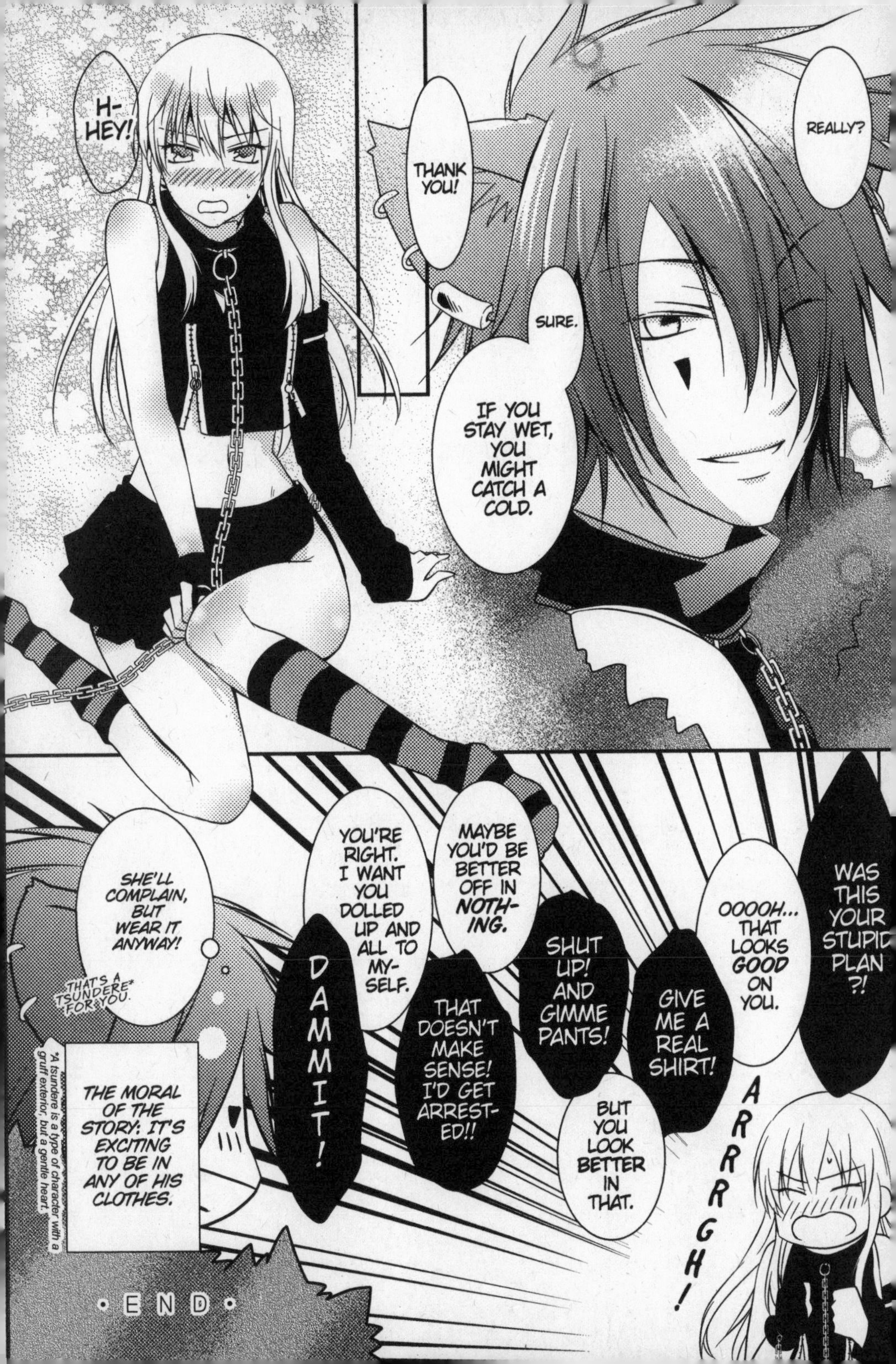
REALLY?
SURE.
IF YOU STAY WET, YOU MIGHT CATCH A COLD.
THANK YOU!
H-HEY!
WAS THIS YOUR STUPID PLAN?!
OOOOH... THAT LOOKS GOOD ON YOU.
GIVE ME A REAL SHIRT!
BUT YOU LOOK BETTER IN THAT.
ARRRGH!
SHUT UP! AND GIMME PANTS!
MAYBE YOU'D BE BETTER OFF IN NOTHING.
THAT DOESN'T MAKE SENSE! I'D GET ARRESTED!!
YOU'RE RIGHT. I WANT YOU DOLLED UP AND ALL TO MYSELF.
DAMMIT!
SHE'LL COMPLAIN, BUT WEAR IT ANYWAY!
THAT'S A TSUNDERE* FOR YOU.
*A tsundere is a type of character with a gruff exterior, but a gentle heart.
THE MORAL OF THE STORY: IT'S EXCITING TO BE IN ANY OF HIS CLOTHES.
•END•

CHESHIRE CAT WALTZ: CHAPTER 6 - POST-MORTEM

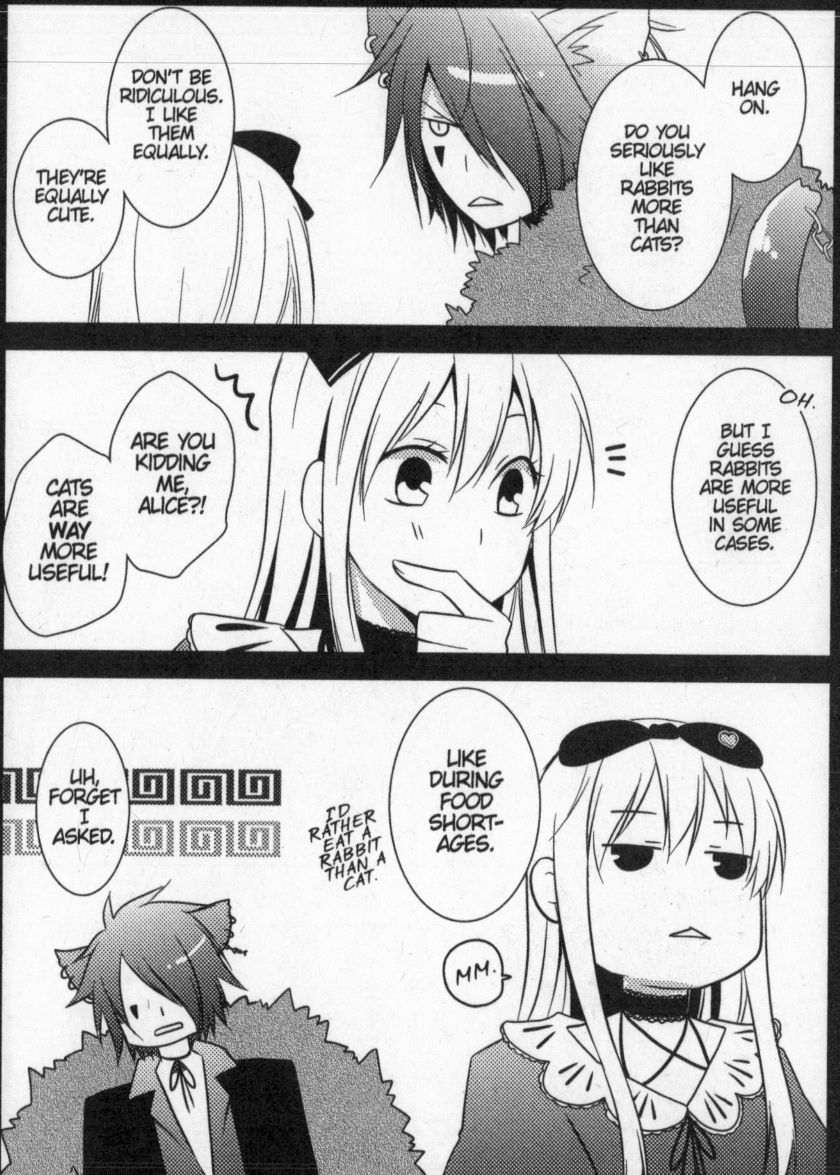
HANG ON.
DO YOU SERIOUSLY LIKE RABBITS MORE THAN CATS?
DON'T BE RIDICULOUS. I LIKE THEM EQUALLY.
THEY'RE EQUALLY CUTE.
OH.
BUT I GUESS RABBITS ARE MORE USEFUL IN SOME CASES.
ARE YOU KIDDING ME, ALICE?!
CATS ARE WAY MORE USEFUL!
LIKE DURING FOOD SHORTAGES.
I'D RATHER EAT A RABBIT THAN A CAT.
MM.
UH, FORGET I ASKED.

CHESHIRE CAT WALTZ: VOLUME 2 - POST-MORTEM

SOMETIMES MY FRIEND (WITH ALICE GAME EXPERIENCE) HELPS ME PREPARE MY SCRIPTS.
HEY, YOU KNOW PAGE X? IN THE PANEL WHERE BORIS IS WITH ELLY AND MOM?
NORMALLY.
MOM...?
*WORKING ON THE PC.
CLICK
CONFIRMATION.
ELLY
BORIS
GRAY?
HE IS THE MOM!
EVEN FOR THE FANS WHO PLAYED THE GAME!
BUT THEY CALL HIM THAT OUT OF LOVE.
GRAY IS MY BRIDE! I WON'T LET ALICE HAVE HIM!
WHEN DID SHE...?

DEEP APPRECIATION!

SORRY FOR ALL THE TROUBLE!
QUINROSE

THANK YOU FOR ALL YOUR HELP!
ASSISTANTS

THANK YOU FOR EVERYTHING!
FRIENDS AND ACQUAINTANCES

AND THANK YOU FOR PICKING UP THIS BOOK!
READERS

THANK YOU VERY MUCH!

WHEN I ADDED GRADIATION ON TOP OF FLAT SCREENTONE FOR THE FUR ON BORIS'S SUIT, IT LOOKED LIKE THE BOSS OF ALL SEA CUCUMBERS--STRONG ENOUGH TO MOVE ON ITS OWN. THAT'S WHY I SETTLED ON THE SCREENTONE YOU SEE NOW.

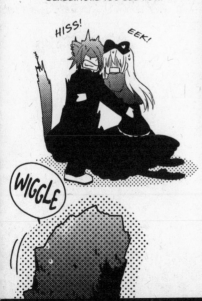

HISS!
EEK!
WIGGLE

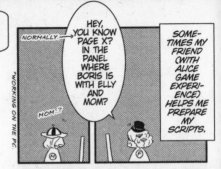

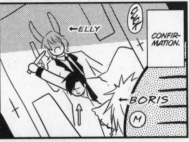

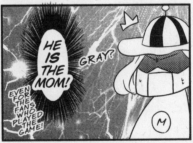

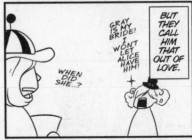

NEXT TIME...

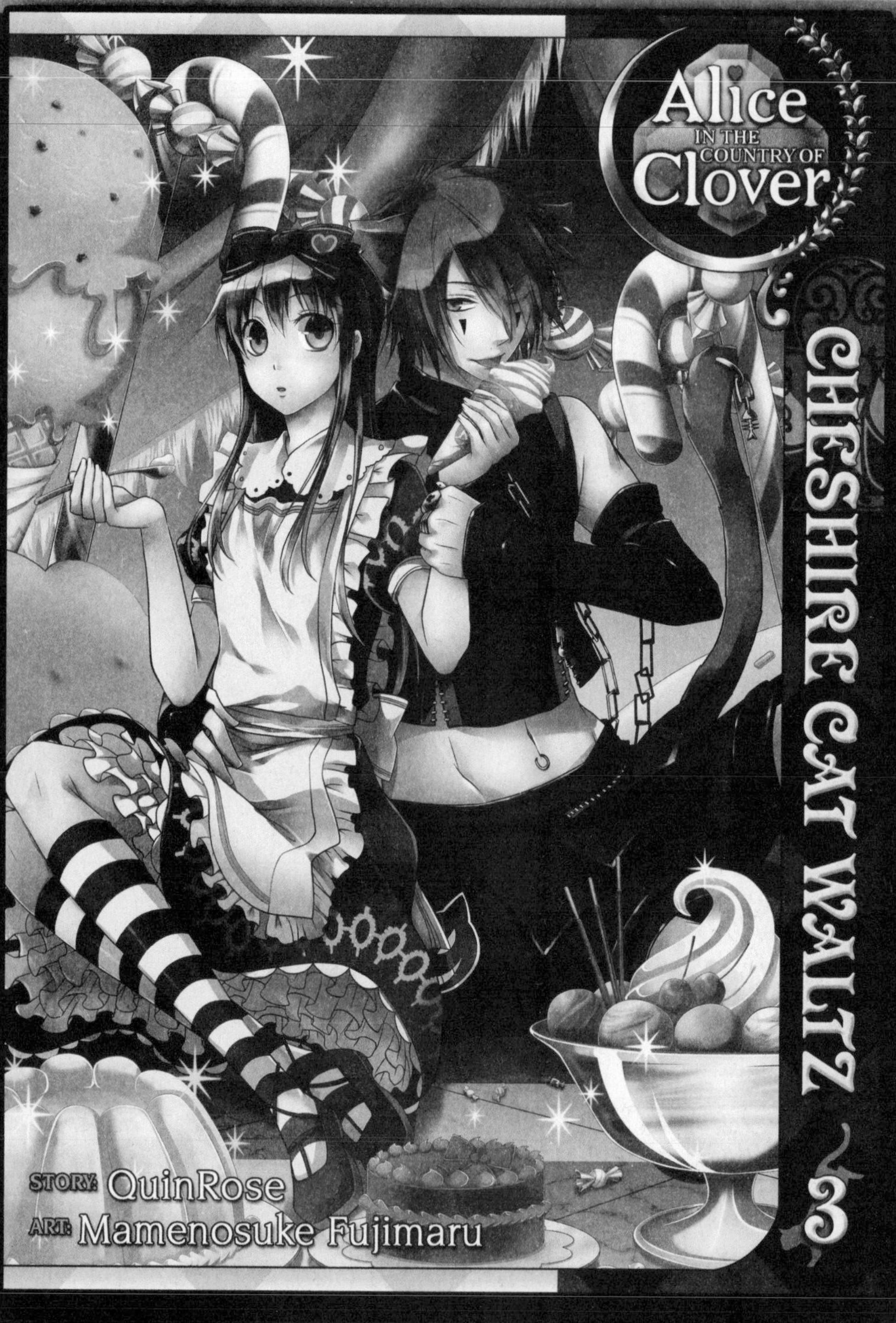
Alice IN THE COUNTRY OF Clover
CHESHIRE CAT WALTZ 3
STORY: QuinRose
ART: Mamenosuke Fujimaru

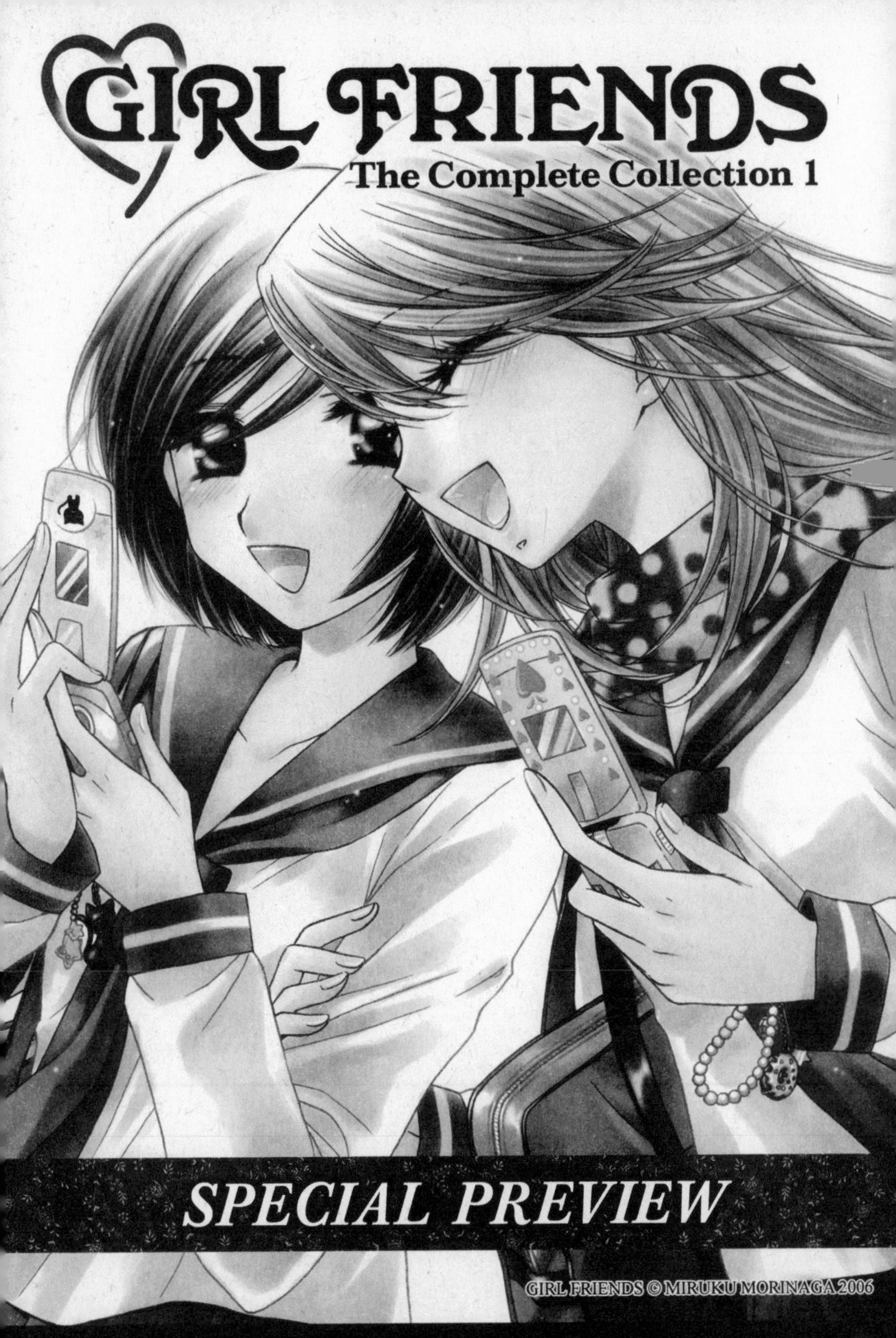
GIRL FRIENDS
The Complete Collection 1
SPECIAL PREVIEW
GIRL FRIENDS © MIRUKU MORINAGA 2006

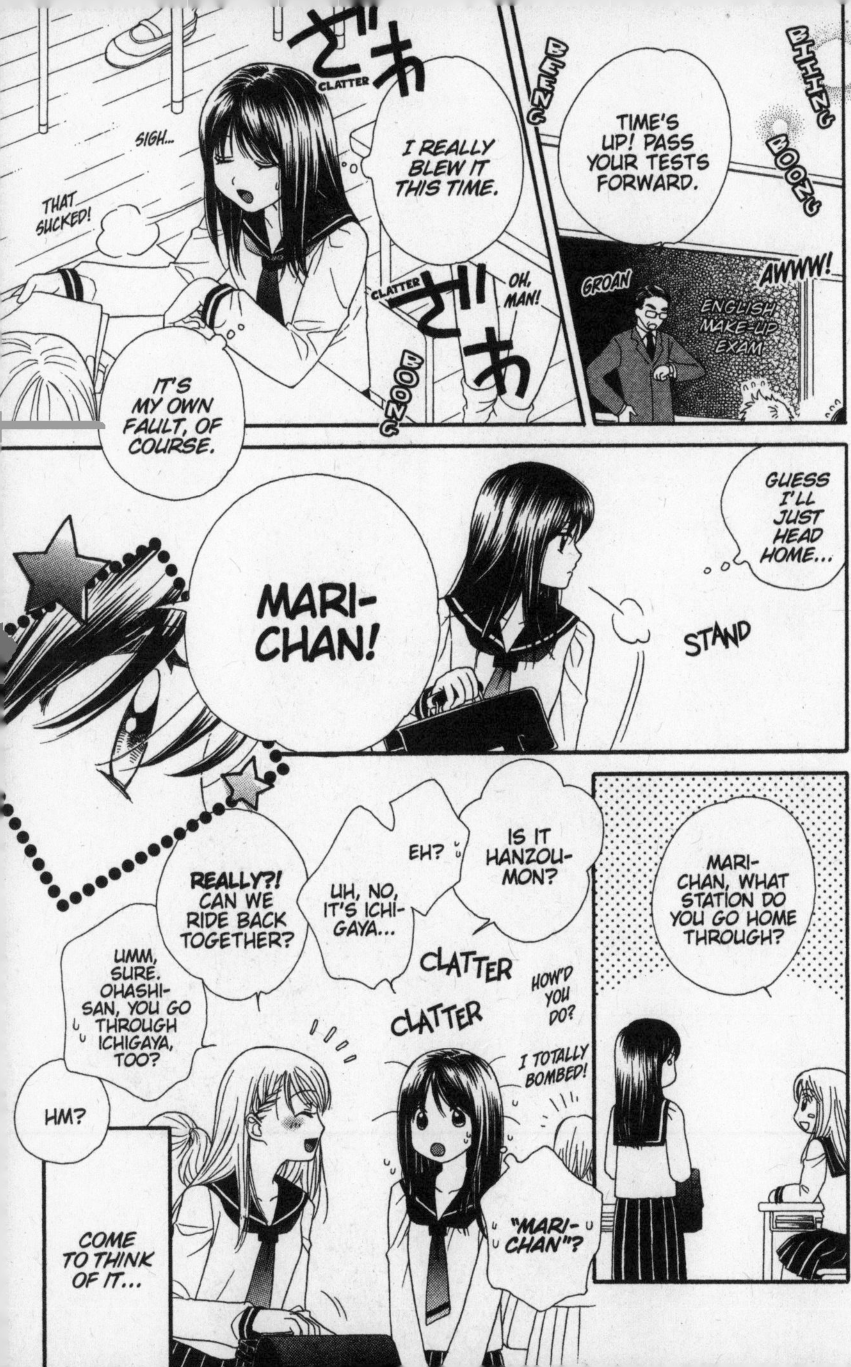
BIIING
BOONG
BEENG
TIME'S UP! PASS YOUR TESTS FORWARD.
AWWW!
GROAN
ENGLISH MAKE-UP EXAM
ざわ
CLATTER
I REALLY BLEW IT THIS TIME.
SIGH...
THAT SUCKED!
ざあ
CLATTER
OH, MAN!
BOONG
IT'S MY OWN FAULT, OF COURSE.
GUESS I'LL JUST HEAD HOME...
STAND
MARI-CHAN!
MARI-CHAN, WHAT STATION DO YOU GO HOME THROUGH?
IS IT HANZOU-MON?
EH?
UH, NO, IT'S ICHI-GAYA...
REALLY?! CAN WE RIDE BACK TOGETHER?
CLATTER
HOW'D YOU DO?
CLATTER
I TOTALLY BOMBED!
UMM, SURE. OHASHI-SAN, YOU GO THROUGH ICHIGAYA, TOO?
"MARI-CHAN"?
HM?
COME TO THINK OF IT...

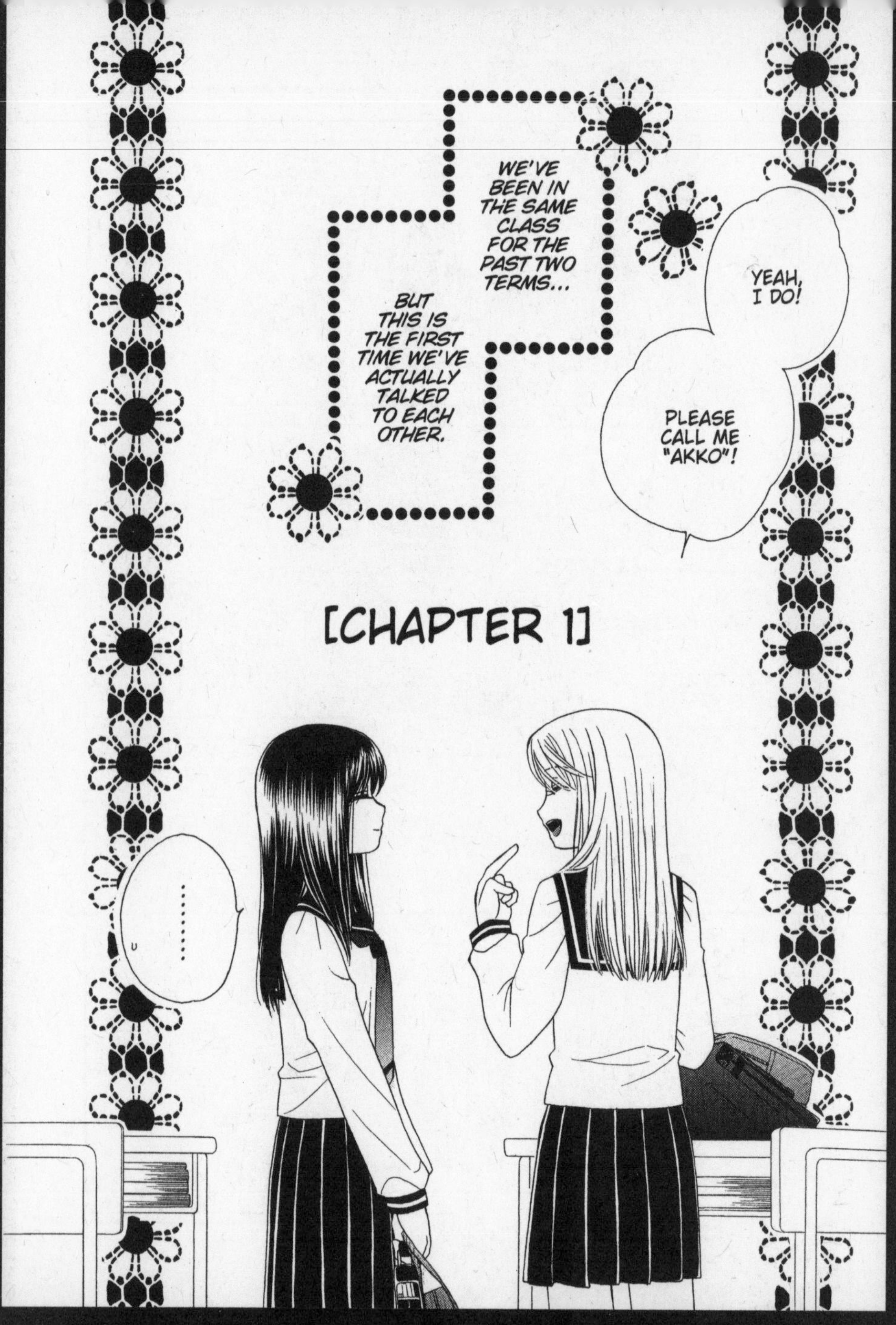
YEAH, I DO!
PLEASE CALL ME "AKKO"!
WE'VE BEEN IN THE SAME CLASS FOR THE PAST TWO TERMS...
BUT THIS IS THE FIRST TIME WE'VE ACTUALLY TALKED TO EACH OTHER.
[CHAPTER 1]
......

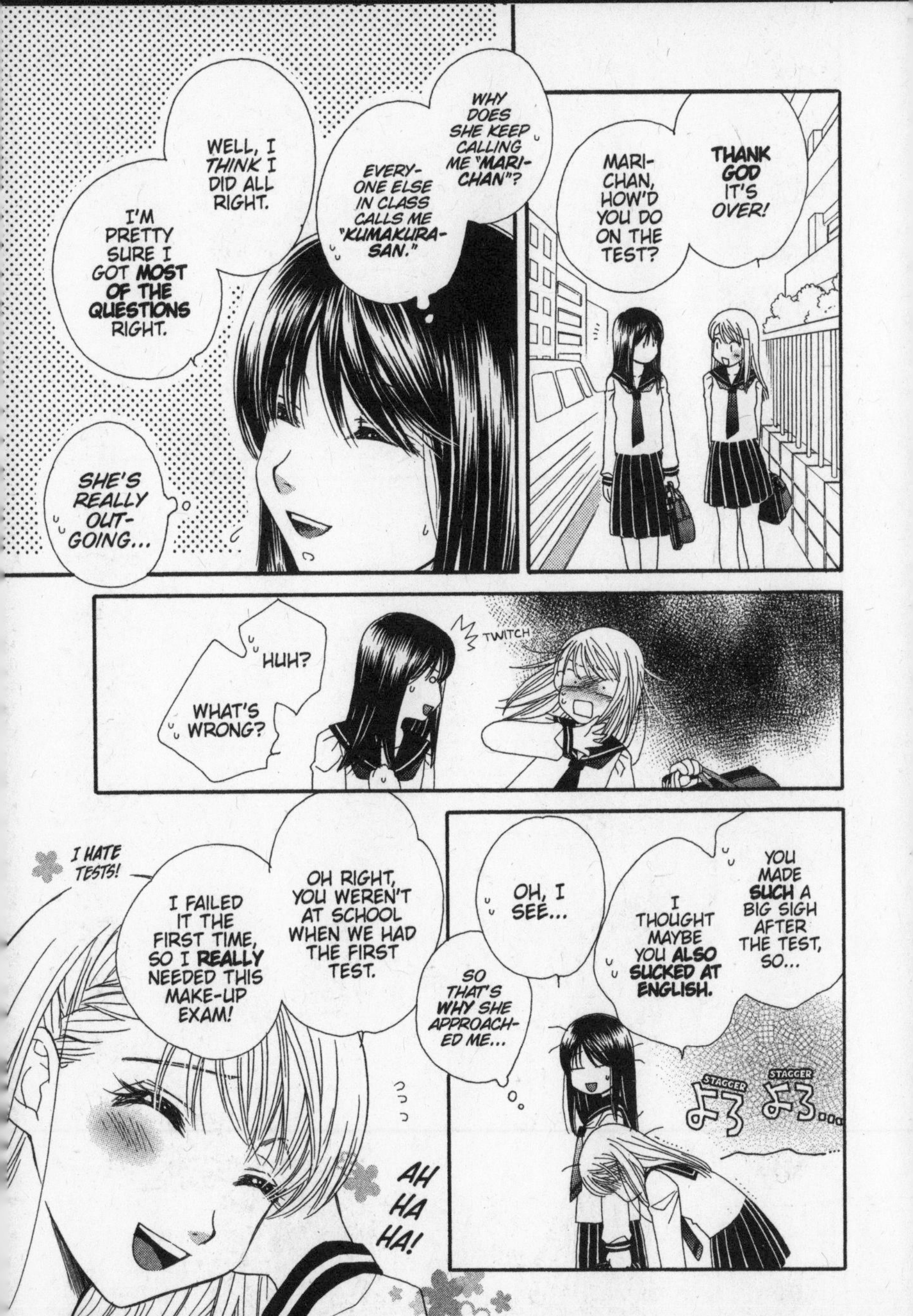
THANK GOD IT'S OVER!
MARI-CHAN, HOW'D YOU DO ON THE TEST?
WHY DOES SHE KEEP CALLING ME "MARI-CHAN"?
EVERY-ONE ELSE IN CLASS CALLS ME "KUMAKURA-SAN."
WELL, I THINK I DID ALL RIGHT.
I'M PRETTY SURE I GOT MOST OF THE QUESTIONS RIGHT.
SHE'S REALLY OUT-GOING...
TWITCH
HUH?
WHAT'S WRONG?
YOU MADE SUCH A BIG SIGH AFTER THE TEST, SO...
I THOUGHT MAYBE YOU ALSO SUCKED AT ENGLISH.
STAGGER STAGGER
よろよろ...
OH, I SEE...
SO THAT'S WHY SHE APPROACH-ED ME...
OH RIGHT, YOU WEREN'T AT SCHOOL WHEN WE HAD THE FIRST TEST.
I FAILED IT THE FIRST TIME, SO I REALLY NEEDED THIS MAKE-UP EXAM!
AH HA HA!
I HATE TESTS!

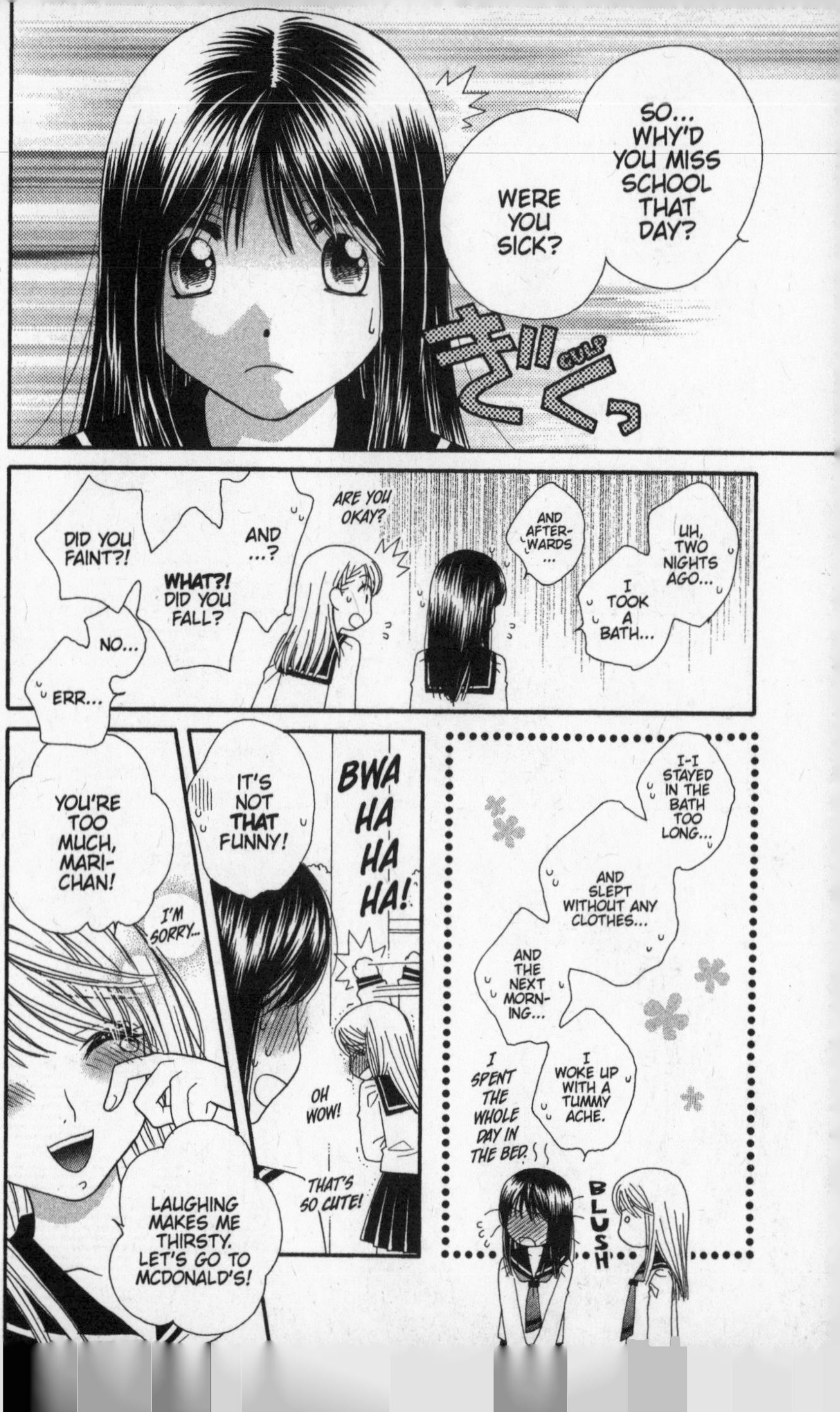
SO... WHY'D YOU MISS SCHOOL THAT DAY?
WERE YOU SICK?
ぎくっ
GULP
UH, TWO NIGHTS AGO...
I TOOK A BATH...
AND AFTER-WARDS...
ARE YOU OKAY?
AND ...?
WHAT?! DID YOU FALL?
DID YOU FAINT?!
NO...
ERR...
I-I STAYED IN THE BATH TOO LONG...
AND SLEPT WITHOUT ANY CLOTHES...
AND THE NEXT MORN-ING...
I WOKE UP WITH A TUMMY ACHE.
I SPENT THE WHOLE DAY IN THE BED.
BLUSH
BWA HA HA HA!
IT'S NOT THAT FUNNY!
OH WOW!
THAT'S SO CUTE!
YOU'RE TOO MUCH, MARI-CHAN!
I'M SORRY...
LAUGHING MAKES ME THIRSTY. LET'S GO TO MCDONALD'S!

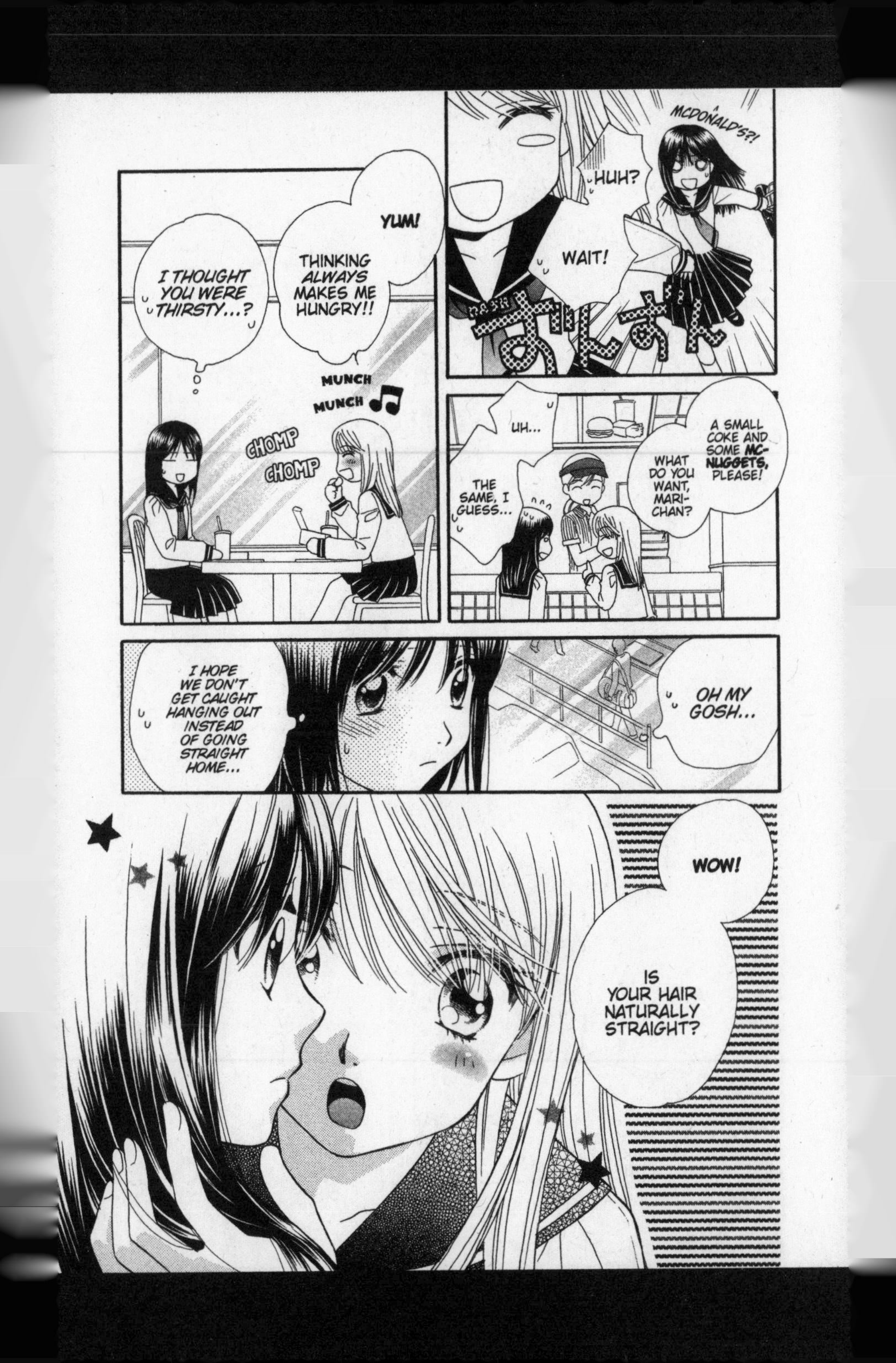
MCDONALD'S?!
HUH?
WAIT!
A SMALL COKE AND SOME MC-NUGGETS, PLEASE!
WHAT DO YOU WANT, MARI-CHAN?
UH...
THE SAME, I GUESS...
YUM!
THINKING ALWAYS MAKES ME HUNGRY!!
I THOUGHT YOU WERE THIRSTY...?
MUNCH
MUNCH
CHOMP
CHOMP
OH MY GOSH...
I HOPE WE DON'T GET CAUGHT HANGING OUT INSTEAD OF GOING STRAIGHT HOME...
WOW!
IS YOUR HAIR NATURALLY STRAIGHT?

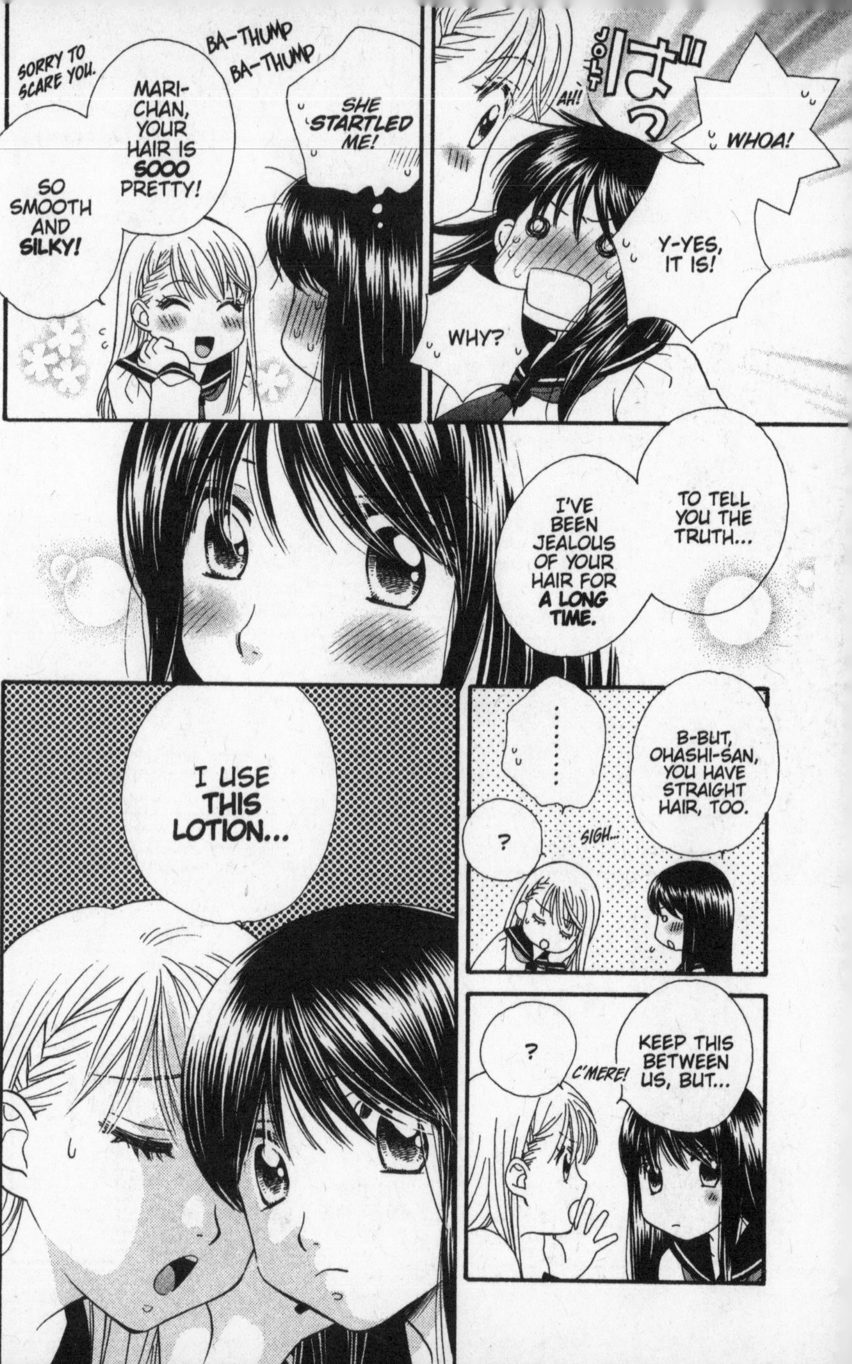
WHOA!
ばっ
JOLT
AH!
Y-YES, IT IS!
WHY?
BA-THUMP BA-THUMP
SHE STARTLED ME!
MARI-CHAN, YOUR HAIR IS SOOO PRETTY!
SORRY TO SCARE YOU.
SO SMOOTH AND SILKY!
TO TELL YOU THE TRUTH...
I'VE BEEN JEALOUS OF YOUR HAIR FOR A LONG TIME.
B-BUT, OHASHI-SAN, YOU HAVE STRAIGHT HAIR, TOO.
......
SIGH...
?
KEEP THIS BETWEEN US, BUT...
C'MERE!
?
I USE THIS LOTION...

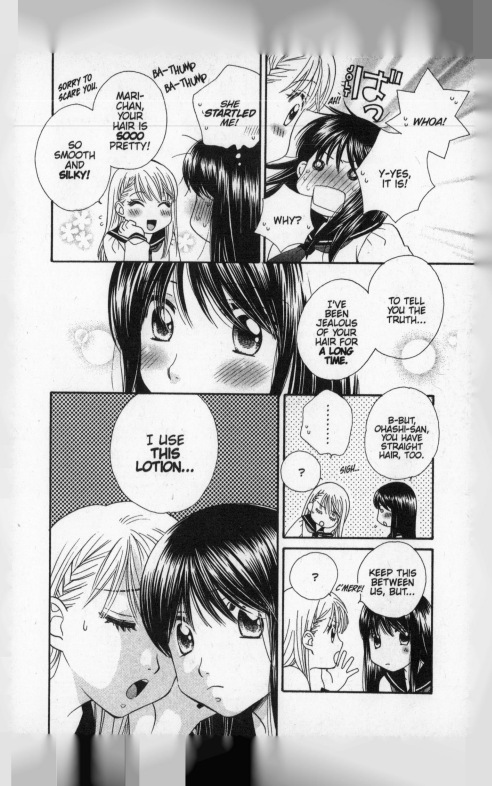

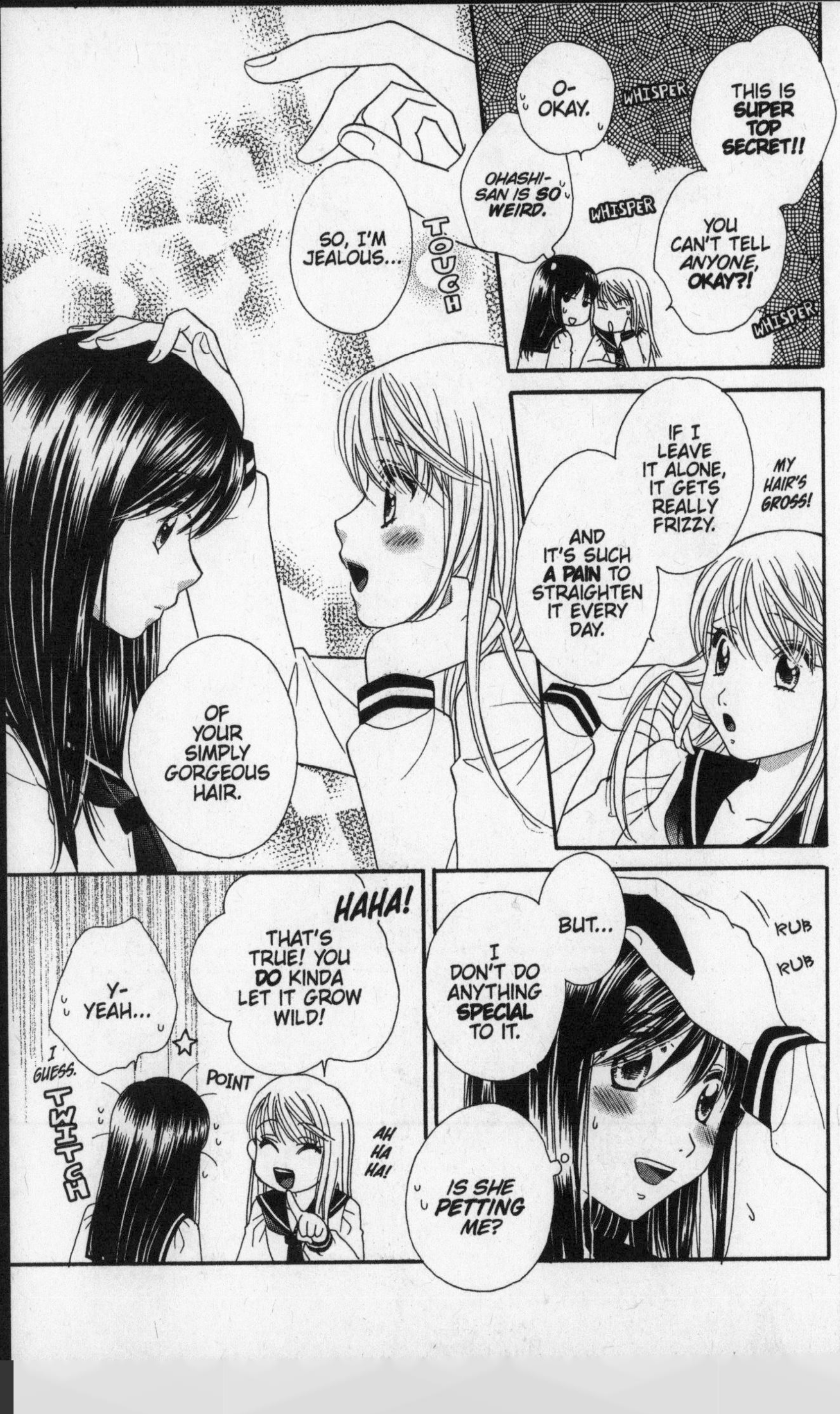
THIS IS SUPER TOP SECRET!!
WHISPER
YOU CAN'T TELL ANYONE, OKAY?!
WHISPER
O- OKAY.
WHISPER
OHASHI-SAN IS SO WEIRD.
MY HAIR'S GROSS!
IF I LEAVE IT ALONE, IT GETS REALLY FRIZZY.
AND IT'S SUCH A PAIN TO STRAIGHTEN IT EVERY DAY.
TOUCH
SO, I'M JEALOUS...
OF YOUR SIMPLY GORGEOUS HAIR.
RUB
RUB
BUT...
I DON'T DO ANYTHING SPECIAL TO IT.
IS SHE PETTING ME?
HAHA!
THAT'S TRUE! YOU DO KINDA LET IT GROW WILD!
AH HA HA!
POINT
Y- YEAH...
I GUESS.
TWITCH

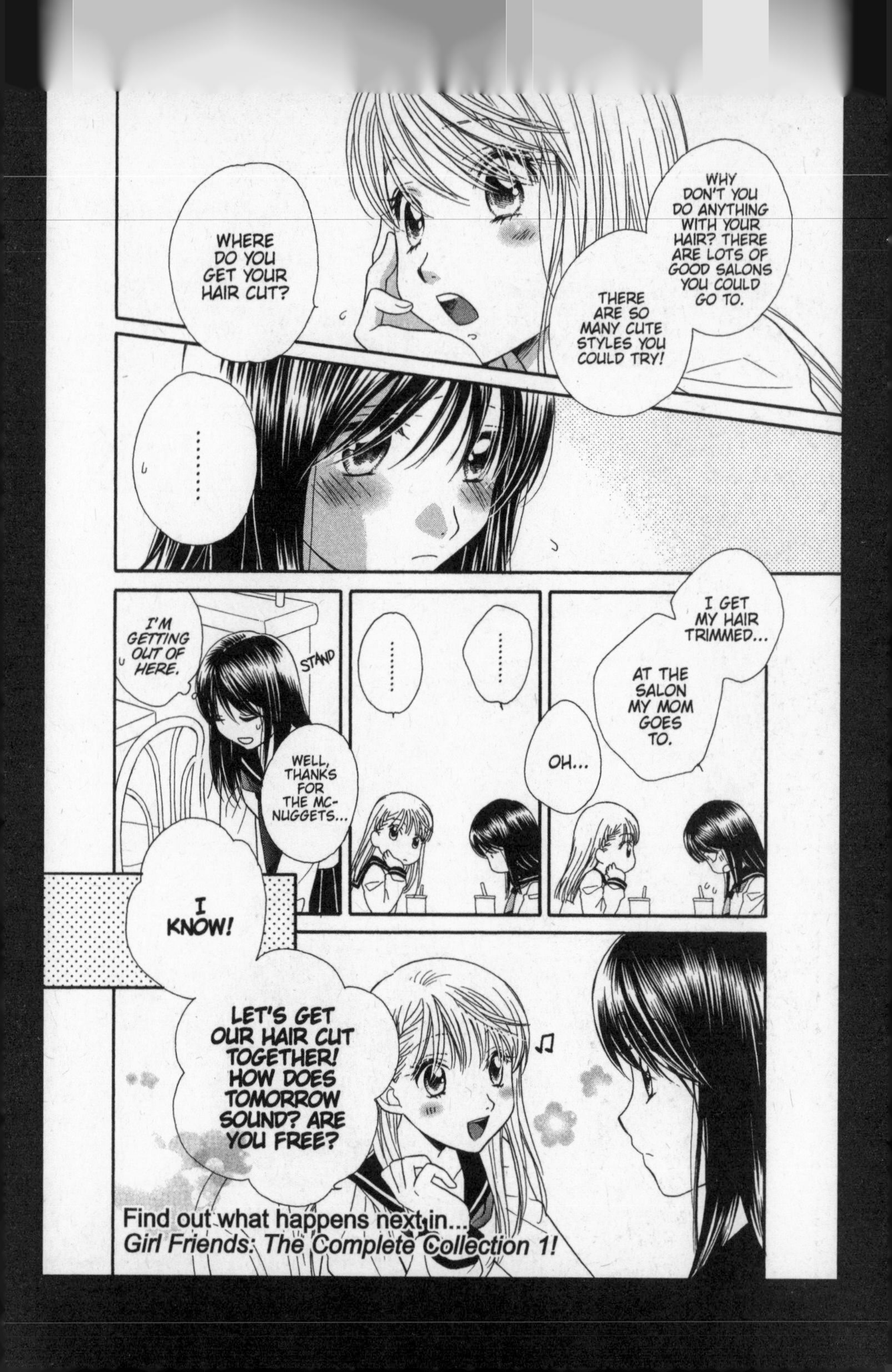
WHY DON'T YOU DO ANYTHING WITH YOUR HAIR? THERE ARE LOTS OF GOOD SALONS YOU COULD GO TO.
THERE ARE SO MANY CUTE STYLES YOU COULD TRY!
WHERE DO YOU GET YOUR HAIR CUT?
......
I GET MY HAIR TRIMMED...
AT THE SALON MY MOM GOES TO.
OH...
......
......
STAND
I'M GETTING OUT OF HERE.
WELL, THANKS FOR THE MC-NUGGETS...
I KNOW!
LET'S GET OUR HAIR CUT TOGETHER! HOW DOES TOMORROW SOUND? ARE YOU FREE?

Find out what happens next in...
Girl Friends: The Complete Collection 1!

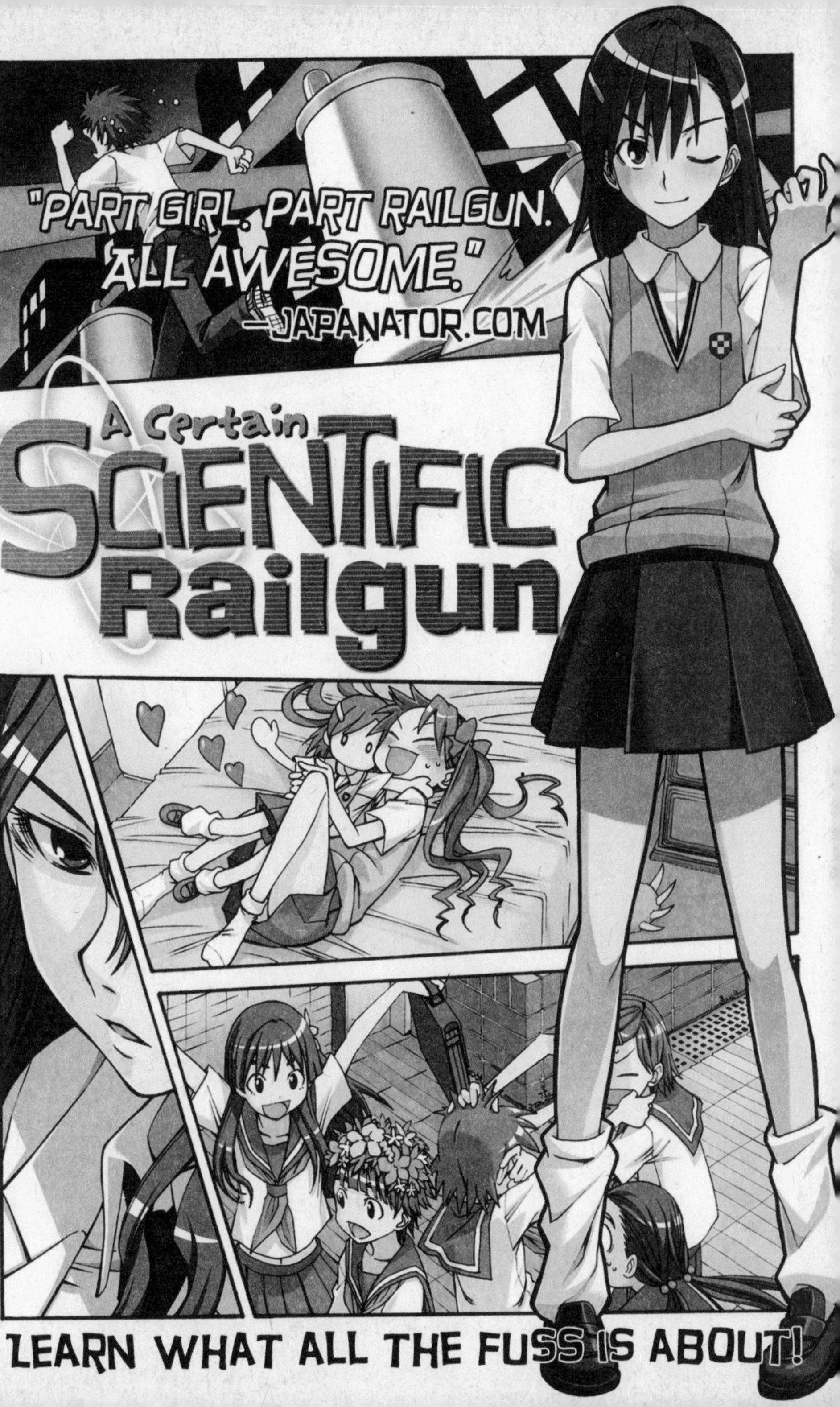
"PART GIRL. PART RAILGUN. ALL AWESOME."
—JAPANATOR.COM
A Certain SCIENTIFIC Railgun
LEARN WHAT ALL THE FUSS IS ABOUT!

Amazing Agent LUNA

Experience All 7
Exciting Volumes!

LUNA

DeFilippis & Weir • Shiei

Luna: the perfect secret agent. A girl grown in a lab from the finest genetic material, she has been trained since [b]... ultimate espio... [agen]t's an assignment ... s given max - high sc... o the

story
Nunzio DeFilippis & Christina Weir • **art** Shiei

visit www.gomanga.com

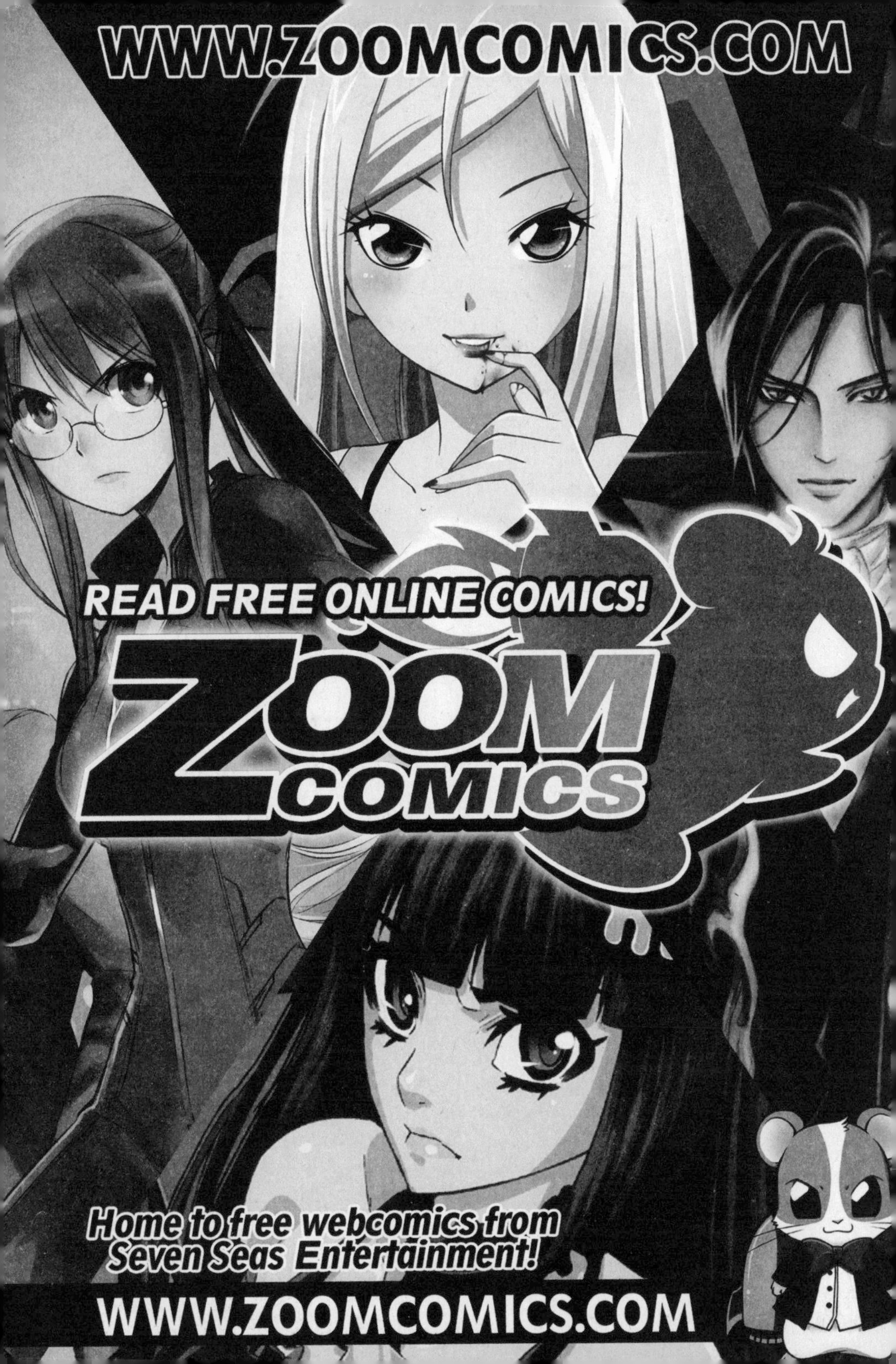
WWW.ZOOMCOMICS.COM
READ FREE ONLINE COMICS!
ZOOM COMICS
Home to free webcomics from Seven Seas Entertainment!
WWW.ZOOMCOMICS.COM